Multimedia and Literacy Development

Representing the state of the art in multimedia applications and their promise for enhancing early literacy development, this volume broadens the field of reading research by looking beyond print-only experiences to young readers' encounters with multimedia stories on the Internet and DVD. Multimedia storybooks include, in addition to static pictures and written text, features such as oral text, animations, sounds, zooms, and scaffolds designed to help convey meaning. These features are changing how young children read text, and also provide technology-based scaffolds for helping struggling readers.

Multimedia and Literacy Development reports experimental research and practices with multimedia stories indicating that new dimensions of media contribute to young children's ability to understand stories and to read texts independently. This is the first synthesis of evidence-based research in this field. Four key themes are highlighted:

- Understanding the multimedia environment for learning
- Designing multimedia applications for learning
- New approaches to storybook reading
- Multimedia applications in classroom instruction.

Written for an international audience of students in university courses on literacy and information technology, researchers, policymakers, program developers, and media specialists, this volume is essential reading for all professionals interested in early literacy and early interventions.

Adriana G. Bus is Professor at Leiden University, the Netherlands. Currently she is working with computer experts, instructional designers, and content specialists on building an Internet environment to promote rich literacy experiences for young children.

Susan B. Neuman is Professor in Educational Studies at the University of Michigan, Ann Arbor, USA, specializing in early literacy development. Previously, she directed the Center for the Improvement of Early Reading Achievement (CIERA) and served as the U.S. Assistant Secretary for Elementary and Secondary Education.

Multimedia and Literacy Development

Improving Achievement for Young Learners

Edited by Adriana G. Bus and Susan B. Neuman

Routledge
Taylor & Francis Group

NEW YORK AND LONDON

First published 2009
by Routledge
270 Madison Ave, New York, NY 10016

Simultaneously published in the UK
by Routledge
2 Park Square, Milton Park, Abingdon, Oxon OX14 4RN

Routledge is an imprint of the Taylor & Francis Group, an informa business

© 2009 Routledge, Taylor and Francis

Typeset in Minion by Wearset Ltd, Boldon, Tyne and Wear
Printed and bound in the United States of America on acid-free paper by
Edwards Brothers, Inc.

Library of Congress Cataloging in Publication Data
Bus, A.G.
Multimedia and literacy development: improving achievement for young
learners/Adriana G. Bus, Susan B. Neuman.
p.cm.
Includes bibliographical references and index.
1. Computers and literacy. 2. Media literacy. 3. Reading (Early childhood) I. Neuman,
Susan B. II. Title.
LC149.5.B875 2008
372.40285–dc22   2008007940

ISBN10: 0-415-98841-1 (hbk)
ISBN10: 0-415-98842-X (pbk)
ISBN10: 0-203-89215-1 (ebk)

ISBN13: 978-0-415-98841-4 (hbk)
ISBN13: 978-0-415-98842-1 (pbk)
ISBN13: 978-0-203-89215-2 (ebk)

Contents

Preface

Today, we are seeing the beginnings of a new technological era with far-reaching consequences for young children's literacy development. The contours of the new literacy environment are already visible. Television, movies, videos, music, video games, and computers have gradually moved from the sideline into the center of young children's daily activities.

This book examines the important ramifications of these new media on children's literacy development. It is an outgrowth of a 3-day international research conference supported by the Royal Netherlands Academy of Arts and Sciences (KNAW), for the purpose of bringing together prominent researchers in multimedia and literacy development. We assembled a truly international group of scholars to study issues concerning new media. Our focus was to explore the potential promise of new media as well as the problems and challenges of becoming literate in such environments.

Throughout the conference, we found a remarkable convergence of studies that highlighted a central theme: when dimensions of media (video, music, and sounds) are constructed to support children's learning, these new technologies contribute significantly to young children's ability to understand stories and to reading texts independently. This is true for average learners, those who have limited proficiency in academic language, and for children with special needs. These studies suggest that children benefit from the intensity of a multimedia intervention for comprehending stories and deriving meaning from print. These findings hold true not only for emerging readers (3- to 5-year-old), but also for beginning children starting to read text independently (6- to 8-year-old).

Our book is designed to highlight four principal areas in which significant developments are occurring: (1) understanding the multimedia environment for learning; (2) designing multimedia applications for learning; (3) new approaches to storybook reading; (4) multimedia applications in classroom instruction. During the colloquium, these four themes were discussed with the purpose of addressing the following questions:

- How do multimedia contribute to becoming literate in the beginning stages of reading?
- Are there specific learning processes that are especially supported by multimedia influences?
- How can we support children (and teachers) to profit maximally from multimedia?

This volume represents the state-of-the-art in multimedia applications and their promise for enhancing literacy development. Chapters highlight the character of the ever-changing multimedia environment, the ways in which we can better design applications for literacy learning, and new approaches for reaching a broader spectrum of learners in school and non-school settings. Together, they reflect the tremendous vibrancy in the field of new media in promoting literacy to enable all children to develop the critical knowledge, skills, and dispositions essential for reading success.

We hope to broaden the focus of reading, looking beyond print-only experiences to encounters with multimedia on Internet, DVD, and other sources. In this respect, our book recognizes that multimedia represents a promising new development for improving achievement for all young learners.

Introduction

Adriana G. Bus and Susan B. Neuman

Minsky warns us of speculating about computers:

> Anything you hear about computers should be ignored, because we are in the Dark Ages. We're in the thousand years between no technology and all technology. You can read what your contemporaries think, but you should remember they are ignorant savages.
>
> (quoted in Brand, 1987, p. 104)

We are only at the beginning of a new technological era with far-reaching consequences for children becoming literate. In today's society, children already are in touch with electronic media. It is thoroughly integrated into the fabric of their lives, with television, movies, videos, music, video games, and computers central to daily activities. Even young children spend on average about two hours a day with electronic entertainment, about as much time as they normally spend playing outside and about three times as much as they spend on average on reading independently or being read to (Rideout, Vandewater, & Wartella, 2003). To an increasing degree, modern media are not just seen as competing with other activities such as reading, but as a stimulus for learning. That is why a growing number of researchers have begun to study how children under 8 years old learn to be literate across a range of printed and electronic media.

It would be ideal if we could experiment and assess the influence of media by creating a virtual world in which children wander in a fantasy world with innumerable examples of written language. Papert (1996), for example, proposed *Mathland*—a virtual world packed with numbers. It was intended to test children's math concepts and the state of their math skills after they had a chance to ramble around this virtual world. By analogy, a virtual *Literacyland* might add to our understanding of how children can learn to read and write with media. By using the computer as a *Literacyland*, children could "ideally" play at real reading from the very beginning instead of the slow, often laborious process of learning to reading at school.

But in place of the virtual *Literacyland*, we have at our disposal the results of experimental research testing aspects of multimedia on literacy learning. And taking into account these growing numbers of studies, the time seems ripe to gather the wealth of information that has accumulated about multimedia and literacy. With financial support from the Royal Netherlands Academy of Arts and Sciences, an international group of scholars convened in June

2006 for 3 days in the home base of the KNAW, the seventeenth century Trippenhuis in Amsterdam, to do just that: to explore theories and data that could explain how multimedia might be used as a tool for developing reading achievement.

Themes Emerging from the Literature

In the past, much of the research on children and media assumed a deficit model in which media were seen as displacing more "valuable" activities. The prevalent view was that children should "run in the sun" instead of being "glued to the screen." Since then, however, studies have shown that media do not replace children's other interests (Neuman, 1988). Children who watch Cookie Monster are also eager to listen to a picture storybook about their favorite character in *Sesame Street*. In fact, media may even positively affect the process of becoming literate: interests generated by programs may stimulate listening to stories. Assuming that almost all children spend a fair amount of time with electronic media, scholars have gradually shifted from a focus on the issue of displacement to the issue of effective programs (e.g., Ennemoser & Schneider, 2007).

As we enter a new technological era, electronic stories have begun to attract attention in research. This is not surprising given that the digitized format of picture storybooks preserves all relevant qualities of print versions such as a narrative and illustrations. One may wonder to what extent encounters with multimedia stories are equivalent to book reading experiences and whether or not, they too stimulate literacy development (e.g., Bus, van IJzendoorn, & Pellegrini, 1995; Frijters, Barron, & Brunello, 2000; Sénéchal, LeFevre, Thomas, & Daley, 1998). Originally, electronic stories were designed like picture storybooks, preserving common features like separate screens analogous to pages in print books (de Jong & Bus, 2003). Text in print was accompanied by oral text that started up with a single mouse click. At each screen, children could get assistance by loading film representations of events or by activating a dictionary.

But gradually the design of electronic books has changed into a format that looks less like a book imitation. Today, most living books include a continuous filmic presentation of the story while the oral text is presented simultaneously. No longer does it include the kind of "edutainment" characteristic of the first generation of products. For example, the digitized version of Mercer Mayer's *Just Grandma and me*—one of the first living stories ever available—included animated illustrations, numerous amusing but nonsensical animations hidden in illustrations, such singing flowers, a dancing picture on the wall, or columns with ants marching over the screen.

The evolution of electronic books and the time children spend with them raises new questions. Should they be considered assets to literacy learning or impediments (Tyner, 1998)? Do additional coherent symbols such as images, sound, and movement act conjointly in helping children construct meaning and generate inferences in new contexts like Neuman's (1997) theory of synergy predicts? Does processing of the animated pictures in concert with the text enhance children's text understanding especially when children lack basic vocabulary or grammatical knowledge (Paivio, 1986)? How relevant is temporal contiguity of verbal and nonverbal information sources in guiding children, i.e., presenting animations congruent with the narration simultaneously rather than successively (Mayer & Moreno, 1998)?

The jury is still out, according to a number of international studies. Some studies have found that children may become distracted from the story language as a result of the graphic and other symbols. Turbill (2001), for instance, concluded that attention to graphic symbols comes at the cost of spoken text. Children rather look than listen ("visual superiority hypothesis"). Labbo and Kuhn (2000) hypothesized that symbols not related to the storyline (edutainment) interfere negatively with story comprehension.

Children may shift from a story-related to a game-playing stance—a shift in cognitive perspective that may interfere with their comprehension of the story (Greenfield et al., 1996). For example, when Labbo and Kuhn asked children to retell an electronic story including inconsiderate edutainment, children seemed to lose themselves in irrelevant details. Such results suggest that inconsiderate programs may coax children into habits of thinking or dispositions toward meaning making that are nonproductive when viewed from the perspective of print-based reading skills.

Similarly, observing kindergarten children sitting at the computer screen, de Jong and Bus (2002) noticed that children seemed especially playful when using an electronic book full of edutainment in search of appealing animations and games. When children had a choice of several options, they picked pictorial and iconic options at the expense of listening to the story text. When compared to a traditional storybook reading by an adult, children who used the electronic book were less successful in retelling the story and had remembered fewer words and sentences from the story text than in their counterparts. In a follow-up experiment with books that included less edutainment (de Jong & Bus, 2004) children learned more yet still seized every opportunity to use the pictorial and iconic options.

These results touch on an essential problem in using electronic media in education. Children may enjoy activities on the computer but they may use the programs differently from what the designer had in mind. For several reasons, the designs of electronic stories may not succeed in focusing children's attention to the story. In other words, programs may not evoke a *reading* stance.

In fact, the CTELL group (Case Technologies To Enhance Literacy Learning) describes similar problems for other software. There often is a gap between what teachers expect children to practice and what children actually do. After a brief period children get bored with learning games and discontinue practicing ("Skill and drill, no thrill") or choose too difficult games and tumble around with characteristics not at all related to the content (a funny man that appears each time they make a mistake). Although teachers might expect children to practice skills, they rarely control whether children indeed pursue these objectives.

Some characterize multimedia as an "easy" medium that requires less mental effort than understanding a story that is read to children (Salomon, 1984) thereby expecting more from book reading than from multimedia stories (Jordan, 2005). On the other hand, only few situations seem to elicit more concentration and attention from young children than computers (Calvert, 2005). Future research most likely is needed supplementing behavioral assessment with psycho-physiological measures to examine this thesis.

Moreover multimedia stories may enhance story and text comprehension as a result of additional information sources ("dual coding theory"). Well-designed living books highlight events by adding features such as sound, music, and film: the camera zooms in on details of the static illustrations in the equivalent picture storybook and some details of pictures are made more dynamic. When the black cat is turned into a green one, we see the animal's color change. The music matches the events and we hear the cat snoring, the witch fall from the stairs, or birds twittering. Nowadays innumerable good examples of digitized picture storybooks are plentifully available even for the littlest ones, retaining all print book qualities but simultaneously adding new features.

In the Netherlands the website Bereslim (www.bereslim.nl) has been launched for 3- to 8-year olds presenting an impressive selection of high points from children's literature that came out during the last 3 years to be completed each year with new award-winning stories. The recent infusion of computers into homes and early childhood classrooms in various countries around the world may make it possible for us to gain insights into children's opportunities for literacy development while interacting with new storytelling media.

Of particular interest is the power of multimedia to enhance learning for children at risk. Do multimedia stories have the potency to call a halt to the depressing cycle of poor comprehension by making stories more accessible to children who struggle with reading? The evidence is inconsistent. On the one hand, there is evidence that interesting visual techniques can distract children from learning verbal material, a phenomenon known as the visual superiority hypothesis (Hayes & Birnbaum, 1980). On the other hand, scholars report corroboration for the hypothesis that short stories, accompanied by a helpful video framework, support children's story recall and interpretation more than stories accompanied by mainly static images (Sharp et al., 1995).

There are also more recent studies providing support for the assumption that graphic and auditory symbols are facilitative of text comprehension (e.g., Uchikoshi, 2005) and language acquisition (e.g., Verhallen, Bus, & Jong, 2006). Questions remain, however, about whether infants and toddlers are able to learn from electronic stories or whether these stories are able to affect infants' and toddlers' communicative abilities (Linebarger & Walker, 2005). There are some studies suggesting that positive effects are reserved for groups over 30 months whereas under that age findings are less promising. There may be a so-called video deficit effect in that age range resulting from perceptual differences between televised and real models (Anderson & Pempeck, 2005).

So far the main focus in research of living books has been on what are the most common multimedia additions: iconic features like hidden animations and animated illustrations. There is a paucity of research testing the effects of so-called computer assistants, a stand-in for adults who now and then appear on the screen to ask questions or supply some help. Such additions to the next generation of living books may make the books not only cognitively but also emotionally more rewarding to young children. In line with previous research of book sharing highlighting the role of intimacy between parent and child (Bus & van IJzendoorn, 1995, 1997), it is imaginable that a computer assistant, who interacts with the child, may neutralize the absence of an adult in encounters with living books. Although it is likely that electronic stories do not replicate entirely the adult–child interactions that occur when reading print-based books, electronic text may function as a unique scaffold that supports children's learning.

Some studies test the hypothesis that additional features may serve as "electronic scaffolds" of reading when word recognition constitutes a major bottleneck in the child's efforts to negotiate text (McKenna, 1998). In the conventional classroom, word recognition problems create serious logistical problems because teachers are limited in the number of students they can assist individually, inevitably limiting the amount of actual reading undertaken by the child. Thanks to electronic books equipped with digitized pronunciations of words and oral renderings of larger textual units, children with reading problems may read more fluently thereby stimulating their comprehension and reading pleasure.

Other scholars, as well, have begun to speculate about the usefulness of computer programs when children's learning behavior is characterized by insufficient control of impulses, problems in regulating attention, and hyperactivity. Students with such executive function deficits are likely to be more vulnerable to competing attractors in the learning environment and need more intense tutoring of learning processes than instruction normally offers (e.g., Meltzer, 2007; Spira, Bracken, & Fischel, 2005). As computer programs have possibilities to ask questions or supply feedback they might help children to stick to learning objectives (Rose & Rose, 2007).

One may argue that television programs and Internet sites with animated picture storybooks create new chances for young children at risk. In lower income families books are scarce and reading is seemingly not encouraged, even though television and computers are ever present. However, a growing number of animated picture storybooks on Internet sites does not automatically imply that low-income children who are most in need enter such sites even when entrance is free. *Sesame Street*, for example, created to close the gap for children from low- and middle-income families, did not cause such effects: on the contrary, as a result of the program, gaps in kindergarten age between middle- and low-income neighborhood children were larger than ever before (Cook et al., 1975). Similar results are reported for children's uses of reading resources in neighborhood libraries. Neuman and Celano (2006) concluded that children from low-income neighborhoods spent a good deal of time in the library on activities that contained little print; children from middle-income neighborhoods spent more time on content applications with more print. Analogously, Internet sites with animated picture storybooks are mainly visited by children already favored in other ways: they are often read to by their parents familiar with the icons of children's literature (Mansens, 2007).

Consequently, as we go forth in this electronic age, we carry with us the recognition that multimedia play a critical role in children's life. We now have a growing array of resources designed to bolster children's growth and development in reading, and to support those who struggle as they face the daunting challenges of decoding and comprehension of text. Despite these hopeful signs, we also must acknowledge that we are far from understanding the intricacies of the new media and their promise for literacy development. We have only an imperfect grasp of the complex interplay between children's culturally laden experiences and their capacity to use new media to promote learning. At the same time, the intellectual energy displayed by the authors of these chapters give testimony to the fact that we will assuredly make enormous intellectual strides in these endeavors to meet the literacy needs of all children.

Contents of the Volume

Our book is designed to highlight four key themes emerging from the literature: (1) understanding the multimedia environment for learning; (2) designing multimedia applications for learning; (3) new approaches to storybook reading; (4) multimedia applications in classroom instruction. Chapters in the volume are clustered round the four issues to address a similar set of issues. Here, we briefly highlight parts and chapters to help you navigate through the book. Throughout chapters, we have attempted to cross-reference one chapter to another to allow for a more in-depth analysis of key ideas.

Part I: Understanding the Multimedia Environment for Learning

Part I essentially sets the stage for subsequent chapters in the volume. The first two chapters provide an overview of how children use media. In Chapter 1, Ellen Wartella and Rebekah A. Richert review the current American context on the effects of media on young children and its impact on their development. They argue that young children are a special audience with very special needs, and that producers need to be cognizant of their development in designing quality programs.

In Chapter 2, Jackie Marsh reports the results of survey data including 1,852 parents and caregivers for trends in media use in the UK. This survey indicates that children are avid users and producers of media from an early age, with great access to a wide variety of media. Early childhood educators, she suggests, would benefit from infusing aspects of popular culture, media, and new technologies into the early years curriculum to support children's motivation and interest in learning about literacy.

These chapters highlight the importance of media in children's lives. In Chapter 3, Susan B. Neuman argues that, in contrast to displacing literacy, multimedia can support it. She argues for a theory of synergy in multimedia and demonstrates through a number of studies that media can have a multiplicative effect on children's literacy development.

In Chapter 4, Paul van den Broek, Panayiota Kendeou, and Mary Jane White substantiate why multimedia approaches to fostering comprehension have considerable potential. They discuss when a synergy of multimedia is most likely to improve comprehension and when multimedia approaches may interfere with comprehension by increasing the attentional load for the comprehenders.

But the promise of media for literacy learning also comes with a caveat: multimedia must be designed in ways that recognize children's development and support the knowledge, skills, and dispositions central to children's successful outcomes in learning to read and write. Together, these chapters provide a strong rationale for the importance of quality instructional design that is addressed in Part II.

Part II: Designing Multimedia Applications for Learning

Part II includes chapters that focus on instructional designs and their applications to literacy development. In Chapter 5, Kathleen Roskos and Jeremy Brueck examine the eBook through the lens of instructional design theory. Their discussion essentially takes us behind the screen to the digital building blocks of multimedia and interactivity in eBooks that help shape children's early literacy experience. In this respect, they propose a "working" analytic framework for examining eBook architecture and design.

In Chapter 6, Mary Ann Evans, Annie Roy-Charland, and Jean Saint-Aubin discuss another strategy for analyzing instructional design: one that focuses on the child's perspective in learning. Following a brief overview of eye movement studies, they speculate on how electronic books might foster literacy development in preschool and kindergarten children. Further, they examine the ways in which eye movement research as a tool might help us better understand children's response to electronic books.

Chapters 7 and 8 examine computers as a tool for literacy learning. In Chapter 7, Eliane Segers focuses especially on the early years, and the potential benefits of computer-supported instruction in language learning for kindergarten classrooms. She describes the instructional design of an educational software program for mainstream children, and its effectiveness on literacy development. Further, she explores the effects of the software program on vocabulary learning for children learning Dutch as a second language, and for those who have special learning needs. In Chapter 8, Victor H.P. van Daal, a scholar with a long-standing reputation in dyslexia research, discusses design features of multimedia instruction for children who struggle in reading. Specifically, he examines the promise of computers as a potential "bootstrap" for helping children with significant reading difficulties.

In Chapter 9, Paul P.M. Leseman, Aziza Y. Mayo, and Anna F. Scheele highlight the design features specially targeted to second language learners and their effects. They examine the role of traditional and new media for bilingual children, proposing a threshold hypothesis to explain children's language development. They argue that new media can be highly effective; however, when children's language skills have reached a certain level of proficiency, they will need additional input that is lexically richer and grammatically more complex to extend their language learning. At this point, traditional media can be especially helpful by involving children in conversations that use rare words with complex meanings, formal taxonomic definitions, and varied use of verb tense.

Together, these chapters highlight the potential and the problematic for considering how new media can be constructed to promote children's literacy development. Quality designs provide new tools for learning, which have tremendous potential for enabling learners who may struggle in reading to become successful.

Part III: New Approaches to Storybook Reading

Part III, "New Approaches to Storybook Reading" includes chapters that examine how multimedia presentations may transform the storybook reading experience. Adriana G. Bus, Maria T. de Jong, and Marian J.A.J. Verhallen in Chapter 10 provide a synthesis of research studies examining the benefits of onscreen stories on second language learners' vocabulary and comprehension development. Reporting on four laboratory experiments with 5-year-olds using traditional and physiological measures (skin conductance), these researchers found that second language learners profited more from onscreen storybooks including film-like visualizations, music, and sound than from static storybooks on the computer. And, more importantly, they make plausible that learning from onscreen digitized storybooks strongly depends on the children's willingness to invest mental efforts during multiple independent exposures to a story.

In Chapter 11, Adina Shamir and Ofra Korat use the instructional design features highlighted in Part II to develop and examine the efficacy of learning using a specially designed eBook. In the first study, they explore three activation features in the eBook, and their impact on literacy skill development. In the second study, they examine educational efficacy of paired or collaborative learning with the same educational eBook in a kindergarten setting. They explore the hypothesis that the eBook is an excellent medium for collaborative activity in learning about literacy.

Television, as well, can be a primary medium for storybook reading. In Chapter 12, Yuuko Uchikoshi explores the educational potential of several popular new shows, such as *Arthur* and *Between the Lions*. Focusing on the potential for second language learners to interact with stories, her research provides powerful evidence that when the "black box" of television produces programs with both educational content and delightful entertainment, children can learn specific skills for literacy development including phonological awareness, letter naming, decoding, and storytelling.

As multimedia storybooks become the norm, and not the exception, some people wonder whether the intimacy and comfort of the storybook reading experience between parents and children will be lost forever. In Chapter 13, Linda D. Labbo challenges that thesis. In her detailed analysis of adult–child interactions, she shows how a 2-year-old and his grandmother shared thinking spaces when reading an electronic story. As the format of eStories continues to blur the distinctions between stories told on paper and stories told on screens, she suggests that we must be open to the differential ways in which adults and children will mediate meaning with multimedia.

Part IV: Multimedia Applications in Classroom Instruction

Part IV brings multimedia into the classroom to examine its efficacy in improving reading instruction. In Chapters 14 and 15, Bette Chambers, and her colleagues at the *Success for All Foundation* explore the potential of embedded multimedia applications in early reading and writing instruction for low-income children. Their research describes an innovative project that examines the impact of Success for All instruction with embedded video clips designed to highlight certain alphabetic principles compared to instruction without video. The authors conclude that embedded multimedia is highly effective in enhancing children's understanding of sound–symbol correspondences. In Chapter 15, using similar design principles, they describe a multimedia application using computers as a tutorial intervention. Especially for children who might have had little success in reading before, Chambers and her colleagues found this approach to be highly motivating for children, and effective in promoting achievement.

In Chapter 16, Iris Levin and her colleagues Michal Schleifer, Rachel Levin, and Tali Freund attempt to bring these principles to scale in a large, nation-wide trial of using multimedia to enhance early literacy in Israel. They focus on the special role of teachers in the program and the role that parents can play in the home. As reported in other chapters throughout the book, their observations and teachers' reports clearly showed that the new medium of electronic books is highly attractive to young children. Further, children's interactions with computers significantly improved their vocabulary and related competencies. Their findings suggested that the educational effects of TV programs and websites in the public domain can expand children's opportunities for literacy learning in schools and homes.

In the final chapter, Michael C. McKenna and Tricia A. Zucker examine the digital features of multimedia from the perspective of an interactive-compensatory model. They examine the presence of supports in media and how they might relate to our understanding of the comprehension process. They also propose an intriguing hypothesis to extend the theory of synergy. They argue that some of the monitoring strategies children learn through their media experiences with supported text will transfer not only to other digital texts but to print situations as well, where conventional supports (footnotes, glossary entries, etc.) are available. This "high road to transfer," might provide substantial evidence for helping young children improve and enhance their literacy achievement.

In sum, we are enthusiastic about the growing sophistication of design principles, research methodologies, and theories that recognize multimedia as an important contributor to literacy development. The convergence of research and theoretical energy from disparate disciplines and perspectives promises to deepen our knowledge of the cognitive underpinnings of media's impact on literacy. And from the convergence, we will improve our capacities to ensure that all children have greater opportunity to achieve in literacy.

References

Anderson, D.R., & Pempeck, T.A. (2005). Television and very young children. *American Behavioral Scientist, 48,* 505–522.

Brand, S. (1987). *The media lab.* New York: Viking.

Bus, A.G., & van IJzendoorn, M.H. (1995). Mothers reading to their three-year-olds: The role of mother–child attachment security in becoming literate. *Reading Research Quarterly, 30,* 998–1015.

Bus, A.G., & van IJzendoorn, M.H. (1997). Affective dimension of mother–infant picturebook reading. *Journal of School Psychology, 35,* 47–60.

Bus, A.G., van IJzendoorn, M.H., & Pellegrini, A.D. (1995). Joint book reading makes for success in learning to read: A meta-analysis on intergenerational transmission of literacy. *Review of Educational Research, 65,* 1–21.

Calvert, S.L., Rideout, V.J., Woolard, J.L., Barra, R.F., & Strouse, G.A. (2005). Age, ethnicity, and socioeconomic patterns in early computer use: A national survey. *American Behavioral Scientist, 48* (5), 590–607.

Cook, T., Appleton, H., Conner, R., Shaffer, A., Tamkin, G., & Weber, S. (1975). *"Sesame Street" revisited.* New York: Russell Sage Foundation.

de Jong, M.T., & Bus, A.G. (2002). Quality of book-reading matters for emergent readers: An experiment with the same book in a regular or electronic format. *Journal of Educational Psychology, 94,* 145–155.

de Jong, M.T., & Bus, A.G. (2003). How well suited are electronic books to supporting literacy? *Journal of Early Childhood Literacy, 3,* 147–164.

de Jong, M.T., & Bus, A.G. (2004). The efficacy of electronic books in fostering kindergarten children's emergent story understanding. *Reading Research Quarterly, 39,* 378–393.

Ennemoser, M., & Schneider, W. (2007). Relations of television viewing and reading: Findings from a 4-year longitudinal study. *Journal of Educational Psychology, 99,* 349–368.

Frijters, J.C., Barron, R.W., & Brunello, M. (2000). Direct or mediated influences of home literacy and literacy interest on prereaders' oral vocabulary and early written language skill. *Journal of Educational Psychology, 92,* 466–477.

Greenfield, P.M., Camaioni, L., Ercolani, P., Weiss, L., Lauber, B.A., & Perucchini, P. (1996). Cognitive socialization by computer games in two cultures: Inductive discovery or mastery of an iconic code? In I.E. Sigel (Series Ed.), P.M. Greenfield, & R.R. Cocking (Vol. Eds.), *Advances in applied developmental psychology: Vol. II. Interacting with video* (pp. 141–167). Norwood, NJ: Ablex.

Hayes, D.S., & Birnbaum, D.W. (1980). Preschoolers' retention of televised events: Is a picture worth a thousand words? *Developmental Psychology, 16,* 410–416.

Jordan, A.B. (2005). Learning to use books and television. *American Behavioral Scientist, 48,* 523–538.

Labbo, L.D., & Kuhn, M.R. (2000). Weaving chains of affect and cognition: A young child's understanding of CD-ROM talking books. *Journal of Literacy Research, 32,* 187–210.

Linebarger, D.L., & Walker, D. (2004). Infants' and toddlers' television viewing and language outcomes. *American Behavioral Scientist, 46,* 1–21

McKenna, M.C. (1998). Electronic texts and the transformation of beginning reading. In D. Reinking, M.C. McKenna, L.D. Labbo, & R.D. Kieffer (Eds.), *Handbook of literacy and technology. Transformations in a post-typographic world* (pp. 45–59). Mahwah, NJ: Lawrence Erlbaum.

Mansens, T. (2007). *Elektronische boeken op internet: Nieuwe kansen voor risicokinderen?* [Electronic stories through the Internet: New chances for children at-risk?] Master thesis, Leiden University, the Netherlands.

Mayer, R.E., & Moreno, R. (1998). A split-attention effect in multimedia learning: Evidence for dual processing systems in working memory. *Journal of Educational Psychology, 90,* 312–320.

Meltzer, L. (2007). *Executive function in education. From theory to practice.* New York: The Guilford Press.

Neuman, S.B. (1988). The displacement effect: Assessing the relation between television viewing and reading performance. *Reading Research Quarterly, 23,* 414–440.

Neuman, S.B. (1997). Television as a learning environment: A theory of synergy. In J. Flood, S. Brice Heat, & D. Lapp (Eds.), *Handbook of research on teaching literacy through the communicative and visual arts* (pp. 15–30). New York: Simon & Schuster.

Neuman, S.B., & Celano, D. (2006). The knowledge gap: Implications of leveling the playing fields for low-income and middle-income children. *Reading Research Quarterly, 41,* 176–201.

Paivio, A. (1986). *Mental representations. A dual coding approach.* Oxford, UK: Oxford University Press.

Papert, S. (1996). *The connected family: Bridging the digital generation gap.* Marietta, GA: Longstreet Press.

Rideout, V.J., Vandewater, E., & Wartella, E.A. (2003). *Zero to six. Electronic media in the lives of infants, toddlers and preschoolers.* Menlo Park, CA: A Kaiser Family Foundation Report.

Rose, D., & Rose, K. (2007). Deficits in executive function processes: A curriculum-based intervention. In L. Meltzer (Ed.), *Executive function in education. From theory to practice* (pp. 287–308). New York: The Guilford Press.

Salomon, G. (1984). Television is "easy" and print is "tough": The differential investment of mental effort as a function of perceptions and attributions. *Journal of Educational Psychology, 76,* 647–658.

Sénéchal, M., & LeFevre, J., Thomas, E., & Daley, K. (1998). Differential effects of home literacy experiences on the development of oral and written language. *Reading Research Quarterly, 32*(1), 96–116.

Sharp, D.L.M., Bransford, J.D., Goldman, S.R., Risko, V.J., Kinzer, C.K., & Vye, N.J. (1995). Dynamic visual support for story comprehension and mental model building by young, at-risk children. *Educational Technology Research and Development,* 43, 25–40.

Spira, E.G., Bracken, S.S., & Fischel, J.E. (2005). Predicting improvement after first-grade reading difficulties: The effects of oral language, emergent literacy and behavior skills. *Developmental Psychology, 41,* 225–234.

Turbill, J. (2001). A researcher goes to school: Using technology in the kindergarten literacy curriculum. *Journal of Early Childhood Literacy, 1,* 255–279.

Tyner, K. (1998). *Literacy in a digital world: Teaching and learning in the age of information.* Mahwah, NJ: Laurence Erlbaum.

Uchikoshi, Y. (2005). Narrative development in bilingual kindergartners: Can Arthur help? *Developmental Psychology, 41,* 464–478.

Verhallen, M.J.A.J., Bus, A.G., & de Jong, M.T. (2006). The promise of multimedia stories for kindergarten children at risk. *Journal of Educational Psychology, 98,* 410–419.

I
Understanding the Multimedia Environment for Learning

1

Special Audience, Special Concerns
Children and the Media

Ellen Wartella and Rebekah A. Richert

The number and type of media platforms have expanded over the past 50 years from the traditional media of television, radio, movies, newspapers, books, and magazines to include other interactive digital media. Interactive media have come of age; and interactive entertainment products intended to be used by children within and out of school settings is growing: CD-ROMs, computers, the Internet, video games (for a variety of handheld and console platforms), interactive toys (including educational talking books), and a variety of wireless software for cell phones and other wireless devices. In short, for today's children, interactive media have become part of the media landscape in which they are growing up. These devices represent the most recent in a century-long introduction of media technologies into the lives of children.

This chapter reviews the American context of what we know about young children and their introduction to media, as well as what young children learn from television and its impact on their development. Most importantly, concerns about young children's use of media are rooted in an understanding that children represent a special audience with special needs.

Media Use and Access

The extent to which American children are growing up with all kinds of media available in their home is striking. From print media through screen media (television, computers) to portable technologies (PDAs and iPods), American children increasingly live in homes that enable them to have media as part of their lives during nearly all of their waking hours. According to a 2005 Kaiser Family Foundation study of a national sample of 2,000 third through twelfth graders, American children live in homes with unprecedented access to media (Roberts, Foehr, & Rideout, 2005). The typical 8- to 18-year-old lives in a home with:

- 3.5 televisions
- 3.3 radios
- 2.9 VCRs/DVD players

- 1.5 computers
- 68% have televisions and 49% have video game players in their bedrooms
- 31% have computers and 20% have Internet access in their bedrooms.

In 2003 and 2006, the Kaiser Family Foundation funded nationally representative surveys of parents of 0- to 6-year-olds, a commonly overlooked population among media researchers (Rideout & Hamel, 2006; Rideout, Vandewater, & Wartella, 2003). These studies demonstrated that in recent years, there has been a proliferation of media for children under 2: from Baby Einstein videos to entire cable channels directed at babies (e.g., Baby First). Children are starting to use screen media at very young ages, both as babies sitting on their parents' laps and as toddlers watching television and videos.

Moreover, American parents have positive attitudes about these media. According to a separate analysis of the Kaiser Family Foundation data by Vandewater et al. (2007), 70% of parents of children under 2 do not follow the 1999 American Academy of Pediatrics' (AAP) guidelines recommending that no child under 2 should watch screen media. Furthermore, the AAP recommended that older children be limited to two hours a day of screen media. According to parents' reports, 56% of 3- and 4-year-olds watch two hours or less on a typical day; and 70% of 5- and 6-year-olds watch more than two hours of screen media on a typical day (Vandewater et al. 2007).

The parents of young children do not always follow the AAP guidelines. One explanation may be that American parents generally feel positively about television created for children. According to Rideout et al. (2003), 40% of mothers of young children believed that television mostly helped children's learning. The mothers were pleased they could make use of the proliferation of educational media for preschool children.

In the past 15 years, the U.S. media landscape has grown from two national television cable networks devoted to children to more than a dozen today; and many of these networks claim to be educational for children. For example, on the U.S. public broadcasting network alone, there were five educational preschool shows aired in the 1990 to 1994 period; whereas in 2006, there were 20 educational shows for children. Add to these numbers the considerable programming on networks (many of which are international in distribution), such as Nickelodeon, Disney, and Cartoon Network, and it becomes clear that there is a plethora of children's programming available to American children.

It is not too surprising, given this context, that young children are spending a large amount of time with screen media. Television watching is a dominant activity of childhood in America today. In 2006, 48% of 0- to 6-year-olds had used a computer and 30% had played video games (Rideout, 2006). A surprising 20% of children between birth and age 2 had television sets in their bedrooms. According to parents, these children spend about 2 hours a day with screen media, which is equivalent to the amount of time parents reported their children spent playing. Although parents rated watching television as the most important of the screen media for these very young children, children also spent time with videos and DVDs (one hour and 18 minutes per day), playing video games (55 minutes per day), and using a computer (50 minutes per day) (Rideout, 2006).

Attention to screen media (television, computers, and videos or DVDs) is a major daily activity of the vast majority of American children under the age of 6. According to Rideout (2006), 83% of American children in this age range use screen media each day. Moreover, even among the youngest children, 61% of those from 6 months to 1 year of age attend to screen media on a typical day. A total of 90% of children aged 2 to 6 are reported to attend to screen media daily. It is clear that screen media are now an important part of American children's introduction to media.

Fifty years ago, children's first medium was print; and although print media use is still a part of American children's typical day, it is giving way to screen media use. For instance, according to Rideout (2006), comparable percentages of American children under 6 are reading or being read to on a typical day (83%), and slightly higher numbers of babies from 6 months to 1 year are more read to (77%) than involved in screen media. However, fewer older (2- to 6-year-olds) children read or are read to than watch screen media (81% of 2- and 3-year-olds and 87% of 4- and 6-year-olds). Screen media are dominating young children's media use, and it appears that early introduction to screen media is occurring either before or simultaneously with introduction to print media.

We are now raising a generation of children who are introduced to screen media at the same time they are introduced to print media. This phenomenon is different from earlier generations of children who typically were introduced to picture books and print media before watching television or other screens. The effect that this increased exposure to screen media may have on development is unclear.

A Special Audience

The media audience of young children, particularly children ages 0 to 6, has a unique set of issues related to media exposure and learning from media, especially screen media. Some of these issues are very practical and basic; others involve the development of more sophisticated cognitive abilities. In particular, we focus on young children's unique characteristics in relation to perception, language, imitation, symbolic representation, and analogical reasoning.

In terms of infant perception, infants do not have adult-like eye coordination until 6 months (Aslin & Jackson, 1979); and visual acuity is very poor at birth, improving over the first year of life (Kellman & Banks, 1998). Infants' auditory perception is much more developed at birth. In fact, newborn infants have the unique ability to discriminate all phonemes in all languages, regardless of the language being spoken around them (Werker, Gilbert, Humphrey, & Tess, 1981). Infants typically begin to lose this ability between 6 and 8 months of age, becoming more adult-like in their discrimination in that they can only discriminate the phonemes that occur within their native tongue (Eilers, Gavin, & Wilson, 1979). Research has demonstrated that repeated exposure to a non-native language through a book-reading interaction increases the length of time for which infants can continue to distinguish particular non-native phonemes. Interestingly, this effect was only demonstrated if the infants heard the non-native language in a live interaction, but not when the exposure was through a DVD (Kuhl, Tsao, & Liu, 2003).

It is also important to consider children's language development in relation to their learning from screen media. On average, children begin to speak their first words around 10 to 12 months of age, and the rate at which they learn new words increases substantially between 22 and 37 months of age (Benedict, 1979). This phase is often called the word spurt. Children's receptive vocabulary (i.e., the words they can understand but do not say) generally develops earlier than their productive vocabulary (i.e., the words they say) (Schafer & Plunkett, 1998). In considering how children learn new words, a large body of research suggests that infants are more likely to learn words for novel objects if a speaker is looking at an object rather than attending elsewhere (e.g., Baldwin, 1993). In fact, it has been argued that infants initially understand words as referent actions similar to gaze and pointing (e.g., Woodward, 2004). Given these factors in how children learn words, we might hypothesize that young children would not initially learn words from television until they are well into the word spurt phase of language development. Recent findings from research in our lab suggests that even after as many as 15 exposures to a video meant to teach infants words, 12- to 15-month-olds demonstrated no learning of these words (Robb, Richert, & Wartella, 2006).

Another aspect related to children's cognitive development as well as their learning from screen media where children can see a model has to do with children's ability to imitate, in particular the development of deferred imitation (i.e., imitation after a delay). Early research on imitation suggests that even neonates will imitate a live model's facial expressions (Meltzoff & Moore, 1977). However, deferred imitation is most often used as the indicator of children's learning through imitating others. In some cases, infants as young as 9 months have demonstrated memory and reproduction of event sequences up to 1 month after seeing the sequence for the first time (e.g., Barr & Hayne, 2000).

Some research has directly explored young children's ability to imitate live versus videotaped models (e.g., Barr & Hayne, 1999; Hayne, Herbert, & Simcock, 2003; Meltzoff, 1988). Typically in this procedure, children are shown various actions that can be done to a puppet or a machine. Some studies have found that 14- and 24-month-olds will imitate specific toy manipulations both immediately after viewing the video and 24 hours later (Meltzoff, 1988). Other researchers have found that 12- to 15-month-olds imitated the live demonstrations even after a 24-hour delay, but they were poor at imitating the televised demonstrations (Barr & Hayne, 1999). A separate study revealed that this deficit in learning from the videotaped models persisted until 30 months of age (Hayne et al., 2003); and further research has indicated that children in this age range need as many as six repetitions of the procedure before imitating from televised demonstrations (Muentener, Price, Garcia, & Barr, 2004).

Findings on children's development of symbolic representation can also inform our understanding of the child audience. Research on children's dual representation difficulties has indicated that children often cannot recognize that something that is very interesting in and of itself can be a source of information for an analogous, real world situation (e.g., DeLoache, 1995). In these studies, after children have been shown a toy Snoopy doll hidden in a model room, they do not look for the real Snoopy in the same place in the actual room without assistance until age 4 or 5. With varying levels of assistance, children as young as $2\frac{1}{2}$ have searched for the real Snoopy doll in its correct place in the real room.

Based on the kind of assistance required for children to solve this task (e.g., using pictures instead of the model), it has been suggested that younger children's difficulty with the model room paradigm is that they cannot see the model room as a source of information because they are interested in the model itself (DeLoache, 1987, 1991). Some of the most compelling evidence for this hypothesis comes from an experiment in which children were convinced that the large room had been shrunk using a shrinking machine (DeLoache, Miller, & Rosengren, 1997). In this case, children as young as $2\frac{1}{2}$ easily found the Snoopy in the life-sized room after seeing the toy Snoopy hidden in a smaller room that was then converted back to its real size by magic.

Similar to children's dual representation problem in the development of symbolic understanding, children may initially view electronic media as an inappropriate source of information about the real world. In this case, we would expect children to be more likely to transfer solutions from live models, and not from media. Indeed, children demonstrated different search patterns when looking for a real toy in a real room after being shown a model toy hidden in a model room depending on how that information was conveyed to them. Children were more likely to search in the correct location for the toy if they were instructed by a live model rather than a videotaped model

(Troseth, Saylor, & Archer, 2006). Interestingly, children's performance in the video condition increased if the televised model first engaged in a contingent interaction with the child.

One last aspect unique to an audience at this age has to do with children's ability to reason analogically. In order for children to demonstrate learning from screen media such as television, videos, or even computers, they must make an analogical connection between the information presented on the screen and the real world. To solve a traditional analogical problem, a child must transfer a solution from an initial story or situation (i.e., a televised episode or computer game) to solve a similar problem in a new context (i.e., a real world problem) (Holyoak & Thagard, 1995). If performed correctly, analogical thinking leads to more efficient processing by helping children apply an old solution to a new problem.

By 2 years, children can transfer solutions if the surface characteristics of the source and target analogs are similar, or the relationship is very simple (Holyoak & Thagard, 1995). For example, 1- and 2-year-old children were able to transfer the solution that a rake would help them pull a toy to within reach, after learning in a prior interaction that a cane could serve that purpose (Brown, 1989). In this case, children were not misled by differing appearances of the rake and the cane, which was painted red and white. They instead were able to map the similarity of action (pulling) from the source problem to the target. Thus, even toddlers learned to transfer a strategy to new situations.

This is not to say that by age 2 children have mastered the ability to make analogical maps. Research on preschool children's ability to transfer problem solutions often employs the paradigm developed by Holyoak and colleagues (Holyoak, Junn, & Billman, 1984). In this paradigm, children are told a story in which a problem is solved and then introduced into a situation in which they could use a similar solution for a novel problem. For example, in the original set of studies, children were told the story of a genie who wanted to transfer his jewels from one bottle into another and could not drop any of the jewels. In order to achieve this goal, the genie used a magic staff to pull one bottle closer to the other bottle and then drops the jewels into it. Children were then presented with a ball problem in which they could use any number of tools (a walking cane, a large piece of posterboard, a hollow tube, scissors, string, tape, paper clips, and rubber bands) to transfer balls from one bowl in front of them to an out of reach bowl. Within this paradigm, Holyoak et al. (1984) have demonstrated that about 30% of 4- to 5-year-old children will produce the analogical solution after hearing the story about the genie, and only 10% of children in this same age group will produce the analogical solution without hearing a story at all.

There are some contextual circumstances that facilitate children's ability to solve analogical problems. These factors include having the characters in the source story be familiar fantasy characters (Holyoak et al., 1984, Experiment

3), having prior experience with solving analogical problems (Brown & Kane, 1988), and memory for the relevant goal structure of the initial story (Brown, Kane, & Echols, 1986). Until children have achieved a more sophisticated level of analogical reasoning ability, they may be less likely to transfer solutions from electronic media because they may not view these media sources as appropriate analogs for real world situations.

Some research has supported this claim. Crawley, Anderson, Wilder, Williams, and Santomero (1999) explored how much information 3- to 5-year-old children learned from either one or five exposures to a *Blue's Clues* episode. They tested for learning of educational content and entertainment content, as well as whether children transferred concepts from games in the episode to different stimuli. They found that children performed worse on the transfer test than on the other learning tests, even after repeated exposures to the episode. In a recent pilot study in our lab, preschool children were less likely to transfer solutions after watching a video than after being read a book (Richert & Abrego, 2007).

In summary, the above findings suggest that very young children have unique perceptual and cognitive difficulties in learning from screen media when the content and formal features are developmentally inappropriate. In particular, children's difficulties in learning from screen media at these young ages appear to be a result of their problems transferring between the screen and the real world, and not necessarily related to their inability to interpret or understand the content. A large body of research suggests that slightly older children do benefit from watching and interacting with educationally focused screen media. These findings are outlined below.

Young Children and Learning from the Media

Most discussions of the role of media, especially television, in young children's development tends to focus on objectionable content children are exposed to, such as violent or commercial content. These discussions typically point out that television is a powerful teacher, and what it teaches is dependent on the content it presents. Rather than focusing on violent or commercial content, we will focus on the specific ways in which planned educational content has been shown to influence young children's learning.

Over the past 50 years, there have been a number of planned educational television programs that have demonstrated the power of television as an educational tool. In the United States, *Sesame Street* is the primary television show that has demonstrated that well-planned, educational programs specifically targeted to the needs of children at specific ages can successfully teach children a planned curriculum. According to the research presented below, children can learn their numbers, letters, science information, math information, and much about the social world from well-produced, educationally oriented screen media.

Exposure in the preschool years to programs designed to be educational has been linked with increased vocabulary (Linebarger & Walker, 2005; Rice, Huston, Truglio, & Wright, 1990; Uchikoshi, this volume), higher scores on standardized measures of problem solving and flexible thinking (Anderson et al, 2000), and higher grades in school (Anderson, Huston, Schmitt, Linebarger, & Wright, 2001). Much of this research has been conducted to examine the effects of *Sesame Street* on young (3- to 5-year-old) viewers. In a major longitudinal study, Rice et al. (1990) demonstrated that *Sesame Street* viewing at age 30 to 36 months predicted vocabulary scores at age 5, controlling for a variety of family factors including parents' education, family size, and parents' attitudes toward television. The authors argued that watching planned educational content as preschoolers sent children on a positive trajectory for schooling and that the positive benefits could be attained even when parents did not co-view *Sesame Street* with their preschoolers.

Anderson et al. (2001) conducted an analysis of high school students' educational achievement and found that adolescents who were frequent viewers of *Sesame Street* at age 5 had significantly better grades in English, science, and mathematics and read more books for pleasure. These students also expressed less aggressive attitudes and reported higher levels of motivation to achieve. In short, planned educational programming can set children on a life course of learning that persists at least through high school. In other words, there is substantial evidence of the power of well-produced, educationally sound, and developmentally appropriate screen media materials to influence positively children's learning, especially for children from ages 3 and older. Further, as is evident from the studies reviewed above, the majority of research on children's learning from educationally planned media has focused on children in the preschool years.

However, a new phenomenon has arisen in recent years in the development of baby media: videos, television shows, computer lapware, and interactive toys. These increasing amounts of media are being targeted to infants in the first 2 years of life. Whether and what babies learn from the baby videos, television shows, and other interactive media now marketed to them is a topic of major interest as researchers examine the claims of baby media marketers about infant learning from such media.

In a variety of reviews of what few studies do exist, Anderson and Pempeck (2005) and Wartella and Robb (2007) have concluded that infants younger than 24 months demonstrate a video deficit effect, namely "young children learn less from television than from equivalent real-life experiences" (Anderson & Pempeck, 2005, p. 511). Explanations for the video deficit effect tend to focus on either the perceptual differences between televised and real models (Schmitt & Anderson, 2002) or the lack of contingent social cues resulting from a videotaped model (Troseth et al., 2006). This effect is typically tested with children between the ages of 1 and 3, depending on the kinds of learning that are being tested.

Evidence of this deficit is apparent in the research outlined in the previous part of this chapter. Children have demonstrated later imitation of televised rather than live demonstrations (e.g., Barr & Hayne, 1999). The video deficit effect has also been documented in children's word learning (Grela, Lin, & Krcmar, 2003) and object retrieval tasks (Troseth, 2003; Troseth & DeLoache, 1998; Troseth et al., 2006). More specifically, children younger than $2\frac{1}{2}$ demonstrated more vocabulary learning from live models labeling objects than from videotaped models or a *Teletubbies* video (Grela et al., 2003).

In contrast to these findings on the video deficit effect, under some conditions, especially when the modeled behavior is very simple, even children younger than 2 have demonstrated learning from a televised model (e.g., Meltzoff, 1988). There is also some evidence from observing babies watching television in their homes that children around 2 years of age can learn new words from television (Lemish & Rice, 1986; Uchikoshi, this volume). These findings suggest that within certain facilitative contexts, even very young children can benefit from exposure to educationally focused screen media.

In summary, young infants' learning from screen media requires a variety of symbolic and representational abilities to allow them to understand the nature of screen messages and their application to the real world. These abilities are likely not available to children until somewhere between 30 and 36 months of age, during which time children develop the ability to decode simultaneously the visual images on the screen and to understand the representational nature of these images. Given these factors, learning from television, whether educationally focused or not, before this age is probably very limited.

This is not to say that young children can never learn from educationally focused media. As some of the above findings indicated, in some circumstances, children younger than 2 did demonstrate word learning and imitation from televised models. In particular, children have demonstrated this learning and transfer if the content is simple and developmentally appropriate and if the exposure is repeated and occurs within a familiar environment. In addition, a large body of work suggests that educationally focused media has positive effects on learning if the exposure occurs in the preschool years. Thus, developers and parents interested in providing the most positive educational screen media to children should consider the perceptual and cognitive issues related to young children's learning and capitalize on those factors most likely to increase children's learning and transfer, rather than developing programs from which children are developmentally unable to learn.

Conclusions

There has been controversy surrounding children's exposure to and learning from screen media as long as these media have existed. This controversy has often centered on children's exposure to violent images and advertising on television. However, current research suggests that screen media can also serve a positive role in educating young children. Despite the evidence of a deficit in learning from television at very young ages, much of the research reviewed above suggests that educationally focused media targeted to the particular cognitive abilities of children at particular ages can be successful at teaching children.

One of the important implications of these findings is the potential usefulness of television as a means of educating children. Consider the case of children who are growing up in at-risk homes. Many children live in homes where they have less access to educational resources, like books or tutors. In addition, many children are growing up in homes in which both parents are non-English speakers; and the children must learn to speak English in order to succeed in school. Providing these children with educationally focused media may prove to be an important educational resource.

A second implication is in reference to educationally-focused media targeted to parents of infants. At these young ages, live interaction is still very important to children's learning and development. Children also have unique difficulties in transferring information from the television to the real world. Although these media appear to have the potential for teaching infants, likely the only thing children younger than 2 learn from these kinds of products is how to use and engage with the products themselves.

Future research should begin to explore young children's learning from interactive media, not just televised images like Labbo's study in this volume. The purveyors of computers, video games, and interactive toys suggest that newer interactive media are powerful teachers. In fact, much of the marketing of these out-of-school interactive media (e.g., CD-ROMs and talking books) involves claims that they are superior platforms for children's learning compared to television, especially because of their interactive nature. In addition, the purveyors of these learning toys argue that their interactive nature engages the children in ways that regular books do not or cannot, and therefore they are superior learning devices. In short, what is always emphasized about new media is their interactive nature. Specification of the mechanisms by which interactivity aids learning from media is a powerful topic for future research, and other chapters in this book examine the power of interactive platforms to aid children's learning at various ages (e.g., Chambers, Cheung, et al. this volume; Shamir & Korat, this volume).

Researchers have suggested that various aspects of interactivity may accelerate children's cognitive development. By allowing children to organize information, provide structure to the activity, adjust the material to suit children's needs and abilities, and receive feedback, interactive technologies may encourage processing that will enhance children's learning and increase their metacognitive abilities by prompting them to think about their cognitive strategies (Calvert, 1999; Krendl & Lieberman, 1988; Papert, 1980). However, to understand whether any given interactive toy or program is a superior educational tool, we need to know much more about how well the child is using that tool and how the interactive medium engages and responds to the child's actions.

As researchers begin to explore children's learning from screen media as opposed to other kinds of stimuli, a picture of children's understanding of screen media has begun to emerge. This picture allows us to understand better both children's learning in particular situations as well as their development in general. This knowledge should inform parents, media producers, and researchers about the most positive ways to use media in early childhood and how to avoid the potential pitfalls of early media exposure.

References

Anderson, D.R., & Pempeck, T.A. (2005). Television and very young children. *American Behavioral Scientist, 48*, 505–522.

Anderson, D.R., Huston, A.C., Schmitt, K.L., Linebarger, D.L., & Wright, J.C. (2001). Early childhood television viewing and adolescent behavior: The recontact study. *Monographs of the Society for Research in Child Development, 66*, 1–147.

Anderson, D.R., Bryant, J., Wilder, A., Santomero, A., Williams, M., & Crawley, A.M. (2000). Researching Blue's Clues: Viewing behavior and impact. *Media Psychology, 2*, 179–194.

Aslin, R.N., & Jackson, R.W. (1979). Accommodative-convergence in young infants: Development of a synergistic sensory-motor system. *Canadian Journal of Psychology, 33*, 222–231.

Baldwin, D. (1993). Infants' ability to consult the speaker for clues to word reference. *Journal of Child Language, 20*, 395–418.

Barr, R., & Hayne, H. (1999). Developmental changes in imitation from television during infancy. *Child Development, 70*, 1067–1081.

Barr, R., & Hayne, H. (2000). Age-related changes in imitation: Implications for memory development. In C. Rovee-Collier, L.P. Lipsitt, & H. Hayne (Eds.), *Progress in infancy research*, Vol. 1 (pp. 21–67). Mahwah, NJ: Erlbaum.

Benedict, H. (1979). Early lexical development: Comprehension and production. *Journal of Child Language, 6*, 183–200.

Brown, A.L. (1989). Analogical learning and transfer: What develops? In S. Vosniadou & A. Ortony (Eds.), *Similarity and analogical reasoning* (pp. 369–412). Cambridge, MA: Cambridge University Press.

Brown, A.L., & Kane, M.J. (1988). Preschool children can learn to transfer: Learning to learn and learning from example. *Cognitive Psychology, 20*, 493–523.

Brown, A.L., Kane, M.J., & Echols, K. (1986). Young children's mental models determine analogical transfer across problems with a common goal structure. *Cognitive Development, 1*, 103–122.

Calvert, S.L. (1999). *Children's journeys through the information age*. Boston: McGraw-Hill College.

Crawley, A.M., Anderson, D.R., Wilder, A., Williams, M., & Santomero, A. (1999). Effects of repeated exposures to a single episode of the television program Blue's Clues on the viewing behaviors and comprehension of preschool children. *Journal of Educational Psychology, 91*, 630–637.

DeLoache, J.S. (1987). Rapid change in the symbolic functioning of very young children. *Science, 238*, 1556–1557.

DeLoache, J.S. (1991). Symbolic functioning in very young children: Understanding of pictures and models. *Child Development, 62*, 736–752.

DeLoache, JS. (1995). Early symbolic understanding and use. In D. Medin (Ed.), *The psychology of learning and motivation*, Vol. 33 (pp. 65–114). New York: Academic Press.

DeLoache, J.S., Miller, K.F., & Rosengren, K.S. (1997). The credible shrinking room: Very young children's performance with symbolic and nonsymbolic relations. *Psychological Science, 8,* 308–313.

Eilers, R.E., Gavin, W.J., & Wilson, W.R. (1979). Linguistic experience and phonemic perception in infancy: A cross-linguistic study. *Child Development, 50,* 14–18.

Grela, B., Lin, Y., & Krcmar, M. (2003, April). *Can television be used to teach vocabulary to toddlers?* Paper presented at the annual meeting of the American Speech Language Hearing Association, Chicago.

Hayne, H., Herbert, J., & Simcock, G. (2003). Imitation from television by 24- and 30-month-olds. *Developmental Science, 6,* 254–261.

Holyoak, K.J., & Thagard, P. (1995). *Mental leaps: Analogy in creative thought.* Cambridge, MA: MIT Press.

Holyoak, K.J., Junn, E.N., & Billman, D.O. (1984). Development of analogical problem-solving skill. *Child Development, 55,* 2042–2055.

Kellman, P.H., & Banks, M.S. (1998). Infant visual perception. In D. Kuhn & R.S. Siegler (Vol. Eds.), *Cognitive, language, and perceptual development,* Vol. 2 (pp. 103–146). In W. Damon (Gen. Ed.), *Handbook of child psychology.* New York: Wiley.

Krendl, K.A., & Lieberman, D.A. (1988). Computers and learning: A review of recent research. *Journal of Educational Computing Research, 4,* 367–389.

Kuhl, P.K., Tsao, F-M., & Liu, H-M. (2003). Foreign-language experience in infancy: Effects of short-term exposure and social interaction on phonetic learning. *Proceedings of the National Academy of Sciences, 100*(15), 9096–9101.

Lemish, D., & Rice, M.L. (1986). Television as a talking picture book: A prop for language acquisition. *Journal of Child Language, 13,* 251–274.

Linebarger, D.L., & Walker, D. (2005). Infants' and toddlers' television viewing and language outcomes. *American Behavioral Scientist, 48,* 624–645.

Meltzoff, A.N. (1988). Imitation of televised models by infants. *Child Development, 59,* 1221–1229.

Meltzoff, A.N., & Moore, N.K. (1977). Imitation of facial and manual gestures by human neonates. *Science, 198,* 75–78.

Muentener, P., Price, K., Garcia, A., & Barr, R. (2004, April). *Transferring the representation: Infants can imitate from television.* Paper presented at the annual meeting of the Eastern Psychological Association, Washington, DC.

Papert, S. (1980). *Mindstorms: Children, computers, and powerful ideas.* New York: Basic Books.

Rice, M.L., Huston, A.C., Truglio, R., & Wright, J.C. (1990). Words from Sesame Street: Learning vocabulary while viewing. *Developmental Psychology, 26,* 421–428.

Richert, R.A., & Abrego, T. (2007). *Preschooler's transfer from fantasy through books and video.* Unpublished manuscript, University of California, Riverside.

Rideout, V.J., & Hamel, E. (2006). *The media family: Electronic media in the lives of infants, toddlers, preschoolers, and their parents.* Menlo Park, CA: The Henry J. Kaiser Family Foundation.

Rideout, V.J., Vandewater, E.A., & Wartella, E.A. (2003). *Zero to six: Electronic media in the lives of infants, toddlers and preschoolers.* Menlo Park, CA: The Henry J. Kaiser Family Foundation.

Robb, M., Richert, R.A, & Wartella, E.A. (2006). *Infants' learning of words from Baby Wordsworth.* Unpublished manuscript, University of California, Riverside.

Roberts, D., Foehr, U.G., & Rideout, V. (2005) Generation M: Media and the lives of 8–18 year olds. Washington, DC: The Henry J. Kaiser Family Foundation.

Schafer, G., & Plunkett, K. (1998). Rapid word learning by fifteen-month-olds under tightly controlled conditions. *Child Development, 69,* 309–320.

Schmitt, K.L., & Anderson, D.R. (2002). Television and reality: Toddlers' use of visual information from video to guide behavior. *Media Psychology, 4,* 51–76.

Troseth, G. (2003). TV guide: Two-year-old children learn to use video as a source of information. *Developmental Psychology, 39,* 140–150.

Troseth, G.L., & DeLoache, J. (1998). The medium can obscure the message: Young children's understanding of video. *Child Development, 69,* 950–965.

Troseth, G.L., Saylor, M.M., & Archer, A.H. (2006). Young children's use of video as a source of socially relevant information. *Child Development, 77,* 786–799.

2

Digital Beginnings

Young Children's Use of Popular Culture, Media and New Technologies in Homes and Early Years Settings

Jackie Marsh

Technological developments have led, over the past three or four decades, to significant changes in the ways in which we communicate and undertake daily tasks involving the reading, writing and creation of texts. The impact of this digital revolution on the lives of young children is rarely considered, yet they are as engaged in the social practices of the "new media age" (Kress, 2003) as the older children, adolescents and adults who surround them. In addition, it is vital that educational institutions respond to these wider social and cultural changes in order that they offer children opportunities to develop skills, knowledge and understanding, which will be of value in the new knowledge economy (Luke & Carrington, 2002). This chapter, therefore, examines some of these themes and offers insights into the new media worlds of our youngest children, focusing on their digital literacy practices and considering ways in which parents support these practices.

This chapter will argue that children are avid users and producers of media from an early age and that these experiences should inform approaches to the teaching and learning of literacy. The chapter will paint a broad picture of young children's media use in order to underpin more detailed analyses of children's interaction with specific media, as outlined in other chapters in this volume. The chapter focuses on young children's use of popular culture, media and new technologies in the home. It is necessary to define these terms before discussing the issues further, given the wide and varied understanding of these terms. "Popular culture" refers to texts, practices and artefacts that are embedded into the daily lives of many young children and includes toys, games, films and television programs and clothes. Much of children's popular culture is shaped by media and new technologies. "Media" is a term used for materials and resources in a range of formats and modes that are used for communication, such as books, comics and magazines, newspapers, television programs and films. "New technologies" is a phrase used to refer to technological innovations that have been made

Vandewater, E.A., Rideout, V.J., Wartella, E.A., Huang, X., Lee, J.H., & Shim, M. (2007). Digital childhood: Electronic media and technology use among infants, toddlers, and preschoolers. *Pediatrics, 119*(5), 1006–1015.

Wartella, E. & Robb, M. (2007). Young children, new media. *Journal of Children and Media, 1*(1), 35–44.

Werker, J.F., Gilbert, J.H., Humphrey, K., & Tess, R.D. (1981). Developmental aspects of cross-language speech perception. *Child Development, 52,* 349–355.

Woodward, A.L. (2004). Infants' use of action knowledge to get a grasp on words. In D.G. Hall & S.R. Waxman (Eds.), *Weaving a lexicon* (pp. 149–172). Cambridge, MA: MIT Press.

possible through digitization. It can include "old" technologies, such as radio and television, which have been transformed through the digital signal, in addition to computers, console games, hand-held computers and mobile phones. Finally, "digital literacy" refers to literacy practices that are mediated through the digital signal. These practices are focused on lettered representation, such as words and letters on screen, although it is recognized that visual images, both still and moving, also play a significant part in children's digital literacy practices. It is important to recognize that young children's meaning-making is increasingly multimodal in nature (Flewitt, in press) and therefore to limit study solely to the written word on paper is to be too narrowly focused on a specific set of practices.

There have been a number of surveys of children and young people's media use over the last decade (Livingstone & Bovill, 1999; Livingstone & Bober, 2005). However, none of these studies have explored the media use of children under the age of 6 in England. The most comprehensive survey to date of this youngest age group is the report *Zero to Six: Electronic Media in the Lives of Infants, Toddlers and Preschoolers* (Rideout, Vandewater & Wartella, 2003). This details the findings from a telephone survey of 1,065 families in the United States. This survey indicated that many young children's lives are media-rich and that they are developing a wide range of skills, knowledge and understanding of media from birth. Children in this study had access to a wide range of technologies in the home and they were using them from a very young age. Parents reported that their children were developing competence in using these technologies from their first years of life.

This use of media and new technologies has raised a number of concerns. There has been a range of "moral panics" (Cohen, 1987) taking place in relation to young children's use of popular culture, media and new technologies. These have included concerns about the perceived negative impact of media on children's emotional, social and cognitive development, in addition to worries about the way in which children are becoming positioned as economic targets by multinational companies (Kenway & Bullen, 2001). These concerns are not to be dismissed in their entirety; there is a need to consider the way in which childhood is being constructed and shaped by specific political, economic and social practices (Buckingham, 2000). Nevertheless, often these anxieties about media and young children are based on misinformation and nervousness about the prospect of a seemingly "runaway world" (Giddens, 2000; Leach, 1968) in which children and young people are the "digital insiders" and adults the outsiders (Lankshear & Knobel, 2004), unsure about where the technology is leading and concerned about losing control. Instead of viewing young children's use of media in purely negative terms, Robinson and Mackey (2003) propose that we embrace an "asset model," a model that examines the positive aspects these encounters with media and technology bring. What Robinson and others (Mackey, 2002) argue is that children's literacy is enhanced and developed through these multiple forms, not diminished. In the study reported in this chapter, therefore, the complex relationships between different aspects of children's popular cultural interests were of interest. Children's responses to a range of technologies and media were explored and the nature of parental involvement in children's use of media was identified.

This chapter also acknowledges the vital role that popular culture plays in the self-identities and self-esteem of young children. Many children develop a sense of themselves through the media, they use the media to perform different identities and try out new roles and their social and cultural worlds are permeated with their favorite popular cultural and media narratives. Activities relating to favorite characters, television programs and films offer a means of forging relationships with family members and friendships with peers (Pahl, 2002); they become the cement that binds together the varied building blocks of their lives. It is important for parents, carers and educators to understand the role that these texts and artefacts play in contemporary childhoods; to dismiss them as "fads" is to underestimate their impact.

In the past, educational institutions have not always valued the cultural practices of childhood (Dyson, 1997). Pushed to the margins of classroom life, popular culture and media have been seen to pose threats to the educational attainment of children (Marsh & Millard, 2005). However, the use of children's popular culture in educational institutions can offer recognition of their identities and the things they value, thus enhancing their self-esteem and motivating them to engage in learning (Dyson, 1997, 2002; Marsh, 2000). In addition, there is a need for educators to consider the ways in which children's literacy practices are changing in the digital age if schools are to keep up with developments. No longer are paper and pencil the preferred modes of communication for many in society (Kress, 2003), including very young children. Examining the way in which these "toddler netizens" (Luke, 1999) are navigating the worlds of technologically-mediated childhoods is a significant task for early years educators in the twenty-first century.

Finding Out about Children's Media Habits

This chapter focuses on the "Digital Beginnings"[1] study, which looked at uses of popular culture, media and new technologies in homes and early years' settings in England (Marsh, Brooks, Hughes, Ritchie & Roberts, 2005). The study consisted of two stages. The aims of the first stage of the study were to identify preschool children's access to and use of popular culture, media and new technologies and to identify parents' and carers' attitudes towards children's use of popular culture, media and new technologies. The aims of the second stage of the study were to identify early years practitioners' current use of media and new technologies and to identify the impact of the introduction of aspects of popular culture, media and new technologies into the early years curriculum.

Twenty early years settings in ten Local Education Authorities (LEAs) in England were randomly selected to take part in the study, 200 in total. The settings were varied in nature. Some, for example, were state funded nurseries, others were privately owned. Other settings were run by volunteers, such as parent and toddler groups. It was important to include a range of child-care settings in the study in order to ensure that the respondents varied in terms of social class, ethnicity and location. The LEAs were spread geographically across England and varied in terms of the type of authority and their demographics. For example, metropolitan authorities were more likely than others to have multicultural communities, whereas authorities in rural areas were more likely to house primarily white communities. The final sample of 1,852 families varied greatly in terms of social class, with families in all social class groups represented. The largest social group represented was lower middle class, blue collar workers, who represented 42% of the sample. A further 30% of the sample was working class and 24% upper middle class and upper class. A total of 78% of the families who took part in the survey identified their children as white, 11% identified their children as Asian or Asian British, 4% Black or Black British, 1% Chinese and 5% Dual Heritage. The survey therefore provided a snapshot of family life across varied social and ethnic groups.

Questionnaires for parents and carers of children attending the 200 settings in the sample were sent out, along with questionnaires for practitioners working in the early years settings. A total of 1,852 parents' questionnaires were returned (which represented a response rate of 27%) and 524 practitioners' questionnaires returned (which represented a response rate of 45%). Sixty parents took part in telephone interviews and 12 practitioners took part in semi-structured interviews.

The questionnaire surveys for parents explored a range of areas. Questions related to the length of time children spent using various media and technologies, the way in which they used them, where they used them and the age at which they first engaged in those practices. Parents' attitudes towards this media use were also explored and the level of their engagement in it determined. The questionnaire surveys for practitioners asked them to identify the range of ICT hardware and software the setting they worked in contained, and required them to detail their use of this hardware and software. The attitudes of the practitioners towards the use of media and new technologies were also explored. Questions in both surveys were varied and included open and closed questions, multiple choice (including the use of a Likert scale) and ranking questions.

In the second stage of the project, once the questionnaire surveys had been returned, nine settings agreed to conduct action research projects in which they introduced an aspect of popular culture, media and new technologies into the foundation stage communication, language and literacy curriculum.

Settings were asked to identify randomly up to eight children for focused observations and data collection at this stage of the project. The total number of children who were involved in Stage 2 of the study was 67; 37 boys and 30 girls, from a range of families in terms of ethnicity and socioeconomic status. Parents of the children were contacted to take part in structured telephone interviews before the start of the project and on its completion. Despite several calls, it was not possible to make contact with all of the parents of the focus children. Interviews took place with 60 parents at the start of the project and 33 parents at the end of the project. These semi-structured interviews explored in greater depth some of the themes identified in the questionnaire survey responses. Interviews conducted with parents at the end of the study focused on the children's responses to the intervention projects in which an aspect of popular culture, media and new technologies was introduced into the foundation stage communication, language and literacy curriculum. Data were quantitatively and qualitatively analyzed.

Next, the general findings of the project in relation to the children's uses of popular culture, media and new technologies will be outlined. I will then discuss briefly how parents and other family members scaffolded children's developing understanding of digital literacy. Finally, I will outline the practices in the early years settings and share some of the findings relating to the work undertaken in the action research projects in order to explore the possibilities offered when the language and literacy curriculum builds on children's home experiences of media and new technologies.

Children's Use of Media and New Technologies in the Home

Overall Use

The study confirmed that children have access to a wide range of media and technologies. The ownership of televisions and video/DVD players is almost universal, with only 2% of homes not having access to these technologies. A total of 81% of families own one or more desktop computers and/or laptops.

Patterns of use are different from patterns of access. However, the data suggest that the children in this study are avid users of a range of technologies and this is a pattern established from birth. On a typical day, the mean number of minutes children engage in screen use (including watching television, watching videos/DVDs, using computers, playing console games and playing handheld games, such as Gameboy) is 126, which is two hours and six minutes.

There has been general concern about the amount of time children engage with screens. However, the children in this study spend an equal period of time playing inside with toys on a typical day as they do in screen use, and Figure 2.1 suggests that children, on a typical day, enjoy a well-balanced diet consisting of varied activities.

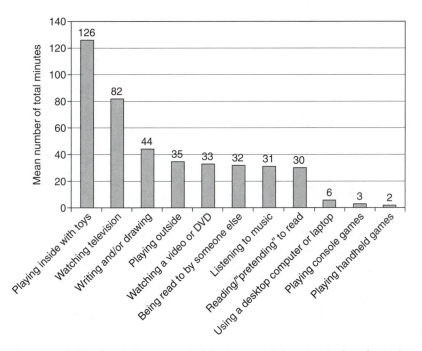

Figure 2.1 Children's activities on a typical day (*n* = 1,731) (source: Marsh et al., 2005).

As Buckingham (2004) suggests, more longitudinal, observational studies of children's media use are needed in order to confirm, or refute, such claims. Nevertheless, the data in this study indicate that the majority of very young children are not excessive users of media, according to parental reports.

A frequent source of anxiety for some is the thought that children and young people's use of media is driving them into engagement in excessive solitary activities. However, this study suggests that this is far from the case. Instead of decreasing time with family members, media use appears to provide opportunities for social interaction. The percentage of children engaging in specific activities entirely on their own is outlined in Figure 2.2. As this illustrates, the activity that appears to be least social in nature is reading/"pretending"[2] to read.

This social use of media may be due to the location of computers and televisions, which are more likely to be placed in family rooms and shared social spaces that facilitate paired and group interaction with media. There was also evidence from the study that many parents purchased educational software for their children and data from the interviews suggest that some of the shared media use related to this, as parents support children's use of the software. However, there is a small minority of parents (9%) who report that their young children were more confident users of technology than themselves. As one parent reported:

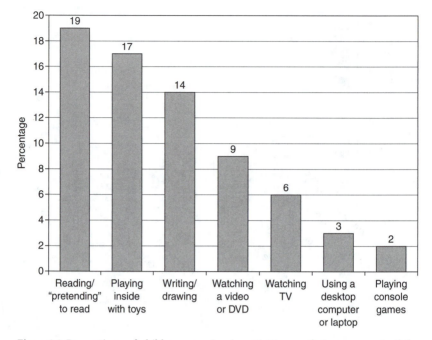

Figure 2.2 Proportions of children engaging in activities on their own, most of the time (*n* = 1,656) (source: Marsh et al., 2005).

INTERVIEWER: How independent is she, would she be able to switch it [the computer] on, put a disc in or click on an icon?

PARENT: Yes.

INTERVIEWER: She's fairly independent, then?

PARENT: She's possibly better than we are ... I don't think she is quite as competent as some, but she is certainly better than we are.

Books

There appears to be little evidence that books were playing a minimal role in children's lives, a fear that is sometimes expressed by those who are concerned about the implications of the new media age (Birkerts, 1998). A total of 75% of children own more than 20 books.

A total of 82% of all children spend time with books on a typical day. Parents report that children read, or "pretend" to read, for an average of 30 minutes on a typical day. They are read to by someone else for an average of 32 minutes. Engaging with books either as an individual or with others, therefore, is the third most frequent activity for children (after playing inside with toys and watching television).

Eighty-one percent of children own books related to their favorite television programs or characters. Sixty percent of parents in the survey feel that these books motivate their child to read or write, and this is supported by data from the interviews with parents, in which many parents state that this is the case for their child:

> He's got the monsters book, he's got the "Bug's Life" book, "Toy Story" book and they are the ones he always goes for. If I say, "Go and choose a book," he will choose generally one of his favourite films. It motivates him to pick a book up in the first place, certainly.

Some parents note that children deliberately relate the books to the film/ television program, drawing on the language experienced with the moving image to retell the stories:

> I mean, he'll sit there and he'll watch the "Jungle Book" on the DVD and then maybe the next couple of days he'll get his books and he'll look at the pictures and say, "Oh, I've seen that bit on the telly." He does sit there and he makes up his own words, do you know what I mean, like he's reading the book.

As Neuman (1995) has suggested, the relationship between television viewing and reading can be positive, as watching television can interest children in related reading material. Children are also motivated to read by comics and magazines that are related to their media interests. What is significant is the synergy between the various media. Children are motivated to move across media by their interests in specific narratives that are embedded in a range of media, not just one, and therefore, as Neuman points out in a chapter in this volume, children's movement across media and the synergy this creates needs close examination.

Computers

Eighty-one percent of all families in the survey report that they own one or more desktop computers and/or laptops. On a typical day, 53% of children aged 0–6 use a desktop computer or laptop at home, 45% for less than an hour, 8% for an hour or more. Forty-two percent of this age group are reported as never using a desktop computer or laptop at home on a typical day. Parents suggest that their children are independent users of computers:

PARENT: We would probably go to the CBeebies web page and have the icon and just click on the characters and play games.
INTERVIEWER: So, she is quite independent, then, in using the computer?
PARENT: She is, she is a very independent girl anyway. She is always batting my hand away.

Parents state that children undertake a wide range of activities on computers, including sending emails, using Internet chatrooms (both with adults as scribes), playing Internet games, writing stories and making cards.

Mobile Phones

Family ownership of at least one mobile phone is almost universal. There appears to be minimal independent use of mobile phones by children in this age group, with only 14% of parents reporting that their child had ever used a mobile phone to make a call and only 1% stating that this had been done independently. However, using phones with the help of others is part of some families' communication practices with their young children:

> Sometimes I put a little bit of money on it just for her to play with her friend because she goes away to the caravan with my mum, her grandma on a weekend, so she will text little pictures to us and things.

It is clear that children are being inducted into mobile phone use from a young age and, whilst not using phones independently for most of the time, are developing understanding of their role, nature and the uses to which they are put in social contexts. In addition to mobile phone practices within the home, toys, sweets, adverts and television programs all reflect this techno-logical landscape of text messages, ring-tones and emoticons and thus the communicative practices related to mobile phones are firmly embedded within the habitus (Bourdieu, 1977) of many contemporary early childhoods.

These data indicate that literacy practices in contemporary childhoods are changing. Emergent literacy is now an established part of early childhood dis-course. Since Marie Clay introduced the term in 1966, the subsequent four decades have led to a richer understanding of the way in which children's engagement in print literacy practices from birth is an integral part of their literacy development. Parents scaffold children's emerging understanding of literacy as a social practice. This is also the case with digital literacy.

Parents support the development of their children's digital literacy skills and understanding in a number of ways, as previous studies have indicated (Marsh, 2004a, 2004b; Marsh & Thompson, 2001). Some parents talk to chil-dren about how narratives cross media and develop children's understanding of the way in which elements of narrative remain constant across media, such as setting, plot and character. Through their television-related play with children, parents enhance children's understanding of character and view-point. Further, some parents scaffold children's developing understanding of the affordances of various modes by talking with them about the different effects of sounds and images when watching televisual narratives. Parents talk to children about the way in which the narratives they encountered cross modes, which may contribute to children's understanding of the concept of transduction (Kress, 2003), that is the process by which semiotic material is transformed as it moves from one mode into another. Observational studies suggest that the way in which parents support children's narrative understanding of multimedia, multimodal texts appears to be similar to the strategies and practices they adopt in relation to print-based texts, in particular using talk to extend children's responses to texts (Marsh, 2004a, 2004b; Marsh & Thompson, 2001).

Overall, the data from Stage 1 of the "Digital Beginnings" (Marsh et al., 2005) study indicate that children in England are immersed in a media-rich world. The findings in this study correlate with other studies of children's media use (Livingston & Bober, 2005; Livingtsone & Bovill, 2002; Rideout et al., 2003). There are differences in relation to age, gender, social class and ethnicity (see Marsh et al., 2005), which emphasizes the importance of ensuring that early years settings and schools offer meaningful and extensive experiences with technology and media in order to exacerbate the digital divide. However, Stage 2 of the study offered some rather worrying findings in relation to children's engagement with media in early years settings, which are detailed below.

Children's Use of Media and New Technologies in Early Years Settings

Although the data from the parents' surveys indicate that children are growing up in homes rich in technological experiences, this does not appear to be the case in relation to the early years settings that the children attend. Practitioners were asked to outline the resources they had for engaging in work that utilized new technologies. Whilst the majority of practitioners work in settings that have at least one television, DVD/video player, desktop computer, CD/audiocassette player or digital still camera, at least a third of practitioners are based in settings that do not own one of these, with the figure rising to 48% lack of ownership in the case of digital still cameras. This figure is higher in relation to video cameras—only 11% of settings own one or more video cameras, a figure that is surprising, given the emphasis on recording children for formative assessment purposes (Clark & Moss, 2001).

The ownership of hardware is reflected in the statistics relating to overall usage. Practitioners were asked which of the ICT hardware they had used in the early years setting in the week prior to the survey. Figure 2.3 indicates that there is little use of hardware other than CD/audiocassette players, desktop computers, televisions and video/DVD players.

However, much of the children's use of computers in some settings appears to be a self-selected activity. Practitioners were asked to specify how often they plan for the use of computers in the setting, both by individual children and by groups. A total of 32% of practitioners report that they rarely (7%) or never (25%) plan for children to use computers individually. This may be due to early years practice in which children are not directed to tasks, but because of inequality of access to technologies in the home, it is

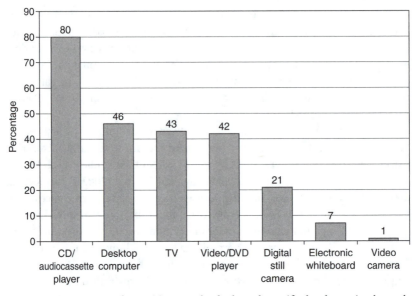

Figure 2.3 Percentage of practitioners who had used specific hardware in the early years setting in week prior to survey (*n* = 514) (source: Marsh et al., 2005).

important that early years settings provide targeted opportunities for children to engage with computers.

Practitioners were asked if they had used computers in the setting in the week prior to the survey. Only 46% had. Children are therefore more likely to use a computer at home, if their families own one (53% of children used a computer at home on a typical day), than in an early years setting. This has obvious consequences for the minority of children who do not have regular access to a computer at home.

One of the barriers to increased use of popular culture, media and new technologies in early childhood settings is lack of subject knowledge in the field (Marsh, 2006). This certainly appears to be the case in this study. Many practitioners suggest that they know little about the use of media and new technologies in the language and literacy curriculum and this affects levels of confidence. Practitioners express more confidence in their levels of expertise in some aspects of popular culture, media and new technologies than others. Seventy-four percent state that they are confident or very confident in their knowledge of children's popular cultural interests, with 55% expressing confidence in their knowledge of how to use these interests in the foundation stage curriculum. But only 32% express confidence in their ability to analyze film and television, and even fewer feel confident with photo-editing software (21%) and film-editing software (5%). Practitioners report higher levels of confidence regarding the use of digital cameras, although there is a sizeable minority (28%) that expressed a lack of confidence.

Age has an impact on the confidence practitioners express towards the use of various technologies. Older practitioners are more likely to feel less confident, and this is also the case in relation to the use of computers. Twenty-five percent of all practitioners state that they do not feel very confident with computers (5% of these not at all confident). However, only 8% of the 18–21 age group feel this way, whilst 42% of the 46–65 age group express this lack of confidence. This appears to corroborate the claims of Lankshear and Knobel (2004), that there appears to be a "digital divide" with regard to digital insiders and outsiders—between people who have been immersed in technology from a young age and people who have had to acquire the skills at a later stage in life.

Practitioners are not complacent about this lack of subject knowledge and confidence, with many suggesting that they would like to improve the situation. Sixty-eight percent of practitioners agree that they would like more information on how to use popular culture productively in the foundation stage, 63% want more training on how to develop children's understanding of media, 58% state that they would like training on developing children's media production skills and 70% agree that they would like more training on how to use ICT in the foundation stage. Comments made by practitioners on open questions in the survey indicate that they are aware of the need to develop children's skills and understanding in relation to new technologies and see this as important for the new media age:

> As educators we need to have a great amount of knowledge on all agendas that will affect a child's future.

> As technology continues to advance apace, and is commonplace in so many educational and employment situations, a good grasp of how to use it will be imperative in future years.

> It is the future—computers are everywhere today and children need the skills to use them.

Early years practitioners, therefore, appear to be keen to develop practice in relation to media and new technologies, but many report that they have not had sufficient professional development opportunities. This needs to be addressed if early years practice in relation to media and new technologies is to be enhanced.

In the second stage of this project, nine early years settings introduced aspects of popular culture, media and new technologies into the communication, language and literacy curriculum. Activities involving media and new technologies included making electronic and digital books, watching and analyzing moving image stories and creating presentations using electronic software.

Table 2.1 The Leuven Involvement Scale—level descriptors

Level 1	No activity
Level 2	Frequently interrupted activity
Level 3	More or less continuous activity
Level 4	Activity with intense moments
Level 5	Sustained intense activity

One of the aims of the study was to examine the impact of these action research projects on the motivation and engagement of children in curriculum activities related to communication, language and literacy. In order to identify this, practitioners were asked, as one of a number of methods, to undertake three observations of children prior to the project and three observations of children during the project, using the *Leuven Involvement Scale for Young Children* (Laevers, 1994).

The levels of involvement are described as follows. A total of 84 observations of 14 children were used for this analysis. As Figure 2.4 indicates, during the project levels of engagement were higher, with 80% of scores at levels 4 and 5 (as opposed to 38% of scores at these levels prior to the project).

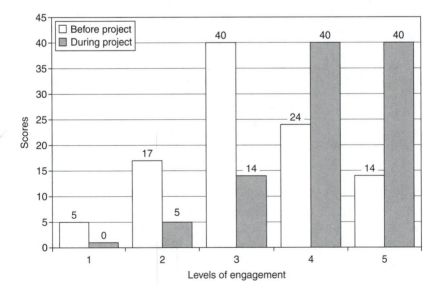

Figure 2.4 Scores on *The Leuven Involvement Scale* prior to and during the project ($n = 84$) (source: Marsh et al., 2005).

Note:
Level 1: no activity; level 2; frequently interrupted activity; level 3: more or less continuous activity; level 4: activity with intense moments; level 5: sustained intense activity.

This relationship between the use of media and new technologies and enhanced engagement in literacy and language activities has been identified in other studies (Marsh, 2000). Indeed, there is evidence to suggest that the use of media does not simply promote engagement, but increases attainment in literacy (Moses, 2008; Primary National Strategy (PNS)/United Kingdom Literacy Association (UKLA), 2004). It is important, therefore, for educators to begin to develop further the use of media and new technologies in order to enhance print-based literacy. However, this should not be the only reason for using such tools in the language and literacy curriculum. It is essential that young children grasp the alphabetic principle, but it is also important that they begin to develop understanding of multimodal texts, become familiar with how word, sound and image work together in a text and identify the affordances of the various modes. These are the skills, knowledge and understanding that children need as we move into an increasingly multimodal, multimedia society. The action research projects, therefore, were important in developing practitioners' subject knowledge and confidence in relation to digital literacy practices. It was also notable that the parents interviewed at the end of the projects were enthusiastic about the impact of the projects on their children, with parents reporting children becoming more excited about attending nurseries during the project and demonstrating greater levels of engagement in digital literacy practices in the home.

Conclusion

This study outlined here has offered a variety of perspectives on the changing worlds of very young children in contemporary society. It has provided evidence of the extensive nature of children's engagement with popular culture, media and new technologies in the home and indicated that this engagement is much more limited in early years settings. The chapter has also considered the outcomes of action research projects in which aspects of popular culture, media and new technologies were introduced into the communication, language and literacy curriculum of early years settings. It is suggested that those educators who have responded to the challenge of the new media age by developing appropriate curricula and pedagogy enable children to build on their digital "funds of knowledge" (Moll, Amanti, Neff, & Gonzales, 1992) and provide them with opportunities to engage fully with the technological, social and cultural demands of the knowledge economy (Luke & Carrington, 2002). Not to develop these pedagogical approaches so is to assign our youngest children to an education which, although generally successful in preparing children for encounters with the written word on paper, is not yet as successful in ensuring they are proficient with the multimodal, multimedia texts and practices that permeate everyday life in the twenty-first century.

Notes

1. The Digital Beginnings study was funded by BBC Worldwide and the Esmée Fairbairn Foundation. For the full report, see the project website: www.digitalbeginnings.shef.ac.uk/.
2. In a previous study (Marsh, 2004a), it was clear that parents did not consider early literacy behavior, such as retelling a story, or pointing to words in a text without one-to-one correspondence, to be "reading," even though early literacy educators do see it as part of the continuum of learning to read (Hall, Larson, & Marsh, 2003). Therefore, the phrase "pretending to read" was added to this survey in order to capture this behavior.

References

Birkerts, S. (1998). Sense and semblance: The implications of virtuality. In Cox, B. (Ed.), *Literacy is not enough: Essays on the importance of reading.* Manchester, UK: Manchester University Press.

Bourdieu, P. (1977). *Outline of a theory of practice,* trans. Richard Nice. Cambridge, UK: Cambridge University Press.

Buckingham, D. (2000). *After the death of childhood: Growing up in the age of electronic media.* Cambridge, UK: Polity Press.

Buckingham, D. (2004). *The media literacy of children and young people: A review of the research literature.* London: Ofcom.

Clark, A., & Moss, P. (2001). *Listening to children: The mosaic approach.* London: National Children's Bureau.

Cohen, S. (1987). *Folk devils and moral panics: The creation of the mods and rockers* (2nd ed.). Oxford, UK: Blackwell.

Dyson, A.H. (1997). *Writing superheroes: Contemporary childhood, popular culture, and classroom literacy.* New York: Teachers College Press.

Dyson, A.H. (2002). *Brothers and sisters learn to write: Popular literacies in childhood and school cultures.* New York: Teachers College Press.

Flewiit, R. (in press). Multimodal Literacies. In J. Marsh & E. Hallet (Eds.), *Desirable literacies: Approaches to language and literacy in the early years* (2nd edn.). London: Sage.

Giddens, A. (2000). *Runaway world: How globalization is reshaping our lives.* London: Routledge.

Hall, N., Larson, J., & Marsh, J. (Eds.) (2003). *Handbook of early childhood literacy.* London, New Delhi, Thousand Oaks, CA: Sage.

Kenway, J., & Bullen, E. (2001). *Consuming children: Education–entertainment–advertising.* Buckingham, UK: Open University Press.

Kress, G. (2003). *Literacy in the new media age.* London: Routledge.

Laevers, F. (1994). *The Leuven Involvement Scale for young children,* LISYC Manual and video tape, Experimental Educational Series No. 1. Leuven, Belgium: Centre of Experimental Studies.

Lankshear, C., & Knobel, M. (2004). Text-related roles of the digitally "at home." Paper presented at the American Education Research Association Annual Meeting, San Diego, April 15, 2004.

Leach, E. (1968). *A runaway world: the 1967 Reith Lectures.* Oxford, UK: Oxford University Press.

Livingstone, S., & Bober, M. (2005). *UK children go online: Final report of key project findings.* London: London School of Economics and Political Science.

Livingstone, S., & Bovill, M. (1999). *Young people, new media: Report of the research project: Children, young people and the changing media environment.* London: London School of Economics and Political Science.

Luke, A., & Carrington, V. (2002). Globalisation, literacy, curriculum practice. In R. Fisher, M. Lewis & G. Brooks (Eds.), *Language and literacy in action.* London: Routledge/Falmer.

Luke, C. (1999). What next? Toddler netizens, Playstation thumb, techno-literacies. *Contemporary Issues in Early Childhood, 1,* 95–100.

Mackey, M. (2002). *Literacies across media: Playing the text.* London: RoutledgeFalmer.

Marsh, J. (2000). Teletubby tales: popular culture in the early years language and literacy curriculum. *Contemporary Issues in Early Childhood, 1*(2), 119–136.

Marsh, J. (2004a). *BBC Child of Our Time: Young children's use of popular culture, media and new technologies.* Sheffield, UK: University of Sheffield.

Marsh, J. (2004b). The techno-literacy practices of young children, *Journal of Early Childhood Research, 2,* 51–66.

Marsh, J. (2006). Tightropes, tactics and taboos: Pre-service teachers' beliefs and practices in relation to popular culture and literacy. In J. Marsh & E. Millard (Eds.), *Popular literacies, childhoods and schooling* (pp. 73–89). London: Routledge.

Marsh, J., & Millard, E. (Eds.) (2005). *Popular literacies, childhoods and schooling.* London: Routledge.

Marsh, J., & Thompson, P. (2001). Parental involvement in literacy development: Using media texts. *Journal of Research in Reading, 24,* 266–278.

Marsh, J., Brooks, G., Hughes, J., Ritchie, L., & Roberts, S. (2005). *Digital Beginnings: Young children's use of popular culture, media and new technologies.* Sheffield, UK: University of Sheffield. Retrieved June, 2006 from: www.digitalbeginnings.shef.ac.uk/.

Moll, L., Amanti, C., Neff, D., & Gonzalez, N. (1992). Funds of knowledge for teaching: Using a qualitative approach to connect homes and classrooms. *Theory into Practice. 31,* 132–141.

Moses, A.M. (2008). Impacts of television viewing on young children's literacy development in the USA: a review of the literature. *Journal of Early Childhood Literacy, 8*(1), 67–102.

Neuman, S.B. (1995). *Literacy in the television age: The myth of the TV effect.* Norwood, NJ: Ablex Publishing Corporation.

Pahl, K. (2002). Ephemera, mess and miscellaneous piles: Texts and practices in families. *Journal of Early Childhood Literacy, 2,* 145–165.

Primary National Strategy (PNS)/United Kingdom Literacy Association (UKLA) (2004). *Raising boys' achievement in writing.* London: HMSO.

Rideout, V.J., Vandewater, E.A., & Wartella, E.A. (2003). *Zero to six: Electronic media in the lives of infants, toddlers and preschoolers.* Washington, DC: Kaiser Foundation.

Robinson, M., & Mackey, M. (2003). Film and television. In N. Hall, J. Larson & J. Marsh (Eds.), *Handbook of Early Childhood Literacy.* London, New Delhi, Thousand Oaks, CA: Sage.

3

The Case for Multimedia Presentations in Learning

A Theory of Synergy

Susan B. Neuman

Since Marshall McLuhan's elliptical phrase, "the medium is the message" (McLuhan, 1964), there has been a continuing and broadening debate on the influence of media in shaping cognition. Much of the debate has focused on whether or to what extent media should be used in instruction and how they might maximize children's learning. The argument centers around the relative role of the characteristic symbol system of such media as television, print, computers, and radio—the combination of pictures, sounds, print—and how these distinctive forms influence information processing demands. A number of scholars have made the case that each medium implicitly cultivates new skills for exploration and internal representation (Reeves & Nass, 2003). Therefore, as children are taught to read, David Olson a noted language theorist claimed (Olson, 1977), "They are learning both to read and to treat language as text" (p. 279).

Extending this theory, Gabriel Salomon (1994) proposed that not only can a medium implicitly teach an information process skill as these scholars had assumed, but by arousing certain attentional processes, it can become internalized as a "scheme of thought." Reporting on a number of intriguing studies, Salomon found that students deficient in cue attending after watching a film were able to internalize the zooming of a camera lens into a stimulus field, thereby increasing their ability to identify details in a visual montage. In another study, using computers to stimulate meta-cognitive skills in reading, students were able to transfer these meta-cognitive modes of representation when given a new condition. While Salomon acknowledges that these features may merely activate already established skills, he contends that these data show evidence that media codes were internalized, schematized, and then applied to new circumstances.

These scholars suggest that the medium itself may serve a particular instructional function, and consequently provide specific learning benefits to individuals. The closer match between the characteristics of the symbol system, the content of instruction, and the strategies to be learned, the easier the instructional message will be to recode and comprehend. In Salomon's original cue-attending study (Salomon, 1974), for example, it was the zooming feature of film that was thought to provide the most effective modeling strategy for students who needed it. Thus, there is the belief that given the proper mix of medium, student needs, and learning tasks, instruction may be more appropriately tailored to meet the specific aptitudes of individual learners.

In contrast to these claims, however, others (Clark, 1994; Pylyshyn, 1981) argue that all kinds of incoming information, regardless of the symbol system, become transformed into internal propositions. Symbolic codes, or pictorial images for that matter, are not a fundamentally different form of cognition, but merely a species of a single form used in all cognitive processing. Clark, for example, in his synthesis of research on learning from media, found no evidence to suggest that symbol systems serve any unique function at all in cognition and learning, arguing that "media are mere vehicles that deliver instruction but do not influence student achievement any more than the truck that delivers our groceries cause changes in our nutrition" (p. 445). It is not the symbolic elements themselves, according to Clark, that influence learning, but how well the symbols are shaped to represent the critical features of a cognitive task. Since a variety of symbol systems might be manipulated to represent a learning goal, the choice of particular media may be less important for learning than the symbol system theories had assumed.

In fact, recently, media scholars (McKenna & Zucker, Chapter 17, and Wartella & Richert Chapter 1, this volume) have come to the conclusion that it may not be productive to continue traditional media research, in which one medium is compared to another. Rather, Kozma (1994) reflects a consensus to shift the focus of research from media as conveyors to media as "facilitators of knowledge construction and meaning making on the part of learners" (p. 13). Consequently, instead of asking, "Are computers more effective than textbooks," we might ask "Do children learn more deeply when materials are presenting using two or more symbol systems—such as words and pictures—rather than one—such as words alone?" The question then becomes: how do we design effective multimedia presentations that foster better understanding for learners?

In this chapter, I will argue that multimedia presentations have the potential to be more powerful interventions especially for children who are at risk—than a single medium alone. In contrast to a zero-sum game inherent in the media effects literature, I suggest there is a critical synergy among media. Specifically, a theory of synergy (Neuman, 1995) is based on two propositions: (a) that there are qualitative differences in the content of each medium's messages; and (b) that the skills acquired from media act conjointly in helping children construct meaning and generate inferences in new contexts. This chapter will explore both propositions, and then suggest the implications for helping at-risk children read and comprehend storybooks.

Qualitative Differences in Media

The first premise of a theory of synergy is that instructional messages from media differ qualitatively. Waxing philosophically, McLuhan in the *Gutenberg Galaxy* (1962) and *Understanding Media* (1964) described every medium of communication as possessing a logic or grammar that constituted a set of devices for organizing experiences. Each medium employs specific symbols to tell a story and structures how individuals process and acquire information. A storybook, for example, uses print and illustrations to convey its message. Television uses both the integration of sound and visual images through movement to tell a story.

Empirically, noted psychologist Alan Paivio (1986) and his colleagues (Sadowski & Willson, 2006) have provided the most coherent theoretical and empirical evidence to, in part, substantiate McLuhan's argument. Paivio proposed a dual-coding theory. His theory suggests that humans have separate information processing channels—one verbal and the other, visual. Each can be activated independently, but there are interconnections between the two systems that allow for dual coding of information. When dual coded, information will be easier to retain and retrieve because of the availability of two mental representations instead of one. Further, Paivio hypothesized, pictures are more likely to activate both coding systems than words, suggesting the mnemonic superiority of the image over the verbal code.

Meringoff and her colleagues (Meringoff et al., 1983) at Harvard's Project Zero were among the first to investigate these distinctive features of learning from video and other media. One study, for example, analyzed children's apprehension of an African folktale presented in either an animated televised form or read aloud from a picture storybook. Verbal retellings indicated that children in the television group used character actions and visual cues to describe the story content, while the read-aloud group responded to aural cues or information not given in the story at all. These findings indicated that the visual presentation influenced the more subtle skills of drawing on one's prior knowledge, supporting Paivio's image superiority effect. Although subsequent media comparison studies (see review, Neuman 1995) have had a somewhat disappointing history with inconclusive empirical results (Mayer, 1997), research on mental representations suggest that verbal ways of representing knowledge may be qualitatively different from pictorial displays.

The distinctiveness of media (Neuman, 1995), however, derives from other critical aspects as well, beside their presentation modes. Among these differences are the particular rules and conventions various media use in their treatment of material, the kinds of content they are likely to make available, their historical legacy, and the particular critical mass audience required by the economics of the industry to stay viable in the marketplace. All these factors suggest that while different media may convey similar material, each will do so in a qualitatively different form.

Qualitative Differences in Processing Demands

Presentation modes, however, are but one aspect of the qualitative differences among media. Other attributes, such as the psychological energy needed to process information, the pacing of information, and level of interactivity can influence how and how much children learn for the media.

To focus specifically on processing differences, Salomon (1984) introduced the construct of amount of invested mental effort (AIME). According to this medial, AIME reflects the level of processing or mental energy needed to be expended to comprehend a medium. Television, with its format and pictures, is regarded by most as an easy medium, requiring little effort to learn. As a result, he argues, children tend to view the medium rather mindlessly, missing valuable opportunities to learn from it. Print on the other hand is perceived as "tough," requiring more AIME, leading to greater in-depth processing. Reporting on the invested mental effort in reading a narrative story or a televised version, Salomon found that sixth graders invested more effort in reading, and made more correct inferences than when viewing the televised version. Further, children in both versions made more correct inferences the more effort they reported investing.

The concept of AIME, however, has been roundly criticized for failing to reflect differences in effort expenditure that may be due to context and purpose (McKenna & Zucker, this volume): television viewing in schools, for example, may reflect a very different AIME than viewing television at home before bedtime. Further, a recent study (Bus, this volume) reported that children's mental-effort expenditure may also vary as a function of view age, type of program, and reading level (expert readers vs. novice). Still, Salomon's concept of AIME highlights a potentially important difference among media: children view certain media more efficaciously than others, which may influence their ability to learn from them.

Another difference between media is its pacing. Some researchers have argued that the pacing of certain media like television or radio may influence how children process information. Singer and Singer (2005), for example, suggested that the invariant pacing of television makes it difficult to retrieve efficiently information from memory. The emphasis on visual images in television, he thought, seemed to favor a holistic interpretation of events, rather than a careful and deeper analysis. Reading, on the other hand, is slower paced—by its very deliberation, it seems to provide an opportunity for greater integration of the material with patterns of memory, and intentions.

Closely related to the pacing of the medium is its level of interactivity. Some media, like television, radio, and film offer only a one-way mode of communication. Although in some cases audience members may interact with these media, it is only at a superficial level (quiz shows; call-in radio programs). Other media that allow children to "click here to continue," controlling the presentation pace, have been shown in preliminary research studies by Mayer and Chandler (2001) to result in better transfer performance.

A large number of critics unfortunately have described these differences in such a way as to suggest that one medium is "good" and another "bad." Such self-declared experts including salesmen (Mander, 1978); journalists (Winn, 1977), and even a hypnotist (Moody, 1980) have claimed that various media, like television "dulls the senses," "trains right brain synapses," and "controls," while reading "develops the powers of imagination and inner visualization." This view has been based on an outmoded conception of learning that conflicts with cognitive theory (Mayer, 2001). Rather, the counter-thesis, described below, is that the skills and information children acquire from their many experiences with media provide them with knowledge and strategies that may ultimately contribute to significant literacy learning gains.

The Active Learner

Suggesting there are qualitatively distinctive features of media leads to a second premise: children can benefit from multiple media presentations (see de Jong & Bus, 2004). In the course of interacting with different media, children use a wide range of physical, perceptual, and cognitive skills. As they engage in each activity, they acquire not only domain-specific information, but strategic knowledge regarding the medium's strengths and limitations. Consequently, the more, the better: in some cases, for example, visually presented moving images may instill insight and understanding far better than verbal descriptions. Other times, learning may require a motoric response, like learning to drive or to fix a car. Learning requires knowledge transformations from many different types of experiences, media-related and others.

Constructing Schemas: the Building Blocks of Knowledge

If we think about how children acquire knowledge, it makes sense that information in distinctive, yet somewhat redundant forms, can enhance learning. Children's earliest experiences are thought to be organized or structured around schemas, described by Rumelhart (1980) as the "building blocks of cognition." Schemas provide children with the conceptual apparatus for making sense of the world around them by classifying these incoming bits of information into similar groupings (Duchan, 2004). Stein and Glenn (1979) in a now-classic analysis for example, provided a compelling case for schema and its usefulness for recalling information about stories. They found that well-read-to children internalized a form of story grammar, which aided in understanding and retelling simple stories. Similarly, schemas have been shown to aid in remembering, recalling, and classifying particular entities into similar groupings (Anderson & Pearson, 1984), building through analogical reasoning a greater repertoire of knowledge.

But what is particularly important in the process of knowledge acquisition is that schemas provide a kind of organizational prosthetic (Stone, Silliman, Ehren, & Apel, 2004) that serves to diminish the information-processing load. Consider, for example, a young child visiting a library for the first time. It is probably a complex and confusing new world. Not only are there new routines to consider, but categories of choices of books, activities, and different locations, and roles of individuals. As the child comes to know the routines, and the schemas of visiting the library, she begins to form a mental representation of certain activities, devoting less mental energy to the structure of the activity than to the content itself. Certain activities, originally confusing, then, become understandable, familiar, and easier to access.

By diminishing the information-processing load, children are able to acquire new information more rapidly. Understanding the basic concept of a "library" for example, enables children to quickly make new associations, creating additional schemas that become increasingly differentiated with more knowledge. Children begin to recognize differences in genres, and text types, and purposes for reading, resulting in greater speed for gathering and remembering information. Knowledge becomes easier to access producing more knowledge networks (Neuman, 2006).

Four Processes

Colleagues in the field of reading and media (Anderson & Collins, 1988; Anderson & Pearson, 1984) have proposed a theoretical model to describe the development of schemas. Regardless of the medium, children actively search for meaning, they strategically examine and attend to certain features of the medium, they construct and interpret meaning, and they use their prior knowledge in acquiring meaning and making inferences.

In a series of studies using think-aloud protocols to elicit children's comprehension of stories in print and televised forms (Neuman, 1995), I found that the interpretive processes of "viewing" stories were strikingly similar to that of "reading" stories. For example, after either watched or read the following episode, they were asked to interpret its meaning:

"The One-Ton Jewel"

Episode 1

SCENE: Detective Office; Carl, Vickie, and Ricardo

VICKIE: [The phone rings] Bloodhound Detective Agency. [someone speaks] White dwarf from outer space? Yes, we'll be discrete.

VICKIE TO RICARDO: Here, you look up the white dwarf. They're stars. Someone's trying to sell a piece of one, and I smell a swindle.

RICARDO: It says here that white dwarfs are dead stars collapsed, shrunk, pressed by their own gravity. The stuff is so heavy you couldn't lift a teaspoon of it. No one knows how much it weighs being nothing that dense could exist on earth. It's got to be a fake.

VICKIE: Fake? How?

RICARDO: I don't know, but I've got a hunch. Carl, run home and borrow a needle and if you have a magnet, bring that too.

Student A response (viewing): [Any questions?] "Nope." [What are you thinking about?]" I think they're going to make a compass out of the magnet and the pin and I don't know what they're going to do with it, but ... maybe they're going to find the direction where the magnetic force is.

Student B response (reading): [What are you thinking about?] "I think they're going to use the magnet to see if the phone call was from outer space. I think something's fishy. Someone wants to make some money."

In this example, although it's clear that Student A had greater prior knowledge of a compass than Student B, both attempted to "read into" the episode. They constructed meaning on the basis of what they knew, read, or watched strategically, each attending to slightly different features of the episode. In over 100 protocols, these patterns were similar: children used similar inferencing strategies to make meaning for both the reading and televised episodes.

These findings are important because it suggests that children actively engage in cognitive processing to construct a coherent mental representation of their experiences. These active processes include paying attention, organizing incoming information, and integrating incoming information with other knowledge.

But it also highlights the fact that meaning making is not media specific. Children apply cognitive processes to incoming information—processes that are intended to help them make sense of the material regardless of medium. Consequently, they will process pictures, spoken words, printed words, and video to enhance their understanding to discover and understand their world.

The Complementarity of Media

The third premise in the theory of synergy is that children's everyday activity is multifaceted, filled with multimedia. Far from being a distraction, these multiple representations of favorite stories and activities enliven children's imaginative lives and help deepen their understanding of favorite characters and events.

Conducting a year-long study with families (Neuman, 1995), and their media habits, it was clear that children's interests often crossed media lines as they looked for opportunities to spend time with their favorite characters and stories. For example, a child's love of a particular character or set of characters like "Spider-man" would find expression through many different media: records, books, video, television, and toys, even lunch boxes and bed sheets. One of the mothers in our study, for example, described her daughter's current interest this way:

> Jennifer's just in love with *Charlotte's Web* right now. She tries to read a chapter when she wakes up in the morning. Then, we bought a video and I thought, "Oh dear"—here she was reading the book. But the video helped her get back into the book again, which surprised me. It brought her back to the book.
>
> She just loves *Templeton*. The video makes it so funny. And she laughs about that. And then when she gets in the book, she laughs, because she knows what's going to happen. Whereas, I could never get into *Templeton*—he was the terrible one. So I think the video has given her a new angle on *Templeton*.

In this case Jennifer's interest in *Charlotte's Web* first began with her teacher reading the book at school. At other times, however, Hannah, her sister became interested in reading as a result of watching television. For example, having seen Lionel, the ravenous reader in *Between the Lions* on television, she bought a little lion and pretended to read just about everything to it. Later, with her mother's help, she even wrote a letter to him to tell him about her favorite series book.

For another family, the Clarkes, videos were occasionally used to encourage reading directly. Scanning a guide each week, the mother would videotape a number of classics including *The Lion, the Witch and the Wardrobe*, and the *Lord of the Rings*, something she wanted the children eventually to read. The videos were used as a way of helping children get into the story, which she later read during their evening story hour.

Cross-media connections were also evident in the home of the single parent Mary-Alice Conley, where television or video often substituted for the children's storybook hour. Mary Alice rarely had time to read to the children. However, favorite books on video were a common future in this household. I would often see the children watch stories like *The Velveteen Rabbit*, or *Green Eggs and Ham*, bought through the school book club. With no one to read the story to him, Alex repeatedly watched the video with intense interest, waiting for his favorite scene, "When all the toys get fired."

In this home, television was often used explicitly by Mary Alice as a catalyst for the children's literacy interactions. Linkages between Alex's interests in *Blue's Clues* and print, for example, were seen in a calendar in his room, a primary vocabulary (and picture) learning game, an alphabet videotape—even a dictionary. Similarly, Mary Alice joined another book club, and ordered many videos for Stacey, who was just beginning to read on her own.

Television, film, and book characters all became embedded in children's pretend activities as well. Characters like "Buzz Lightyear" were used in such common play themes as good versus evil, marriage and family, and fear of monsters. In fact, it was not uncommon for the children to invite particular friends over to play a favorite story.... On some occasions, the older children invited their young brother or sister to join in, but only if they were able to follow the story structure. When they did not, play was interrupted, as in the case when Jennifer yelled to her sister, "C'mon Leah, remember in Toy Story you've got to have a problem!" Such awareness of the implicit rules of the narrative was probably learned through multiple exposures to both video and print experiences.

The sheer variety of connections between media suggests that children's interests tended not to remain medium specific. Seeking time beyond the immediate media experience, children pursued their favorite stories and characters through multiple exposures with different media. In fact the distinctions between media became increasingly blurred, as the children moved freely back and forth from visually oriented media (i.e., television, video games, movies) to print-oriented media (books, toy books, advertising circulars). Thus, contrary to displacing worthwhile activities, these observations indicated that access to media often served as a resource for children's emerging interests. Rather than conflict, there was a complementarity between children's media activities; children were the active agents in choosing leisure activities. Their media uses were guided by their interests and their practical assessment of attractive alternatives.

A Theory of Synergy

Synergy, however, goes beyond the assumption of complementarity. It assumes that the whole is greater than the sum of its parts. Considering their distinctive characters, a theory of synergy suggests that each medium's physical features, its structure, its method of handling material, may add a new dimension to children's knowledge and the means they employ to attain new knowledge. Thus, rather than detract from literacy, some amounts of media activity—computers, television, video, and other media—may expose children to an additional set of processing tools, which in combination with others, contributes to children's ability to interpret events. Since children apparently engage in inferencing strategies in different media, it is possible that these cognitive abilities are refined through practice and enhanced through their applications in another medium. For example, in examining third and fourth graders' recall and inferential abilities, I found that the students who were given multimedia exposures of a similar story recalled more story structural elements than those students receiving repeated exposures through one medium alone.

Consequently, there may be a spiraling effect. A greater facility to process information and greater access to resources may enhance children's capability to acquire new information. Conducting perhaps the most comprehensive set of studies, Richard Mayer (2001) reported that multimedia presentations can promote children's learning. Students performed better on transfer and retention tests when presented with a multimedia presentation than through print alone.

Implications of a Theory of Synergy

Although the concept of synergy requires further hypothesis testing, this area of research suggests several important implications in using media to foster learning. First and foremost, it suggests we need to shift the focus of our research from media as mere conveyors of methods to media as facilitators of content and knowledge and meaning-making for different learners.

A theory of synergy is based on the premise that existing medium presentations are qualitatively different, and that used wisely, multiple media presentations can quantitatively improve children's learning. It also suggests that using critical design features, as scholars like Richard Mayer (2001) have demonstrated (spatial contiguity, temporal contiguity, coherence, modality and redundancy), we might use this synergy principle to construct multimedia presentations that further enhance transfer and retention.

Second, although much less is known about who learns best from multimedia, initial studies (see review, Mayer, 2001) suggest that children who have limited prior knowledge seem to benefit more, as shown in evidence of higher retention and transfer than others. These results, if further replicated, might have enormous implications for poor readers. Although the results are preliminary, it seems that verbal and visual representations tend to bootstrap children's knowledge while in the process of learning the basic skills of decoding. For children with limited prior knowledge, such bootstrapping might be especially useful in helping them establish initial schemas at the very outset of hearing or listening to a story, leading to better comprehension of materials. For example, in our study using the "One-Ton Jewel," we found one poor reader interpreting the "white dwarf" as a dead "rap" star, setting her whole interpretation of the story in a search about music schema.

Third, research (Neuman, Roskos, Wright, & Lenhart, 2007) has demonstrated that repeated readings of stories positively influence children's story comprehension. Children seem to be able to use new vocabulary, and recall story details in more elaborated forms after hearing a story multiple times. Our experience suggests that repeated experiences with stories in multiple media, however, might be superior to multiple applications in the same medium.

When only words are presented and heard, the most likely cognitive process will be to decipher words, organize words, and integrate words with prior knowledge. Yet when words, pictures, and moving images are presented, for example, then learners can also engage in selecting images, or organizing images and integrating words, pictures, and moving images. In other words, children benefit from a "redundancy effect" (Neuman et al., 2007). Considering the distinctiveness of medium presentations, and that each is a delivery system for information, then it makes sense that multiple deliveries of information are better than only one delivery.

This is especially true when one delivery system is "blocked" perhaps because the learner does not learn well from that format, or because they need more practice in that format before becoming independent. Think of the young child who is eager to learn to read, but doesn't have the benefit of a caregiver reading to her on a regular basis. Multiple media learning gets in through another route. Given that knowledge and information are so central to children's comprehension of text, multiple media's capacity to provide redundant information can create a critical safety net.

Fourth, if Gabriel Salomon's hypothesis of AIME (Salomon, 1984) holds true for future applications, it suggests that entry into learning specific topics might be enhanced through media that are "easy," followed by media that are more "tough." In other words, feeling more efficacious in learning a topic might curtail the vicious cycle of low self-esteem, and low achievement documented in Keith Stanovich's (1986) now-classic Matthew Effect. Conventional instructional messages have relied heavily on verbal information—one system only. Multimedia learning offers a potentially powerful way for children to understanding things that would be very difficult to grasp from words alone.

The Challenges to Synergy

Children's interactions with media, however, are not immune to influence from the environment. What children take away from multiple media, how they use it, and how literate they become from it, are shaped to a large extent by how media are mediated—by the parent, caregiver, and teacher. For example, in our studies, parents influenced the educative potential of media by linking children's interests directly with literacy-related materials. Cross-media connections were made intentionally to spark children's reading interests. In this respect, children's interests were taken seriously by their parents, were shaped and transformed to reflect the educational priorities established by their families. Consequently, in contexts where the mediation influences reinforce literacy practices, children's experiences with media will serve to support and enhance their emerging concepts of print.

In addition, there are skills involved in using media. Cues provided by the medium itself that direct and guide children can be informally taught through conversations with caregivers and children. Acquiring the set of skills inherent in each medium help orient children to its language and grammar, and these processes enable children to come to understand and anticipate story events.

Finally, while the virtue of books is widely accepted, as an avenue for learning, other media like television, video, pictures have only rarely been acknowledged. What we now know is that these media, too, have the capacity to be used constructively for learning. Just as children are exposed to a steady diet of genres and levels of reality and fantasy in reading, so too, should they be exposed to stories in a variety of media presentations. Such experiences may enrich children's understanding of stories and events, and extend their engagement in literacy practices and literacy learning.

References

Anderson, D., & Collins, P. (1988). *The impact on children's education: Television's influence on cognitive development* (Working Paper No. 2). Washington DC: Office of Educational Research and Improvement.

Anderson, R.C., & Pearson, P.D. (1984). A schema-theoretic view of basic processes in reading comprehension. In P.D. Pearson (Ed.), *Handbook of reading research* (pp. 255–291). New York: Longman.

Clark, R.E. (1994). Media will never influence learning. *Educational Technology Research and Development, 42,* 21–30.

de Jong, M., & Bus, A. (2004). The effects of electronic books in fostering kindergarten children's emergent story understanding. *Reading Research Quarterly, 39,* 378–393.

Duchan, J. (2004). The foundational role of schemas in children's language and literacy learning. In C.A. Stone, E. Silliman, B. Ehren & K. Apel (Eds.), *Handbook of language and literacy: Development and disorders* (pp. 380–397). New York: Guilford Press.

Kozma, R.B. (1994). Will media influence learning? Reframing the debate. *Educational Technology Research and Development, 42,* 7–19.

McLuhan, M. (1962). *The Gutenberg galaxy.* Toronto: University of Toronto Press.

McLuhan, M. (1964). *Understanding media.* New York: Signet Books.

Mander, J. (1978). *Four arguments for the elimination of television.* New York: William Morrow.

Mayer, R., & Chandler, P. (2001). When learning is just a click away: Does simple user interaction foster deeper understanding of multimedia messages? *Journal of Educational Psychology, 93,* 390–397.

Mayer, R.E. (1997). Multimedia learning: Are we asking the right questions, *Educational Psychologist, 32,* 1–19.

Mayer, R.E. (2001). *Multimedia learning.* New York: Cambridge University Press.

Meringoff, L., Vibbert, M., Char, C., Fernie, D., Banker, G., & Gardner, H. (1983). How is children's learning from television distinctive? Exploiting the medium methodologically. In J. Bryant & D. Anderson (eds), *Children's understanding of television: Research on attention and comprehension* (pp. 151–180). New York: Academic Press.

Moody, K. (1980). *Growing up on television: The TV effect.* New York: Times Books.

Neuman, S.B. (1995). *Literacy in the television age: The myth of the TV effect* (2nd ed.). Norwood, NJ: Ablex.

Neuman, S.B. (2006). The knowledge gap: Implication for early literacy development. In D. Dickinson & S.B. Neuman (eds), *Handbook of Early Literacy Research* (pp. 29–40). New York: Guilford Press.

Neuman, S.B., Roskos, K., Wright, T., & Lenhart, L. (2007). *Nurturing knowledge: Linking literacy to math, science, social studies and much more.* New York: Scholastic.

Olson, D.R. (1977). From utterance to text: The bias of language in speech and writing. *Harvard Educational Review, 47,* 84–108.

Paivio, A. (1986). *Mental representations: A dual coding approach.* Oxford, UK: Oxford University Press.

Pylyshyn, Z.W. (1981). The imagery debate: Analogue media versus tacit knowledge. *Psychological Review, 88,* 16–45.

Reeves, B., & Nass, C. (2003). *The media equation: How people treat computers, television, and new media like real people and places.* New York: Cambridge University Press.

Rumelhart, D.E. (1980). Schemata: The building blocks of cognition. In R.J. Spiro, B.C. Bruce, & W.F. Brewer (Eds.), *Theoretical issues in reading comprehension* (pp. 34–58). Hillsdale, NJ: Erlbaum.

Sadowski, M., & Willson, V. (2006). Effects of a theoretically based large-scale reading intervention in a multicultural urban school district. *American Educational Research Journal, 43*, 137–154.

Salomon, G. (1974). Internalization of filmic schematic operations in interactions with learners aptitudes. *Journal of Educational Psychology, 66*, 499–511.

Salomon, G. (1984). Television is "easy" and print is "tough": The differential investment of mental effort as a function of perceptions and attributions. *Journal of Educational Psychology, 76*, 647–658.

Salomon, G. (1994). *Interaction of media, cognition, and learning.* Hillsdale, NJ: Erlbaum.

Singer, D., & Singer, J. (2005). *Imagination and play in the electronic age.* Cambridge, MA: Harvard University Press.

Stanovich, K.E. (1986). Matthew effects in reading: Some consequences of individual differences in the acquisition of literacy. *Reading Research Quarterly, 21*, 360–406.

Stein, N., & Glenn, C. (1979). An analysis of story comprehension in elementary school children. In R.O. Freedle (Ed.), *Advances in discourse processing* (Vol. 2, pp. 53–120). Norwood, NJ: Ablex.

Stone, C.A., Silliman, E., Ehren, B., & Apel, K. (eds) (2004). *Handbook of language and literacy: Development and disorders (challenges in language and literacy).* New York: Guilford.

Winn, M. (1977). *The plug-in drug.* New York: Viking Press.

4

Cognitive Processes During Reading

Implications for the Use of Multimedia to Foster Reading Comprehension

Paul van den Broek, Panayiota Kendeou, and
Mary Jane White

The ability to read and comprehend texts is critical for successful functioning in society as well as for lifelong learning. Despite enormous efforts by researchers, educators, and policymakers, many children struggle to learn to read. In the United States, over one-third of fourth grade students and one-quarter of eighth grade students cannot read at a basic level (National Center for Education Statistics (NCES), 2005). These reading difficulties often persist into adulthood: approximately 23% of U.S. adults meet only basic reading proficiency levels (NCES, 2004). In Canada, although the average performance of students on measures of reading tends to be in the upper quartile (Coulombe, Tremblay, & Marchand, 2004), approximately 30% of all students tested every year perform well below their grade level. Similar situations are described in other countries, including in Europe. For example, in the Netherlands, where reading achievement tends to be near the top amongst European countries (Mullis, Martin, Gonzalez, & Kennedy, 2001), 10–15% of Group 6 (equivalent to fourth grade in the USA) children do not have adequate reading skills (Verhoeven, Biemond, Gijsel, & Netten, 2007).

It is not surprising, then, that with the increasing availability of electronic media in schools and at home, multimedia approaches are more and more frequently proposed as effective means to promote reading comprehension. In the United States nearly every child lives in a home with at least one television and many children live in homes with multiple televisions, computers, internet access, video players, and video game systems (e.g., Rideout, Vandewater, & Wartella, 2003). The availability of computers, video display systems, and so on, has increased dramatically in educational settings as well (Pelgrum & Plomp, 1991). Thus, multimedia indeed provide a potential tool for teaching skills that have proven to be difficult to teach for a substantial segment of the population.

To realize this potential, it is important to have a thorough understanding of the nature of the reading process, and of factors that may lead to failure in reading. In this chapter, we provide an overview of the cognitive processes that take place during reading comprehension. We focus on reading comprehension in our review because few, if any, existing intervention programs are successful in improving comprehension. For example, the U.S. Institute of Education Sciences reviewed 24 well-known reading intervention programs and found evidence of six having consistent and reliable positive effects on basic alphabetic skills (phonemic awareness, phonological awareness, letter recognition, print awareness, and phonics), but none to have reliable positive effects on comprehension (Beginning Reading: What Works Clearinghouse, 2007). Thus, there is a particularly dire need for interventions that focus on comprehension. Moreover, as we will discuss, multimedia use has a particularly strong potential for improving comprehension processes. After describing the cognitive products and processes involved in reading comprehension, we explore implications for using multimedia to foster comprehension.

Cognitive Processes During Reading Comprehension

When considering reading comprehension, it is important to distinguish the *product*—what the reader has extracted from the text after reading is complete—and the *process* of reading—the combined activities by the reader as he/she proceeds through the text. From an educational point of view we ultimately are interested in the product, but it is through the process that such product is constructed and that its quality is determined. Indeed, for a comprehension intervention to be effective it must affect the reading process. Interestingly, virtually all reading comprehension interventions propose activities that are presumed to influence processing and thereby alter the product—although in research on these interventions only the product is actually tested (Pearson & Hamm, 2005; Pressley, Graham, & Harris, 2006; Rapp, van den Broek, McMaster, Kendeou, & Espin, 2007). What follows is a brief overview of the essential properties of the reading product and process, respectively.

The Product of Reading Comprehension: A Coherent Representation

Central to successful comprehension is the construction of a coherent mental representation of the textual information by the reader (Goldman & Varnhagen, 1986; Graesser & Clark, 1985; Kintsch & van Dijk, 1978; Trabasso, Secco, & van den Broek, 1984; Zwaan & Singer, 2003). This representation combines the various pieces of information in the text with relevant information from the reader's semantic (i.e., background) knowledge; importantly, this information from text and background knowledge is connected through meaningful relations. Together, these pieces of information and their interconnections form a network in the reader's mind. This representation is the foundation on which the reader can build for specific reading purposes and types of comprehension and that the reader uses to perform tasks such as retelling, identifying the theme, applying the knowledge presented in the text, evaluating and esthetically appreciating the text, and so on.

The idea units in a text can be connected via many different types of meaningful relations, but two types have been found to be particularly important, referential and causal relations. These two types of relations are found in the comprehension of virtually any kind of text and, moreover, they are required for the identification of most other types of relations. Consider the following sentence pair:

(1)   The lady gave the waiter $100.
      He returned to give her the change.

Most skilled readers will infer that "he" and "she" in the second sentence refer to "waiter" and "the lady" in the first sentence. These are examples of referential connections. Most readers will also infer that the waiter returned to give the lady change *because* she had given him $100 and, moreover, infer that this happened in the context of a restaurant where the lady had ordered and consumed a meal or drink, that the meal or drink cost less than $100, and so on. These are examples of causal inferences.

Such relations can be found in narrative texts, but also in informational texts. Consider the following sentences:

(2)   The moon exerts gravitational pull on the earth.
      Thereby it contributes to the development of life on earth.

For this example, most readers have little difficulty identifying the referential relation between "it" in the second sentence and "the moon" in the first sentence. They experience much more difficulty, however, identifying the causal relation between the two sentences. This is striking because, unlike in example (1), the text explicitly tells the reader that a causal relation exists between the two sentences. Thus, the pair of sentences in example (2) actually is more "user friendly" than the pair in example (1). The difficulty arises because most readers do not readily have available the background knowledge that would allow them to identify the causal relation. Motivated readers will search their semantic memory (background knowledge) for potential explanation as to how the two events are causally connected (usually coming up with incorrect inferences about the involvement of tides rather than correct inferences about the role of the electromagnetic field in shielding the developing life on earth from lethal cosmic rays). This example illustrates that referential and causal relations play an important role in comprehension of expository texts as well as in comprehension of narratives. In addition, it illustrates that background knowledge plays an important role in the identification of meaningful relations between text units.

Together, the two examples illustrate yet another aspect of inference generation, namely that inferences may be fast, automatic as in example (1) or slow, strategic and effortful as in example (2). We will return to this aspect when we discuss the inferential processes during reading.

In these examples, the semantic relations occur between two adjacent sentences. In real texts they are much more complicated. For example, the majority of relations span considerable distances in the text, sometimes many pages. Moreover, more often than not causal relations require the coordination of multiple text elements, not just two. As a result, even a short

Table 4.1 Introductory excerpt of *Tuk the Hunter*, based on an Inuit fairy tale (numbers indicate idea units)

1. This is the story of a boy
2. who lived in the Arctic.
3. He wanted to show that he could be brave by hunting for big animals
4. like his father who was a great hunter.
5. Some people do not like the idea of hunting,
6. but his family relies on animals for most of their food and clothing needs.
7. Although he was still too young to go on hunting trips
8. and prove how brave he could be,
9. he listened carefully to everything his father told him
10. and was given many of the hunting chores.
11. He helped ready the dogsled for each trip
12. and had learned how to sharpen the hunting spears and knives.

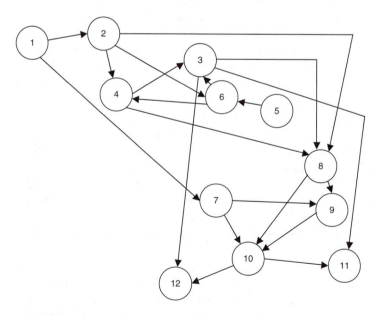

Figure 4.1 Relational network representing idea units and causal relations for excerpt of *Tuk the Hunter*.

text can involve many interconnections. This is illustrated in the short text excerpt presented in Table 4.1. Figure 4.1 depicts the relational network for this excerpt, with nodes indicating the idea units numbered in the Table and arrows indicating the major causal relations. For a complete network, other types of relations would be included as well. This illustration shows that even for very simple texts, the number of potentially identified relations can be quite large.

Evidence from Proficient Readers

There is considerable evidence that proficient readers construct networks such as those just described. These readers are more likely to remember idea units in a text that have many connections to other idea units in the text (Fletcher & Bloom, 1988; Goldman & Varnhagen, 1986; Trabasso & van den Broek, 1985; van den Broek, 1988). In the example in Table 4.1, readers are more likely to remember idea unit 3 (Tuk wanted to show that he could be brave), which has five causal connections than idea unit 5 (Some people object to hunting) that has only one causal connection. Likewise, they are more likely to include highly connected idea units when summarizing a text and to rate these idea units more important than less connected idea units. Furthermore, when a reader, upon having completed reading, is reminded of one part of the text this activates other parts related to it more than unrelated parts even if these unrelated parts are closer in the text (O'Brien & Myers, 1987). This is also reflected in proficient readers' answers to questions about a text they have read: the answers tend to follow the semantic connections (Goldman, 1985; Graesser & Clark, 1985; Graesser et al., 2007; Trabasso, van den Broek, & Liu, 1988).

Evidence from Beginning and Struggling Readers

Network representations also capture how young and beginning readers comprehend the texts they read. They too remember and consider important idea units that have many causal relations more often than idea units with few relations (Goldman & Varnhagen, 1986; Lynch & van den Broek, 2007; van den Broek, 1989). Children's ability to identify semantic relations between parts of a text is related to reading skills, and distinguishes between good and poor readers (Oakhill, Cain, & Bryant, 2003; Oakhill, 1994; Wolman, 1991; Wolman, van den Broek, & Lorch, 1997). Moreover, training beginning readers in identifying relations leads to improved comprehension (Medo & Ryder, 1993).

Comprehension at the younger age levels in elementary school and even younger children, in preschool and kindergarten, has been studied using non-textual media, such as auditory presentation or presentation of TV stories (Kendeou et al., 2005; van den Broek et al., 2005a). Again, the results show clearly that even these very young children make causal and other inferences and establish meaningful relations between elements of the events that they experience. For example, when 4- and 6-year-old children watch television programs such as *Sesame Street*, they remember events with many causal connections better than events with few connections and answer questions by following the connections in the network (van den Broek, Lorch, & Thurlow, 1996; see also Trabasso & Nickels, 1992). Indeed, when appropriate materials and testing techniques are used, even 2-year-old children have been found to identify causal relations between simple sets of events they experience (e.g., Bauer, 1997; Wenner & Bauer, 2001).

Although the principles of representation are remarkably consistent across age groups, there are systematic age and skill differences in the actual relations included in the representations. In general, children and adults with limited proficiency (i.e., young children or, within an age group, those with comprehension difficulty) more readily identify connections between overt, concrete events and other idea units whereas more proficient comprehenders frequently include more abstract and internal connections, such as those to the goals and feelings of characters (Lynch & van den Broek, 2007). Likewise, whereas beginning or struggling readers focus on identifying relations between individual events, more proficient comprehenders connect clusters of idea units as well, for example by identifying themes or connecting to titles (van den Broek, Lynch, Naslund, Ievers-Landis, & Verduin, 2003; Williams, 1993; for a review of developmental trends in inference generation during event comprehension, see van den Broek, 1997, and van den Broek et al., 2005).

Thus, the construction of a coherent representation, in which the individual idea units are interconnected with each other and with background knowledge, is central to (reading) comprehension at all ages and skill levels. This extends to preschool children and—important in the context of the possible use of multimedia to foster comprehension—across media (see also Diakidoy, Stylianou, Karefillidou, & Papageorgiou, 2005; Lorch & Sanchez, 1997; Paris & Paris, 2003).

Representations Across Media

The fact that coherent representations—and the same sets of relations, such as causal and referential ones—play an important role in comprehension at different ages and skills, and in different media, opens the door for the possible use of nonreading contexts (i.e., media other than text, which depend less on basic reading skills such as orthography, letter and word decoding) to promote and develop the comprehension skills that are used during reading. Such use would depend, however, on the extent to which the skills used to identify the underlying relational structure of a narrative in one medium are similar to those used in a different medium. It is possible that although (causal/referential) networks are important for comprehension in different media, the skills to arrive at such representations depend crucially on the medium and, hence, that the skills necessary to arrive at a representation differ according to the unique properties of the different media. Moreover, it would depend on the extent to which such skills are stable over development, with the ability to identify relations and arrive at a coherent network representation at one age predicting that at a later age.

To determine the stability of coherence-building skills across media and age groups and to determine the relations of these skills and basic reading skills such as word decoding and vocabulary, we asked 4- and 6-year-old children to listen to audiotaped and watch televised authentic children's narratives (Lynch et al., in press) and then to retell these narratives (to a little friend, a stuffed bear, who had been sleeping through the narratives). They also answered comprehension questions, designed to gauge factual as well as inferential understanding and completed tests of vocabulary and word decoding skills. Although the older children in general remembered more and correctly answered more questions than did the younger children, both age groups were remarkably sensitive to the underlying structure of the narratives. Both 4- and 6-year-old children recalled a greater percentage of events with more causal connections than events with fewer connections. This pattern became stronger with age, but was very robust for each age group.

The children's performances on the comprehension measures for the two types of media, audio and televised, were strongly correlated with one another for both 4- and 6-year-old children. Likewise, skills associated with word decoding (i.e., phonological awareness, letter identification, and, for 6-year-olds, word identification) were interrelated, but they showed few if any correlations with narrative comprehension. Thus, sensitivity to the causal structure appears to generalize across media but is independent from decoding skills, at least for children who are 4 and 6 years old: children that were very sensitive to the causal structure of narratives presented in one medium tended to be very sensitive to the causal structure of narratives in the other medium as well.

This study comprised the first phase in a longitudinal study, in which these same children were retested every 2 years until they were 8 and 10 years old, respectively (Kendeou, van den Broek, White, & Lynch, 2007; van den Broek et al, 2005). At each testing point, the children were tested using the same procedures, with the exception of a few modifications. Both audio and television narratives were replaced to make them age appropriate and, at the later points, phonological tests were not included. Furthermore, and most relevant to the current topic, when the children were 8 and 10 years old they also were presented with written stories and asked to recall and answer questions on these stories. This design allowed us to investigate the development of comprehension skills in different media, their relation to other language skills, and their contribution to later reading comprehension.

The results from the longitudinal phases indicate that for each age group (4, 6, 8, and 10 years old), audio and television comprehension were strongly interrelated. When reading comprehension was included (for the oldest age groups), comprehension measures for all three media (audio, television, written texts) were interrelated. For all age groups, comprehension skills in the various media were not systematically related to basic language skills, phonological awareness, and letter/word identification. Interestingly, vocabulary played a "swing role," in that it was moderately related to both comprehension and basic language skills (see Dickinson, McCabe, Anastasopoulos, Peisner-Feinberg, & Poe, 2003; Pearson, Hiebert, & Kamil, 2007; Whitehurst & Lonigan, 1998). The same patterns emerged when the data were analyzed using factor analytic techniques.

To determine whether early comprehension processes—found to be similar across media and to develop independently from basic language skills—predict comprehension performance at a later age, hierarchical regression and path modeling analyses were performed on the data for each cohort of children. The results indicate that preschool narrative comprehension skills for each cohort predicted later narrative comprehension across audio and television media. Importantly, the results for the 8- and 10-year-old children indicate that the early comprehension performance predicts later reading comprehension, over and above basic language skills and vocabulary.

In summary, the results of this longitudinal study suggest that narrative comprehension skills are remarkably similar across the media and age groups in this study, and that they start to develop in parallel with basic language skills well before the children begin to read. Furthermore, when the children begin to read, the developing comprehension skills join with basic language skills in determining their reading comprehension performance.

The Process of Reading Comprehension: Inference Generation in the Context of Limited Attention

To gain an understanding of the process by which readers construct an interconnected network representation as they proceed through a text, it is useful to consider this process from the perspective of a reader of a text.

As the reader proceeds through the text, he or she can attend to only a small subset of all the information that is presented by or relevant to the text at any one time. This reflects the fact that humans have *limited attentional capacity* or *working memory* (e.g., Engle, 2002; Just & Carpenter, 1992). As a result, as the reader encounters new information from the text or activates new information from his/her background knowledge, some information currently in the focus of attention needs to be discarded or deactivated. Thus, the process of reading the text as a whole resembles that of a fluctuating landscape that unfolds over time (Kintsch & van Dijk, 1978; Rapp & van den Broek, 2005; Tzeng, van den Broek, Kendeou, & Lee, 2005; van den Broek,

Young, Tzeng, & Linderholm, 1999), with new information being activated, currently activated information being either held on or deactivated, and previously deactivated information becoming activated again.

It is worth exploring what determines the factors that determine the fluctuations in activation, the unfolding landscape, during reading because of a second property of the comprehension process, namely that direct semantic connections between two idea units can only be established if the two units are co-activated, i.e., activated in the reader's focus of attention, at the same time (Brownstein & Read, 2007; Fletcher & Bloom, 1988; Just & Carpenter, 1992; Kintsch & van Dijk, 1978; van den Broek et al., 1999). Consequently, successful comprehension depends to a large part on the amount of processing capacity or working memory a reader has available and on his/her ability to allocate this attention effectively and efficiently to the most relevant information in the text and their background knowledge.

Individual differences in the capacity of working memory have been found to be closely related to differences in comprehension ability in general (Oakhill & Yuill, 1986), and inference generation in particular (Virtue, van den Broek, & Linderholm, 2006). Likewise, the way in which the reader allocates the available attentional capacity strongly determines the ultimate representation that is constructed for the text (Linderholm & van den Broek, 2002; Narvaez, van den Broek, & Barron-Ruiz, 1999; van den Broek, Lorch, Linderholm, & Gustafson, 2001).

The allocation of available attentional capacity depends on two factors: the standards of coherence that the reader employs and his/her toolbox of strategies for inference making (e.g., van den Broek & Kremer, 1999). For example, good readers adjust their distribution of attention to their particular reading goals, whereas poor readers fail to adjust their attention. A reader's standards reflect when he or she feels that the text has been understood adequately. These standards differ across individuals and even within an individual depending on the reading circumstances (van den Broek, Risden, & Husebye-Hartman, 1995).

To grasp the role that standards of coherence and attention allocation play in the achievement of successful comprehension, it is useful to take a more detailed look at what information is available to the reader as he/she reads a text segment. At any point, there are four sources of information available to the reader. The two most obvious sources are the current input—i.e., the sentence that is currently being read—and the information that remains activated from reading the previous sentence—i.e., the information that is carried over in working memory. The third source is the text that has been read so far but that is not activated in the reader's mind anymore—i.e., prior text that once was activated but subsequently has been deactivated as the reader proceeded. The fourth source is the reader's background knowledge. Whereas the first two sources (current input and carry over from the preceding input) are primarily a function of the reader's capacity, the latter two (prior text and semantic knowledge) are the results of extra activities performed by the reader. Some of these activities are not under the control of the reader (e.g., simple, automatic spread of activation from attended idea units that are associated to it: to take an example from the earlier illustration, "waiter" is associated with "restaurant"), but others are under the reader's control—and are most readily open to intervention and training (see van den Broek, Rapp, & Kendeou, 2005b, for a review).

Thus, as the reader reads a new sentence in the text, information from this new sentence and carry over from the preceding sentence is activated. In addition, some information from prior text and the reader's general semantic knowledge will be activated. If these sources of information provide adequate information to meet the reader's standards for coherence then the reader will simply proceed to the next sentence. If they do not provide adequate information to meet the reader's standards then the reader will engage in strategic activities aimed at attaining the missing coherence, such as reactivating information from the prior text by looking back in the text or searching one's memory for the text and searching one's semantic background knowledge to make inferences that provide coherence.

In summary, the reading process is a balancing act, in which the reader tries to find a compromise between limited attentional capacity and his/her standards for coherence. The success of this process depends on whether the reader has the appropriate standards of coherence and facility with the metacognitive, inferential strategies necessary to attain these standards. Many adult readers have difficulty with both aspects of reading comprehension, young children do so even more. Not only are young children still acquiring an understanding of the standards of coherence to which their comprehension should be held and of the range of strategies that they can use to attain the standards, when reading they also have to divide their limited attentional capacities to basic language processes such as decoding (van den Broek & Kremer, 1999). Instructional activities aimed at developing children's understanding of standards of coherence and of available comprehension strategies outside of the text medium, therefore, have great educational potential.

The Use of Multimedia Approaches in Influencing the Process of Reading Comprehension

The findings in the preceding sections indicate that significant development of comprehension skills takes place during preschool years, simultaneously but separately from basic language skills. Moreover, comprehension performance at the age of 4 years predicts reading comprehension performance at the age of 8. Finally, to a considerable degree these comprehension skills generalize across media. These findings suggest that interventions based on non-textual contexts can be used profitably to foster the development of comprehension skills in young children. Indeed, well-known reading compre-hension programs such as Reciprocal Teaching (Palincsar & Brown, 1984) and Peer Assisted Learning Strategies (PALS; Fuchs, Fuchs, Mathes, & Simmons, 1997) use auditorily presented stories to model and practice com-prehension skills. Indeed, the research reviewed above suggests multiple ways in which both television and auditory presentation of narratives can be used to foster comprehension development even at preschool age (Kendeou et al., 2005; Kendeou et al., 2007; Lynch et al., in press; van den Broek et al., 2005a).

An understanding of the cognitive processes involved in comprehension and of potential sources of failure suggests how multimedia approaches (in addition to or instead of a textual approach) may be used to foster compre-hension. There are two principal ways in which comprehension can be improved: (a) multimedia can be used to assist in comprehension of a particular piece of information and (b) multimedia can be used to foster development of comprehension strategies that the child can apply to other situations, including reading. The distinction between these two ways is similar to that between reading to learn and learning to read.

Improving Comprehension of Specific Content

Multimedia approaches to improve comprehension of specific content will be effective in so far as they promote the construction of a correct, coherent representation of the presented information. It is important to note that mul-timedia approaches may help or hinder in the task of constructing such a representation by identifying semantic relations (Brunyé, Taylor, Rapp, & Spiro, 2006; Rapp, 2006). Mayer (2001) has proposed several principles that increase the likelihood that multimedia use will be beneficial. These principles were developed for the combination of text with pictures, a relatively modest use of multimedia, but they can easily be adapted for more ambitious use of multimedia such as television, computers, internet, and so on. Most relevant to the construction of a coherent representation are the principles of spatial contiguity (i.e., learning is better when corresponding information is pre-sented closely together in the different media), temporal contiguity (i.e., learning is better when corresponding information is presented close in time in the different media), and coherence (i.e., learning is better when irrelevant information is not included).

These principles are directly relevant in the context of the cognitive processes that take place during comprehension. Indeed, in order for two idea units to be connected by the comprehender, they need to be activated simultaneously (Brownstein & Read, 2007). Spatial and temporal contiguity contribute to simultaneous activation of the to-be-connected idea units, whereas information that is activated yet not-be-connected will consume pre-cious attentional capacity and thereby interfere with the construction of the desired representation.

On the one hand, the use of multiple media may direct attention to the connections between individual bits of information by encouraging co-activation of the to-be-connected information and, moreover, by highlighting the kind of connection in ways that the text alone could not do. For example, a multimedia approach may reduce the demands on the child to decode printed letters and words, thereby releasing attentional resources to devote to the idea units and their connections. As a second example, text almost inevitably presents information in a sequential order. As a result, multiple causality (a particular outcome event is caused by several antecedents) is inherently difficult to recognize because all but the most recently mentioned causes may be deactivated by the time the outcome event is mentioned. Media that do not suffer from such strict sequentiality (e.g., animation, television, diagrams) would be able to keep the combined antecedents active in the comprehender's focus of attention, thereby increasing the likelihood of recognition of the multiple causality (e.g., Graesser & Olde, 2003).

On the other hand, the use of multimedia by definition increases the attentional load for the comprehender. As a result, the ability to select the important information may be compromised. For example, when narratives are presented in televised format, young children will pay undue attention to loud and flashy, but unimportant events, as compared to the same narratives presented in auditory form (van den Broek et al., 1996; Wenner, 2004). This problem frequently is compounded when multimedia are used to motivate or increase interest in the comprehender by highlighting human interest anecdotes or interesting details. Although these anecdotes and details may increase the general interest the comprehender has in the topic, they likely will siphon attention from the comprehension processes themselves. Indeed, such "seductive detail" has been found to interfere considerably with comprehension by adults (e.g., Harp & Mayer, 1998) and, even more strongly, by children (e.g., Garner, Gillingham, & White, 1989).

In summary, a multimedia approach is most likely to improve comprehension and learning of specific information over text alone if it increases the attention the child can devote to the to-be-connected information. If it does not increase such attention, then it will have no benefit or, worse, may have a detrimental effect.

Fostering Comprehension Strategies

The second possible application of multimedia approaches is to teach children skills and strategies that they can apply to any comprehension situation, including reading. There are several reasons that multimedia approaches may be useful in this respect. First, they allow the child to recognize and practice comprehension strategies without the need to negotiate developing basic language skills, such as decoding, at the same time. Second, the use of multimedia may sustain the interest of the child more easily than text alone would (but keep in mind the above-mentioned caveat that such interest may detract as well). Third, multimedia approaches have the potential to make the consequences of a child's comprehension processes more obvious (to the child) than text alone could do. For example, there is considerable evidence that even adult readers have difficulty recognizing inconsistencies between different ideas in a text or between their own background knowledge and the text (e.g., Kendeou & van den Broek, 2005, 2007; Rapp & Kendeou, 2007; van den Broek & Kendeou, 2008). By using multimedia such as animation a child's inferences may be visualized, alerting the child to potential failures in his/her comprehension processes (see also Bus et al., this volume).

Multimedia approaches may assist the child develop an understanding of what it means to comprehend—i.e., develop standards for coherence—and learn and practice strategies for attaining the standards. Judicious use of multiple media may provide the child with feedback on his or her comprehension, and may give the child the opportunity to practice the application of strategies when initial comprehension turns out to be inadequate. Furthermore, as mentioned, limited language decoding skills may hamper a child in demonstrating comprehension skills or, worse, in acquiring and practicing comprehension skills. For example, questioning techniques have proven to be among the most effective ways of fostering comprehension in text contexts, but only for older children who do not have to negotiate decoding difficulties at the same time (van den Broek et al., 2001b). By avoiding or reducing the need to rely on these skills, the door opens for the child to test and develop his or her comprehension strategies.

Conclusions

A central component of comprehension is the identification of semantic relations between ideas, events, and facts, and the construction of coherent representation of these interrelations. The ability to do so is essential to successful reading comprehension, but this ability starts to develop well before a child begins to read. The processes and skills involved in comprehension in different media overlap considerably. As a result, multimedia approaches to fostering comprehension have considerable potential, both with regard to comprehending specific information and with regard to developing strategies that can be applied in a range of comprehension situations.

Improvement in comprehension of specific information as well as the development of generalizable comprehension skills will only occur if multimedia activities are strategically selected and combined. Thus, it is not the use of multimedia per se that fosters comprehension, but it is the strategic use of the various media in such a way that the comprehending child engages in relevant processes in which he or she otherwise would not engage.

In this respect, the use of multiple media rests as much on the commonalities in comprehension processes between media as on the fact that each medium elicits these common processes in a unique fashion. For example, some media allow the comprehending child to influence the pace at which information is presented (e.g., text, websites) whereas other media present information at a pace not controlled by the child (e.g., audio and television presentations). As a result, the demands on working memory are somewhat different in these various situations. Interventions that make strategic use of the common and unique properties of different media, are most likely to foster the desired comprehension processes.

Acknowledgments

This project was supported by grants from the Center for the Improvement of Early Reading Achievement (CIERA), the Center for Cognitive Sciences at the University of Minnesota, and the National Institute of Child Health and Human Development (HD-07151). Paul van den Broek received support through Golestan and Lorentz fellowships from the Netherlands Institute for Advanced Study and from the Guy Bond Endowment for Reading Research, University of Minnesota. Panayiota Kendeou was supported by a McGill Researcher Grant.

References

Bauer, P.J. (1997). Development of memory in early childhood. In N. Cowan (Ed.), *The development of memory in childhood* (pp. 83–111). Sussex, United Kingdom: Psychology Press.

Beginning Reading: What Works Clearinghouse (2007). Institute of Education Sciences. Retrieved August 14, 2007, from http://ies.ed.gov/ncee/wwc/reports/beginning_reading/index.asp.

Brownstein, A.L., & Read, S.J. (2007). Situation models and memory: The effects of temporal and causal information on recall sequence. *Memory, 15*(7), 730–745.

Brunyé, T.T., Taylor, H.A., Rapp, D.N., & Spiro, A.B. (2006). Learning procedures: The role of working memory in multimedia learning experiences. *Applied Cognitive Psychology, 20*, 917–940.

Coulombe, S., Tremblay, J.-F., & Marchand, S. (2004). *International adult literacy survey: Literacy scores, human capital and growth across fourteen OECD countries*. Retrieved April 28, 2008, from www.statcan.ca/english/research/89-552-MIE/2004011.pdf.

Diakidoy, I-A.N., Stylianou, P., Karefillidou, C., & Papageorgiou, P. (2005). The relationship between listening and reading comprehension of different types of text at increasing grade levels. *Reading Psychology, 26*(1), 55–80.

Dickinson, D.K., McCabe, A., Anastasopoulos, L., Peisner-Feinberg, E., & Poe, M. (2003). The comprehensive language approach to early literacy: The interrelationships among vocabulary, phonological sensitivity, and print knowledge among preschool-aged children. *Journal of Educational Psychology, 95*, 465–481.

Engle, R.W. (2002). Working memory capacity as executive attention. *Current Directions in Psychological Science, 11*, 19–23.

Fletcher, C.R., & Bloom, C.P. (1988). Causal reasoning in the comprehension of simple narrative texts. *Journal of Memory and Language, 27*(3), 235–244.

Fuchs, D., Fuchs, L., Mathes, P.G., & Simmons, D.C. (1997). Peer assisted learning strategies: Making classrooms more responsive to diversity. *American Educational Research Journal, 34*(1), 174–206.

Garner, R., Gillingham, M.G., & White, C. (1989). Effects of "seductive details" on macroprocessing and microprocessing in adults and children. *Cognition and Instruction, 6*, 41–57.

Goldman, S.R. (1985). *Handbook of discourse processes*. Mahwah, NJ: Erlbaum.

Goldman, S.R., & Varnhagen, C.K. (1986). Memory for embedded and sequential story structures. *Journal of Memory and Language, 25,* 401–418.

Graesser, A.C., & Clark, L.F. (1985). *Structures and procedures of implicit knowledge.* Norwood, NJ: Ablex.

Graesser, A.C., Louwerse, M.M., McNamara, D.S., Olney, A., Cai, Z, & Mitchell, H.H. (2007). Inference generation and cohesion in the construction of situation models: Some connections with computational linguistics. In F. Schmalhofer & C. Perfetti (Eds), *Higher-level language processes in the brain* (pp. 289–310). Mahwah, NJ: Erlbaum.

Graesser, A.C., & Olde, B.A. (2003). How does one know whether a person understands a device? The quality of the questions the person asks when the device breaks down. *Journal of Educational Psychology, 95*(3), 524–536.

Harp, S.F., & Mayer, R.E. (1998). How seductive details do their damage: A theory of cognitive interest in science learning. *Journal of Educational Psychology, 90,* 414–434.

Just, M.A., & Carpenter, P.A. (1992). A capacity theory of comprehension: Individual differences in working memory. *Psychological Review, 99,* 122–149.

Kendeou, P., Lynch, J.S., van den Broek, P., Espin, C., White, M.J., & Kremer, K.E. (2005). Developing successful readers: Building early narrative comprehension skills through television viewing and listening. *Early Childhood Education Journal, 33,* 91–98.

Kendeou, P., & van den Broek, P. (2005). The effects of readers' misconceptions on comprehension of scientific text. *Journal of Educational Psychology, 97,* 235–245.

Kendeou, P., & van den Broek, P. (2007). The effects of prior knowledge and text structure on comprehension processes during reading of scientific texts. *Memory and Cognition, 35,* 1567–1577.

Kendeou, P., van den Broek, P., White, M., & Lynch, J. (2007). Preschool and early elementary comprehension: Skill development and strategy interventions. In D.S. McNamara (Ed.), *Reading comprehension strategies: Theories, interventions, and technologies* (pp. 27–45). Mahwah, NJ: Erlbaum.

Kintsch, W., & van Dijk, T.A. (1978). Toward a model of text comprehension and production. *Psychological Review, 85,* 363–394.

Linderholm, T., & van den Broek, P. (2002). The effects of reading purpose and working memory capacity on the processing of expository text. *Journal of Educational Psychology, 94,* 778–784.

Lorch, E.P., & Sanchez, R.P. (1997). Children's memory for televised events. In P.W. van den Broek, P.J. Bauer, & T. Bourg (Eds.), *Developmental spans in event comprehension and representation: Bridging fictional and actual events* (pp. 271–291). Hillsdale, NJ: Erlbaum.

Lynch, J., & van den Broek, P. (2007). Understanding the glue of narrative structure: Children's on- and off-line inferences about characters' goals. *Cognitive Development, 22*(3), 323–340.

Lynch, J.S., van den Broek, P., Kremer, K.E., Kendeou, P., White, M., & Lorch, E.P. (in press). The role of narrative comprehension in early literacy. *Reading Psychology.*

Mayer, R.E. (2001). *Multimedia learning.* New York: Cambridge University Press.

Medo, M.A., & Ryder, R.J. (1993). The effects of vocabulary instruction on readers' ability to make causal connections. *Reading Research and Instruction, 33,* 119–134.

Mullis, I.V.S., Martin, M.O., Gonzalez, E.J., & Kennedy, A.M. (2003). *PIRLS 2001 International Report: IEA's Study of Reading Literacy Achievement in Primary Schools.* Chestnut Hill, MA: Boston College.

Narvaez, D., van den Broek, P., & Barron-Ruiz, A. (1999). Reading purpose, type of text, and their influence on think-alouds and comprehension measures. *Journal of Educational Psychology, 91,* 488–496.

National Center for Education Statistics. (2004). Executive summary of adult literacy in America: A first look at the results of the National Adult Literacy Survey. Retrieved August 31, 2004 from http://nces.ed.gov/naal/resources/execsumm.asp#litskills.

National Center for Education Statistics. (2005). The nation's report card: 2005 assessment results. Retrieved July 9, 2006 from http://nces.ed.gov/nationsreportcard/nrc/reading_math_2005/.

Oakhill, J. (1994). Individual differences in children's text comprehension. In M.A. Gernsbacher (Ed.), *Handbook of psycholinguistics* (pp. 821–848). San Diego, CA: Academic Press.

Oakhill, J.V., Cain, K., & Bryant, P.E. (2003). The dissociation of word reading and text comprehension: Evidence from component skills. *Language and Cognitive Processes, 18*, 443–468.

Oakhill, J., & Yuill, N. (1986). Pronoun resolution in skilled and less skilled comprehenders: Effects of memory load and inferential complexity. *Language and Speech, 29*, 25–36.

O'Brien, E.J., & Myers, J.L. (1987). The role of causal connections in the retrieval of text. *Memory and Cognition, 15*, 419–427.

Palincsar, A.S., & Brown, A.L. (1984). Reciprocal teaching of comprehension: Fostering and monitoring activities. *Cognition and Instruction, 1*, 117–175.

Paris, A.H., & Paris, S.G. (2003). Assessing narrative comprehension in young children. *Reading Research Quarterly, 38*, 36–76.

Pearson, P.D., & Hamm, D.N. (2005). The assessment of reading comprehension: A review of practices—past, present, and future. In S.G. Paris & S.A. Stahl (Eds.), *Children's reading comprehension and assessment* (pp. 13–69). Mahwah, NJ: Erlbaum.

Pearson, P.D., Hiebert, E.H., Kamil, M.L. (2007). Vocabulary assessment: what we know and what we need to learn. *Reading Research Quarterly, 42*, 282–296.

Pelgrum, W.J., & Plomp, T. (1991). *The use of computers in education worldwide: Results from the IEA Computers in Education survey in 19 educational systems.* Oxford, UK: Pergamon Press.

Pressley, M., Graham, S., & Harris, K. (2006). The state of educational intervention research as viewed through the lens of literacy intervention. *British Journal of Educational Psychology, 76*, 1–19.

Rapp, D.N. (2006). The value of attention aware systems in educational settings. *Computers in Human Behavior, 22*, 603–614.

Rapp, D.N., & Kendeou, P. (2005). Revising what readers know: Updating text representations during narrative comprehension. *Memory and Cognition, 35*, 2019–2032.

Rapp, D.N., & van den Broek, P. (2005). Dynamic text comprehension: An integrative view of reading. *Current Directions in Psychological Science, 14*, 276–279.

Rapp, D.N., van den Broek, P., McMaster, K.L., Kendeou, P., & Espin, C.A. (2007). Higher-order comprehension processes and struggling readers: A perspective for research and intervention. *Scientific Studies of Reading, 11*, 289–312.

Rideout, V.J., Vandewater, E.A., & Wartella, E.A. (2003). *Zero to six: Electronic media in the lives of infants, toddlers, and preschoolers.* Menlo Park, CA: The Henry J. Kaiser Family Foundation.

Trabasso, T., & Nickels, M. (1992). The development of goal plans of action in the narration of a picture story. *Discourse Processes, 15*(3), 249–275.

Trabasso, T., Secco, T., & van den Broek, P.W. (1984). Causal cohesion and story coherence. In H. Mandl, N.L. Stein, & T. Trabasso (Eds.), *Learning and comprehension of text* (pp. 83–111). Hillsdale, NJ: Erlbaum.

Trabasso, T., & van den Broek, P. (1985). Causal thinking and the representation of narrative events. *Journal of Memory and Language, 24*, 612–630.

Trabasso, T., van den Broek, P.W., & Liu, L. (1988). A model for generating questions that assess and promote comprehension. *Questioning Exchange, 2*, 25–38.

Tzeng, Y., van den Broek, P., Kendeou, P., & Lee, C. (2005). The computational implementation of the landscape model: Modeling inferential processes and memory representations of text comprehension. *Behavior Research Methods, 37*, 277–286.

van den Broek, P. (1988). The effects of causal relations and hierarchical position on the importance of story statements. *Journal of Memory and Language, 27*, 1–22.

van den Broek, P. (1989). Causal reasoning and inference making in judging the importance of story statements. *Child Development, 60*, 286–297.

van den Broek, P.W. (1997). Discovering the cement of the universe: The development of event comprehension from childhood to adulthood. In P.W. van den Broek, P.J. Bauer, & T. Bourg (Eds.), *Developmental spans in event comprehension and representation: Bridging fictional and actual events* (pp. 321–342). Mahwah, NJ: Erlbaum.

van den Broek, P., & Kendeou, P. (2008). Cognitive processes in comprehension of science text: The role of co-activation in confronting misconceptions. *Applied Cognitive Psychology, 22*, 335–351.

van den Broek, P., Kendeou, P., Kremer, K., Lynch, J.S., Butler, J., White, M.J., et al. (2005a).

Assessment of comprehension abilities in young children. In S. Stahl & S. Paris (Eds.), *Children's reading comprehension and assessment. Center for the Improvement of Early Reading Achievement (CIERA)* (pp. 107–130). Mahwah, NJ: Erlbaum.

van den Broek, P., & Kremer, K. (1999). The mind in action: What it means to comprehend. In B. Taylor, M. Graves, & P. van den Broek (Eds.), *Reading for meaning* (pp. 1–31). New York: Teacher's College Press.

van den Broek, P., Lorch, E.P., & Thurlow, R. (1996). Children's and adult's memory for television stories: The role of causal factors, story-grammar categories, and hierarchical level. *Child Development, 67*, 3010–3028.

van den Broek, P., Lorch, R.F., Linderholm, T., & Gustafson, M. (2001a). The effects of readers' goals on inference generation and memory for texts. *Memory & Cognition, 29*, 1081–1087.

van den Broek, P., Lynch, J., Naslund, J., Ievers-Landis, C.E., & Verduin, K. (2003). The development of comprehension of main ideas in narratives: Evidence from the selection of titles. *Journal of Educational Psychology, 95*, 707–718.

van den Broek, P., Rapp, D., & Kendeou, P. (2005b). Integrating memory-based and constructionist processes in accounts of reading comprehension. *Discourse Processes, 39*, 299–316.

van den Broek, P., Risden, K., & Husebye-Hartman, E. (1995). The role of readers' standards for coherence in the generation of inferences during reading. In R.F. Lorch, Jr. & E.J. O'Brien (Eds.), *Sources of coherence in text comprehension* (pp. 353–373). Hillsdale, NJ: Erlbaum.

van den Broek, P., Tzeng, Y., Risden, K., Trabasso, T., & Basche, P. (2001b). Inferential questioning: Effects on comprehension of narrative texts as a function of grade and timing. *Journal of Educational Psychology, 93*, 521–529.

van den Broek, P., Young, M., Tzeng, Y., & Linderholm, T. (1999). The Landscape model of reading: Inferences and the online construction of memory representation. In H. van Oostendorp & S.R. Goldman (Eds.), *The construction of mental representations during reading* (pp. 71–98). Mahwah, NJ: Erlbaum

Verhoeven, L., Biemond, H., Gijsel, M., & Netten, A. (2007). Taalvaardigheid Nederlands: Stand van zaken in 2007. (Reading proficiency in the Netherlands: The status in 2007). Nijmegen: Expertisecentrum Nederlands.

Virtue, S., van den Broek, P., & Linderholm, T. (2006). Hemispheric processing of inferences: The effects of textual constraint and working memory capacity. *Memory & Cognition, 34*, 1341–1354.

Wenner, J.A. (2004). Preschoolers' understanding of narrative goal structure in narratives. *Memory, 12*, 193–202.

Wenner, J., & Bauer, P.J. (2001). Bringing order to the arbitrary: One to two-year olds' recall of event sequences. *Infant Behavior and Development, 22*, 585–590.

Whitehurst, G.J., & Lonigan, C.J. (1998). Child development and emergent literacy. *Child Development, 69*, 848–872.

Williams, J.P. (1993). Comprehension of students with and without learning disabilities: Identification of narrative themes and idiosyncratic text representations. *Journal of Educational Psychology, 85*, 631–642.

Wolman, C., van den Broek, P., & Lorch, R.F. (1997). Effects of causal structure on immediate and delayed story recall by children with mild mental retardation, children with learning disabilities, and children without disabilities. *Journal of Special Education, 30*, 439–455.

Wolman, C. (1991). Sensitivity to causal cohesion in stories by children with mild mental retardation, children with learning disabilities, and children without disabilities. *Journal of Special Education, 25*, 135–154.

Zwaan, R.A., & Singer, M. (2003). Text comprehension. In A.C. Graesser, M.A. Gernsbacher, & S.R. Goldman (Eds.), *Handbook of discourse processes* (pp. 83–121). Mahwah, NJ: Erlbaum.

II
Designing Multimedia
Applications for Learning

5

The eBook as a Learning Object in an Online World

Kathleen Roskos and Jeremy Brueck

The electronic equivalent of the storybook is the eBook and it is proliferating as a reading source for young children in a media-saturated world. Most major publishing houses, and many major libraries now offer eBook collections for young children. The New York Public Library, for example, lists a collection of 329 eBooks for young children (http://ebooks.nypl.org/ 812DC61A-F967-4795-8E061D9044D2A000/10/206/en/BrowseChildren.htm), including many childhood favorites and a variety of genres. eBooks are commercially available for iPods, cell phones, home computers, CD players, and television monitors in cars. Flexible, portable, and entertaining, eBooks offer a completely new reading environment for early reading experiences at a very young age.

But, are eBooks good for children? Are they on par with the wonderful children's books we all know and love as adult readers to young children—the likes of *Where the Wild Things Are* (Sendak, 1988), *Goodnight Moon* (Brown, 1947), and *Are You My Mother?* (Eastman, 1960)? Can they support young children's emerging literacy skills just like traditional storybook reading can do (Bus, van IJzendoorn & Pellegrini, 1995)? We don't know the answers to these questions—yet, as with all things electronic, eBooks are rapidly becoming a part of everyday life with little scrutiny as to what they might mean for children's early literacy development and learning. This spread is risky given the significance of early literacy experiences in emergent literacy. Considerable research indicates that time spent reading storybooks must be time spent well for strong early literacy development (Bus, 2001). It's time to press the pause button on the eBook for a closer look if we are to make the best use of this new, media-rich resource in an increasingly online world.

We can examine the eBook as a storybook reading resource from several different angles. Do eBooks represent quality children's literature? Do they support children's developing literacy knowledge? Are they well designed for use by young children, similar to conventional books that are attractive, easy to hold and manipulate? Following the trail of these questions to some practical answers would be worthwhile, no doubt. But we are not going there in this chapter. Rather we pursue a less-traveled route—one that focuses on the technical side of the eBook, which has to do with how it is built—its mechanics.

Recall that childhood curiosity about what makes a clock "tick?" Well ... our immediate interest in eBooks is something like that. Our purpose in this chapter is to explore what makes an eBook "tick" as a material resource of early literacy knowledge and skill.

We begin the chapter by providing some background on early childhood eBooks—their beginnings, some design studies, and instructional potential. Then we move *behind the screen*, so to speak, to describe learning objects as the digital building blocks of eBook design and construction. From this vantage point, we propose two prototype tools for analyzing and evaluating the eBook architecture as a learning resource in early literacy education.

Methodologies and analytic tools are needed to inform the design and construction of eBooks as beneficial mediators of early literacy experiences. What makes a book a good book is the superb integration of both content and structure. The eBook is no different in that its quality is found in the artful combination of digital media and message. To ensure high quality eBooks for emerging young readers requires closer scrutiny of them as a form of "edutainment"—and for this we need new methods, new tools, and new insights.

The eBook for Young Children: Gadget or Learning Resource?

The market for children's eBooks has been steadily increasing since 2000 when companies like Adobe and Microsoft developed ways to sell eBooks that could be downloaded but not easily copied. In their simplest form, children's eBooks are computer files that act much like a book with a title, pages, and chapters; they feature illustrations and perhaps internal hyperlinks that allow the reader to maneuver around the book. In their more complex form, children's eBooks are a kind of software that includes sounds, animations, a read-aloud capability, and other multimedia additions. *Thinking Reader*™, for example, is a software program that offers books of unabridged award-winning literature into which prompts, hints, models answers, and instant feedback are embedded for immediate feedback. Some eBooks require special devices to be read, such as those by Gemstar eBook reader, while others can be opened on personal computers, handhelds, and cell phones. Various terms are used to refer to the spectrum of children's eBooks, such as talking books, living book, CD-ROM storybook, interactive book, computer book. Different degrees of complexity, routes of access and use of terms make the children's eBook market confusing indeed.

Several attempts have been made to describe eBook design and construction from a literacy learning perspective. Pioneers in this effort, Anderson-Inman and Horney (1997) proposed four criteria that distinguish the eBook from other media:

- text presented visually on screen;
- presence of a book metaphor, i.e., a table of contents, chapters, pages;

- an organizing theme or topic;
- multimedia to support or enhance on-screen text.

eBook design, they argued, consisted of embedding multimedia in the online text. An eBook, for example, might contain a notational function allowing note-taking and glossing in a text box—much like a reader might do in a conventional book.

Focusing on the impact of eBooks on literacy development, Labbo and Kuhn (2000) described eBook design and construction from a considerate/inconsiderate text perspective (Armbruster & Anderson, 1984). In a screen-by-screen analysis of two eBooks (*Arthur's Teacher Trouble* [Brown, 1986]; *Stellaluna* [Cannon, 1993]), they examined features of interactivity and congruence with the storyline. They observed that online considerate text—true to the storyline—supported literacy skills, such as word recognition. But they also noted design problems impacting eBook quality. How to manipulate new digital conventions (e.g. pop-ups) to produce more considerate texts for better comprehension, for example, is not well specified. How to construct the interface between content and digital elements for the young, emerging reader also lacks a knowledge base, such as research-based design principles and descriptors of technical quality.

Focused more squarely on the technical design of eBooks for young children, de Jong and Bus (2003) developed an analytic method that specified digital elements of eBook construction. They coded a corpus of 55 commercial eBooks for features of multimedia, interactivity, print quality, and quality of "hotspots" (click locations for audio, images, or animation). Their analysis revealed generally weak designs in this corpus with many eBooks containing low quality multimedia additions, limited interactivity between child and text, and, unfortunately, hotspots irrelevant to the storyline. eBook design for early literacy, they concluded, is not yet a high art—an observation corroborated by Korat and Shamir (2004) in a replication study.

But so what about design and construction of eBooks? Is there any evidence in the first place that these multimedia books contribute to children's developing literacy skills? Well, some.... Still in its infancy, eBook literacy research suggests that multimedia features can improve inference skills in story reading (Trabasso & Van den Broeck, 1985) and that game-like interactivity can stimulate story comprehension (de Jong & Bus, 2002; Labbo & Kuhn, 2000; Shamir & Korat, 2007) and word learning, especially when children's attention is guided to these purposes (McKenna, 1998; Shamir & Korat, 2006).

eBooks also compel young children to be more active readers from the "get-go"—to choose where to focus, inspect words and images, negotiate the reading environment, and explore different perspectives (Hassett, 2006a). In short, the eBook environment invites young children to play—and this is a powerful motivator for engaging with print and its related cognitive processes, such as active, critical learning (Gee, 2003).

Digital Building Blocks

So … let's face it. Although different from our well-worn, comfortable storybooks, eBooks are definitely more than a passing fad or another electronic gadget. They offer a potentially rich material resource for literacy learning at an early age. And as everyday life fast-forwards in an online world, they are likely to stay. Still, even as eBooks may join the ranks of our beloved storybooks, they are not like conventional books. So … what makes an eBook tick?

An eBook, like any book, is made from raw materials. The modern book is made from paper and ink with illustrational inserts (e.g., photos) interspersed (much more these days than in the past). The eBook is made from digital stuff called learning objects. What are learning objects (hereafter referred to as LOs)? They are the building blocks of computer-based instruction (Downes, 2003) composed of digital assets such as images, audio files, video clips, texts, and animated objects. An LO may be as large as an online course and as small as a photo, although smaller objects are preferred for their reusability (Gibbons, Nelson, & Richards, 2000). Let's say you click on the word *gazebo* at an online garden shop. A photo bank of different gazebo styles fills the screen along with short texts describing the dimensions of each one. This is an LO built from digital raw materials, including images (photos) and text.

On a grand scale, an eBook may be considered an LO in and of itself—a large, chunky instructional object. This works, but treating an eBook as a whole instructional chunk only yields generalities about its design qualities as an instructional resource. A more granular inspection of its assets is more fruitful for purposes of learning about and appreciating eBook design and design principles. Our focus, therefore, is on the *primary individual LOs* of an eBook that are built from digital assets and contribute to the early reading environment.

Much like a well-built house results from quality building materials and thoughtful design, a well-built eBook reflects quality LOs assembled in ways that engage, motivate, and "teach." Several prominent instructional designers in the computer-based instruction field have developed guidelines and specifications for building high quality LOs that contribute to powerful learning architectures for developing new knowledge and skills (see, for example, Clark & Mayer [2003] on developing eLearning courses and Aldrich [2005] on educational simulations).

For a concrete sense of what an LO is and how it works, let's look at several in that "old favorite" eBook, *The Cat in the Hat* (see Riverdeep, Inc., 2001). First: know that this electronic book is organized into three primary options for storybook reading. The "Read To Me" section is basically an audio read aloud of the *Cat in the Hat* much like the conventional storybook format of reading to a child. The "Let's Play" section highlights pages that contain hotspots (multimedia click locations) that children can explore in the course of the storybook reading. The "Options" section allows children to focus just on the screen-pages that contain the hotspots without progressing through the entire story. Our examples of LOs are retrieved from page one of the Let's Play option of this eBook. For descriptive purposes, the page consists of a short four-line stanza, located in the center of the page. It is surrounded by a variety of objects, including toys (e.g., a ball), furniture, wall art, a fish bowl, a window, and a door. The two main characters (boy and girl) are present along with, of course, the "cat in the hat" (Giesel, 1957). All total this screen shot contains 19 LOs, so it's a busy screen-page. To move things along, we'll describe sets of these LOs.

We turn first to LO 1.1–1.5 located in the center of the screen-page and focused on the four-line stanza: *I know it is wet/And the sun* [picture of a sun] *is not sunny/But we can have/Lots of good fun that is funny* (see Riverdeep, 2001). This set of objects is built from three to four digital elements—text, audio, images, and/or animation. Each LO activates the written text of the book in some way. A click on the *hat* (1.1), for example, produces a read aloud of the stanza with simultaneous highlights of text chunks in yellow (e.g., *I know it is wet*). Clicking on the word *wet* (1.3) highlights the word followed by an audio of the word—*wet*—plus an animated image of falling rain. The sequence ends with the plop! plop! sound of raindrops. All of these LOs contain information that helps children match speech to print or to develop comprehension at the word level.

Next we consider the LO set numbered 1.6–1.11 toward the left side of the screen pane. It consists of six objects—ball, bicycle, plant, wall art, racket, and window. The digital elements of this set include audio, images, and animation, but no text. The purpose is to *play with* certain items, but not in a print-oriented way. Clicking on LO 1.6 (*ball*), for example, allows it to be moved about the screen with the target of getting it into the basket in the right hand corner. The ball has to be up high in the right hand pane in order to get it to plummet into the basket below. (It's a challenge!) Clicking on the six different items and manipulating them takes some time—but it's playful. The information embedded in the LO is motor-skill related (e.g., eye–hand coordination), not literacy related, and the feedback is linked to following through on the motor sequence.

In LO set 1.12–1.13 (the boy and girl) and also LO 1.17 (the cat) at the center of the screen, the interaction supports oral language comprehension, thus the set is more closely aligned with early literacy. The digital elements of audio, image, and animation are built around story-related talk. The *boy* (LO 1.12), for example, says *Wow! A six foot tall cat.* This commentary embellishes the storyline and therefore contributes to comprehension of the story. The information contained in this LO set is literacy related, helping the emerging reader to check for understanding of the storyline as well as to elaborate on it.

The final set of LOs (1.14–1.16; 1.18–1.19), toward the right hand of the screen pane, mimics those on the left, combining digital elements to support *play with* different items on the screen-page. Clicking on LO 1.18 (*door and bird*) causes the door to open and the bird to fly out and say *It's much drier in here than that soggy old tree/So it's in this house I want to be*, then hide under the desk. The LO provides practice in eye-tracking skills. Keeping your eye on that bird supplies the action and immediate feedback (if you can do it).

This hotspot-filled screen is one of 15 similar screen-pages in *The Cat in the Hat.* The LOs that compose this screen are in a 40–60 split between early literacy and motor play, so the latter receives more exercise in this environment. Projecting on the basis of this one screen-page, we could surmise this eBook (as a material resource) supports early literacy ... sort of. The building blocks of the eBook—the LOs—contribute to a supportive learning environment for early literacy, but modestly. This may be alright if eBook story reading includes rich adult–child interaction from one screen-page to the next. But it may give us pause if the eBook serves a "child-minding" role while adults are busy doing other things. While some eBook exposure to early literacy skills is better than none, is it enough?

From our brief exposure to LOs in this example we can recognize at least this: you can't judge an eBook by its cover. Behind the screen, more is going on than meets the eye to shape the early reading experience. There are LOs at work that constitute the built environment, and these digital building blocks may more or less support an early experience. If eBooks, especially as a form of edutainment, are to support early literacy, then we need to pay closer attention to the design quality of LOs for this purpose—as early literacy instructional objects in the online environment.

What To Look For in an LO

In the online world, much discussion is focused on the description and storage of LOs, and for a practical reason: reusability. The manufacture of LOs is not cheap, and these instructional objects are projected to be the staples of online K-16 education in the future (Fletcher, Tobias, & Wisher, 2007). Toward the goal of more accessible, sharable, and reusable LOs, a number of cataloguing schemes have been proposed. These range from basic models, such as the Sharable Content Objects Reference Model or SCORM (www.adlnet.org), to more elaborate schemes such as the Learning Object Indexing Scheme (Epsilon Learning). Full treatment of such "tagging" systems is beyond the scope of this chapter. Suffice it to say that these schemes provide organizational frameworks for describing LOs in online instructional resources. Drawing on these frameworks, we can identify and examine LOs in eBooks for young children, and in undertaking this descriptive groundwork make progress toward a better understanding of the eBook as an instructional resource in the early years.

In Table 5.1, we propose a "starter" framework for examining LOs in eBooks designed for young children. The framework is organized into three categories of design:

- graphic design (how elements are visually presented);
- learning design (how elements demonstrate an instructional purpose);
- interface design (how elements explain use).

Each category includes a set of features that represent it. The graphics category, for example, includes essential features of visual coherence, such as composition. The learning design category contains the basic features of instruction—the "learn-about" loop of topic, purpose, and outcome (e.g., *learn about* frogs [topic] to recognize them [purpose] and to remember what they look like [outcome]). The interface design category addresses fundamentals, such as user control of the LO. The framework, therefore, offers an easy-to-use tool for examining some basic features of individual LOs.

To apply the framework, users first need to identify the primary LOs in a material. Recall that learning objects are built from a few basic digital raw materials, namely image, audio, video, text. Usability is the guiding principle of selection. A primary LO should be large enough to support learning yet small enough to be accessed and reused without much modification. Once identified and "tagged" each LO can be examined for evidence of features in the three design categories.

Let's return to LO 1.3 from *The Cat in the Hat* to see how our exploratory tool works. The LO has to do with the word *wet*. Applying the tool to this small LO, we can observe several of its features. The graphic design, for example, includes complementary graphic elements of color and size to highlight the word *wet*. Both visual balance and placement in the line of text are

Table 5.1 Framework for examining design of primary learning objects

Category	Feature	Present	
		Yes	No
Graphics	Complementary graphic elements (color, size, line, shape)		
	Visually balanced graphic elements		
	Complementary placement of object with text		
Learning	Instructional purpose		
	Instructional content		
	Assessment (feedback)		
Interface	Choice of formats		
	Control of object		
	Conventions of use		

present. In the category of learning, the purpose is clear: to "say" the word (audio) and to "tell" what it means (animation of falling rain), and thus the instructional content is evident. But there is no evidence of an assessment feature to check outcomes of the interaction (e.g., *Now ... you say the word.*). As for design related to use, evidence of choice in the format or control of it, for that matter, is not there. Once clicked, the LO is triggered and cannot be adapted. The LO is a familiar one, though, and follows on-screen conventions, such as clicking.

All in all, this small LO about the word *wet* reflects several features of design in essential design categories. Applying the tool to all the LOs in *The Cat in the Hat*, or even a representative sample of them, can reveal patterns that place us in a better position to describe the internal design of this eBook. And good eBooks, we are arguing, should reflect good internal designs that encourage and facilitate active, critical early literacy learning.

How To Look at the LO Structure

At this point, we have proposed a relatively simple analytic framework for observing several high-level design features of individual LOs. Our exploratory tool has the capacity to locate a set of features in an LO. But: that's as far as it can go. The tool lacks criteria for judging the quality of LO features. We might expand the function of the tool by combining it with other eBook evaluation tools. Shamir and Korat (2006), for example, proposed an evaluation framework for selecting eBooks as storybooks for young children. Based on a developmental scale (Haughland & Wright, 1977) and related research (de Jong & Bus, 2003), they developed a set of evaluation questions around six criteria: age appropriate, child control, clear instructions, independence, process orientation, and technical features. Positive responses to a majority of the questions indicate a high quality eBook that supports early literacy. Combining our tool with more holistic frameworks, such as this one, widens its applicability in research and design, as well as its utility in judging overall eBook quality.

Yet we are not completely satisfied with this option. Still needed, we would argue, is a more precise tool that probes the internal design of an LO if we are to know what makes an eBook "tick." Understanding internal design, we think, lays the groundwork for insights about technical quality and ultimately of excellent instructional design. But, to "see" inside the LO, we need schematics that permit a close inspection of each LO and how different LOs combine to support early literacy in the eBook environment. To achieve this technical goal, we have come up with a *blueprint key* for making blueprints of individual LOs. The *blueprint key*, like the analytic framework we outlined above, is a prototype tool with the potential to support research and development of high quality eBooks as early literacy educational resources.

The *blueprint key* can be used to array the basic structure of a built LO. It consists of a relatively small set of symbols that represent basic digital assets and common screen navigators. The set is displayed in Figure 5.1. The digital assets, or raw materials of an LO, are on the left hand side of the key and the screen navigators, or interface items, on the right hand side. Five digital assets are represented: images (e.g., photos), audio files, video clips, text segments, and the combined asset (e.g., an animated asset). Four conventional navigators are included: scroll up, scroll down, the button (defined navigation), and the pop-up. Using these symbols, blueprints of individual LOs can be generated to examine the internal design of an LO.

To see how the *blueprint key* works, let's return to LO 1.3 (the word *wet*) in the *Cat in the Hat*. A blueprint of this small LO is provided in Figure 5.2. The LO structure is displayed above the *blueprint key*. Note that this is a simple LO built from three digital assets (text, image, and audio) and just one navigator (the button). The word *wet* is highlighted in the text. When the navigator is applied (click button) the LO is triggered, complementing the audio of the word *wet* with an image and sounds of dripping rain. The LO is instructional, in short, because it "reads" the word aloud and demonstrates the meaning of the word with image and audio assets. The LO blueprint for *wet* shows us how it works in the environment, and provides a

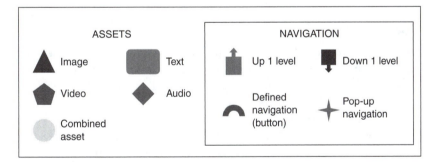

Figure 5.1 Learning object architecture.

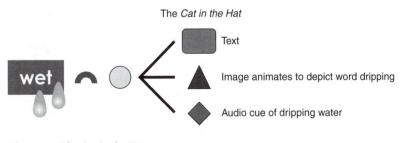

Figure 5.2 The Cat in the Hat.

point of reference for examining others, as well as the overall learning architecture of the screen-page.

Our brief example attempts to illustrate the potential of the *blueprint key* as an analytic tool for displaying the schematics of individual LOs from small to large, simple to complex, in part and as a whole. As a tool, the *blueprint key* can also facilitate rendering the overall LO architecture of an eBook as an instructional resource. We are now at a point where we can see what makes an eBook tick. And we can ask more particular questions. How many LOs are structurally the same, setting up redundancy in the eBook? How many are different, thus creating novelty? Are LOs progressively more challenging, pulling emerging readers to the edge of their literacy development? How are LOs networked to support learning early literacy concepts and skills? Questions like these pique our curiosity about how LOs shape the eBook reading environment and in turn children's early literacy experience in it. They are the technical, but they are also probing questions that pull us forward into what Herbert Simon (1996) referred to as *sciences of the artificial*—research at that thin boundary between conceptual ideas and real tools, that place where idea and object become fused in the design process (pp. 131–132). *Here*, albeit difficult to imagine, is where LOs are built for instruction and "harmonized" for learning. And it is here that we need to focus our attention if we are to improve the design quality of eBooks as educational resources in early literacy experience.

Where From *Here*?

eBooks for young children are like storybooks we know and love in some ways. But they are also different in ways that profoundly change the storybook as a source of early literacy experience. How eBooks contribute to young children's literacy development and learning in an ever-widening online world is largely unknown. We need new tools to examine these new-age books so we might study them and use this resource more wisely in creating supportive learning environments for emerging readers. In our chapter, we propose two analytic tools for examining and describing the eBook learning architecture with an eye to the learning potential of this resource.

One of these tools is a framework for describing critical design features of instructional objects (LOs) in eBooks—their potential to appeal, encourage interaction, and inform. Based on the premise that good design reflects good principles of learning, locating what is present (or not) in an object is the basis of evaluation. The other is a symbol key for making blueprints of LO architecture(s). This is a more precise tool for making schematics of individual LOs that illustrate how they are built, how they function, and how they network in the eBook environment. Both tools permit closer inspection of what makes an eBook tick, and from here to study the LO structures that support early literacy experience.

Still … our readers may wonder why we dwell on these technicalities, since it is the quality of adult–child interaction that—in the end—optimizes the eBook reading experience as an educational resource. And so it is. Yet the fact remains that often the eBook is a trusted form of edutainment that requires minimal adult involvement, and in this instance design matters. When adults rely on the medium for the message—*reading is important and here's how it works*—good design is essential in building an *environment* for rich literacy experience.

Environment, whether classroom-real or online-virtual, is a powerful force in human learning. Like all environments, the eBook contains possibilities for action, and when activated by the learning child, these potentials become meaning-makers (Barab & Roth, 2006). Designing rich eBook environments for early literacy development, however, is a new *science of the artificial* in the early literacy field. Research is needed about the adequacy of current eBook designs, about instructional objects that enhance the eBook learning architecture, about ways to represent early literacy knowledge in the internal design of LOs, and about networking LOs for instruction. Cross-disciplinary studies and joint investigations involving instructional designers and content specialists hold out the best hope of developing design methodologies that result in high quality eBooks for early literacy learning. Design at the boundary between concept and real artifact is never simple, requiring the integration of multilayers of structures and links to achieve an internal grammar that informs. For this, content expert and instructional designer must work together to create powerful digital mediators for learning. We have proposed prototype tools that may contribute to this line of research and briefly showed how they might be applied. And in this effort, we tried to catch and share a glimpse of the "wizardry" behind the screen that makes the eBook tick (tock).

References

Aldrich, C. (2005). Learning by doing: A comprehensive guide to simulations, computer games, and pedagogy in e-learning and other educational experiences. San Francisco: John Wiley & Sons.

Anderson-Inman, L., & Horney, M. (1997). Electronic books for secondary students. *Journal of Adolescent and Adult Literacy, 40*(6), 486–491.

Armbruster, B.B., & Anderson, T.H. (1984). Producing "considerate" expository text: Or easy reading is damned hard writing (Reading Education Report No. 46). Urbana, IL: Center for the Study of Reading.

Barab, S., & Roth, W. (2006). Curriculum based ecosystems: Supporting knowing from an ecological perspective. *Education Researcher, 35*(5), 3–13.

Bus, A.G. (2001). Joint caregiver–child storybook reading: A route to literacy development. In S.B. Neuman & D.K. Dickinson (Eds.), *Handbook of early literacy research* (pp. 179–191). New York: Guilford Press.

Bus, A.G. van IJzendoorn, M.H., & Pellegrini, A.D. (1995). Joint book reading makes for success in learning to read: A meta-analysis on intergenerational transmission of literacy. *Review of Educational Research, 65,* 1–21.

Clark, R.C., & Mayer, R.E. (2003). *E-Learning and the science of instruction: Proven guidelines for consumers and designers of multimedia learning.* San Francisco, CA: Jossey-Bass/Pfeiffer.

de Jong, M.T., & Bus, A.G. (2002). Quality of book-reading matters for emergent readers: An experiment with the same book in a regular or electronic format. *Journal of Educational Psychology, 94*, 145–155.

de Jong, M.T., & Bus, A.G. (2003). How well suited are electronic books for supporting literacy? *Journal of Early Childhood Literacy, 3*(2), 147–164.

Downes, S. (2003). Learning objects in a wider context. Paper presented at the CADE National Research Council, June.

Fletcher, J.D., Tobias, S., & Wisher, R.A. (2007). Learning anytime, anywhere: Advanced distributed learning and the changing face of education. *Educational Researcher, 36*(2), 96–102.

Gee, J.P. (2003). *What video games have to teach us about learning and literacy.* New York: Palgrave Macmillan.

Gibbons, A.S., Nelson, J., & Richards, R. (2000). The nature and origin of instructional objects. In D.A. Wiley (Ed.), *The instructional use of learning objects.* Bloomington, IN: Association for Educational Communications and Technology. Retrieved May 2006, from, www.reusability.org/read/chapters/wiley.doc.

Giesel, T.S. (1957). *The Cat in the Hat.* New York: Random House.

Hassett, D.D. (2006a). Signs of the times: The governance of alphabetic print over "appropriate" and "natural" reading development. *Journal of Early Childhood Literacy, 6*(1), 77–103.

Hassett, D.D. (2006b). Technological difficulties: A theoretical frame for understanding the non-relativistic permanence of traditional print literacy in elementary education. *Journal of Curriculum Studies, 38*(2), 135–159.

Haughland, S.W., & Wright, L. (1977). *Young children and technology: A world of discovery.* London: Allyn & Bacon.

Korat, O., & Shamir, A. (2004). Do Hebrew electronic books differ from Dutch electronic books? A replication of a Dutch content analysis. *Journal of Computer Assisted Learning, 20*(4), 257–268.

Labbo, L.D., & Kuhn, M.R. (2000). Weaving chains of affect and cognition: A young child's understanding of CD-ROM talking books. *Journal of Literacy Research, 32*(2), 187–210.

McKenna, M.C. (1998). Electronic texts and the transformation of beginning reading. In D. Reinking, M.C. McKenna, L.D. Labbo, & R.D. Kieffer (Eds.), *Handbook of literacy and technology: Transformations in a post-typography world* (pp. 45–59). Mahwah, NJ: Erlbaum.

Riverdeep Interactive Learning, Ltd. (2001). Dr. Seuss Enterprises, LP. Dr. Seuss Properties and (1997) Dr. Seuss Enterprises, LP. The Learning Company, *The Cat in the Hat,* copyright, 1957 by Dr. Seuss Enterprises. Version 1.0 Windows/Macintosh CD-ROM.

Shamir, A., & Korat, O. (2006, June). The educational electronic book as a tool for supporting children's early literacy. Presentation at the KNAW Conference: Amsterdam, the Netherlands.

Shamir, A., & Korat, O. (2007). Developing an educational e-book for fostering kindergarten children's emergent literacy. *Computers in the Schools, 24*(1/2).

Simon, H.A. (1996). *The sciences of the artificial.* Cambridge, MA: MIT Press.

Trabasso, T., & van den Broek, P. (1985). Causal thinking and the representation of narrative events. *Journal of Memory and Language, 24*, 612–630.

Children's Literature Cited

Brown, M.W. (1947). *Goodnight moon.* New York: Harper & Row Publishers, Inc.

Brown, M. (1986). *Arthur's teacher trouble.* Toronto, Canada: Little, Brown, and Company.

Cannon, J. (1993). *Stellaluna.* Orlando, FL: Harcourt, Inc.

Eastman, P.D. (1960). *Are you my mother?* New York: Random House.

Sendak, M. (1988). *Where the wild things are.* New York: Harper Collins.

6

A New Look at an Old Format

Eye Tracking Studies of Shared Book Reading and the Implications for eBooks and eBook Research

Mary Ann Evans, Annie Roy-Charland, and
Jean Saint-Aubin

Stories have long been told as a way of presenting, transmitting and preserving the collective memories and knowledge of a culture—the settings in which it has been, its characters, events and practices, and its points of view and beliefs. As such stories of the past have been a way of making sense of the present. In addition the content of stories may explain a reason for something, provide a moral caution, or describe exemplary behavior to which to aspire. Thus oral stories have always had an instructive or teaching function, as well as that of entertainment and wonder.

However most recently in our literate societies, the educational function of both written and oral stories has been extended to their potential impact on children's reading development or their ability to make sense of written text. With respect to the literacy development functions of stories, telling stories to young children is thought to expand their oral vocabulary (see citations later under heading *Vocabulary Knowledge*), increase their comprehension of syntax (Crain-Thorenson & Dale, 1992), create an understanding of the schemata or organization of stories (Purcell-Gates, 1988; Sulzby, 1985), and foster skill in intratextual linking devices and written language patterns (Pappas, 1987). In the case of stories read from books, the printed format is thought additionally to develop children's orthographic knowledge and understanding of the conventions of print (Goodman, 1980, 1986; Pick, Unze, Brownell, Drozdal, & Hopman, 1978; Sulzby, 1996; Wells, 1985).

For young children who cannot read, this is largely achieved through the mediation of a older reader who brings the printed book to life as the oral storyteller, engaging the child in the book as an object and in the words and pictures that appear on its paper pages. We began our series of studies to try to document what young children attend to when being read storybooks as a way of understanding what the book itself versus the adult mediator brings about in book reading interactions. We have applied the technique of monitoring young children's eye fixations when read books presented on a computer screen, applying a new tool to the study of an old one.

In this chapter we present a brief overview of eye movement studies and our findings as a basis for speculating on electronic books fostering literacy development in preschool and kindergarten children and on eye movement research as a tool for understanding children's response to them. For Landoni and Gibb (2000),

> the result of integrating classical book structure, or rather the familiar concept of a book, with features which can be provided within an electronic environment, is referred to as an electronic book, which is interpreted as an interactive document which can be composed and read on a computer.

Following their definition we have generally adopted the term electronic book (or eBook) in this chapter, although various other labels have been used such as multimedia books, living books, animated books, and interactive books. In addition we have concentrated the age range of 4- and 5-year-olds or nonreaders. As Lankshear and Knobel (2003) noted, there is a particular paucity of research on technology and literacy concerning children ages 0 through 8.

Overview of Eye Movement Research

Since the very first work on reading, researchers have been interested in eye movements. Bent over the subject's shoulder, with a mirror placed on the adjacent page of a book, researchers observed that, during reading, eyes moved in saccadic movements from left to right rather than in a continuous manner, and between these saccadic movements that the eyes remained immobile (see Brown, 1895 and Javal, 1879, cited in Wade, Tatler, & Heller, 2003; Huey, 1908). These first eye movement explorations of saccades and fixations, measures that still remain important phenomena in eye movement research, are discussed as part of the first era of research on eye movements by Rayner (1998, 1999). The second era as described by Rayner coincided with the behaviorist movement in psychology. Consequently, work on eye movements during these years was mostly dedicated to providing descriptive information about eye movements in reading. The empirical activity was intense and marked by Tinker's (1946) and Buswell's (1935) classical studies in reading and in perception respectively. However, after years of empirical activity with little theoretical developments about the cognitive processes highlighted by eye movements, eye movement research came to a standstill, with very few studies conducted between the 1950s and 1970s. At the beginning of the 1970s, a third era began. New technological advancements allowed more precise measures of eye movements, computers allowed processing of larger amounts of data, and theories on cognitive processes in language and reading had evolved to allow the study of eye movements as a way to collect information related to these processes. In the current fourth era, a large number of research domains, both applied and fundamental, incorporate eye movement monitoring. Eye movement patterns are studied in perception (van den Berg & van Loon, 2005; Brenner, Meijer, & Cornelissen, 2005), in verbal and spatial memory (Tatler, Gilchrist, & Land, 2005; Traxler, Williams, Rihana, & Blozis, 2005; Tremblay, Saint-Aubin, & Jalbert, 2006), in attention (Crundall, Chapman, & France, 2005), in language comprehension and production (Brown-Schmidt, Byron, & Tanenhaus, 2005), in cognitive processes in adult reading (Roy-Charland, Saint-Aubin, Klein, & Lawrence, 2007), in neuroscience (Crawford, Higham, & Renvoize, 2005; Sailer, Eggert, & Straube, 2005), in comparative psychology (Sasaoka, Hara, & Nakamura, 2005), and most recently, as we will discuss more thoroughly, in shared book reading with children (Evans & Saint-Aubin, 2005; Justice, Skibbe, Canning, & Lankford, 2005b; Roy-Charland, Saint-Aubin, & Evans, 2007).

Eye Movement Apparatus and its Use in Research with Children

Multiple types of apparata have been used to monitor eye movements with adults (Rayner, 1998), including surface electrodes, video-based pupil monitoring, infrared Purkinje image tracking, and search coils attached like contact lenses to the surface of the eyes. These allow different levels of precision both in the measurement of location of fixations and latencies of movements. (For more information see Underwood, 1998.) Some systems such as the search coil attached to the eye are extremely invasive. Similarly all apparata that require that the head be constrained to limit head movements are also unusable with children. Recent developments with video-based systems have made eye tracking systems more friendly in being easier to calibrate, less invasive, and less sensitive to head movements.

However, even with video-based systems, eye movement monitoring with children is associated with many challenges and requires considerable skill on the part of the experimenter. Using our experience testing children with the Eye Link II system, we will highlight a number of general issues related to the use of eye tracking with children.

The SR Research Ltd. EyeLink II system is a video-based pupil tracking apparatus developed by Eyal Reingold (University of Toronto). As shown in Figure 6.1, the EyeLink II system uses a lightweight headband adjusted on the participant's head. Three cameras are mounted on the headband. The first two, located underneath the participant's eyes, follow the movements of the pupil and must be adjusted for each participant at the beginning of the testing session. The third camera located approximately in the middle of the participant's forehead does not require any adjustment. In addition, sensors are located on each of the corners of the monitor and, in conjunction with the

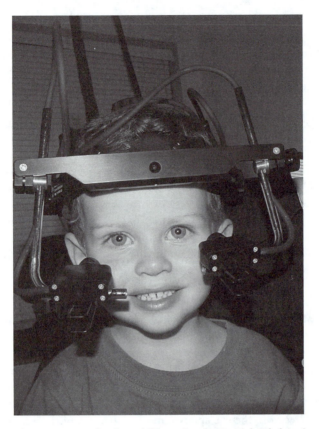

Figure 6.1 A preschool age child wearing the EyeLink II helmet in our laboratory.

camera located on the middle of the headband, allow compensation for head movements. In sum, the cameras and sensor system allow simultaneous tracking of both eyes and head position for head-motion compensation. Consequently, even if the participant moves his or her head, the apparatus can accurately follow the movements of the pupil on the computer screen.

The head mounted nature of EyeLink II deserves comment. First, not all video-based pupil tracking systems are head mounted. For instance, the Tobii eye tracking system or the recent EyeLink 1000 Desktop system are not mounted on the head. Such a system could be easier to use with children because children cannot interfere with the system by touching it. Despite the higher probability of a decalibration due to children's interactions with the headband, head mounted equipment can nevertheless, confer an advantage. We find that giving the children a photograph of themselves wearing the head mounted equipment is highly appreciated by both parents and children, and it is a strong incentive for classmates to take part in our studies.

All video-based pupil tracking apparata, be they head mounted or remote desktop mounted systems, require a similar calibration procedure. The calibration procedure must be performed to insure that the data collected correspond to the location and duration of the participant's eye movements. For the system to be calibrated, the participant must successively fixate on a small dot that appears at various locations on the screen. Participants have to fixate and keep their eyes still on the dot until it moves to another location. When the dot does move, the participant has to fixate it again in its new location. This task must be performed with minimal head movements for the calibration to be accurate. With the EyeLink II system calibration can be achieved by using between 3 and 12 dot locations on the screen. After looking at each dot location once, the dot is presented a second time at each of the locations at which it appeared first. For successful calibration, participants must precisely look at the dot location both times with the mean deviation between both measures smaller than a set criterion (often 1°). If the required precision is not achieved, the calibration procedure must be performed yet again.

Although all video-based systems need a similar calibration procedure, they are not all equally demanding on subjects. Broadly speaking, there is a positive relationship between the precision of the equipment and the demands on subjects during calibration. At one end of the continuum, systems such as EyeLink II or EyeLink 1000 require the head to be relatively still during calibration and at least three dots must be fixated twice. At the other end of the continuum, calibration with systems like Tobii can be achieved despite extreme head motion and with a single dot. Reflecting the very different demands on children during calibration, these systems provide very different levels of information about eye behavior. EyeLink II and 1000 provide extremely high temporal and spatial resolution eye data, allowing insight into not only coarse gaze position information, but also very accurate information regarding saccade metrics and fixation onset times and durations. Tobii, given its lower sampling rate, provides no information on saccade events and comparatively poor fixation onset and duration information. On the other hand, Tobii permits very stable tracking of eye position by reducing errors caused by headband slippage, muscle tremor, and environmental vibration. Thus, at present there is a trade off between ecological validity as a result of the ease of use and quality of information provided that researchers need to consider in selecting an eye tracking system.

Issues Using Eye Movement Monitoring with Children

Because monitoring children's eye movements is at an early stage of development, to the best of our knowledge, challenges associated with the procedure have not been documented. Here, in addition to documenting those challenges, we present innovative solutions that we developed and successfully applied. Obviously, this is mostly relevant for high accuracy systems requiring a more elaborate calibration.

The first major challenge of testing young children (4- or 5-years old) is that, contrary to adults, most children are unaware that they are able to move their eyes without moving their head. Thus children's natural tendency is to rely solely on head movements to fixate the dots in the different locations. To circumvent this problem, practice is required before the experiment begins. For instance, children can be asked to follow the tip of a pencil while the experimenter moves it in different angles until the child is successfully able to move the eyes without head movements.

The second specific challenge with children is that children's calibration accuracy deteriorates with number of calibration attempts, while that of adults usually improves. Adults are increasingly able to fixate the dot more accurately without head movements and they improve in their ability to keep their gaze still in a specific location of the screen. Consequently, the failure to calibrate an adult on the first attempt is not a problem, as the adult will improve in the next attempt. With children, the reverse happens. Over calibration attempts, children become less attentive, move their head more often, and are less able to keep their eyes still on the calibration dot. Thus it is of paramount importance to practice with them without the equipment. Once the equipment is on the child's head, one often has but a single chance to calibrate.

A more technical consideration relates to the number of presentation locations to be used for the calibration. As mentioned previously, the higher number of locations used for the calibration, the more accurate the calibration can be. Typically with adults, nine locations are used. With children a sort of intuitive skill must be developed to reduce the number of dot locations for feasibility without compromising accuracy. Children's motivation and ability to perform the calibration task declines drastically as the number of tested locations increases (recall that each dot location must be fixated twice). As the number of presented dots increases, children become less accurate in their fixation behaviors and the probability of failing to reach the criterion increases. Such calibration failure results in excluding the child from the study.

Generally with young children we have used fewer locations for the calibration procedure. First, although some children are able to calibrate with more points, it is not possible to anticipate which children will be able to do so. Thus this reduces the likelihood of losing participants on these grounds. Second, should a young child decalibrate during the experiment by scratching the head or touching the headband, the calibration procedure must be redone within the experiment. With 4- and 5-year-old children we use a three-point calibration procedure (Evans & Saint-Aubin, 2005) and with children from kindergarten to Grade 4 (5 to 9 years old) a five-point calibration procedure, although we have found that this constitutes a challenge for kindergarten children (Roy-Charland, Saint-Aubin, & Evans, 2007).

In addition to the number of calibration locations, the calibration dot per se also presents a hurdle. While adults will willingly fixate a small black dot, children do not easily comply. In addition to their rapid loss of interest at looking at black dots, children do not look at each dot for a sufficient amount of time. The calibration procedure requires both that the child fixate it precisely, and that the eyes remain stable on the dot for a given amount of time. It is our experience that girls were much more likely to comply with the requirement than boys. To avoid creating biased samples with children, SR Research Ltd. developed, at our request, a variant of the calibration procedure in which the dot is replaced by the tiny face of a cartoon character. With this procedure children tended to look at the cartoon character longer, and to keep fixating and exploring it with our encouragements such as, "Have you seen his red hat," or "Can we see his teeth?" to redirect their attention to and maintain it on the calibration point in a game-like fashion.

In sum, we feel we have begun a new research era in the field of eye movement monitoring in which the equipment can be used with young children. The main challenges associated with testing young children are now known and specific procedures specifically adapted to them have been developed. This does not imply that testing children with eye trackers is easy, but it is clearly possible. Now that the procedure has been developed, what have we learned about storybook reading to children with this technology?

Young Children's Response to Shared Storybook Reading

Parents and teachers often read storybooks to young children and are advised to do so by experts with the premise that doing so will help their children learn to read. While the extent to which shared reading contributes to emergent literacy skills has been debated (e.g. Bus, van IJzendoorn & Pellegrini, 1995; Dunning, Mason, & Stewart, 1994; Lonigan, 1994; Payne, Whitehurst, & Angel, 1994; Scarborough & Dobrich, 1994), the relationships are found frequently enough to conclude that something is going on in this interaction—likely in the way in which the adult mediates the interaction and the child's attention—to foster children's emergent literacy development and subsequent reading skill. However the materials themselves would also be thought to play a role, this being a critical issue when children read books on their own. Emergent literacy encompasses a broad range of knowledge spanning phonological awareness (the ability to reflect on and manipulate the phonemes or sounds in spoken language); letter name and letter sound knowledge, conceptions of print (e.g., linearity, direction in which it is read, title pages in books), semantic knowledge (vocabulary and concepts), and the structure of extended text (e.g., narrative schemas). (See Whitehurst & Lonigan, 1998 for an overview.) For this chapter we have selected two areas on which to focus—print knowledge and vocabulary knowledge.

Print Knowledge

Within preschool and kindergarten classrooms, in which reading books to children typically occurs with a group of children from a book held far away and potentially out of view, it is little wonder that the frequency of shared reading does not predict letter knowledge and beginning reading skills (Meyer, Stahl, Wardrop, & Linn, 1994; Reese, 1995; Vellutino & Scanlon, 2001). However in one-to-one shared reading the book is in full view, physically close to the child, and the pages with their print and illustrations spread out for easy visual inspection. This physical arrangement, coupled with findings showing at least a modest relationship between the frequency of shared book reading and children's literacy development, naturally leads one to think that the books in themselves foster literacy development by drawing children's attention to print on the pages. For this to happen and to benefit children's familiarity with letters, acquisition of letter–sound correspondences, and recognition of individual words, children would need to attend to the print during this activity. Various design characteristics of books might be expected to stimulate such attention. Smolkin, Conlon and Yaden (1988), for example, specified five aspects of books that would make print more salient: (a) print within the illustrations such as speech balloons or labels on the illustrated objects; (b) print looking different such as a change of font, color, or size; (c) print that forms an object or pattern itself such as print snaking across the page; (d) print presented in a three dimensional fashion; and (e) print in which letters are isolated from the rest of the background.

While reading entails many skills—linguistic, conceptual, and orthographic—which shared reading might foster, two recent investigations from our laboratory and that of Laura Justice and colleagues (Justice et al., 2005b) lead one to question whether varying the design characteristics of static books can in itself result in substantial gains in the alphabetic and orthographic knowledge of nonreaders. Using a head mounted eye tracker, both studies directly examined the duration of preschoolers' eye fixations on print and the accompanying illustrations when read storybooks books converted into digitized files and presented on computer screens.

In the first study in our work (Evans and Saint-Aubin, 2005) parents of five children ages 48 to 61 months read five storybooks to their child. These children could name on average 13 letters of the alphabet and were unable to read nine simple words selected from the books. The books varied in the layout of the text and illustrations with three of the books having colorful illustrations and two having simple monochrome line drawings. In one book the text appeared across the top and bottom of the illustration, with one word highlighted in bold uppercase letters. In a second, the text was displayed on the left or right facing page opposite the illustration and each text page began with a large decorated letter seven times the size of the text, which consisted of an average of 36 words per page. In a third, the text appeared in speech bubbles within the illustrations. Finally, in the two books with simple line drawings, there were only an average of seven words per page presented in a uniform font on the page facing the illustration.

Regardless of the nature of the print and illustrations, children rarely looked at the print. Over the total duration of reading the five books, children on average spent a total of ten minutes fixating the illustrations and just 22 seconds fixating the text. None of the children fixated any of the words printed in bold uppercase letters. The ratio of time on illustration to time on text was 27:1 for this book. Large decorated letters were potentially slightly effective in gaining the child's attention, in that one child fixated on the letter on two of the seven pages and another fixated on the letter on three of them. However three of the five children focused on just one or none of these letters, resulting in an overall ratio of time on illustration to time on text of 24:1. All of the children fixated on some text appearing in speech bubbles within the illustrations but this most often seemed to occur when children encountered these speech bubbles while following the contours or objects in the illustrations, such as the curvature of a large pumpkin or the handle on the end of a shovel. Children did not explore the text in these bubbles, fixating only one location within them, and quickly moving on to more of the illustration. Thus for this book, the ratio of time on illustration to time on text was again 27:1. For the two books with simple line drawings and clear separate text, the ratios were widely different—42:1 and 17:1. Most recently we have replicated this among first graders in showing that, if the text exceeds their reading skill, they revert to the behavior of younger nonreaders, looking at the pictures and fixating the text less than 7% of the time (Roy-Charland, Saint-Aubin, & Evans, 2007).

In a related study by Evans, Williamson & Pursoo (2008) we videotaped book reading interactions. From the videotapes we calculated children's gaze direction at pages with print versus illustrations. After each book had been read to the child, we also tested their memory for print targets that had been made salient in the books through combinations of color, size, and font changes, and for nonsalient parts of the illustrations. Here again the ratio of time looking at the illustrations to time looking at the text was 27:1 among children age 3 to 5 years. All age groups performed better than chance in recognizing parts of the illustrations, all of which had not been mentioned in the text and all of which were insignificant elements of the illustrations. In contrast none of the age groups performed beyond chance in recognizing aspects of the text that had been made visually salient. Thus we are not convinced that the design features of books that we manipulated reliably influence children's attention to print.

Justice and her colleagues (Justice et al., 2005b) took a slightly different approach by identifying print zones within two books and quantifying the

Figure 6.2 Sample pages from storybooks used in Experiment 1 of Evans & Saint-Aubin (2005) (source: Copyright©2005 by the estate of Ruth Krauss. Used by permission of HarperCollins Publishers).

Notes

The circles superimposed on each picture represent the fixations of a participant. The diameter of the circles is proportional to the duration of the fixations they represent. The top panels represent two typical children when read *The Happy Egg* (simple illustrations; Krauss, 1967). The bottom panels represent two typical children when read *Les Vaches Voyageuses* (text left; Lebel & Daigneault, 1991). These samples illustrate that there were very few fixations on the text and no significant difference in fixations between books with attractive colorful illustrations and monochromatic simple ones.

extent to which children's eye fixations were within these print zones. One book had "print salient text" in which a third of the print zones or regions of print were within speech bubbles or surrounded completely by the illustrations. In the other book, all of the print zones were separate from the illustrations. Their ten participants were slightly older than ours, ranging in age from 50 to 69 months and knew on average 20 letters of the alphabet. Justice et al. found that the duration of fixations within three minutes of reading time in the print zones was uniformly low, on average under just five seconds for the print salient book and under three seconds for the other book, regardless of children's alphabetic knowledge. Proportionally more of the children's fixations were in the print zones for the print salient book (6% versus 2.5%). This led the authors to conclude that such "print salient" books should be used by educators to encourage the development of children's print awareness. However no mention is made of whether the size of the print zones was equal for the two books. Moreover in the absence of experimental research to show this effect, and given our findings from a wider sampling of book designs, we feel that this conclusion cannot be made. In addition research remains to be conducted on how much incidental attention to unfamiliar letterforms is needed to breed familiarity with and recall of printed forms in young children to allow the conclusion that such design features will enhance print awareness.

This is not to say that books cannot incorporate design features significantly, in a practical sense, to increase young children's attention to print, but rather that we do not know this yet and that much research needs be done to specify design features and their effect. Electronic media offer possibilities beyond that of static books in being able to animate the letters to dance, flash, morph, etc., and in being able to include visual markers to highlight text as it is read, such as balls bouncing along the text or moving shading. This would be thought to capture significantly children's attention and encourage them to interact with the print actively to examine it in a way that reading to the child from a static, paper-format book does not do, and thus foster an understanding of the appearance of print and alphabetic knowledge.

A recent study by Gong and Levy (in press) however, leads one to be cautious about the extent to which visual highlights on the text of electronic books can readily improve young children's print knowledge. Six storybooks were presented on a computer to 4-year olds assigned to one of four conditions. In the standard baseline condition, a voice read the text. In a second, a ball bounced along the words in synchrony as each word was read. In a third, two words on each page violated the way printed words look (e.g., contained uppercase letters in medial positions, backwards letters, letters spaced too far apart). When the ball bounced to it, the voice said "Oh oh" and after three seconds the printed word was corrected on the screen and the story continued. The fourth condition was the same as the third except that the child had to click on the violated word in order for the correct word to be displayed and for the story to continue. Pre- and post-tests consisted of the Wide Range Achievement Test-3 and a print discrimination task (Levy, Gong, Hessels, Evans, & Jared, 2006) in which children choose which pair of words that "Mommy could read," with one of the pair violating the appearance of printed words. Their results showed that neither children in the standard baseline condition nor bouncing ball condition made significant gains on the print discrimination task, whereas those in the other two conditions did. Thus visual highlights on the text while it was read were ineffective. With respect to letter knowledge, children in all the conditions except the standard condition improved slightly. However it should be noted that children in the bouncing ball condition had the highest scores at pre-test, suggesting possible confounds with other uncontrolled variables influencing letter knowledge acquisition across the study.

This "failure of highlighting" for young children is corroborated by Evans Williamson and Pursoo (2008) who had implemented two conditions of book reading: one in which the adult pointed to the text as it was read, and one in which she did not. It was found that if the adult pointed to the text, children's attention to print for the 5-year olds increased over a standard reading condition, and their ability to recognize the salient print targets moved to beyond chance. However, this pointing to the text had no effect on the children in the 3- and 4-year-old age groups.

Thus, simple highlighting of text appears to have limited effect on the print specific skills of children under age 5 but may be effective for older children. However, much research remains to be done in directly examining the focus of children's attention to animated displays of letters and text and their effects for different ages of children and stages of reading development. In addition situations in which animated illustrations combine with animated text should be studied to determine if they result in reduced attention to print. Eye tracking studies offer the possibility of seeing what young children are attending to in such displays.

Vocabulary Knowledge

In our first eye tracking study, the amount that children looked at the print did not vary with the length of the text heard, but time looking at the illustrations increased as length of the text read increased. In effect, the longer the storybook, the more the child looked at the pictures. This led us to wonder whether children's attention to the various pictured content items in the illustration was in concert with the spoken content of the text.

In a second study reported by Evans and Saint-Aubin (2005), we manipulated the text to provide two equivalent versions that highlighted different aspects of the illustrations, these aspects being small and otherwise insignificant details in the illustrations. Participants were children ages 4 and 5 who correctly named eight letters of the alphabet and could read none of five simple words sampled from the story. Again with the technology of an eye tracker, we measured visual fixations in the zone or area surrounding the highlighted content versus the area encompassing the rest of the illustration, as well as fixation on the printed text. The findings in the previous part of this chapter regarding attention to print were replicated. Children spent an average of seven seconds on the text and two minutes on the illustrations. However the results further showed that where children looked in the illustrations could be manipulated according to the content of the text read to them, in that children fixated an illustrative detail more when it was mentioned in the text. Thus children appeared to direct their attention to the illustrations according to the semantic content of what was read to them.

The fact that children appear to process the pictures in concert with the text points to the role of the illustrations in enhancing their understanding of the text. In fact previous research has documented the facilitative role that pictures play in young children's comprehension of the storyline in traditional paper books (Guttman, Levin, & Pressley, 1977; Lesgold, Levin, Shimron, & Guttman, 1975) and electronic storybooks (Miller, Blackstock, & Miller, 1994; Neuman, 1989; Segers, Takke, & Verhoeven, 2004; Shamir & Korat, this volume; Sharp et al., 1995; Verhallen, Bus, & de Jong, 2006).

It also points to the role that illustrations may play in fostering vocabulary knowledge. The most reliable findings about the benefits of shared book reading center around gains in semantic knowledge, although it should be noted that studies have dealt primarily with the acquisition of new words rather than gains in the depth of meaning in known words. Young children's literature typically contains a higher percentage of rare words and more varied vocabulary than is found during conversations, toy play, mealtime, routine care giving interactions, and prime television programs (Dunn, Wooding, & Herman, 1977; Hayes & Ahrens, 1988; Hoff-Ginsberg, 1991), making it a "natural" medium for fostering vocabulary development.

Several studies have reported increments in children's understanding of novel words introduced in storybooks read to them (Biemiller & Boote, 2006; Brabham & Lynch-Brown, 2002; Eller, Pappas & Brown, 1988; Elley, 1989; Ewers & Brownson, 1999; Leung & Pikulski, 1990; Penno, Wilkinson, & Moore, 2002; Robbins & Ehri, 1994; Sénéchal & Cornell, 1993; Wasik & Bond, 2001). When the characteristics of studies showing gains in vocabulary acquisitions are examined, it is apparent that experiments, interventions, and field studies showing the greatest association between novel vocabulary in storybooks and semantic gains had some combination of the following characteristics: (a) the books were read multiple times—at least three; (b) there were multiple occurrences of each novel word in the text; (c) the novel words were clearly illustrated by the pictures and specifically pointed to by the reader; (d) the novel words were important to the text; (e) the meaning of the novel words was clear from the context, picture, or explanation of adults; (f) the novel words introduced were largely nouns; (g) the child was asked to repeat the words, retell the story, and/or engage in activities related to the words' meanings. Under some combination of the above conditions, averaging across studies, children showed increased understanding of about 20% of novel words in storybooks in a post-test situation.

Not all studies, however, have reported a positive association between shared book reading and vocabulary development. For example Beals and Tabors (1995) found no relation between rare words used in book reading conversations and children's receptive vocabulary scores. This may be because when unusual words are encountered during reading, most parents continue with the story without pausing to explain them, and children rarely ask for clarification (Pursoo, Evans, & Shaw, 2005; Tabors, Beals, & Weizman; 2001). Thus our most recent study (Evans, Saint-Aubin, Roy-Charland, & Allen, 2006) examined how closely children 4- and 5-years old "read" the pictures in concert with the text and their use supporting text clues to identify novel vocabulary items as reflected by their eye movements.

Half of the 15 target words in the text across three short storybooks were high frequency words, and half low frequency words. For each book, a mirror version was created in which all high frequency words in the original version were replaced by their low frequency word counterparts and vice versa. Each version was used with half of the children. The illustrations and text were shown on a computer screen to the adult and child, seated on the adult's lap, for the adult to read to the child as she normally would. Clues to the words in the form of a subsequent sentence containing a high frequency word (or words) describing the target item followed in close or more distal proximity to the target word. As each target word was read, a signal was entered into the online Eyelink data file and the lag between the target word being spoken by the adult and target item in the illustration being fixated by the child was calculated. After each book was read, children were tested on their receptive knowledge of the words by asking them to select the spoken word from among pictured alternatives showing parts of the illustrations appearing in the books. Half of these low frequency words had appeared in the storybook version read to them and half had not.

Here as seen in Figure 6.3 the appearance of the printed text was considerably denser and smaller than in our studies focusing on children's attention to print and to text, and we did not expect children to fixate it. Regardless of whether the illustration accompanied a high or low frequency word, children fixated the print just six seconds versus the pictures about 160 seconds—a ratio of 27:1. These figures are strikingly similar to what was presented earlier when the print was manipulated to be more salient. This again shows that the physical appearance of text does not substantially influence the extent to which nonreaders attend to the text versus the pictures. With respect to children's attention to rare and common words mentioned in the text, it took longer for

Figure 6.3 Sample pages from storybooks used in Evans, Saint-Aubin, Roy-Charland, and Allen (2006) (source: *Les Vaches Voyageuses*, Lebel & Daigneault, 1991. Permission granted by Éditions Pierre Tisseyre Inc.).

Notes

The black circles superimposed on the pictures represent the fixations of the participant. The diameter of the circles is proportional to the duration of the fixations they represent. For graphic simplicity only the fixations that occurred between the target word, circled in blue, being read by the adult and the first fixation by the child on the corresponding object are presented in the figure. The arrows between fixations represent the order in which fixations occurred. The upper panel presents fixations by one participant when the target word embedded in the text was a high frequency label; the lower presents the same when the target word was a rare synonym. As shown in these samples, the reaction times, calculated from the moment the target word was read to when target object was first fixated, were on average longer for the rare word than the frequent word.

children to fixate the part of the picture corresponding to rare words than to common ones. In addition, the interaction of the proximity of the clues to meaning and the novelty of the words did not affect the time it took children to fixate the novel words. Finally, there was no difference in children's accuracy on the post-test in identifying rare words or common words heard in the text and illustrated in the pictures and those that had not been in the books.

Together these results show three things. One is that a single mention of a word and accompanying illustration does not readily facilitate the acquisition of new vocabulary. This single reading of the books had little effect on children's acquisition of the meaning of the new words within them. The second is that children's current level of semantic understanding guides their visual attention to the parts of the pictures in the text read to them, in that the pictures of rare words were fixated more slowly. The third is that young children have difficulty quickly integrating and applying clues from known words to novel words when listening to books as shown by no difference in lag when the known clues were close to or farther away from the unfamiliar word. This may explain why previous research has shown a Matthew effect with the vocabulary of 4- and 5-year-old children with higher vocabulary knowledge increasing more than those of children with lower pre-test scores (Nicholson & Whyte, 1992; Robbins & Ehri, 1994; Sénéchal, Thomas, & Monker, 1995).

What are the implications for eBooks? Given that it appears that for children to acquire the meanings of new words, the corresponding pictures need to be clearly illustrated and explicitly pointed to, electronic books may be a powerful medium for teaching vocabulary. Such books can animate the corresponding part of the illustration as it is spoken to allow children to orient quickly to novel words regardless of background knowledge. In fact, Verhallen, Bus, and de Jong (2006) have shown that four encounters with a multimedia book that animated aspects of the setting, characters, events, and resolutions resulted in greater vocabulary gains than similar exposure to a static electronic book counterpart among second language learners.

Adult Mediation during Shared Book Reading

In this chapter, for the purpose of brevity we have not discussed studies of the way in which adults scaffold children's interactions with books and elaborate the text. There is a growing literature on this, including early and recent studies of parent reading books to toddlers and babies (e.g., DeLoache & DeMendoza, 1987; Ninio & Bruner, 1976; Wheeler, 1983), to preschoolers (e.g., Danis, Bernard, & Leproux, 2000; Haden, Reese, & Fivush, 1996; Hammett, Van Kleeck, & Huberty, 2003; McArthur, Adamson, & Deckner, 2005; Reese, 1995; Shapiro, Anderson, & Anderson, 1997), in different SES groups (e.g., Baker, Mackler, Sonnenschein, & Serpell, 2001; Hockenberger, Goldstein, & Haas, 1999), to children with special needs (e.g., Kaderavek & Justice, 2005; Woude & Barton, 2001), and to children in the early school grades who are taking on the reading role (e.g., Bergin, Lancy, & Draper, 1994; Evans, Baraball, & Eberlee, 1998; Evans, Moretti, Shaw, & Fox, 2003; Hannon, Jackson, & Weinberger, 1986; Mansell, Evans, & Hamilton-Hulak, 2005; Stolz & Fischel, 2003; Tracey & Young, 2002).

These studies demonstrate that adults play an active and important role in engaging the child, by elaborating the text, asking questions, and relating the content of the print, the story, and the illustrations to the child's experience, and by coaching children decode the words when they take on the reader role. A concern over interactive storybooks is that parents may confer upon them the "role of the surrogate adult in the reading process" (Underwood, 2000). The widely varying nature and quality of electronic books (see reviews by de Jong & Bus, 2003; Korat & Shamir, 2004), coupled with children's interest in bells and whistles of interactive hotspots, along with our eye movement work showing that young children's attention is not necessarily where one thinks it might be, should add to this malaise. For example, de Jong and Bus (2002) found that 4- and 5-year olds, who had repeated access to an electronic story-book with hotspots that animated the illustration and gave access to games, preferred the games and animations and actually heard about only half of the text heard by children using a paper storybook. The former children also made less progress in word reading. Similarly research by Trushell and col-leagues (Trushell, Burrell, & Maitland, 2001; Trushell & Maitland, 2005; Trushell, Maitland, & Burell, 2003) has shown that among 8- and 9-year-old children, cued animations and sound effects interfered with inferential under-standing and storyline recall.

In addition, no research was found in preparing this chapter on how parents use electronic storybooks, and whether and how they direct their chil-dren's interaction with these media when they are in use. Moreover one might even question whether interactive electronic books would have the effect of minimizing the mediation role that parents now typically play when reading to children. Adults can discern that a child does not understand, is off task, or is working with too difficult material, and can provide just-in-time adjustments and supports to meet the child's needs. On the other hand, if electronic books were designed properly, they could potentially uniformly do what parents often do not. For example, when reading to young children, including preschoolers who are in the process of learning the alphabet in North American society, parents rarely comment on aspects of the print (Evans et al., 2006; Justice & Ezell, 2000; Yaden, Smolkin, & Conlon, 1993). Similarly parents rarely offer an explanation of unfamiliar vocabulary encountered during shared book reading (Pursoo et al., 2005; Tabors et al., 2001), even though explicit verbal explanations facilitate vocabulary acquisi-tion (Brett, Rothlein, & Hurley, 1996; Elley, 1989; Justice, Meier, & Walpole, 2005a; Penno et al., 2002).

Concluding Comments

This chapter has described methodology points in eye tracking research and what we have found in our studies of shared book reading with young children using this technological tool. We have done so for three main reasons. One has been to challenge assumptions about shared book reading, what children do when being read to, and the mechanism by which benefits, real or purported, may occur. The second has been to speculate on whether and how electronic books could remedy what we will temporarily call for the purpose of this sentence the "limitations" of traditional paper storybooks. The third has been to dangle the possibility of applying eye tracking methodology in the future to young children interacting with electronic books as a window on their cognitive engagement. The challenges of doing so, however, will be considerable in arriving at accurate data, but this is not seen as impossible.

Finally we wish to leave the reader with a last thought to complicate the notions of effect and value in different designs of books, be they electronic or traditional paper format. The research literature is overwhelmingly biased towards the "eduvalue" of children's books, shared book reading, and most recently, electronic books. This review is equally guilty in exploring children's cognitive responses to various design characteristics. However, it must be borne in mind that different users approach storybooks with different goals. In our most recent study (Audet, Evans, & Williamson, 2006) we developed a survey to assess the goals that parents have for shared book reading, consisting of 36 items reflecting five factors. Responses were received from parents of 294 children in grades junior kindergarten through three (roughly ages 4 through 8). At every age level, the two highest rated goal areas—indistinguishable from each other in the ratings and significantly higher than cognitive goals—were those of "fostering enjoyment of reading" (e.g., to enjoy hearing a good story); to develop respect for literature, to make reading a habit, and "bonding with the child" (e.g., to share quality time, to experience physical closeness, to strengthen child–parent relationship). To quote Cyndi Lauper's feminist anthem (1983; original lyrics by Robert Hazard, 1979), sometimes "girls just wanna have fun." A challenge for the design of both electronic and traditional books, and caregiver interventions with these media, is to provide an appropriate balance of affect/enjoyment and stimulation/eduvalue to meet the goals of parents, teachers, and children without sacrificing either.

References

Audet, D., Evans, M.A., & Williamson, K. (June, 2006). Goals for parent–child shared book reading. Paper presented at the Canadian Psychological Association, Calgary, Canada.

Baker, L., Mackler, K., Sonnenschein, S., & Serpell, R. (2001). Parent's interactions with their first-grade children during storybook reading and relations with subsequent home reading activity and reading achievement. *Journal of School Psychology, 39*, 415–438.

Beals, D.E., & Tabors, P.O. (1995). Arboretum, bureaucratic and carbohydrates: Preschoolers' exposure to rare vocabulary at home. *First Language, 15*, 57–76.

Bergin, C., Lancy, D.F., & Draper, K.D. (1994). Parents' interactions with beginning readers. In D.F. Lancy (Ed.), *Children's emergent literacy: From research to practice* (pp. 53–73). Westport, CT: Greenwood Publishing Corp.

Biemiller, A., & Boote, C. (2006). An effective method for building meaning vocabulary in primary grades. *Journal of Educational Psychology, 98*, 44–62.

Brabham, E.G., & Lynch-Brown, C. (2002). Effects of teacher's read aloud styles on vocabulary acquisition and comprehension of students in the early elementary grades. *Journal of Educational Psychology, 94*, 465–473.

Brenner, E., Meijer, W.J., & Cornelissen, F.W. (2005). Judging relative positions across saccades. *Vision Research, 45*, 1587–1602.

Brett, A., Rothlein, L., & Hurley, M. (1996). Vocabulary acquisition from listening to stories and explanations of target words. *Elementary School Journal, 9*, 415–422.

Brown, A.C. (1895). The relation between the movements of the eyes and the movements of the head. *Nature, 52*, 184–188.

Brown-Schmidt, S., Byron, D.K., & Tanenhaus, M.K. (2005). Beyond salience: Interpretation of personal and demonstrative pronouns. *Journal of Memory and Language, 53*, 292–313.

Bus, A.G., van IJzendoorn, M.H., & Pellegrini, A.D. (1995). Joint book reading makes for success in learning to read: A meta-analysis on intergenerational transmission of literacy. *Review of Educational Research, 65*, 1–21.

Buswell, G.T. (1935). *How people look at pictures*. Chicago: University of Chicago Press.

Crain-Thorenson, C., & Dale, P.S. (1992). Do early talkers become early readers: Linguistic precocity, preschool language and emergent literacy. *Early Child Development and Care, 271*, 210–237.

Crawford, T.J., Higham, S., & Renvoize, T. (2005). Inhibitory control of saccadic eye movements and cognitive impairment in Alzheimer's disease. *Biological Psychiatry, 57*, 1052–1060.

Crundall, D., Chapman, P., & France, E. (2005). What attracts attention during police pursuit driving? *Applied Cognitive Psychology, 19*, 409–420.

Danis, A., Bernard, J-M., & Leproux, C. (2000). Shared picture-book reading: A sequential analysis of adult–child verbal interactions. *British Journal of Developmental Psychology, 18*, 369–388.

de Jong, M.T., & Bus, A.G. (2002). Quality of book-reading matters for emergent readers: An experiment with the same book in a regular or electronic format. *Journal of Educational Psychology, 94*, 145–155.

de Jong, M., & Bus, A. (2003). How suitable are electronic books to support literacy? *Journal of Early Childhood Literacy, 3*, 145–155.

DeLoache, J.S., & DeMendoza, O.A. (1987). Joint picture book interactions of mothers and 1-year-old children. *British Journal of Developmental Psychology, 5*, 111–123.

Dunn, J., Wooding, C., & Herman, J. (1977). Mothers' speech to young children: Variation in context. *Developmental Medicine and Child Neurology, 19*, 629–638.

Dunning, D.B., Mason, J.M., & Stewart, J.P. (1994). Reading to preschoolers: A response to Scarborough and Dobrich (1994) and recommendations for future research. *Developmental Review, 14*, 324–339.

Eller, R.G., Pappas, C.C., & Brown, E. (1988). The lexical development of kindergarteners: Learning from written context. *Journal of Reading Behavior, 20*, 5–24.

Elley, W.B. (1989). Vocabulary acquisition from listening to stories. *Reading Research Quarterly, 24*, 174–187.

Evans, M.A., Barraball, L., & Eberlee, T. (1998). Parental responses to miscues during child-to-parent book reading. *Journal of Applied Developmental Psychology, 19*, 67–84.

Evans, M.A. Mitchell, K., Reynolds, K., Mansell, J., Pursoo, T., Spere, K., et al. (June, 2006). Parental goals and print referencing during shared book reading with 4-year-olds. Paper presented at Canadian Language and Literacy Research Network, Charlottetown, Canada.

Evans, M.A., Moretti, S., Shaw, D., & Fox, M. (2003). Parent scaffolding in children's oral reading. *Early Education and Development. Special Issue: Vygotskian perspectives in early childhood education, 14*, 363–388.

Evans, M.A., & Saint-Aubin, J. (2005). What children are looking at during shared storybook reading. *Psychological Science, 16*, 913–920.

Evans, M.A., Saint-Aubin, J., Roy-Charland, A., & Allen, L. (June, 2006). Reading pictures: Preschoolers eye fixations on illustrations during shared book reading. Paper presented at the Royal Netherlands Academy of Arts and Sciences Colloquium: "How media can contribute to early literacy," Amsterdam.

Evans, M.A., Williamson, K., & Pursoo, T. (2008). Preschoolers' attention to print during shared reading. *Scientific Studies of Reading, 12*, 106–129.

Ewers, C., & Brownson, S. (1999). Kindergartners' vocabulary acquisition as a function of active versus passive storybook reading, prior vocabulary, and working memory. *Reading Psychology, 20*, 11–20.

Gong, Z., & Levy, B.A. (in press). Four-year-old children's acquisition of print knowledge during electronic storybook reading. *Reading and Writing: An Interdisciplinary Journal.*

Goodman, Y.M. (1980). The roots of literacy. In M. Douglass (Ed.), *Forty-fourth yearbook of the Claremont Reading Conference* (pp. 1–32). Claremont, CA: Claremont Reading Conference.

Goodman, Y.M. (1986). Children coming to know literacy. In W.H. Teale & E. Sulzby (Eds.), *Emergent literacy: Writing and reading* (pp. 1–14). Norwood, NJ: Ablex.

Guttman, J., Levin, J.R., & Pressley, M. (1977). Pictures, partial pictures, and young children's oral prose learning. *Journal of Educational Psychology, 79*, 473–480.

Haden, C., Reese, E., & Fivush, R. (1996). Mothers' extratextual comments during storybook reading: stylistic differences over time and across texts. *Discourse Processes, 21*, 135–169.

Hammett, L.A., Van Kleeck, A.V., & Huberty, C.J. (2003). Patterns of extratextual interactions during book sharing with preschool children: A cluster analysis study. *Reading Research Quarterly, 38*, 442–468.

Hannon, P., Jackson, A., & Weinberger, J. (1986). Parents' and teachers' strategies in hearing young children read. *Research Papers in Education, 1*, 6–25.

Hayes, D.P., & Ahrens, M.G. (1988). Vocabulary simplification for children: A special case of "motherese?" *Journal of Child Language, 15*, 395–410.

Hockenberger, E.H., Goldstein, H., & Hass, L.S. (1999). Effects of commenting during joint book reading by mothers with low SES. *Topics in Early Childhood Special Education, 62*, 15–27.

Hoff-Ginsberg, E. (1991). Mother–child conversation in different social classes and communicative settings. *Child Development, 62*, 782–796.

Huey, E. B. (1908). *The psychology and pedagogy of reading.* New York: Macmillan. (Reproduced by MIT Press, Cambridge, MA, 1968.)

Javal, L.E. (1879). *Physiologie de la lecture et de l'écriture.* Paris: F. Alcan.

Justice, L.M., & Ezell, E. (2000). Enhancing children's print and word awareness through home-based parent intervention. *American Journal of Speech-Language Pathology, 9*, 257–269.

Justice, L.M., Meier, J., & Walpole, S. (2005a). Learning new words from storybooks: An efficacy study with at-risk kindergarteners. *Language, Speech and Hearing Services in Schools, 3*, 17–32.

Justice, L.M., Skibbe, L., Canning, A., & Lankford, C. (2005b). Preschoolers, print and storybooks: An observational study using eye movement analysis. *Journal of Research in Reading, 28*, 229–243.

Kaderavek, J.N., & Justice, L.M. (2005). The effect of book genre in the repeated readings of mothers and their children with language impairments: A pilot investigation. *Child Language Teaching & Therapy, 21*, 75–92.

Korat, O., & Shamir, A. (2004). Do Hebrew electronic books differ from Dutch electronic books: A replication of a Dutch content analysis. *Journal of Computer Assisted Learning, 20*, 257–268.

Kraus, R. (1967). *The happy egg.* Chicago: J. Philip O'Hara.

Landoni, M., & Gibb, F. (2000). The role of visual rhetoric in the design and production of electronic books: The visual book. *Electronic Library, 18*, 190–201.

Lankshear, C., & Knobel, M. (2003). New technologies in early childhood literacy research: A review of research. *Journal of Early Childhood Literacy, 3*, 59–82.

Lauper, C., Greenwich, E., & Kent, J.B. (1983). Girls just wanna have fun. [Recorded by Cyndi Lauper] On *She's so Unusual*. [R. Chertoff, Producer]. Epic Records.

Lebel, G., & Daigneault, M. (1991). *Les vaches voyageuses* [The travelling cows]. Montreal, Quebec: Éditions Pierre Tisseyre.

Lesgold, A.M., Levin, J.R., Shimron, J., & Guttman, J. (1975). Picture and young children's learning from prose. *Journal of Educational Psychology, 67*, 636–642.

Leung, C.B., & Pikulski, J.J. (1990). Incidental learning of words meanings by kindergarten and first-grade children through repeated read aloud events. *National Reading Conference Yearbook, 39*, 231–239.

Levy, B., Gong, Z., Hessels, S., Evans, M.A., & Jared, D. (2006). Understanding print: Early reading development and the contributions of home literacy experiences. *Journal of Experimental Child Psychology, 93*, 63–93.

Lonigan, C. (1994). Reading to preschooler exposed: Is the emperor really naked? *Developmental Review, 14*, 303–323.

McArthur, D., Adamson, L.B., & Deckner, D.E. (2005). As stories become familiar: Mother–child conversations during shared reading. *Merill-Palmer Quarterly, 51*, 389–411.

Mansell, J., Evans, M.A., & Hamilton-Hulak, L. (2005). Developmental changes in parents' use of miscue feedback during shared book reading. *Reading Research Quarterly, 40*, 294–317.

Meyer, L.A., Stahl, S.A., Wardrop, J.L., & Linn, R. (1994). Effects of reading storybooks aloud to children. *Journal of Educational Research, 88*, 69–85.

Miller, L., Blackstock, J., & Miller, R. (1994). An exploratory study into the use of cd-rom storybooks. *Computers and Education, 22*, 187–204.

Neuman, S. (1989) The impact of different media on children's story comprehension. *Reading Research and Instruction, 28*, 38–47.

Nicholson, T., & Whyte, B. (1992). Matthew effects in learning new words while listening to stories, In C.K. Kinzer & D.J. Leu (Eds.), *Literacy research, theory, and practice: Views from many perspectives. Forty-first yearbook of the National Reading Conference* (pp. 499–503). Chicago: National Reading Conference.

Ninio, A., & Bruner, J. (1976). The achievement and antecedents of labelling. *Journal of Child Language, 5*, 1–15.

Pappas, C.C. (1987). Exploring the textual properties of protoreading. In R. Steele & T. Threadgold (Eds.), *Language topics: Essays in honour of Michael Halliday* (pp. 137–162). Amsterdam: John Benjamins.

Payne, A.C., Whitehurst, G.J., & Angel, A.L. (1994). The role of home literacy environment in the development of language ability in preschool children from low-income families. *Early Childhood Research Quarterly, 9*, 427–440.

Penno, J.F., Wilkinson, I.A.G., & Moore, D. (2002). Vocabulary acquisition from teacher explanation and repeated listening to stories: Do they overcome the Matthew effect? *Journal of Educational Psychology, 94*, 23–32.

Pick, A.D., Unze, M.G., Brownell, C.A., Drozdal, J.G., & Hopman, M.R. (1978). Young children's knowledge of word structure. *Child Development, 49*, 669–680.

Purcell-Gates, V. (1988). Lexical and syntactic knowledge of written narrative held by well-read to kindergartners and second graders. *Research in the Teaching of English, 22*, 128–160.

Pursoo, T., Evans, M.A., & Shaw, D. (June, 2005). Parental elaboration of novel vocabulary during shared book reading. In M.A. Evans (Chair) Perspectives on shared book reading and its contribution to children's development I. Symposium presented at the Canadian Psychological Association, Montreal.

Rayner, K. (1998). Eye movements in reading and information processing: 20 years of research. *Psychological Bulletin, 124*, 372–422.

Rayner, K. (1999). What have we learned about eye movements during reading? In R.M. Klein & P. McMullen (Eds.), *Converging methods for understanding dyslexia* (pp. 23–56). Cambridge, MA: Massachusetts Institute of Technology Press.

Reese, E. (1995). Predicting children's literacy from mother–child conversations. *Cognitive Development, 10*, 381–405.

Robbins, C., & Ehri, L. (1994). Reading storybooks to kindergarten children helps them learn new vocabulary words. *Journal of Educational Psychology, 6*, 54–64.

Roy-Charland, A., Saint-Aubin, J., & Evans, M.A. (2007). Eye movements in shared book reading with children from kindergarten to Grade 4. *Reading and Writing: An Interdisciplinary Journal, 20*, 909–931.

Roy-Charland, A., Saint-Aubin, J., Klein, R.M., & Lawrence, M. (2007). Eye movements as direct tests of the GO model for the missing-letter effect. *Perception & Psychophysics, 69*, 324–337.

Sailer, U., Eggert, T., & Straube, A. (2005). Impaired temporal prediction and eye–hand coordination in patients with cerebellar lesions. *Behavioural Brain Research, 160*, 72–87.

Sasaoka, M., Hara, H., & Nakamura, K. (2005). Comparison between monkey and human visual fields using a personal computer system. *Behavioural Brain Research, 161*, 18–30.

Scarborough, H.S., & Dobrich, W. (1994). On the efficacy of reading to preschoolers. *Developmental Review, 14*, 245–302.

Segers, E., Takke, L., & Verhoeven, L. (2004). Teacher-mediated versus computer-mediated storybook reading to children in native and multicultural classrooms. *School Effectiveness and School Improvement, 15*, 215–226.

Sénéchal, M., & Cornell, E. (1993). Vocabulary acquisition through shared reading experiences. *Reading Research Quarterly, 28*, 361–374.

Sénéchal, M., Thomas, E., & Monker, J. (1995). Individual differences in 4-year-old children's acquisition of vocabulary during storybook reading. *Journal of Educational Psychology, 87*, 218–229.

Shapiro, J., Anderson, J., & Anderson, A. (1997). Diversity in parental storybook reading. *Early Child Development and Care, 127–128*, 47–59.

Sharp, D.L.M., Bransford, J.D., Goldman, S., Risko, V.J., Kinzer, C.K., & Vye, N.J. (1995). Dynamic visual support for story comprehension and mental model building by young at-risk children. *Educational Technology Research and Development, 43*, 25–42.

Smolkin, L.B., Conlon, A., & Yaden, D.B. (1988). Print salient illustrations in children's picture books: The emergence of written language awareness. *National Reading Conference Yearbook, 37*, 59–68.

Stoltz, B.M., & Fischel, J.E. (2003). Evidence for different parent–child strategies while reading. *Journal of Research in Reading, 26*, 287–294.

Sulzby, E. (1985). Children's emergent reading of favorite storybooks: A developmental study. *Reading Research Quarterly, 20*, 458–481.

Sulzby, E. (1996). Roles of oral and written language as children approach conventional literacy. In C. Pontecorvo, M. Orsolini, B. Burge, & L.B. Resnick (Eds.), *Early text construction in children* (pp. 25–46). Hillsdale, NJ: Erlbaum.

Tabors, P.O., Beals, D.E., & Weizman, Z.O. (2001). You know what oxygen is? Learning new words at home. In Dickinson, D.K. & Tabors, P.O. (Eds.), *Beginning literacy with language* (pp. 93–110). Baltimore: Brookes.

Tatler, B.W., Gilchrist, I.D., & Land, M.F. (2005). Visual memory for objects in natural scenes: From fixations to object files. *Quarterly Journal of Experimental Psychology A: Human Experimental Psychology, 58A*, 931–960.

Tinker, M.A. (1946). The study of eye movements in reading. *Psychological Bulletin, 43*, 93–120.

Tracey, D.H., & Young, J.Y. (2002). Mothers' helping behaviours during children's at-home oral-reading practice: Effects of children's reading ability, children's gender, and mothers' educational level. *Journal of Educational Psychology, 94*, 729–737.

Traxler, M.J., Williams, R.S., Rihana, S., & Blozis, S.A. (2005). Working memory, animacy, and verb class in the processing of relative clauses. *Journal of Memory and Language, 53*, 204–224.

Tremblay, S., Saint-Aubin, J., & Jalbert, A. (2006). Rehearsal in serial memory for visual-spatial information: Evidence from eye movements. *Psychonomic Bulletin & Review, 13*, 452–457.

Trushell, J., Burell, C., & Maitland, A. (2001). Year 5 pupils reading an "Interactive Storybook" on CD-ROM: Losing the plot? *British Journal of Educational Psychology, 32*, 389–401.

Trushell, J., & Maitland, A. (2005). Primary pupils' recall of interactive storybooks on CD-ROM: Inconsiderate interactive features and forgetting. *British Journal of Educational Psychology, 36*, 57–66.

Trushell, J., Maitland, A., & Burell, C. (2003). Pupils' recall of an interactive storybook on CD-ROM. *Journal of Computer Assisted Learning, 19,* 80–89.

Underwood, D.D.M. (2000). A comparison of two types of computer support for reading development. *Journal of Research in Reading, 23,* 136–148.

Underwood, G. (1998). *Eye guidance in reading and scene perception.* Oxford, UK: Elsevier.

van den Berg, A.V., & van Loon, E.M. (2005). An invariant for timing of saccades during visual search. *Vision Research, 45,* 1543–1555.

Vellutino, F.R., & Scanlon, D.M. (2001). Emergent literacy skills, early instruction, and individual differences as determinants of difficulties in learning to read: The case for early intervention. In S.B. Neuman & D.K. Dickinson (Eds.), *Handbook of early literacy research* (pp. 229–255). Cambridge, UK: Cambridge University Press.

Verhallen, M.J.A.J.M., Bus, A.G., & de Jong, M.T. (2006). The promise of multimedia stories for kindergarten children at risk. *Journal of Educational Psychology, 9,* 410–419.

Wade, N.J., Tatler, B.W., & Heller, D. (2003). Dodge-ing the issue: Dodge Javal, Hering, and the measurement of saccades in eye-movement research. *Perception, 32,* 793–804.

Wasik, B.A., & Bond, M.A. (2001). Beyond the pages of a book: Interactive book reading and language development in preschool classrooms. *Journal of Educational Psychology, 93,* 243–250.

Wells, G. (1985). Preschool literacy-related activities and success in school. In D.R. Olson, N. Torrance, & A. Hildyard (Eds.), *Literacy, language, and learning: The nature and consequences of reading and writing* (pp. 229–255). Cambridge, UK: Cambridge University Press.

Wheeler, M.P. (1983). Context-related age changes in mothers' speech: Joint book reading. *Journal of Child Language, 10,* 259–263.

Whitehurst, G.J., & Lonigan, C.J. (1998). Child development and emergent literacy. *Child Development, 68,* 848–872.

Woude, J.V., & Barton, E. (2001). Specialized corrective repair sequences: Shared book reading with children with histories of specific language impairment. *Discourse Processes, 32,* 1–27.

Yaden, D.B., Jr., Smolkin, L.B., & Conlon, A. (1993). Preschooler's questions about pictures, print convention, and story text during reading aloud at home. *Reading Research Quarterly, 24,* 189–214.

7

Learning from Interactive Vocabulary Books in Kindergarten

Looking Back, Looking Forward

Eliane Segers

The most important problem in the teaching machine area is not the design of the machine itself but rather the design of good instructional material.

(Carter, 1961, p. 708)

In the last two decades of the twentieth century, the computer has entered the lives of children both at home and in school. Kindergartners also are given access to computer games, and stories read to them by the computer. A popular example is the series of living books designed by the Brøderbund Company, in which a story is told and various "hotspots" can be clicked on for a funny reaction. The goal of this type of software program is mainly entertainment, although educational aspects are always stressed, leading to the popular term "edutainment." However, software programs that are strictly educational have also been developed, based on the belief that the computer can enhance learning and even help children who lag behind in critical skills like vocabulary learning.

Not all parents and teachers have been equally enthusiastic about using computers in kindergarten, however. They associate working with computers with the negative effects of watching too much (violent) television (cf. Wartella, this volume). Kindergartners are thought to be too young and too vulnerable to work with computers. This is probably true for playing violent games, or surfing the internet. But, as with watching television, software with an educational goal and quality design can have positive effects. Computers in schools can also introduce a new dimension to teaching. Kindergarten teachers are often unaware of the possibilities for computers in the classroom (Labbo, 2000), and there is still a need for examples of good practices. Most early research focused on case studies or inventories of teachers' knowledge, attitudes, or practices (Landerholm, 1995). Only a very few attempts have examined the potential of using computers to help children with reading problems (for an overview, see Ehri et al., 2001).

The present chapter will examine the potential benefits of computer-supported instruction in language learning for kindergarten classrooms. It will describe the design of an educational software program for mainstream children, and its effectiveness on literacy development. I will present the effects of the software program on vocabulary learning for mainstream children, those learning Dutch as a second language, and those who have special learning needs, as well as physical and multiple disabilities.

After this overview, I will reflect on the following questions from the past. Is the computer a useful tool in kindergarten? What is the task of the teacher in using the educational software? What do children with special needs need? I will then conclude with a discussion of present research as well as ideas and possibilities for the future in the interesting area of literacy development and computer technology in kindergarten.

Treasure Chest with the Mouse

Using computers to enhance vocabulary has traditionally focused on electronic books, relying on the well-known fact that storybook reading is an important factor in vocabulary growth (Bus, van IJzendoorn, & Pellegrini, 1995). However, to enhance further vocabulary learning by computer, especially in the case of second language learners, additional materials beside interactive stories might enhance learning by inserting vocabulary games. Vocabulary learning then becomes the purpose of the activity, instead of a contextual benefit. This has led to an extended version of interactive books (cf. de Jong & Bus, 2003) known as *interactive vocabulary books* (Segers & Vermeer, 2008). In this sort of software different types of vocabulary games are connected to a story that is being told. Words are presented in a more explicit manner, enhancing the possibilities of enlarging vocabulary.

Schatkist met de Muis (Treasure Chest with the Mouse, TCM: Verhoeven, Segers, & Mommers, 1999), the computer software that was used in our studies, is an example of such an interactive vocabulary book. It was designed for 4- and 5-year-old children with special attention for those with language difficulties. The program includes four main literacy objectives, aligned with the Kindergarten standards in the Netherlands: (1) becoming familiar with books and stories, (2) enlarging vocabulary, (3) enhancing metalinguistic awareness, and (4) discovering the alphabetic principle.

In TCM, a story with story pictures as anchors is presented (Bransford, Sherwood, Hasselbring, Kinzer, & Williams, 1990). When children first play, they click on an icon of a little book, and listen to a story. The story is short, about 300 words, and consists of high-frequency words that kindergarteners with a limited vocabulary should be expected to understand. At the end of each story fragment, a parrot puppet at the bottom of the screen asks a question, which the children then answer by clicking somewhere in the picture. In this way, the children are actively involved in the story. Help is provided if the child cannot answer the question, and eventually the correct answer is given, so the child always can continue to play. At the end of the story, the child is asked to arrange the pictures in the correct order.

The next time the child enters the storybook, he or she can choose to listen to the story again or immediately start playing the vocabulary games, which are described below. Different vocabulary games can be played, all using the story pictures as a playing field. The story pictures all represent a fairly closely woven semantic network with numerous relations: a bakery, a living room, a forest, or a supermarket.

There are four types of games. The first, is a pointing game that requires children to point at the objects the parrot asks for ("Can you click on the table in the kitchen?"). The second is a shifting game that requires the child to move an object to a particular place in the picture. The parrot asks the child, for example, to place the apron on the boy in the kitchen (see Figure 7.1). This game is of special interest for learning prepositions, which can be particularly problematic for young children. Third, is a yes/no game where the child must decide whether an object belongs in the picture or not. The parrot asks, for example, whether you can buy a carrot in a bakery. And the fourth is a coloring game, in which objects in the picture have to be painted or decorated. The parrot asks the child, for example, to paint the curtains red or make the curtains flowered.

When the child demonstrates success with these games, two other vocabulary games become available. The first is a pointing game in which the parrot

Figure 7.1 Screen example: the child is asked to place the apron on the boy in the kitchen (source: © mijnnaamishaas.nl, drawing and animation by Thijs C. Aarts).

breaks the words into syllables (e.g., Can you point to the kit-chen ta-ble?). The second involves a word being written on the screen with the graphemes lighting up as the parrot slowly pronounces the word. These two games stimulate not only vocabulary acquisition but also metalinguistic awareness or the ability to reflect on units of language.

As can be seen in the upper left above the picture in Figure 7.1, the child has to answer five questions per session. The figures above the picture turn green, yellow, or red depending on the number of attempts it takes the child to answer a question correctly. When answering the five questions, the child cannot be interrupted by switching from one thing to the next. Each of the five available CD-ROMs contains 200 questions with 50 questions per picture. This is the software we examined in our studies.

Effectiveness of the Software Program

Teacher Reading Versus Computer Reading

In a first study (Segers, Takke, & Verhoeven, 2004), we attempted to find out whether there were differences in story comprehension and vocabulary learning after kindergartners in native and multicultural classrooms in the Netherlands listened to a story read to them by the computer or by the teacher. Especially for immigrant children, vocabulary gain from listening to a story read to them by the computer could be valuable, since that would give them the means to enhance independently their vocabulary. If immigrant children could be shown to learn when the computer reads to them (see in the introduction to this chapter), this could be a helpful tool in trying to bridge the gap between them and native children. The study explored differences in story comprehension and vocabulary learning in children in native and multicultural kindergarten classrooms when listening to a story read to them by the computer or the teacher. The children came from four different schools. The population of two of these schools consisted of native children only; the other two schools had a population of mainly immigrant children from Turkey and Morocco. The results showed that children (41 native and 30 immigrant) learned new words, both from listening to their teacher and from listening to the computer. However, immigrant children learned more words and had better story comprehension when the teacher read the story, probably because more scaffolding took place. However, all children learned from listening to a story read to them by the computer. Many questions remain on how the computer-read story should be designed for optimal effectiveness. This will be discussed later in this chapter.

In the field of children with special needs, a similar question was asked. Can children with cerebral palsy keep their attention on a story when it is read to them by the computer instead of the teacher? This was tested with 18 children who entered a school for children with physical and multiple disabilities (Segers, Nooijen, & de Moor, 2006). An experimental group ($n =$ 9) listened to a story read to them by the computer. The control group ($n = 9$) had the same story read to them by a teacher. The results showed that children with cerebral palsy were as capable of keeping their attention on the story when it was read to them by the computer as when it was read to them by the teacher. Again, many questions remained on how the computer-read story should be designed for optimal effectiveness, especially since the software was not designed for this population.

Studies comparing humans to computers are intriguing and tempting to conduct. However, Reinking (2001) argued that the question of whether the computer can be compared to the teacher is in fact not the right question to ask. One should not try to have the computer compete with humans, but rather make use of the computer's special characteristics. The additional vocabulary games that are available in TCM are an example of such special characteristics. They can provide practice that is hardly possible for a kindergarten teacher to provide to her class. One teacher in our studies mentioned that the computer could present the language to a child in a meaningful, interactive way and in a greater amount than she could during a school day, because of the number of children in the class. The research on this part of the software is described below.

Research on Vocabulary Learning by Computer

The effects of the software on vocabulary learning have been studied elaborately. In two first pilot studies, we studied immigrant children from two different schools in their first ($n=20$) or second ($n=30$) year of kindergarten (Segers & Verhoeven, 2002). The youngest children spent six 15-minute sessions working with the story and vocabulary games and the older children worked in three 25-minute sessions. In each session, two children were taken out of the classroom to a quiet room in the school to work at the computer. Significant learning gains were found.

We then implemented the software in a mainstream school setting with 30 native and 37 immigrant children in their first and second year of kindergarten who attended one of two locations of the same school (Segers & Verhoeven, 2003). Children worked with the computers in a large room in their school under the supervision of volunteer parents in 15-minute sessions, twice weekly during half a school year. The parents provided little assistance, simply answering any questions the children might have (cf. Klein & Darom, 2000). When compared to a control group of 97 children from two different mainstream schools that did not use the software, a significant effect of the computer intervention was found on words that could be learned in the software. However, no effect on a standardized vocabulary test was found. It was observed that especially second language learners who came to kindergarten with little or no knowledge of the Dutch language had difficulties in working with the software in the beginning. Native children had higher learning gains in their first school year, whereas immigrant children had higher learning gains in their second year of kindergarten, when they had a basic Dutch vocabulary.

The software was also studied in other populations. We found learning effects in a group of children ($n = 28$) in special education (average IQ = 77.8) in an intervention consisting of six 15-minute sessions (Segers & Verhoeven, 2008) and in a small group of nine children with special needs (aged between 48 and 72 months), although the effects for this latter group were less clear-cut (Segers, Nooijen, & de Moor, 2006). The positive effect was found between post-test and retention and not between pre-test and post-test. This can partly be explained by the fact that the story was also read to the control group ($n = 9$), that did not play the vocabulary games. The main conclusion of these studies was that such special children are in need of special software that is better designed for their needs.

TCM in Retrospective: Options for the Future

TCM was one of the first rather advanced educational software programs for kindergartners in the Netherlands. The impact was high, and it is currently used in most kindergartens in the country. The effectiveness was shown in diverse populations, and significant learning effects were found.

However, conducting the research gave new insights for potential improvements in the design and development of new software. For example, the way new vocabulary is taught could be improved. In TCM, new words are presented in the context of the story picture of the anchor story, and little verbal context is given. This may be too difficult for children with little or no knowledge of the language. This was apparent in the learning gains of the children. In a study by Segers and Vermeer (2008), another software program is described that presents new words to children in various semanticizing games (cf. Nation, 2001). These are followed by games in which word knowledge is tested. If the child makes a mistake in a semanticizing game, feedback is given in the form of a description of the word. For second language learners, this software provides an option to also present words in their first language, thus helping out those children who have little knowledge of the second language. Learning gains shown by this software program were almost twice as high as in TCM. An explanation could be found in the amount of time spent on the intervention, but could also be due to the different approaches. These different types of approaches in vocabulary learning by computer need more attention in future research.

A second potential improvement would be to make the software more adaptive to the vocabulary level of the child (see also Segers & Vermeer, 2008 Pragmatic reasons prevented us from doing so in TCM, but the fact remains that some children now often are playing games in which most of the words that are presented are already known by the child, whereas other children can be confused because they hardly know any of the words. For example, if a child is able to click on a cow when asked to, the next level should be to name the parts of the cow (tail, udder, and so on), or to present other farm animals, thus enlarging the semantic network.

Third, the motivational aspect should be improved upon (cf. Donker, 2005). TCM is fun and playful, but not all games provide this in the same amount. For example, the feedback indicating a good answer in the pointing game consists of a sound or short animation, but there is no element of surprise. In the yes/no game, the feedback for a wrong answer is often funnier than for a right answer. In one question, for example, the child is asked whether a real car belongs in the living room. If the child clicks "yes," a life-size car is projected in the living room, which is always a cause for laughter and an encouragement to play the game more often (and give more wrong answers). However, the fact that a child might knowingly give wrong answers in order to receive the funnier feedback does not really matter since the child still becomes familiar with the vocabulary. In enhancing motivational aspects, such as humorous feedback, there is a thin line between educational and edutainment software and it is important that the entertaining part is supportive of the learning. Bus, de Jong, and Verhallen (2006) reported that 90% of the multimedia effects in a computer read story are inconsistent with the story, which shows that there is a lot of room for improvement (and thus potential learning gain) in this area.

Reflection on Questions from the Past

The first question from the past was whether the computer is a useful tool in kindergarten. The above overview shows that it is. Of course this was not only shown in studying TCM, but also by other researchers who showed the positive learning gains from young children listening to interactive storybooks (Terrell & Daniloff, 1996; Johnston, 1997; Ricci & Beal, 2002; de Jong & Bus, 2003, 2004; Verhallen, Bus, & de Jong, 2006). The computer has earned a place in the kindergarten classroom; a few computers form a corner to play in, just as the corner with building blocks, the kitchen-corner and so on. It is important that the software that is placed on these computers is suitable for the group of children that play with it. This means that the contents must have educational value that is adaptive to the level of the child, but on the other hand are also playful. A boring but educational game will not work because children will lose interest quickly. The challenge is to combine insights from research with the creativity of game designers.

The second question from the past addressed the task of the teacher. My own research did not yet involve the teacher enough, since I was mostly interested in the effectiveness of the software on its own, but Nir-Gal and Klein-Pnina (2004) showed how 5- and 6-year olds had higher learning gains when their computer time was mediated by the teacher, instead of very little or no mediation. Saude and colleagues (2005) analyzed the training needs of teachers and plan to set up and evaluate a training program in ICT and education for kindergarten teachers, focusing on use, function, role, and form of curricular inclusion of ICT. This type of research can help enhance the knowledge in this area.

Furthermore, Kuhn (2001) argued that the computer should be taken out of the corner and integrated into the classroom. This does not contradict what I mentioned earlier about a few computers forming a corner in a kindergarten classroom. It means that the effectiveness of software can be boosted if it is integrated in what is going on inside the classroom. An example would be insuring that the contents of the software are in line with a theme that is central for a few weeks in the school. The teacher may read a story to the children that they can have read to them again by the computer and the computer can ask other questions than the teacher did. Vocabulary games can be played in the group and repeated or expanded on the computer in different settings, and so on. This way new words are learned in different settings (cf. Nation, 2001), which should enhance the learning effects of each of the components in the program.

The third question asked about the needs of children with special needs. The answer can be simple. They need special software and they need more attention by researchers in studying what, if anything, should change in order to tailor software to their needs. Perhaps software used in mainstream schools, as was used in my own research, is also suitable for some groups of children with special needs, but it is more likely that adaptations will enhance positive effects. As a follow up of the Bio Bytes program mentioned in the introduction, Lingua bytes is now being developed in the Netherlands, which will provide software intervention to enhance literacy in children with special needs.

A Glimpse of the Future

What will the future bring? More and more attention is being paid to the special characteristics of the computer. New types of games are being developed that do not use the computer as a mechanic teacher or as an advanced cassette recorder. An interesting idea in this line is being explored at the National Center for Language Education in the Netherlands. An immersive game was developed called *Mijn naam is Haas* (My name is Hare; www.mijnnaamishaas.nl). As in TCM the goals are to enhance story understanding and vocabulary development, but the way this was undertaken is completely different. *My name is Hare* is an interactive narrative game, in which children create their own story by following the basic idea that Hare has lost his memory and is trying to regain it. In this case, children do not have to use the mouse to click on objects on the screen (as is the case in almost all other educational software). The mouse functions as their drawing pencil by which they draw their own story. The first assignment for the child is to draw a road for Hare leading to the forest. This road is then integrated in the story (see Figure 7.2a). Hare then faces such challenges as crossing water or climbing a mountain. The child can help him by drawing a bridge or a ladder. The system uses a feedback loop structure to guide the child through such a problem situation. Hare's instructions with regard to drawing the right solution get more specific every time the child goes through the loop again. In Figure 7.2b the problem was that it started to rain, so the child had to draw an umbrella.

Other problems can arise in the game, such as being asked to help a flock of sheep over the water, helping a cow to find food, and so on. There is no standard sequence of problems, they arise according to the landscape that is drawn and even then the problems cannot be predicted. New vocabulary is introduced via these problem situations, and as the game develops, the surroundings become more colorful and more skills are required from the child. Formative evaluations are being conducted at the moment. This idea shows what could be done in the future if one takes a step back and invents new possibilities for the computer to enhance children's literacy.

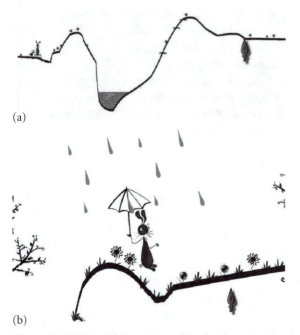

(a)

(b)

Figure 7.2 (a) The child can draw a line that becomes the road for Hare; (b) The child had to draw an umbrella to prevent Hare from getting wet in the rain (source: © mijnnaamishaas.nl, drawings and animations by Thijs C. Aarts).

The present book gives an overview of lines of research that are currently being followed: researchers are focusing on the search for optimal features (see chapters by Bus et al. and Shamir & Korat), such as advanced methodology eye-tracking is used to gain more precise information about the focus of attention (see chapter by Evans), and other behavioral measures are taken into account (e.g., Bus) as well as cognitive demand (e.g., Roskos), environmental effects (e.g. Marsh), and the effects of using the first language for second language learners (e.g., Leseman) are being studied.

As became clear in the previous paragraph, research should also continue to explore the role of the teacher, and keep paying attention to children with special needs. Research should also focus on optimal design features. For example, even in 2007, little is known about design aspects for these young computer users. How many buttons are optimal? How many levels are understandable? How large should the buttons be? Donker (2005) made an interesting contribution, although for a somewhat older age group (6- and 7-year olds learning to read). She described well designed educational software as software that makes children enjoy themselves, work/play at their own level of development, and gives motivational feedback. Her study focuses on one specific computer program. She had children fill in questionnaires, observed them while playing with the software, and had them think-aloud, thus gathering information about the usability of the program and motivational aspects to work with it. She also studied mouse behavior and, contrary to Joiner, Messer, Light, and Littleton (1998) found that drag and drop is more suitable than click-move-click. Age differences could have caused the different effects, since children were younger in the latter study. She also found that objects need to be at least 1 square centimeter in order to prevent unnecessary time to try to click on the object. Cooperation between researchers in the field of (special) education and human–machine interaction could be valuable in this line of research.

Conclusion

The present chapter began by a trip down memory lane as to the questions that were asked in the past. Reservations about having the computer in classrooms in kindergarten, questions about how to use computers, and questions from the field of special education were addressed. An elaborate description was given on the design and study of one software program, which gave insights in these questions. A reflection on the past turned to a look at the future in which researchers and practitioners work together on new and challenging software that can enhance literacy in a meaningful, fun, and effective way.

References

Bransford, J.D., Sherwood, R.D., Hasselbring, T.S., Kinzer, C.K., & Williams, S.M. (1990). Anchored instruction: Why we need it and how technology can help. In D. Nix & R. Spiro (Eds.), *Cognition, education and multimedia: Exploring ideas in high technology*. Hillsdale, NJ: Erlbaum.

Bus, A., de Jong, M., & Verhallen, M. (2006). CD-ROM talking books: A way to enhance early literacy? In M. McKenna, L.D. Labbo, R.D. Kieffer, & D. Reinking (Eds.), *International handbook of literacy and technology. Volume II* (pp. 129–142). Mahwah, NJ: Lawrence Erlbaum.

Bus, A.G., van IJzendoorn, M.H., & Pellegrini, A.D. (1995). Joint book reading makes for success in learning to read. A meta-analysis on intergenerational transmission of literacy. *Review of Educational Research, 65,* 1–21.

Carter, L.F. (1961). Automated instruction. *American Psychologist, 16,* 705–710.

de Jong, M.T., & Bus, A.G. (2003). How well suited are electronic books to supporting literacy? *Journal of Early Childhood Literacy, 3,* 147–164.

de Jong, M.T., & Bus, A.G. (2004). The efficacy of electronic books in fostering kindergarten children's emergent story understanding. *Reading Research Quarterly, 39,* 378–393.

Donker, A. (2005). Human factors in educational software for young children. Unpublished Doctoral dissertation. Amsterdam: PI Research.

Ehri, L.C., Nunes, S.R., Willows, D.M., Schuster, B.V., Yaghiub-Zadeh, Z., & Shanahan, T. (2001). Phonemic awareness instruction helps children learn to read: Evidence from the National Reading Panel's meta-analysis. *Reading Research Quarterly, 36,* 250–287.

Johnston, C.B. (1997). Interactive storybook software: Effects on verbal development in kindergarten children. *Early Child Development and Care, 132,* 33–44.

Joiner, R., Messer, D., Light, P., & Littleton, K. (1998). It is best to point for young children: A comparison of children's pointing and dragging. *Computers in Human Behavior, 14,* 513–529.

Klein, P.S., & Darom, N.E. (2000). The use of computers in kindergarten, with or without adult mediation: Effects on children's cognitive performance and behavior. *Computers in Human Behavior, 16,* 591–608.

Kuhn, M. (2001, April). Taking computers out of the corner: Making technology work in the classroom. *Reading Online, 4.* Retrieved February 8, 2007 from www.readingonline.org/electronic/elec_index.asp?HREF=/electronic/kuhn/index.html.

Labbo, L.D. (2000). 12 things young children can do with a talking book in as classroom computer center. *Reading Teacher, 53,* 542–546.

Landerholm, E. (1995). Early childhood teachers' computer attitudes, knowledge, and practices. *Early Child Development and Care, 109,* 43–60.

Nation, I.S.P. (2001). *Learning vocabulary in another language.* Cambridge, UK: Cambridge University Press.

Nir-Gal, O., & Klein-Pnina, S. (2004). Computers for cognitive development in early childhood: The teacher's role in the computer learning environment. *Information Technology in Childhood Education Annual, 16,* 97–119.

Reinking, D. (2001). Multimedia and engaged reading in a digital world. In L. Verhoeven & C. Snow (Eds.), *Literacy and motivation* (pp. 195–221). Mahwah, NJ: Erlbaum.

Ricci, C.M., & Beal, C.R. (2002). The effects of interactive media on children's story memory. *Journal of Educational Psychology, 94,* 138–144.

Saude, S., Carioca, V., Siraj-Blatchford, J., Sheridan, S., Genov, K., & Nuez, R. (2005). Developing training for early childhood educators in information and communications technology (ICT) in Bulgaria, England, Portugal, Spain and Sweden. *International Journal of Early Years Education, 13,* 265–287.

Segers, E., Nooijen, M., & de Moor, J. (2006). Vocabulary training with the computer in kindergarten children with special needs. *International Journal of Rehabilitation Research, 29,* 343–345.

Segers, E., Takke, L., & Verhoeven, L. (2004). Teacher-mediated versus computer-mediated storybook reading to children in native and multicultural classrooms. *School Effectiveness and School Improvement, 15,* 215–226.

Segers, E., & Verhoeven, L. (2002). Multimedia support in early literacy learning. *Computers & Education, 39,* 207–221.

Segers, E., & Verhoeven, L. (2003). Effects of vocabulary computer training in kindergarten. *Journal of Computer Assisted Learning, 19,* 559–568.

Segers, E., & Verhoeven, L. (2008). ICT support in kindergarten for children at risk. In L. Verhoeven & C. Kinzer (Eds.), *Interactive literacy education. Facilitating literacy environments through technology* (pp. 77–94). Mahwah, NJ: Lawrence Erlbaum.

Segers, E., & Vermeer, A. (2008). Vocabulary learning by computer in kindergarten: The possibilities of interactive vocabulary books. In O.N. Saracho & B. Spodek (Eds.), *Contemporary perspectives on science and technology in early childhood education* (pp. 149–166). Charlotte, NC: Information Age Publishing.

Terrell, S.L., & Daniloff, R. (1996). Children's word learning using three modes of instruction. *Perceptual and Motor Skills, 83,* 779–787.

Verhallen, M.J., Bus, A.G., & de Jong, M. (2006). The promise of multimedia stories for kindergarten children at risk. *Journal of Educational Psychology, 98*(2), 410–419.

Verhoeven, L., Segers, E., & Mommers, C. (1999). *Schatkist met de muis* (Treasure chest with the mouse). Tilburg, the Netherlands: Zwijsen.

8

Struggling Readers and Multimedia

Victor H.P. van Daal

Books are, without doubt, disappearing (Trushell, 2000). They are being replaced by hypertexts—texts that are only available through the use of a computer. Even schoolbooks are disappearing. The following example may be a good illustration. At the start of the 2006/2007 school year, all schoolbooks for secondary education in the Dutch town of Breda in the south of the Netherlands had been made accessible through the internet (some books were scanned into a computer, other books were made available in digital form by the publishers). This had already happened in many other places before and it will undoubtedly happen more in the future. This development might be perceived as a big relief for struggling readers who might no longer have to deal with books!

However, struggling readers will need more than just books replaced by another medium. They will need specific help with activities they cannot undertake independently. Consequently it makes sense to examine the complex needs of struggling readers to determine what types of scaffolds might best support their learning needs.

Difficulties in Learning to Read

Struggling readers encounter a variety of difficulties in decoding and comprehending text. Cross-linguistic research and within particular languages indicate a number of key challenges. For example, Elbro (2005) examined why reading skill develops so slowly in Danish and English compared to German. His research highlighted a number of factors that prevented students from making simple one-to-one relationships between letters and sounds, for example, (1) digraphs, that is, two or more letters are used to represent one sound (e.g. *sj-*, *sch-* and *-ng*), (2) context-dependent letter pronunciations, e.g., vowel length is governed by the number of following consonant letters, and (3) entirely unpredictable pronunciations of certain letters in words. Such deviations are widespread in English and Danish, but less frequent in other languages. It was found that non-words with digraphs (*sjål*) were harder to read for Danish, English and German speaking children than non-words of identical length with respect to sounds (*jål*) or letters (*spål*). He also noted that non-words with a conditional vowel letter sound (*gosse*) were harder to read than non-words with a regular letter vowel sound (*goser*).

Van der Leij and van Daal (1999; in preparation) followed a group of dyslexic readers for 3 years and compared their reading skills (in Dutch) with both reading-matched and chronological-matched controls. We found that: (1) dyslexic children were slower and less accurate than the controls at each level of increasing difficulty of the words, along dimensions such as the length and the syllabic complexity of the word; (2) dyslexic children were able to learn to read words of increasing complexity, but took more time than controls; (3) having reached the mastery of a certain type of word difficulty did not make them any faster in mastering the next level of difficulty: they had to start from scratch again with learning to read words at a new difficulty level; and (4) having reached a nearly 100% accuracy level across all types of difficulties, the dyslexic readers were still slower than controls at reading words.

These findings suggest that orthographic complexities present difficulties to beginning readers because they have to learn a letter-to-sound system that cannot be predicted with 100% certainty. Dyslexic children face even more severe and long-lasting difficulties because of the intrinsic problems with phonological processing (e.g., Share, 1995).

Prevention, Intervention and Compensation

Various approaches have been used to tackle these problems. Usually these approaches are categorized as: prevention, intervention and compensation. Through preventive activities, we attempt to avoid reading problems. The classic example of a prevention study is one carried out by Lundberg, Frost and Petersen (1988) who successfully trained children on phonological skills before they received formal reading instruction. Intervention is the term used for remedial activities undertaken once it becomes apparent that a child has problems. Intervention has had a long tradition, initially based on the work of Samuel Orton in the US around 1925. Compensatory activities are mostly used with older struggling readers, when it has not been possible to (fully) remediate basic reading skills.

Although prevention, if possible, is essential, we take the position that it is critically important to support children when they are actually encountering difficulties in language. In other words, there are limitations to a prevention perspective. For example, a series of prevention programs (four different designs, but all aimed at intervening before children start learning to read) developed in the Dutch National Programme on Dyslexia did not produce substantial transfer effects. That is, children who profited from the prevention programs that were aimed at improving phonological skills did not do any better at reading 1 year later on than children who received syntactical and morphological training (van Otterloo, van der Leij, & Henrichs, in press). These results are at odds with the outcomes of older non-computerized intervention programs reported by Lundberg, Frost and Petersen (1988) who found long-lasting effects of phonological awareness training in kindergarten. It might well be that computerized forms of prevention and intervention are less beneficial for struggling readers. Further research will have to determine if face-to-face contact is essential.

Prevention in combination with continuing intervention might represent the most potent strategy for helping struggling readers. Starting early could be advantageous in at least two ways. First, most children would get a head start, and hopefully become independent readers at a very early stage. We know, for example, that independent reading is the best accelerator for becoming a fluent reader and for profiting from instruction at school. Second, we can easily select the children who might need extra help. The earlier we can address and treat the difficulties, the more cost-efficient it usually is (e.g., Vellutino et al., 1996; Torgesen, 2001).

For older struggling readers, multimedia might serve as a tool to provide compensatory instruction. These students will need frequent skill practice and content rich instruction. Computers could be extremely efficacious in bootstrapping reading skills while students grapple with grade-level subject matter.

Briefly, we will describe some of the features that are central in learning to read, and how computers might enhance prevention, intervention and compensation for struggling readers.

Learning to Read

It is generally accepted that children learn more easily to read if they have already a well-developed vocabulary and if they have some awareness of the sound structure of the language. This is called phonological awareness. Moreover, if children are able to apply these sounds to their letter names, they are likely to be successful in reading.

However, reading is not just being able to decode words. Readers must be fluent and immediately recognize written words. According to Share (1995) item-specific information is stored in memory. Written (orthographic), spoken (phonological) and meaning (semantic) representations of each specific word becomes more and more specified and interconnected over time. Every word has its own word-specific representation in memory, which strengthens with multiple encounters. For that reason it is important to read a lot.

Because repeated reading can be seen as rather tedious, it has never caught on. Yet, the computer offers some attractive possibilities. Underwood (2000), for example, examined the effects of two popular computer programs, *SuccessMaker*, a practice and drill program, and *Arthur's Teacher Trouble*, a talking book. Surprisingly, children became very motivated even with the practice and drill program. By increasing motivation, students learned more from the programs.

Recently programs have been designed that combine the principles of repeated reading and the teaching of specific subskills. For example, programs that combine repeated reading, phonological awareness and decoding such as the WordBuild program (McCandliss, Beck, Sandak, & Perfetti, 2003; Harm, McCandliss, & Seidenberg, 2003) are becoming widely used to help struggling readers.

Multimedia and Struggling Readers

Responding to the needs of struggling readers, multimedia applications have developed in primarily two forms. The first is computerized versions or extensions of basal reader programs. These programs come with a standard reading method and may differ from each other in several ways. In some reading methods the accompanying computer program offers additional practice for struggling readers, in others all children go through the same program, more or less in the same pace. They typically contain several types of practice, ranging from training phonological skills to text reading.

The second are programs designed to assist struggling readers and older dyslexics in comprehending texts. These programs do not teach reading skills, but support users by reading aloud texts, and even web pages. Kurzweil 3000 (www.kurzweiledu.com/), for example, scans books while keeping the original layout, including pictures, drawings and tables. The spoken text can be exported and listened to as an MP3 file. It also supports the import of a wide variety of file types. The program can store difficult words in memory, and may contain several dictionaries. Also, it provide writing supports including a simple spelling checker, a device that shows homophone words, mind mapping programs that predict the word that children are typing.

These programs focus on a number of key skills.

- Phonological skills. They concentrate on the training of subskills that have to do with the understanding of the sound structure of the language (Yopp, 1988) and include practicing blending, segmenting, rhyming and similar. An example is the program evaluated by Reitsma and Wesseling (1998) in which children had to compare two spoken words that were presented one after the other, the first presented in segments followed by a whole word sound.
- Word reading with speech feedback. An example of this feature can be found in van Daal and Reitsma (1993). In this program a child clicks on a button, indicating the format of feedback (either in segments or whole word), and the computer provides the word sound in digitized speech. It also provides an unsolicited version, in which the feedback is presented in every word.
- Flash words (a word is briefly presented on the screen). This is probably the most popular form, because it is so easy to program.

However, it is unclear what just flashing a word will do. Therefore Yap and van der Leij (1993) combined it with presenting letter clusters first, either in spoken or written form, and required the children to indicate whether or not the cluster was part of the later on presented word.

- Text reading with speech feedback. Here the students read stories on the computer and they can indicate when they need assistance from the computer. They either click on a word, mark a sentence or just set the cursor somewhere in the text, and the computer will read the word, sentence or story for them. The first programs offered feedback at word level by presenting the whole word sound or the sound in some other format (Olson & Wise, 1992).

- Talking books. This is a relative new form of "reading while listening" or "listening while reading." Implemented in the form of a Daisy disk (a special kind of CD player originally designed for blind people), it involves video and simultaneously audio of the reading of a book. Tools like the "reading pen," a pen that moves over the print, while it is being read, also belong to this category. Originally "talking books" were developed for pre-readers and contained lots of pictures and other animations aiming at promoting vocabulary acquisition. Since then, talking books are also available for adults who might enjoy the simultaneous stimulation.

- Authoring programs. These include programs like Clicker (www.cricksoft.com/us/products/clicker/), which allow teachers to import pictures, texts and sounds for designing programs specially targeted for children's needs. Through a website experiences and materials can be exchanged.

Features of Multimedia for Struggling Readers

At one time, computer memories were built big to allow for the storage of digitized speech and for programs to generate text to speech. Computers were thought to be very helpful in reading instruction and reading remediation for several reasons. Instruction, for one, could be individualized designed for learning independently and at one's own pace. Further, training could be adapted to the specific needs of an individual learner. In addition, errors could be quickly modified to enhance instant feedback.

These features have been realized in all modern programs. Whether digitized speech or text-to-speech is used, the user is free to "let the computer talk," as (s)he desires. The quality of text-to-speech has improved considerably over the years and is now highly intelligible and comes close to natural speech. Laptop computers can provide all facilities and can easily be used at any location so that the learner can work independently, privately and at his own pace. Tools that can deliver speech-to-text have even become smaller than laptop computers and can be used anywhere, such as the Reading Eye (www.applica.no), a small hand-hold apparatus that scans, stores and reads aloud any text.

More closely related to the process of learning to read are advantages including immediate feedback, repetition and sustaining the attention of the learner. With these characteristics the "time on task" can be considerably increased, especially important for struggling beginning readers. Giving feed-back is implemented in most programs, though it has become apparent that feedback should not be provided in a rigid way by reinforcing all correct answers, or by "punishing" the user for wrong answers. It generally works better when every now and then a pat on the shoulder is given, and errors are completely ignored. However, it is important to keep track of errors in both good and poor readers in order to see whether these errors are systematic. In the case of systematic errors, it is the task of the program (nowadays most programs are constructed in such a way that they can do this) or human tutor to concentrate on these errors. Struggling readers need repetition for over-learning.

The learning process can more precisely be structured (van Daal, 1993), a characteristic of most modern programs, using near-perfect language. There-fore in many programs designers have preferred the use of digitized speech over the use of synthesized speech (van Daal, 1993).

Another relevant issue is the use of the help function. Spaai (1994) who concentrated on independent learning with the computer found that help functions were extremely useful for students' independent work. In other words, it helps them teach themselves (Share, 1995) and rely less often on the teacher. If they are able to read the word on their own, the computer can provide the spoken form of the word after the student has read the word. This procedure of reinforcing correct responses has been implemented by Stru-iksma (2003), who combined the reading of a limited set of words by a student on a computer with a human tutor who gave feedback when needed. Obviously, the role of the teacher has changed: from teacher-driven instruc-tion to learner-driven instruction.

Finally, given that the computer offers a variety of possibilities that are thought to be helpful to the student who is struggling to read, its efficiency should be evaluated. Even if computers are effective, we are still left with the question of whether they are more efficient than the teacher (Ellermann, 1991).

What is the Effect of Multimedia Applications?

A program known as the Stanford project, aimed at completely replacing the teachers by computers. It was the first project to be evaluated. It did not, however, live up to the expectations, especially when field results were taken into account (Fletcher & Atkinson, 1972). The main reason is that it was not cost efficient; programs for initial reading ran on mainframe computers in the early years and they were very expensive. Slavin (1991) evaluated IBM's Writing to Read program in a meta-analysis study by looking at 29 separate studies. He concluded that the efficiency of the program was very low, and that the costs in comparison to the learning effects were too high, a conclusion that is in line with other reviews of the program (Krendl & Williams, 1990).

Computer costs, of course, have decreased significantly since then. New evaluation studies have examined the relation between computers and learning.

Seven reviews since 1990 have evaluated the use of computer-assisted instruction (CAI) and beginning reading. Two used a meta-analytic technique and found effect sizes of 0.25 ($SE = 0.07$) and 0.16 ($SE = 0.08$), Kulik and Kulik (1991) and Ouyang (1993), respectively.

Qualitative reviews were conducted by Torgesen and Horen (1992), van der Leij (1994), Wise and Olson (1998) and by the National Institute of Child Health and Human Development (2000), which were generally positive. Reviewing some 20 studies dealing with a wide range of reading subskills, they reported that talking computers appeared to be a promising technique. However, Torgesen and Horen (1992) pointed out that much work needed to be done to integrate better the computer within the curriculum. In some countries, this is being done with basal reading programs prescribing how and when to use the computer.

Qualitative studies conducted by van der Leij (1994) and Wise and Olson (1998) concerned the use of computers with reading-disabled children. Van der Leij (1994) found that studies that concentrated on a specific subskill were generally more effective than multi-componential programs. Wise and Olson (1998) reviewing their own series of experiments concluded that the talking computers combined with phonological awareness training had a positive effect on the learning results, especially in children with relatively stronger phonological skills.

In order to assess the efficiency of computers, however, it is not sufficient to look at whether children do fare better with the computer in comparison with a control group. We also need to look at the size of the effect. Although many of the aforementioned studies seem to show positive effects, the effect sizes were small, around 0.20 with a standard error of around 0.07.

The most recent review available is the one by Blok, Oostdam, Otter and Overmaat (2002) in which studies undertaken in the period 1990–2000 were reviewed. Examining studies that focused on beginning readers, they categorized the studies along a variety of criteria to find out what features of the computer programs appeared to work best. In particular, they looked at 45 studies that reported on 75 experimental conditions on a large host of characteristics.

The main results of their study are as follows. The combined effect size was 0.25 with a standard error of 0.056. Experimental subjects were on the average 0.25 standard deviations better off than students in the control condition. The variance of the effect sizes was 0.083, which means that there were considerable differences in effect sizes between the studies. A total of 34% of the variance could be explained by entering the effect size at pre-test into the equation. Language of instruction explained another 27% of the variance, studies conducted with English as medium of instruction obtained effect sizes that were 0.319 *SD* larger than non-English studies. No other variable was related to effect size at the post-test. Thus the conclusions were very straightforward: computer-assisted instruction had only a modest effect. The effect was a bit larger when the program was conducted in English and when the experimental group was already better at the pre-test.

This result is in line with previous research (Kulik & Kulik, 1991; Ouyang, 1993). Nevertheless it was very disappointing. These results essentially replicated those of previous reviews.

Systematic reviews of interventions in adult literacy and numeracy have been carried out by Torgeson, Porthouse and Brooks (2003, 2005). However, the authors concluded that most studies lacked methodological quality and that therefore it had been difficult to draw conclusions about which particular forms of intervention are effective.

However there is a good example of a methodologically rigorous study to date. Higgins and Raskind (2005) examined reading passages silently with the assistance of a reading pen and reading passages silently without using a reading pen by 14-year-old students. The effect of using a pen after an extensive training in using the various functions of the pen had a medium to large effect size: 0.66.

Interesting Developments

Although the view just sketched does not seem to be so optimistic, some new developments, which could make a difference, should be mentioned. At Carnegie Mellon Jack Mostow and his colleagues work on the Reading Tutor, a fully computerized system (www.cs.cmu.edu/~listen/) in which the main feature is that it recognizes human speech. The user's task is to read aloud from the screen. The Reading Tutor intervenes when the reader makes mistakes, gets stuck, clicks for help or is likely to encounter a difficulty. It claims that even with barely 20 minutes of use per day, versions of the Reading Tutor have produced substantially higher comprehension gains than current practices in controlled studies lasting several months. The Reading Tutor improves reading comprehension, because it helps students to recognize words effortlessly so that they can devote more attention to comprehension. However, decoding practice by itself does not necessarily improve comprehension, because it is likely that children will only become better comprehenders when they practice both word decoding and understanding in context.

The Way Forward: A Methodology to Assess the Effect of Multimedia Programs

In conclusion, it would be worthwhile to define a methodology for efficacy assessment of computer programs, not only for struggling readers, but also applicable to multimedia programs for pre-readers. However, a standard needs to be set. A sensible choice would seem to take one-to-one tuition with a human tutor as a baseline.

First, the program must be modular and must have many optional features. These requirements should be met in order to be in a position to conduct relatively cost-effective short-term studies. Moreover, with various modules or options to be tested each at a time, it can be relatively easily assessed which components do work.

Second, modules and options should target at a specific learning goal of the curriculum for reading. In the case of multimedia for pre-readers a curriculum is obviously not relevant, but in order to assess whether talking books and similar programs work, a learning goal must be clearly defined. For example, when repeatedly reading an eBook, a sensible choice would be to include recall of the story as a dependent variable (e.g., de Jong & Bus, 2003).

Third, it is advisable that the research on the effects of multimedia should be embedded in a theoretical framework. The research will be of more value if it can add to our knowledge of the reading process, and the optimal strategies for teaching reading. In the case of pre-readers, this goal must be expanded to "how can we best prepare children for learning to read," and in struggling readers to "how can we best intervene or provide compensatory programs that are targeted to their needs."

Finally, it is of utmost importance that this kind of evaluation research is conducted using sound research methodologies, including the use of sensitive pre- and post-tests, delayed post-tests, baseline assessments (the aforementioned one-to-one tuition), transfer tests, etc. (e.g., Adèr & Mellenbergh, 1999; Adèr, Mellenbergh & Hand, 2007).

In conclusion, some features of multimedia applications could really be beneficial to struggling readers. However, evaluation research is still badly needed to assess the efficiency of multimedia applications. Through solid research it should be assessed whether multimedia applications are more effective than one-to-one tuition.

References

Adèr, H.J., & Mellenbergh, G.J. (Eds.) (1999). *Research methodology in social, behavioural and life sciences.* London: Sage.
Adèr, H.J., Mellenbergh, G.J., & Hand, D.J. (Eds.) (2007). *Advising on research methods: A consultant's companion.* Johannes van Kessel Publishing, the Netherlands: Huizen.

Blok, H., Oostdam, R., Otter, M.E., & Overmaat, M. (2002). Computer-assisted instruction in support of beginning reading instruction: A review. *Review of Educational Research, 72*, 101–130.

de Jong, M.T., & Bus, A.G. (2003). How well suited are electronic books to supporting literacy? *Journal of Early Childhood Literacy, 3*, 147–164.

Elbro, C. (2005). Literacy acquisition in Danish: A deep orthography in cross-linguistic light. In R.M. Joshi & P.G. Aaron (Eds.), *Handbook of orthography and literacy* (pp. 31–45). Mahwah, NJ: Lawrence Erlbaum.

Ellermann, H.H. (1991). MIR: A monitor for initial reading. Unpublished Doctoral Thesis, Technical University, Eindhoven, the Netherlands.

Fletcher, J.D., & Atkinson, R.C. (1972). Evaluation of the Stanford CAI program in initial reading. *Journal of Educational Psychology, 63*, 597–602.

Harm, M.W., McCandliss, B.D., & Seidenberg, M.S. (2003). Modeling the successes and failures of interventions for disabled readers. *Scientific Studies of Reading, 7*, 155–182.

Higgins, E.L., & Raskind, M.H. (2005). The compensatory effectiveness of the Quicktionary Reading Pen II on the reading comprehension of students with learning disabilities. *Journal of Special Education Technology, 20*, 31–39.

Krendl, K.A., & Williams, R.B. (1990). The importance of being rigorous: Research on Writing to Read. *Journal of Computer-based Instruction, 17*, 81–86.

Kulik, C.C., & Kulik, J.A. (1991). Effectiveness of computer-based instruction: An updated analysis. *Computers in Human Behavior, 7*, 75–94.

Lundberg, I., Frost, J., & Petersen, O. (1988). Effects of an extensive program for stimulating phonological awareness in preschool children. *Reading Research Quarterly, 23*, 263–284.

McCandliss, B.D., Beck, I., Sandak, R., & Perfetti, C. (2003). Focusing attention on decoding for children with poor reading skills: Design and preliminary tests of the word building intervention. *Scientific Studies of Reading, 7*, 75–104.

National Institute of Child Health and Human Development. (2000). *Report of the National Reading Panel.* Washington, DC: U.S. Government Printing Office.

Olson, R.K., & Wise, B.W. (1992). Reading on the computer with orthographic and speech feedback: An overview of the Colorado Remediation Project. *Reading and Writing: An Interdisciplinary Journal, 4*, 107–144.

Ouyang, R. (1993). A meta-analysis: Effectiveness of computer-assisted instruction at the level of elementary education (K-6). Indiana: University of Pennsylvania.

Reitsma, P., & Wesseling, R. (1998). Effects of computer-assisted training of blending skills in kindergartners. *Scientific Studies of Reading, 2*, 301–320.

Share, D.L. (1995). Phonological recoding and self-teaching: Sine qua non of reading acquisition. *Cognition, 55*, 151–218.

Slavin, R.E. (1991). Reading effects of IBM's "Writing to Read" program: A review of evaluations. *Educational Evaluation and Policy Analysis, 13*, 1–11.

Spaai, G.W.G. (1994). The use of speech feedback in an interactive reading programme for beginners. Unpublished Doctoral Thesis, Technical University, Eindhoven, the Netherlands.

Struiksma, A.J.C. (2003). Lezen gaat voor [Reading comes first]. Unpublished Doctoral Thesis, University of Amsterdam.

Torgesen, C., Porthouse, J., & Brooks, G. (2005). A systematic review of controlled trials evaluating interventions in adult literacy and numeracy. *Journal of Research in Reading, 28*, 87–107.

Torgesen, C.J., Porthouse, J., & Brooks, G. (2003). A systematic review and meta-analysis of randomised controlled trials evaluating interventions in adult literacy and numeracy. *Journal of Research in Reading, 26*, 234–255.

Torgesen, J.K. (2001). The theory and practice of intervention: Comparing outcomes from prevention and remediation studies. In A.J. Fawcett (Ed.), *Dyslexia: Theory and good practice* (pp. 185–202). London: Whurr Publishers.

Torgesen, J.K., & Horen, N.M. (1992). Using computers to assist in reading instruction for children with learning disabilities. In S.A. Vogel (Ed.), *Educational alternatives for students with learning disabilities* (pp. 159–181). New York: Springer Verlag.

Trushell, J. (2000). The future of the book. *Journal of Research in Reading, 23*, 103–109.

Underwood, J.D.M. (2000). A comparison of two types of computer support for reading development. *Journal of Research in Reading, 23,* 136–148.

van Daal, V.H.P. (1993). Computer-based reading and spelling practice for young dyslexics. Unpublished Doctoral Thesis, Free University, Amsterdam.

van Daal, V.H.P., & Reitsma, P. (1993). The use of speech feedback by normal and disabled readers in computer-based reading practice. *Reading and Writing: An Interdisciplinary Journal, 5,* 243–259.

van der Leij, A. (1994). Effects of computer-assisted instruction on word and pseudoword reading of reading-disabled students. In K.P. van den Bos, L.S. Siegel & D.J. Bakker (Eds.), *Current directions in dyslexia research* (pp. 251–267). Lisse, the Netherlands: Swets & Zeitlinger.

van der Leij, A., & van Daal, V.H.P. (1999). Automatization aspects of dyslexia: Speed limitations in word identification, sensitivity to increasing task demands, and orthographic compensation. *Journal of Learning Disabilities, 32,* 417–428.

van der Leij, A., & van Daal (in preparation). Development in developmental dyslexia.

van Otterloo, S.G., van der Leij, A., & Henrichs, L.F. (in press). Early home-based intervention in the Netherlands for children with genetic risk of reading disabilities.

Vellutino, F.R., Scanlon, D.M., Sipay, E., Small, S., Pratt, A., Chen, R., et al. (1996). Cognitive profiles of difficult-to-remediate and readily remediated poor readers: Early intervention as a vehicle for distinguishing between cognitive and experiential deficits as basic causes of specific reading disability. *Journal of Educational Psychology, 88,* 601–638.

Wise, B.W., & Olson, R.K. (1998). Studies of computer-aided remediation for reading disabilities. In C. Hulme and R.M. Joshi (Eds.), *Reading and spelling: Development and disorders* (pp. 473–487). Mahwah, NJ: Lawrence Erlbaum.

Yap, R., & van der Leij, A. (1993). Computergestuurde remediering van dyslexie door het opvoeren van de herkenningssnelheid van subwoordeenheden [Computer-based remediation of reading disability by sub-lexical speed training]. *Pedagogisch Studiën, 70,* 402–419.

Yopp, H.K. (1988). The validity and reliability of phonological awareness tests. *Reading Research Quarterly, 23,* 159–177.

9

Old and New Media in the Lives of Young Disadvantaged Bilingual Children

Paul P.M. Leseman, Aziza Y. Mayo, and
Anna F. Scheele

There is increasing interest in the use of new media. In particular, educational television, computer and video games, as well as animated electronic picture books are the focus of a good deal of recent attention in early childhood. There are good reasons for this interest. First, society is changing. The introduction in society at large and in schools in particular of modern information technology has repercussions for how we try to prepare young children for school and society. Preparing children only with "traditional media"— printed books, conversations about topics of general interest, songs and rhymes, oral stories—runs the risk of being ill-matched to the new demands (Shaffer, 2006). Second, "traditional" media are a less efficient means of stimulating children's language development and emergent school skills to some extent in low income and ethnic minority communities, because of the demands they put on the parents. Attempts to improve the home language and literacy environment to promote low income children's language and emergent literacy often run up against parents' own lack of skills (van Tuijl, Leseman, & Rispens, 2001). Preparing children with a different first language for participation in the second language context of school may fail because the parents are not sufficiently proficient in the second language. New media might provide for alternative ways to promote language and other skills in low literate and bilingual homes. Third and most important, new media *are already present* in young children's lives. Home computers and electronic games have found their way into many homes. Electronics for education and entertainment play a major role in the lives of adolescents and adults, and this role is expected to increase further (Duimel & de Haan, 2007; Mullen, Martin, Gonzales, & Kennedy, 2003).

However, little is known about how young children actually use new media, or its social and cultural connections. Moreover, little is known about the educational potential or, for that matter, the educational hazards of new media. To what extent do new media replace (and in that sense compete with) traditional media? What are the losses and what are the gains? In this chapter we will address the questions raised here. We will concentrate on the role of new media in young preschoolers' language development, in monolingual as well as bilingual contexts, using data from a recent study among Dutch, Turkish-Dutch and Moroccan-Dutch families with 3-year-olds.

Learning Language from Old Media

The important role of traditional media, such as personal conversations, shared book reading and singing songs and rhymes in preschool children's language and literacy development is well documented (Beals, 2001; Bus, van IJzendoorn & Pellegrini, 1995; Hoff, 2006; Leseman & van Tuijl, 2006; Sénéchal & Lefevre, 2002; Weizman & Snow, 2001; Whitehurst & Lonigan, 1998). Further, the use, both quantitatively and qualitatively, of traditional media differs strongly between families of different social classes or ethniccultural communities (Brooks-Gun & Markman, 2005; Leseman & van Tuijl, 2006).

Traditional media influence children's language and literacy development in several ways. Rhymes and songs are reported to increase children's phonological skills, important for learning to read. Shared book reading increases young children's insight in the formal aspects of written language, such as the arbitrary symbolic relation between the written and spoken form. Children acquire letter knowledge from home literacy activities long before reading instruction starts (Sénéchal & Lefevre, 2002). Further, traditional media are known to influence vocabulary, grammatical competence and language comprehension (de Jong & Leseman, 2001; Storch & Whitehurst, 2002). Frequently occurring activities in the home, such as talking about children's experiences, sharing memories, explaining and discussing topics of general interest, like animals, dinosaurs, knighthood in the Middle Ages, provide children with lexically and grammatically rich language input (Beals, 2001; Haden, Haine, & Fivush, 1997). These kinds of activities help children learn the use of specific, technical vocabulary, the use of conventional definitions and the use of complex sentences that express abstract relationships, functions and processes (cf. Huttenlocher, Vasilyeva, Cymerman, & Levine, 2002; Weizman & Snow, 2001).

Shared book reading, for example, presents the child with coherently interrelated sentences that contain new, often rare words in a semantically rich context that helps the child to grasp the elaborate meanings of these words. It often sets the stage for talking about extra-textual, semantically related, topics of general interest, and stimulates the use of specific, rare vocabulary and elaborate grammatical constructions (Hammett, van Kleeck, & Huberty, 2003). A vivid illustration of the complex language used in children's storybooks is presented in the box below.

Examples of Language Use in Picture Books for Preschool Children

Men and machines began work as lorries tipped mountains of bricks and sand, drainpipes and planks, ladders and poles, and piles of tiles over the grass and wild flowers.
From: Molly Brett (1993). *Tom Tit Moves House.* London: Medici Society Ltd.

When frog finds a teddy bear all alone in the forest, he takes him home. He plays football with him in the daytime, and tells him stories in the evening to teach the little bear to talk, which indeed he does! One day he doesn't want to play anymore, or to say anything. He wants to go home, but that doesn't mean he can't come back again, does it?

From: Max Velthuijs (2004). *Frog Finds a Friend.* London: Andersen Press.

In a recent study with Dutch speaking, nonreading 4-year-olds, we found moderate to strong correlations between the kind of home language and literacy activities mentioned above and children's use of so-called academic language in story retelling (Leseman, Scheele, Mayo, & Messer, 2007). Children's emergent academic language in story retelling was reflected by the relatively high information density of their utterances and the use of infrequent words at the lexical level, the use of elaborate tense and aspect, the declarative mood and clause combining at the sentence level, and the use of cohesiveness strategies and explicit discourse structuring at the text level.

In sum, when used frequently and in a linguistically elaborate way, traditional media provide important contexts for language learning that goes beyond mere vocabulary acquisition. Yet, given the existing socioeconomic and ethnic-cultural divides between children in many cultures, might new forms of media provide for additional opportunities for learning language and related skills?

Learning from New Media

In contrast to traditional media, the impact of new media—television, video games, computers and computer games—on children's literacy development is more heavily debated. Traditionally, there have been concerns that new media might displace the old forms at the expense of optimal development (see Neuman, this volume). Large-scale surveys among adults have revealed a steady decline of the use of traditional media, especially in reading for pleasure. Anecdotal reports suggest that children now favor video and computer games. Yet it is still unclear how such broad cultural changes may affect the home learning environments of young children.

To date, only a few studies have examined new media use with young children (see Wartella et al., this volume). In 2003, the Kaiser Family Foundation issued a survey in the USA among 1,000 parents on the media-use of very young children from 6 months to 6 years of age. Using data from this survey, Anand and Krosnick (2005) reported on the relationships between time spent on different traditional and new media and demographic characteristics. In the preschool period, children spent time watching television and videos (or DVDs). Playing video and computer games increased steadily with age. Time spent on book reading also increased with age, but significantly at a slower pace.

The study also highlighted socioeconomic and ethnic divides. Time spent on book reading (a traditional medium) by young children was highest for higher educated white families. Television and video watching (newer media), on the other hand, was highest for lower educated English speaking African-American families. Playing video and computer games and other forms of computer use by young children (newest media) was somewhat higher in lower educated families, although the differences were marginal between other groups. For very low educated, media use was low.

Computers with internet access and electronic game devices vary among nations. In the Netherlands, for instance, internet access of families had reached almost 100% in 2005 (Duimel & de Haan, 2007). Children and adolescents use computers, electronic games and the internet more than any other age group. A study by the Kaiser Family Foundation (1999) among children and youth from age 2 to age 18 found that, by the end of the last century, electronic media had surpassed book reading and play for pleasure in children's and youth's daily life. According to the Zero to Six study (Kaiser Foundation, 2003) even very young children spent already many hours a week playing with electronic media. In the Netherlands, 4- to 6-year-olds spend on average 2 hours a day on television and new media, of which approximately half an hour is playing with electronic games (Nikken, 2002).

Averages, however, can be misleading. There still is a digital divide. Computers and the internet are used less often among low income ethnic minority groups than in middle and high income white groups (Meszaros, 2004). Even with almost universal access to electronic media, as in the Netherlands, there remains a qualitative divide. Children and youth from lower educated families tend to use electronic media mainly for entertainment, whereas children and youth from higher educated families tend to use electronic media mainly for (school-related) educational purposes (Duimel & de Haan, 2007).

The increased use of television and video raises an important question: can these newer media support children's learning equal to that of traditional media? Might they be superior for helping children learn from real life experiences?

Initial experimental studies with children under 3 years of age, unfortunately, suggest the opposite. Children in these studies have shown consistently poorer performance in understanding visualized or spoken instructions from television or video. For example, a study by Anderson and Pempek (2005) found that although young children did learn from television or video, learning was less efficient, requiring more trials than learning from real life experiences. Similarly, young preschoolers *can* learn vocabulary from television and video, yet again less efficiently than from real life social interaction with their parents (Naigles & Kako, 1993). Television may be even less efficient as a medium for language learning when grammar is concerned (Naigles & Mayeux, 2001). Extensive exposure to so-called background television—for instance, when the caregiver is watching a program or film, or when the television is just on—appears to have a negative impact on development. An experimental study by Evans and her colleagues (2004), for example, revealed that background television distracted children, disturbed their play and diminished their interactions with adults.

The influence of traditional and new media on language development in bilingual contexts is an understudied topic. Several studies have examined the effects of traditional media like book reading on language development in bilingual children. The results generally reveal that book reading in the first and second language is indeed associated with first and second language development in a *language-specific* way. One study is of particular interest. This study compared the benefits of television watching and book reading on a sample of 3- and 4-year-old Spanish-English bilingual children. Results indicated that exposure to conversations and shared book reading was far more strongly related to vocabulary acquisition than exposure to television.

In summary, some research suggests that the newer media might compete for preschoolers' attention, and lead to declines in time spent on real life experiences and social interaction. However, studies using detailed measures of television watching by Wright and her colleagues (2001) and Linebarger and Walker (2005) sketch a more nuanced picture. For instance, Linebarger and Walker (2005) used logs to register in detail the amount of television viewing and the specific programs watched from the age of 6 months till 3 years in a sample of 51 predominantly Caucasian, middle income families. They found that children's receptive and productive vocabulary was slightly reduced with greater total amount of television viewing, but expressive communication skills, including the uses of gestures, were slightly increased. Moreover, a few specific television programs, which were narrative storybook-like, appeared to stimulate overall language development substantially.

A few studies to date examined the developmental effects of new electronic media. A mixed picture emerges. There are some obvious negative effects related to extensive electronic media use. Scholars have shown linkages between television and obesity and other health problems, social isolation, gender stereotyping and imitation of violent behavior (Anderson & Bushman, 2001). Most of these studies (see introduction, this volume), however, are based on correlational evidence, and thus, cannot accurately determine cause.

There are other studies, however, that have shown the benefits of electronic games on the improvement of children's visual, spatial and computer skills. For example, Shaffer (2006) reported that certain electronic games, such as *The Sims*, may improve complex reasoning and strategic thinking, in contrast to those games that required only repetitive standard reactions. Green and Bavelier (2003) conducted an experiment with players who were new to video games. He watched as they engaged in a dynamic, action-oriented video game with multiple moving objects. Randomly assigned control subjects were presented with an alternative video training, which was more static, object-oriented. At post-test, subjects shown the more dynamic game had improved visual attention, which generalized to other, non-electronic tasks as well. The control group, however, failed to show any of the cognitive advantages found for the experimental group at post-test. Clearly, then, the type of game is crucial.

A growing body of evidence concerns the effects on language, text comprehension and emergent literacy of *electronic storybooks* as a form of high quality, educationally oriented new electronic media (see Bus et al., in this volume). Electronic storybooks are basically animated storybooks that present a story on the computer screen, while a computer voice reads the story to the child. The electronic storybook can be used interactively, allowing the child to click on animated features, to repeat part of the story, to return to the beginning and listen to the story once again. Several multimedia features can be added. De Jong and Bus (2004) found that 4- to 5-year-old children learned vocabulary and story understanding equally well from an animated electronic picture book and a traditional static picture book that was read to them by an adult. Verhallen, Bus and de Jong (2006) presented evidence that the use of interactive animated storybooks with multimedia features (sound, film) with 5-year-old children at risk, including bilingual children, impacts children's vocabulary, syntactic knowledge and story comprehension more than a static version of the same story. The results of these studies converge on Uchikoski's finding (see chapter, this volume) that educational, storybook-like television programs can stimulate overall language development. Moreover, new developments in electronic media, in particular the addition of multimedia features, promise even stronger impact on language learning. Whether or not high quality electronic media are actually used by families with young children—especially those in high risk groups—however, remains an open question.

Traditional and New Media in Dutch and Immigrant Families in the Netherlands

As part of a larger study of language and literacy development, 161 mothers of 3-year-old children, 58 Dutch, 55 Turkish-Dutch and 48 Moroccan-Dutch, were personally interviewed (for details about sampling, measurements and procedures, see Scheele, Mayo & Leseman, 2007). Turkish participants were all first or second generation immigrants, who spoke Turkish as their first language and Dutch as their second language. These immigrants in the Netherlands have shown a high degree of Turkish language maintenance. This is explained by the strong orientation toward the homeland Turkey, the strong tendency to marry spouses from Turkey and, perhaps most importantly, the easy access to Turkish language use through official media (newspapers, television). Moroccan participants in the study were all of Berber descent. They were first or second generation immigrants speaking Tarifit, a variant of Berber as their first language, Moroccan-Arabic and sometimes French as their second and third language and Dutch always as their newest language. The Berber group was particularly interesting because Tarifit is not a scripted language, not used in education or in official institutions in Morocco. Although the orientation toward the homeland and the marriage patterns in the Moroccan-Berber community in the Netherlands did not differ from the Turkish community, the degree of first language maintenance was lower.

A structured questionnaire was used in personal interviews asking mothers to rate using five point scales how often particular activities involving the child normally occurred at home. The scale points ranged from 1 (never) to 5 (at least once a day). The list of activities presented to the mothers focused on "traditional media" and "newer media" most tied to language and literacy development (cf. Leseman & van Tuijl, 2006). Traditional media included having personal conversations with the child, sharing memories, talking about topics of general interest, reading storybooks, information books and ABC-letter books to the child, teaching and reciting rhymes, singing songs, and telling tales and stories. "New(er) media" included watching television or video/films, using computers with educational software and animated storybooks, and using computers or electronic game devices for playing games for entertainment. We also distinguished between television programs with an educational purpose and television programs with a entertainment purpose. For instance, *Sesame Street* was considered an educational television program for children, whereas the cable network Jetix, which broadcasts mainly cartoons, was considered entertainment. For all media types, scales were constructed for at least two to five inter-correlated items. All scales had satisfactory Cronbach's alphas, which ranged from 0.71 to 0.83. Scale estimates, however, did not reveal the frequency of activities. Figure 9.1 presents the results for the three groups.

Figure 9.1 shows that electronic educational media were rather frequently used by the Dutch and Turkish 3-year-olds in this study, however far less frequently by the Moroccan children. The use of educational electronic media was reported by the Dutch and Turkish mothers to be on average "once a month to once a week." The use of electronic entertainment equipment was comparatively frequent in the Turkish group. However, average scores can be misleading. Combining answers on a number of questions regarding computer use at home, 31% of the Dutch families, 38% of the Turkish families and 67% of the Moroccan families in the sample reported *no* computer or a similar electronic device used by young children.

According to the mothers, the use of television was more frequently used than traditional media activities. In particular programs for children were watched more often in most families. Child programs, educational and entertainment programs alike, also broadcasted by the Turkish national television in Turkish language were available on most cable networks in the Netherlands. Berber or Moroccan-Arabic television, however, was lacking. Arabic television was available on some networks but the language was Standard-Arabic, which differs considerably from Moroccan-Arabic.

Time spent watching television varied somewhat. Dutch 3-year-olds, according to the mothers, watched television or video for about 1½ hours per

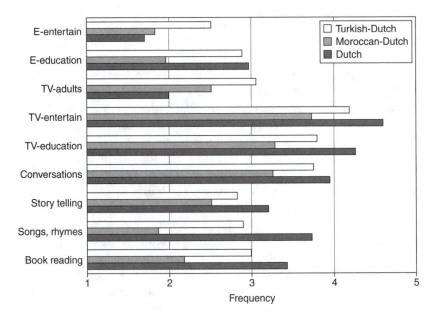

Figure 9.1 Self-reported frequency of use of media with 3-year-old Dutch, Moroccan-Dutch and Turkish-Dutch children (1 = "never, or once a year at most"; 5 = "at least once a day").

day, Turkish children, about $2\frac{1}{4}$ hours and Moroccan children, almost 3 hours per day, twice the time of the Dutch children.

Finally, traditional media use, on average, predominated across all groups, especially personal conversations with the child. Although relatively frequent overall, shared book reading and songs and rhymes revealed rather large differences between the three groups. Turkish and Moroccan families reported much less shared book reading than the Dutch. In Dutch families, on average, shared book reading happens a few times per week, whereas in Turkish families, only a few times per month, and in Moroccan families, only a few times per year. In the Turkish and the Moroccan group, a reported number of families, 7% and 41% respectively, never read to their children. This could be due to lack of literacy skills and a lack of reading materials in their first and best developed language, Tarifit.

Moroccan families differed from other families in their use of rhymes and songs with young children: 44% of the Moroccan mothers reported never to sing songs or to recite rhymes with their children, against only 4% in the Turkish group and 0% in the Dutch group.

Media and Languages

The impact of traditional and new media use on children's language development depends, among many other factors, on the language(s) that are used (Patterson, 2002). For instance, the effect of shared book reading on Dutch vocabulary development may depend on whether or not the books read are in Dutch. Stressing the mediating role that adults play in helping children to learn, it could be that passive media like television or songs without further interaction with adults on language development may be limited.

On the other hand, a number of studies have shown that frequently repeated, highly predictable language input, as in rhymes, songs, prayers and moralistic stories, with a ritualistic character, provide both lexical and grammatical input for implicit language learning (Sokolov & Snow, 1994). Therefore, the question is whether this implicit learning mechanism also works with passive *second language input* through songs, television, video and electronic media. The relevance of the question is clear. In homes where a different language is spoken than in the larger society, media such as radio, television and electronic games may be the main ways in which young children are introduced to the majority language.

To find some answers to these questions, the mothers in our study were asked to detail the language, or languages, used with particular media. This information gave us an interesting insight into the multilingualism of early childhood in present day society. For instance, the typical Moroccan family provided its child with input from Tarifit, Moroccan-Arabic, Standard-Arabic (via religious activities and Arabic television networks), French (due to the secondary school system in Morocco and previous migration), English (via songs, films and television programs) and Dutch, including the local dialect of Dutch (often via older siblings, who already attended primary school). The typical Turkish family provided fewer different languages, but in addition to standard Turkish, a Turkish dialect (predominant), and Dutch and a Dutch dialect, there was often Standard-Arabic and English, and sometimes German or another European language due to previous migration. Even most of the Dutch families provided their children with at least two languages to substantial degree, Dutch and English (mainly through songs).

To obtain a more precise insight into the role of traditional and new media in children's language development, the reported frequencies per media type were multiplied with a factor representing language use. First, the role of media as contexts for Dutch language input to the children was determined by weighing frequency of use as an indicator of exposure with the language used. The reported frequencies of media use were then multiplied with 1 if only Dutch was used, 0.5 if a mixture of Dutch and other languages was used and 0 if mainly other languages were used. Figure 9.2 presents the estimated impact of media as contexts of Dutch language input for the three groups. Note that a maximum score of 5 indicated that the medium concerned was used frequently (at least once a day) and always only with Dutch (language weight 1), whereas a score of 0 would indicate that either the medium was never used or the language was always another language than Dutch.

According to the mothers, Dutch 3-year-olds received Dutch language input through a variety of media. In addition to the traditional media, they also used the newer media. For Turkish and Moroccan children, the pattern was quite different. Only television matched the impact found for the Dutch

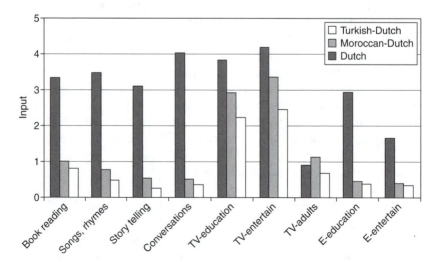

Figure 9.2 Input of Dutch (as second language) × media for Dutch, Moroccan-Dutch and Turkish-Dutch 3-year-old children.

children. All other media, including the traditional media, apparently played a less important role in providing Dutch language input to the Turkish and Moroccan children in this study.

Second, the role of media in providing *first language* input was different (Dutch for the Dutch, and Turkish and Tarifit for the Turkish and Moroccan children respectively).

Here in Figure 9.3, the traditional media of personal conversations and story telling were now equally prominent contexts of first language input for all three groups. The medium of book reading was now seen as important for first language input in the Turkish group, although still clearly below the impact found for the Dutch group. Interestingly, the role of the newer media switched. Children's television was not seen as important for first language input than as a medium for Dutch language input. In contrast, adult television for the Turkish children and electronic media for the Turkish and, to a lesser extent, the Moroccan children were more important as contexts for first language input than for Dutch language input.

Furthermore, there were interesting differences between Turkish and Moroccan groups. Media provided less first language input for the Moroccan children than for the Turkish children. These results might reflect the sociolinguistic and socio-historical constraints mentioned above. Typically there have been few traditional or newer media available for children in the Tarifit language.

Media Use and Language Development

Media and languages come together in different ways in young children's lives and provide a mixed array of inputs for language learning. To examine the

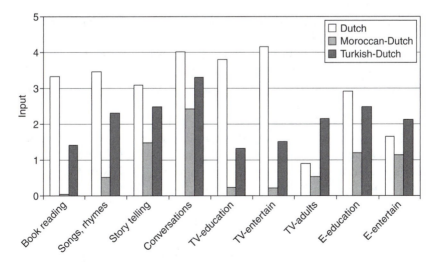

Figure 9.3 Input of First Language × media for Dutch, Moroccan-Dutch, and Turkish-Dutch 3-year-old children.

relations of exposure to different media and languages with children's language and cognitive development, correlations were computed with children's scores on vocabulary tests in Dutch, Tarifit and Turkish respectively on a general cognitive ability measure. Vocabulary tests came from the Diagnostic Test for Bilingual Research, developed by the Dutch national educational testing service. Test words were derived from a large database of words considered to be important for success in primary school. The Dutch, Tarifit and Turkish tests were constructed as parallel tests, using test words with roughly the same frequency of use in the three languages (Cronbach's alphas ranged from 0.83 to 0.89). A cognitive ability composite was created by taking the mean, after z-transformation, of a concept-knowledge test (knowledge of quantity concepts, colors, shapes), assessed in the child's first language, and a forward digit span and dot-matrix visuo-spatial span test, with the test instruction in the child's first language (Cronbach's alpha was 0.68).

Briefly, the pattern of correlations (summarized here due to space considerations), reveal an interesting pattern: overall, in all three groups the degree of Dutch language input through the traditional media was moderately correlated with Dutch vocabulary. In the Moroccan group, in addition to the traditional media, watching television (both education programs for children and entertainment programs for adults) and electronic games for entertainment were significantly correlated with Dutch vocabulary, suggesting that for Moroccan 3-year-olds the new media provided important additional sources for Dutch language learning. In the Turkish group, watching Dutch television was not correlated, although electronic media was with Dutch vocabulary.

In contrast, in the Dutch group apparently none of the new media was significantly related to language development. Perhaps this pointed to a threshold effect. It could be that the Dutch language proficiency of the Dutch children was already too advanced in order for child television or electronic media to have additional positive influence. In contrast, the Moroccan and Turkish children appeared to benefit from television watching and playing computer and video games.

Subsequent analyses revealed that for first language learning, traditional media provided the most important input. The positive effect of shared book reading in Tarifit on Moroccan children's Tarifit vocabulary gains could have been the result of the conversation about the book. Of course these data are suggestive. Longitudinal and experimental research studies are needed to support a causal interpretation of the relations that were found between input and vocabulary. Nonetheless, the present findings are in agreement with other studies demonstrating the important role of input in language development (cf. Hoff, 2006; Huttenlocher et al., 2002; Weizman & Snow, 2001).

Social-Ecological Factors and Media × Language Choice

We also examined whether media use was related to socioeconomic and ethnic-cultural divides. Socioeconomic status of the family was based on the education level of the parents and the social prestige of their jobs. Parents' own uses of literacy was based on six questionnaire items, asking the interviewees how often they read books, newspapers and other forms of print, and how often they wrote postcards, letters or texts for work (Cronbach's alpha of the scale was 0.75). We also examined a measure of experienced stress from daily hassles related to child rearing and household tasks, based on the short Dutch version of the Daily Hassles Questionnaire, designed by Crnic and Greenberg (1990). In addition, we looked at parenting beliefs by using a sub-scale of the Dutch version of Block and Block's Child Rearing Practices Report (Deković, 1989). Both questionnaires were carefully translated by bilingual researchers who spoke Tarifit or Turkish as their native language. The scales had roughly the same reliabilities in the three groups (Cronbach's alphas ranged from 0.75 to 0.81).

Even *within* the three samples, our analyses revealed interesting patterns: there were significant differences in the ways in which parents provided language input to their children using different media. Traditional media were the preferred strategy of the higher educated and more literate parents. The Moroccan group revealed additional possible determinants, which reflect the difficult social position of this group in present Dutch society. Family size was related to time spent television viewing, and negatively related to personal interaction.

Higher educated parents tended to have smaller families. Also the level of reported stress due to a heavy load of child care and household tasks was relatively high in the Moroccan group, at least compared to the Dutch mothers (the Turkish mothers also reported a high level of stressing daily hassles, though lower than the Moroccan mothers). A likely consequence of enhanced stress was that the mothers are less able to interact with their children and more inclined to use the television as a soother. Finally, the child rearing beliefs of the Moroccan mothers were more traditional authoritarian than Turkish and the Dutch parents.

For brevity, the correlations of parent and family characteristics with first language input by media are not presented here. Both in the Turkish and Moroccan group SES and parental literacy were not correlated with new and old media use in the first language.

Conclusion

The term "video-deficit" often refers to the potential detrimental effects on young children's language and cognitive development of increasing use of new media, in particular television, video and electronic video and computer games (Anderson & Pempek, 2005). Some suggest that when young children are exposed each day to long hours of television programs for adults, as a form of so-called *background television*, they miss critical opportunities for play, interaction and stimulation.

However, educational television programs that follow the linguistic structures of narrative books, and electronic animated picture books and video games that afford strategy use may contribute to language and cognitive development (Green & Bavelier, 2003; Linebarger & Walker, 2005; Verhallen, Bus, & de Jong, 2006; Wright et al., 2001). Our work is compatible with these findings. However, they also indicate that the role of the traditional media is still very much present in children's lives.

The role of new media for bilingual children represents an exciting new area to explore. Our research suggests that for immigrant parents, highly accessible new media, such as television and electronic devices, in addition to traditional media may be important initial sources of second language learning for young children. In this study, we found small, but significant positive correlations of exposure to Dutch television and Dutch electronic games with children's Dutch vocabulary.

Yet at the same time, we ventured a threshold hypothesis to explain children's language development. New media can be highly effective; however, when children's language skills have reached a certain level of proficiency, they will need additional input that is lexically richer and grammatically more complex to extend their language learning. At this point, traditional media can be especially helpful by involving children in conversations that use rare words with complex meanings, formal taxonomic definitions and varied use of verb tense.

The lack of positive correlations between the exposure to new media with vocabulary in the Dutch group, and the same finding regarding vocabulary in the first language in the Moroccan and Turkish group were considered an indication of such a threshold effect. In all groups, the traditional media of talking and reading with children in both first and second language appeared to be more consistently and stronger related to language development than the newer media (cf. Patterson, 2002).

Although little direct research is available, it is likely that the choices parents make are also related to family characteristics, child rearing beliefs and parenting styles. If parents believe in the usefulness of early stimulation through verbal interaction and if they think that parents play an important role in preparing children for school, it will guide them in choosing educational and developmentally appropriate options (Leseman & van Tuijl, 2006; cf. Liang, Fuller, & Singer, 2000). If, however, they value quiet and obedient children, then they might be less inclined to evaluate new media with respect to educational objectives.

Therefore, parent education is critically important for helping children use media most effectively in their development (Shaffer, 2006). Traditional media and newer media, together, offer highly promising avenues for increasing children's opportunities for enhancing language, and literacy learning in the early years.

References

Anand, S., & Krosnick, J.A. (2005). Demographic predictors of media use among infants, toddlers, and preschoolers. *American Behavioral Scientist, 48*, 539–561.

Anderson, C.A., & Bushman, B.J. (2001). Effects of violent video games on aggressive behavior, aggressive cognition, aggressive affect, physiological arousal, and prosocial behavior: A meta-analytic review of the scientific literature. *Psychological Science, 12*, 353–359.

Anderson, D.R., & Pempek, T.A. (2005). Television and very young children. *American Behavioral Scientist, 48*, 505–522.

Beals, D.E. (2001) *Eating and reading: Links between family conversations with preschoolers and later language literacy.* Baltimore: Brookes Publishing.

Brooks-Gun, J., & Markman, L.B. (2005). The contribution of parenting to ethnic and racial gaps in school readiness. *Future of Children, 15*, 139–168.

Bus, A.G., van IJzendoorn, M.H., & Pellegrini, A.D. (1995). Joint book reading makes for success in learning to read. A meta-analysis on intergenerational transmission of literacy. *Review of Educational Research, 65*, 1–21.

Crnic, K.A., & Greenberg, M.T. (1990). Minor parenting stresses with young children. *Child Development, 61*, 1628–1637.

de Jong, M.T., & Bus, A.G. (2004). The efficacy of electronic books in fostering kindergarten children's emergent story understanding. *Reading Research Quarterly, 39*, 378–393.

de Jong, P.F., & Leseman, P.P.M. (2001). Lasting effects of home literacy on reading achievement in school. *Journal of School Psychology, 39*, 389–414.

Deković, M. (1989). *Measuring dimensions and patterns of child rearing: Dutch version of the Block Child Rearing Practices Report (CRPR).* Nijmegen, the Netherlands: Department of Family Studies (internal publication).

Duimel, M., & de Haan, J. (2007). *Nieuwe links in het gezin. De digitale leefwereld van tieners en de rol van hun ouders* [New links in the family. The digital world of youth and the role of their parents]. Den Haag, the Netherlands: Sociaal Cultureel Planbureau.

Evans, M.K., Pempek, T.A., Kirkorian, H.L., Frankenfield, A.E., & Anderson, D.K. (2004, May). The impact of background television on complexity of play. Paper presented at the Biennial International Conference for Infant Studies, Chicago.

Green, C.S., & Bavelier, D. (2003). Action video game modifies visual selective attention. *Nature, 423*, 534–537.

Haden, C.A., Haine, R.A., & Fivush, R. (1997). Developing narrative structure in parent–child reminiscing across the preschool years. *Developmental Psychology, 33*, 295–307.

Hammett, L.A., van Kleeck, A., & Huberty, C.J. (2003). Patterns of parents' extratextual interactions with preschool children: A cluster analysis study. *Reading Research Quarterly, 38*, 442–467.

Hoff, E. (2006). How social contexts support and shape language development. *Developmental Review, 26*, 55–88.

Huttenlocher, J., Vasilyeva, M., Cymerman, E., & Levine, S. (2002). Language input and child syntax. *Cognitive Psychology, 45*, 337–374.

Leseman, P.P.M., Scheele, A.F., Mayo, A.Y., & Messer, M.H. (2007). Home literacy as a special language environment to prepare children for school. *Zeitschrift für Erziehungswissenschaft, 10*(3), 334–355.

Leseman, P.P.M., & Van Tuijl, C. (2006). Cultural diversity in early literacy development. In S.B. Neuman & D.K. Dickinson (Eds.), *Handbook of early literacy research. Volume 2* (pp. 211–228). New York: Guilford Press.

Liang, X., Fuller, B., & Singer, J. (2000). Ethnic differences in child care selection: The influence of family structure, parental practices, and home language. *Early Childhood Research Quarterly, 15*, 357–384.

Linebarger, D.L., & Walker, D. (2005) Infants' and toddlers' television viewing and language out-comes. *American Behavioral Scientist, 48,* 624–645.

Meszaros, P.S. (2004). The wired family. *American Behavioral Scientist, 48,* 377–390.

Mullen, I.V.S., Martin, M.O., Gonzalez, E.J., & Kennedy, A.M. (2003). *PIRLS 2001 international report.* Boston: International Study Center Boston College.

Naigles, L.R., & Kako, E.T. (1993). First contact in verb acquisition: Defining a role for syntax. *Child Development, 64,* 1665–1687.

Naigles, L.R., & Mayeux, L. (2001). Television as incidental language teacher. In D.G. Singer & J.L. Singer (Eds.), *Handbook of children and media* (pp. 135–152). Thousand Oaks, CA: Sage.

Nikken, P. (2002). *Kind en media: Weet wat ze zien* [Child and media: Know what they see]. Amsterdam: Boom.

Patterson, J.L. (2002). Relationships of expressive vocabulary to frequency of reading and television experience among bilingual toddlers. *Applied Psycholinguistics, 23,* 493–508.

Rideout, V.J., Vandewater, E.A., & Wartella, E.A. (2003). *Zero to six: Electronic media in the lives of infants, toddlers, and preschoolers.* Menlo Park, CA: Kaiser Family Foundation. Retrieved July 20, 2007, from www.kff.org.

Roberts, D.F., Foehr, U.G., Rideout, V.J., & Brodie, M. (1999). *Kids and media @ the new millennium.* Menlo Park, CA: Kaiser Family Foundation. Retrieved July 20, 2007, from www.kff.org.

Scheele, A.F., Mayo, A.Y., & Leseman, P.P.M. (2007). *Home language environment of mono- and bilingual children and their language proficiency.* Utrecht, the Netherlands: Utrecht University (manuscript under review).

Sénéchal, M., & Lefevre, J. (2002). Parental involvement in the development of children's reading skill: A five-year longitudinal study. *Child Development, 73,* 445–460.

Shaffer, D.W. (2006). *How computer games help children learn.* New York: Palgrave Macmillan.

Sokolov, J.L., & Snow, C.E. (1994). The changing role of negative evidence in theories of language development. In C. Gallaway & B.J. Richards (Eds.), *Input and interaction in language acquisition* (pp. 38–55). Cambridge, UK: Cambridge University Press.

Storch, S.A., & Whitehurst, G.J. (2002). Oral language and code-related precursors to reading: Evidence from a longitudinal structural model. *Developmental Psychology, 38,* 934–947.

van Tuijl, C., Leseman, P.P.M., & Rispens, J. (2001). Efficacy of an intensive home-base educational intervention programme for 4- to 6-year-old ethnic minority children in the Netherlands. *International Journal of Behavioral Development, 25*(2), 148–159.

Verhallen, M.J.A.J., Bus, A.G., & de Jong, M.T. (2006). The promise of multimedia stories for kindergarten children at risk. *Journal of Educational Psychology, 98,* 410–419.

Weizman, Z.O., & Snow, C.E. (2001). Lexical input as related to children's vocabulary acquisition: Effects of sophisticated exposure and support for meaning. *Developmental Psychology, 37,* 265–279.

Whitehurst, G.J., & Lonigan, C.J. (1998). Child development and emergent literacy. *Child Development, 69,* 848–872.

Wright, J.C., Huston, A.C., Murphy, K.C., St. Peters, M., Piñon, M., Scantlin, R., et al. (2001). The relations of early television viewing to school readiness and vocabulary of children from low-income families: The Early Windows Project. *Child Development, 72,* 1347–1366.

III
New Approaches to Storybook Reading

10

How Onscreen Storybooks Contribute to Early Literacy[1]

Adriana G. Bus, Marian J.A.J. Verhallen, and
Maria T. de Jong

Today's children increasingly encounter fictional stories through television, Internet sites, videotapes, and DVDs. According to a survey in the census of 2000 of more than 1,000 parents (e.g., Rideout, Vandewater, & Wartella, 2003), children in the age range of 0 to 6 watch television for 1–2 hours a day whereas they spend about half an hour per day reading. In less educated families, television and DVD occupy an even more prominent place in the reality of 3- to 5-year-olds: the 3.5 hours on weekdays soar to up to 6 hours a day in the weekend (Zeijl, Crone, Wiefferink, Keuzenkamp, & Rijneveld, 2005). In the Netherlands, where information technology is widely available, we notice effects of computer programs on young children's literacy experiences in the home. According to a recently published survey (Mullis, Martin, Gonzalez, & Kennedy, 2003), 9% of Dutch families dispose of educational software related to reading, a number that has probably grown ever since. Expectations are that the share of onscreen storybooks in young children's activities will further increase during the coming decennia, probably even faster than up until now (Marsh, this volume), thereby causing a gradual shift from adults reading books to young children to young children independently experiencing electronic versions of those same storybooks. Thus there is an increasingly urgent need for a response to the question of how helpful solitary exposure to storybooks on the screen can be, especially now that we see an explosion in electronic media marketed directly at the very youngest children in our society (Marsh, this volume; Wartella & Richert, this volume).

For a considerable time, book sharing with young children has been one of the prototypical and iconic aspects of literacy in the preschoolers' social world. If it was not the single most important activity for developing knowledge required for eventual success in reading, it certainly was one of the most important activities (Bus, van IJzendoorn, & Pellegrini, 1995). As this literacy activity will be more and more replaced by solitary encounters with digitized storybooks in the near future, we need to study the consequences for children's literacy (de Jong & Bus, 2002, 2004; Verhallen & Bus, 2007; Verhallen, Bus, & de Jong, 2006). Like the print books that have long been read to children many electronic books seem to have the potential to accomplish similar effects. They can familiarize children with book language—one of the pillars of literacy. Unlike the language in daily communication, language in books is complex. It includes subordinate clauses, passive constructions, unknown expressions, and idioms—all features that make text more difficult to understand than interactive talk. Storybooks give the opportunity to familiarize with complex language. Language with such features would not have been presented to young children were it not for the fictional stories to which young children feel attracted (Bus, 2001).

The onscreen versions of picture storybooks mostly include an oral rendition of the text thus enabling solitary book exposure without an adult as intermediary (Reinking, Labbo, & McKenna, 1997). Onscreen storybooks for the very young may also include other additional formal features by which they may become easier to understand than "normal" print books. Visual features include cuts, pans, dissolves, and special effects; auditory features include music and sound effects; and more holistic characteristics include pacing (rates of scene and character change), physical movement (action), and variation. Nowadays these features are used to present many types of messages, program themes, and story plots (Wright & Huston, 1983). Even Rembrandt van Rijn's famous painting *Night Watch* did not escape this trend. The British film director Peter Greenaway transformed this seventeenth century's painting into a multimedia experience by successively highlighting objects and persons and adding sounds and music, thus reconstructing a criminal act committed more than 400 years ago that had remained unrevealed until then.

The result of adding formal features is a film-like visualization of the storybook coordinated with the oral text. For example, when the text explains that the witch is waving her wand, the animation depicts the witch waving her magic wand and her cat changing from black to green. Besides the rich visualizations, sounds and music are added to support story understanding. When the witch starts worrying about her cat the music slows down and when the cat is happy again and starts "purring" we can hear the cat. According to a content analysis of 55 electronic books published in the Netherlands between 1995 and 2002 (de Jong & Bus, 2003), 69% of electronic books that were available in that period employed rich visualizations, sounds, and music. The same content analysis led up to the conclusion that some of the sounds and animations in the onscreen storybooks may be perhaps appealing and humorous to young children but, nonetheless, irrelevant to the story they accompany and inconsistent with traditional notions of meaning-making processes and comprehension (de Jong & Bus, 2003; Shamir & Korat, this volume). For example, with the click of a mouse a tea towel morphs into a dove, or flowers in a pot start dancing: all animations that are not related to the story.

For our current research we ruled out books that mainly offer engaging but largely peripheral animations and other effects because they encourage children to think of onscreen picture storybooks as games as a number of studies has made manifest (cf. de Jong & Bus, 2002; Greenfield, Camaioni, Ercolani, Weiss, Lauber, & Perucchini, 1996; Labbo & Kuhn, 2000). The focus is on onscreen storybooks with multimedia additions that give added value to illustrations without violating the original story content and that preserve the story text.

Consumption of Images Instead of Listening to the Narration

Theoretically it is conceivable that live-action video and other formal features of multimedia books overwhelm the child because they divert attention from the language, resulting in lower story comprehension and language development (Hayes, Chemelski, & Birnbaum, 1981). According to this hypothesis the richness of multimedia symbols in multimedia presentations may engage most attention from young children at the expense of verbal information processing (Hayes & Birnbaum, 1980; Hayes et al., 1981). The "crowdedness" of televised presentations, requiring children to process simultaneously through multiple modalities, might cause difficulties due to hypothesized limits of children's working memory even when the additions are relevant to story comprehension (Neuman & Koskinen, 1992; Neuman, this volume). As the availability of additional sources of information indeed engages learners in unnecessary cognitive activities that impose a heavy load on working memory, children may benefit most from static onscreen storybooks with, as the only additional multimedia feature, an oral rendition of text but without sound, music, visual, or other special effects.

Evidence in the literature gathered so far does not support the notion that literacy in electronic environments has more to do with the consumption of images than listening to the narration (e.g., Gibbons, Anderson, Smith, Field, & Fischer, 1986; Sharp, Bransford, Goldman, Risko, Kinzer, & Vye, 1995), and neither do the outcomes of our research (de Jong & Bus, 2004; Verhallen et al., 2006; Verhallen & Bus, 2007). Our studies are inconsistent with the expectation that the "crowdedness" of televised presentations, requiring children to process simultaneously through multiple modalities, causes difficulties due to the hypothesized limits of children's working memory. For instance, the de Jong and Bus (2004) study compared effects of children's independent reading of stories electronically with effects of the same stories in print versions read aloud to children by grown-ups. The subjects were normally developing 4- to 5-year-old kindergarten children. If the electronic environments had interfered with listening to the narration de Jong and Bus would have found that animated pictures distracted children from figuring out the meaning of oral text and memorizing the language. Instead, they found that electronic storybooks with live-action video did not reduce inculcation of the story language. Results revealed that children's familiarity with the language after independently experiencing electronic versions of books is comparable with their scores after repeated adult-led book encounters.

Synergy of Multiple Media

In follow-up studies we examined the potential role of new media in the development of kindergarten children learning Dutch as a second language. We argued that this group of pupils (one that is growing all over the world) might be more inclined to focus on visual information at the expense of listening to the language. As a consequence of lags in understanding the narrative text, the nonverbal information may be more accessible than the (oral) text. Even when these pupils have been taught Dutch in school for some time, age-appropriate storybooks include many unknown words and sentence structures that are unknown to these children. As the film-like representation is more helpful for them to understand the story, they may ignore the narrative text. Instead of this negative scenario it is also conceivable that their understanding of the language benefits from additional information sources. Spoken text with static pictures, normally the main source for understanding stories, may not be enough to comprehend the narrative text when children are lagging in language skills. Storybooks with additional information sources may provide a better framework than static picture storybooks for understanding stories and their phrasing and remembering linguistic information from these stories. If there are many gaps in children's understanding of the story, text film-like representations, music, and sounds may add new dimensions to the means that children employ to attain understanding of the language. Thus, rather than detracting from the storyline and story language, information sources commensurate with the events of the story, may expose children to an additional set of processing tools, which in combination with oral text contributes to young children's ability to understand the story and to learn new words from multiple exposures (cf. Calvert, Huston, Watkins, & Wright, 1982; Neuman, this volume).

Paivio's (1986) model of dual-coding can explain how it is possible that processing through multiple modalities does not interfere with language acquisition due to hypothesized limits of children's working memory. Following this model, two different classes of information, one specialized for information concerning nonverbal objects and events and the other for dealing with language, are handled cognitively by separate systems of representation that are structurally and functionally distinct. Thus, working memory capacity for nonverbal representations does not interfere with working memory capacity for verbal representations, and vice versa. This model can also explain how the nonverbal representations can be beneficial for language acquisition. The *words-with-visualizations* treatment encourages the building of referential connections between elements in the verbal representations and in the visual representations, thus helping to understand and memorize new vocabulary and unknown language structures (Mayer & Moreno, 1998). The two systems operate independently but interconnections between the two systems trigger activity in the other, thus promoting children's understanding of the story language. Children may not memorize "worried" until the camera has zoomed in on the worried face of the witch while the text "Winnie was worried" is spoken out loud. Images, sounds and emotions facilitate language understanding and memorization.

To test the hypothesis that especially children scoring at the lower end of language proficiency may benefit from multiple media we exposed children with scores below the 25th percentile of a standardized language test to one of two digitized versions of the same picture storybook. The static version resembled the book version except for the oral rendition of the text; in the other more dynamic version, live-action video replacing the static pictures was coordinated with an oral rendition of the text. If a synergistic treatment is indeed helpful we may expect that film-like additions are effective. Of course, a "rich" electronic book can only work out this way when the participants in this study—second-language learners from low educated families—can benefit from film-like information sources. However, we can make a reasonable case for that since few, if any, children live in circumstances that actively exclude a television or computer. Almost all contemporary children have learned to process film information, that is, to process the grammar of cut, pans, zooms, and edit, into their final interpretation.

Again, there was no support for the hypothesis that additional visual, sound, and music effects interfere with second-language learners' language development even though all participants in this experiment had serious gaps in their understanding of the narration. According to pretest scores they had serious gaps in understanding the book-based vocabulary. On average they were unacquainted with about 10% of the story's vocabulary. Consistent with the hypothesis that multiple information sources support language development, we found that children lagging in language skills benefit most from the digitized storybook with film-like visualizations and other additions (Verhallen et al., 2006). Since there was no help or support by grown-ups during book encounters, the results are representative for solitary exposure to onscreen picture storybooks. After multiple exposures to a book with—as the only additional multimedia feature—an oral rendition of text, the 5-year-old participants improved their story understanding to some extent but more so after repeated exposures to the version with rich visualizations, sounds, and music. Retellings that originally consisted mainly of jumping from one action to the next without explaining the connections between actions were replaced by more coherent retellings actually explaining the transitions between actions, a finding that is not too surprising when we take into account that the film-like version of the storybook, more so than the static version, enables some story understanding without understanding the story language. Multimedia may make children more sensitive to the importance of the goals and intentions of the protagonists although we cannot be certain that the participants indeed understood how those implied elements set a train of actions in the story in motion.

More surprising is the finding that, after four readings—a single exposure was never enough to benefit from a storybook—the film-like onscreen electronic book was more beneficial for children's language development than multiple encounters with static books. The participants, all at the lower end of language proficiency, learned about seven out of 40 words unknown according to a pre-test when they were exposed to the rich version, twice as many as the average number of words they learned when they were exposed to the version with merely static pictures; then they learned at most three or four new words. This effect is even more remarkable when we consider that the text was less well suited to deriving the meaning of unknown words as a consequence of the high proportion of unknown words (about 10% of all words).

We have to examine further whether or not these initial results in this new domain of research will hold in the future now that even children from low socioeconomic status families and minorities have more contact with digitized storybooks that include rich visualizations, sounds, and music. Critics argue that the effects so far are at best temporary. They expect that most children become increasingly adept at using digitized storybooks through television programs, free Internet sites, or (cheap) CD-ROMs and DVDs and at dealing with a storybook format that increasingly incorporates an Internet style with graphs, colored text, pop-ups, and various font sizes. They expect that multimedia additions will stop being incentives for learning because over time a saturation effect would develop.

Effects of Multimedia in a Linguistically Advantaged Sample

According to Sharp and colleagues (Sharp et al., 1995) film-like additions are profitable especially when book-reading experiences are out of children's reach in traditional verbal settings. Children's language proficiency lags behind and there are many gaps in understanding to fill by guessing at the meaning of the story text. If this is true an exact replication of the intervention should turn out differently when kindergarten children are more advanced in language and literacy skills. Greater listening and imaginative skills may enable these children to process oral text alone more adequately and to expand their understanding of syntax and vocabulary without the availability of additional nonverbal information sources. Given that for those children text with static pictures, normally the main sources for understanding stories, is enough for an emerging comprehension of narratives they will benefit as much from digitized versions with static pictures as from "rich" onscreen storybooks. The interventions thus have different effects in groups of linguistically advantaged and disadvantaged kindergarten children especially when books are static. Exposure to these storybooks may rather widen than narrow the gap as a function of language proficiency thus being a classic example of what Stanovich (1986) called the Matthew effect. The linguistically "rich" get richer whereas the "poor" get poorer. By contrast, the books enriched with action video may reduce the initial gaps in ability to understand the story and story language. Children with a low level of language proficiency may catch up when onscreen storybooks include film-like pictures.

To examine the hypothesis that intervention effects vary as a result of children's linguistic proficiency we replicated the Verhallen et al. (2006) experiment in a linguistically more advanced group; they originated from similar low educated minority families but, unlike the subjects of the previous experiment, scored about average on a standardized language test (C-level). The results were on the whole consistent with our expectations. A synergy in multimedia (Neuman, this volume) did not cause a multiplicative effect in the linguistically more advanced sample. Since this group benefited about equally from both the static and video format there is no support for the hypothesis that they need a synergy of multiple media to figure out unknown words and sentence structures. It is only when children have fewer background experiences to help them understand the storyline and derive the meaning of unfamiliar words and sentences that they need the intensity of a synergistic intervention. As Figure 10.1 illustrates for expressive book-based vocabulary,

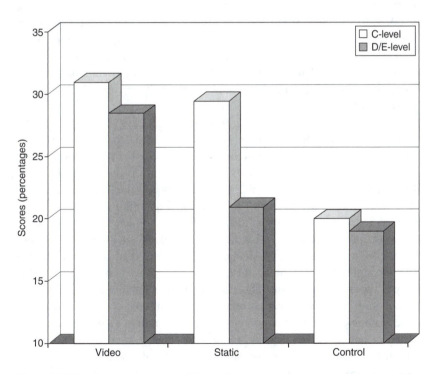

Figure 10.1 Vocabulary scores according to the post-test (in percentages) adapted for the pre-test score; C-level: ranking between 25th and 50th percent; D/E-level: ranking below 25th percent.

the initial differences between the linguistically "rich" (level C) and "poor" (level D/E) increase when the only multimedia addition to onscreen storybooks is an oral rendition of text. By contrast, differences fade when children are exposed to storybooks enriched with visual, sound, and music effects.

Amount of Invested Mental Effort

Adults are mostly not available to raise children's interest in an onscreen storybook and to give children food for thought about the story events by asking questions unless children are very young, as the 2-year-old in Labbo's study (Labbo, this volume). When storybook encounters have become a more solitary activity in older age groups, the extent to which children enable or allow electronic environments to affect them may become critical (Salomon & Leigh, 1984). When children view onscreen storybooks rather mindlessly each time they repeat the story, they may miss valuable opportunities to profit from solitary exposure to onscreen storybooks. There are conflicting opinions about children's mental effort when they process onscreen stories. Televised stories are often perceived as an "easy" medium eliciting less mental effort than book reading (Salomon, 1984). This has led to the conclusion that book-reading routines are preferable to viewing stories on television, Internet sites, or DVD. In the view of other scholars there are few, if any, situations that provoke as much concentration and attention as computer games, even leading some experts to voice high hopes for computer programs (Calvert, Rideout, Woolard, Barr, & Strouse, 2005). "If we could mobilize all that energy for … learning to read!" stated Seymour Papert (1996), the Doctor Spock of computer education.

In line with our previous finding that film-like books support learning the latter view—computers mobilize energy—may best match how linguistically "poor" children respond to onscreen books. Children invest more mental effort when the film-like book adds new dimensions to the means that children employ to attain understanding of the story and the language. It is also conceivable that as a result of all the additional qualities, children are more inclined to continue investing mental efforts to understand more details during each new encounter with a video storybook. When, on the other hand, they perceive the task to be too demanding relative to the frustration after the first encounter with the book, they are unlikely to sustain effort when the story is repeated once more. Thus, when children's ability is held constant, the amount of invested mental effort during multiple encounters with an onscreen book may be a function of the support children experience from the materials and a raised amount of invested energy may boost effects of repeated exposures to a story on language development. As children understand more we expect them to be more willing to continue investing mental effort during multiple exposures. A similar model seems to apply to television viewing (e.g., Anderson & Lorch, 1983; Bickham, Wright, & Huston, 2001;

Huston & Wright, 1983). When children perceive a television program as comprehensible they are more inclined to continue watching and listening, thus learning more from the program. When, instead, children perceive the program as too easy or too difficult, they discontinue watching and prefer other activities to watching television.

We (Verhallen & Bus, 2007) found evidence for the hypothesis that the amount of invested mental effort is a function of the support the children experience. According to the comparatively high number of skin conductance responses linguistically "poor" children were more active when the book included multiple information sources. The differences in effort did not manifest until the story was repeated several times. A synergy of multiple media maintains the amount of invested mental effort at a high level for at least four story exposures whereas mental effort begins to reduce after one or two repetitions when there is only an oral rendition of text combined with static pictures. In other words, in groups of linguistically "poor" children the willingness to maintain mental effort at a high level during story repetition seems stronger as the storybook is more "redundant."

We assessed skin conductance as a measure of what Salomon and Leigh (1984) indicated as AIME—Amount of Invested Mental Effort. According to studies in cognitive domains, this measure is a sound indicator for the extent to which children enable or allow materials to influence them. For instance, an elevated skin conductance activity occurs when children invest efforts in

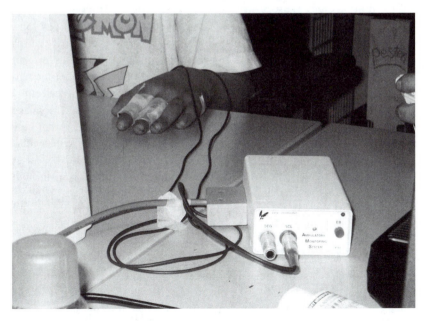

Figure 10.2 Monitoring skin conductance.

solving mental arithmetic problems or anagrams (e.g., Dawson, Schell, & Filion, 2000; Pecchinenda & Smith, 1996). We used an ambulatory monitoring device to register skin conductance (see Figure 10.1). There is seldom a one-to-one relation between a psycho-physiological measure and psychological construct, such that a given individual physiological event can be associated with one and only one psychological construct, and vice versa (Ravaja, 2004). So, to confirm the present findings, we need follow-up studies that include alternative technologies for tracing the amount of invested mental effort, such as pupillary reflexes assessed with the help of eye trackers (Evans et al., this volume).

Reinking (1994) was among the first to suggest monitoring skin conductance responses as an indicator of comprehension difficulty and anxiety during processing an onscreen storybook. He argued that this line of research might instigate a new generation of Living Books with built-in tools to monitor children's efforts during storybook exposure as an instrument to match programs to children's needs. For instance, as online registration of skin conductance indicates that effortful attempts to understand the onscreen storybook are declining, the story presentation may be adapted accordingly. This was another consideration that has led us to start exploring physiological measures in the context of electronic stories; with success so far.

AIME as a Generative Mechanism through which Video Storybooks Improve Language Learning

Video additions may cause a direct effect on learning by providing children with a guide to select the important or central content in the visualizations. Like a spotlight on a stage the action video helps children to coordinate words and fixed word combinations with images and sounds, thus helping to form associations. Salomon's model (Salomon & Leigh, 1984) predicts instead an indirect effect: learning depends on the amount of invested mental effort elicited by the storybook. The book encounters are profitable and language grows only when children remain actively engaged in "processing" what they see and hear every time the story is repeated. By applying the logic of mediation analysis (Baron & Kenny, 1986) we found most evidence for the latter model: invested mental effort functions as a generative mechanism through which qualities of the electronic book improve language learning.

As Figure 10.3 illustrates, the amount of invested mental effort is a mediator between book characteristics and language acquisition. There is a causal chain according to which a synergy of multiple information sources promotes mental effort, which in turn enables learning. Another notable result was that it is not enough when the amount of invested mental effort is high during a few sessions and then declines as we observed in the static condition. It is only when children are actively engaged not just once or twice but actually continue to invest mental effort for at least four exposures to a book, as we found

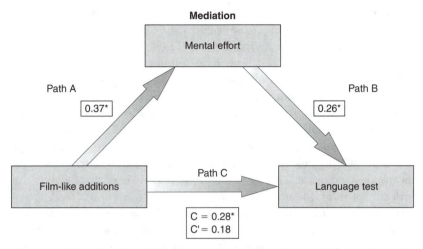

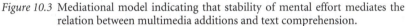

Figure 10.3 Mediational model indicating that stability of mental effort mediates the relation between multimedia additions and text comprehension.

Notes
*$p < 0.05$
The numbers on the arrows are standardized regression coefficients.

for the onscreen video storybook, that they have a chance to learn so far unknown words and phrases. Thus we can make a reasonable case for the conclusion that an external characteristic variable as a synergy of multiple media takes on internal significance by sustaining children's invested mental efforts for at least four exposures. Children are more willing to invest mental effort for multiple sessions when the zooms, cuts, and other techniques in the onscreen storybooks provide them with a guide to select the important or central content in the visualizations, just as a spotlight on a stage tells the audience where to look.

Conclusions, Implications, and Future Directions

The data we collected so far underscore the potential of computer-enhanced, picture storybooks. However, not all onscreen storybooks with the potential to transform young children's book encounters into a solitary activity are as effective. In particular, children who have limited linguistic luggage—a growing group all over the world—need the intensity of a synergistic intervention as they have fewer background experiences to help them understand the storyline and derive the meaning of unfamiliar words and sentence structures. Our research so far focused on children who were taught Dutch for a year at least. We cannot extrapolate from these results that linguistically "poor" children under 5 with an even lower level of language proficiency also profit from storybooks enriched with visual, sound, and music effects. Increasingly, children who are much younger than those in our experiments are spending time with media like those in our experiments, but, due to potential detrimental effects, these children may just be staring at the animated pictures without processing the story (Lewin, 2003).

Even when computer programs have features that enable young non-conventional readers to "read" picture storybooks independently, it is not self-evident that they benefit from these programs. Children learn new language from independent encounters with onscreen storybooks only when they allow or enable the material to influence them. The findings so far suggest that certain qualities of the computer program contribute to the extent to which children are willing to invest efforts during multiple independent exposures. The onscreen storybooks with an oral rendition of text, rich pictures, sounds, and music, rather than just an oral rendition of text combined with static visualizations, made children invest mental effort for at least four exposures. Note also that the present findings are inconsistent with the often-raised hypothesis that children discontinue investing mental efforts when film-like images have betrayed most of the storyline after one or two encounters (e.g., McKenna & Zucker, this volume; Van Daal, this volume). The results so far indicate that it is just the opposite. Linguistically disadvantaged children continue effortful processing in later sessions only when the storybook is "redundant" and includes additional information sources.

No doubt, well-designed book-based programs on television, DVD, and Internet sites that include multimedia might be a great way of promoting at-risk children's story understanding and linguistic skills. By organizing classroom routines with onscreen video storybooks as a central element, teachers have a powerful tool at their disposal to treat language deficits—one of the two main sources of reading problems (Juel, 2006). As yet the position of "Living Books" in classrooms is of minor importance, even though computers are winning ground in preschool and kindergarten. In Dutch schools it is promoted to present static onscreen versions of picture storybooks with an oral rendition of text as the only multimedia feature; a format that, according to our findings, is not profitable for the linguistically disadvantaged pupils who are most in need of exposure to storybooks. The finding that the linguistically "poor" show more spontaneous mental investment in understanding film-like storybooks, thereby creating the requirements for profiting from independent exposure to onscreen storybooks, argues for a cultural shift in which room should be made for televised onscreen storybooks in classrooms. It may be true that book sharing with an adult produces similar or even much better results (Bus, 2001) but high quality adult support as a main element of book sharing is often not practicable in school or at home (e.g., Bus, Leseman, & Keultjes, 2000).

We close with two issues high on our research agenda. First, does intensifying individual onscreen storybook reading experiences in a classroom environment over a longer period reduce the vocabulary deficits of children from families of lower socioeconomic or minority status? To examine lasting effects on linguistic knowledge we need experiments in which routine exposure to onscreen storybooks is stimulated for a period of at least 3 months. Second, can new forms of cognitive apprenticeship scaffold or support youngsters' language development? A computer pal throwing in questions to be answered by clicking on a picture and providing feedback to children's answers may, to some extent, replace the grown-up's role in traditional book reading sessions.

We invite the educational and research community to join us in answering these and other intriguing questions so we may be better prepared as a field to make the best use of computer resources such as onscreen picture storybooks at home and as a component of the curriculum in regular or remedial classrooms.

Note

1. Preparation of this manuscript was supported by an award (411–02–506) from the Netherlands Organization for Scientific Research (NWO) to Adriana G. Bus.

References

Anderson, D.R., & Lorch, E.P. (1983). Looking at television action or reaction? In J. Bryant & D.R. Anderson (Eds.), *Children's understanding of television: Research on attention and comprehension* (pp. 1–33). New York: Academic Press.

Baron, R.M., & Kenny, D.A. (1986). The moderator mediator variable distinction in social psychological research: Conceptual, strategic and statistical considerations. *Journal of Personality and Social Psychology, 51*, 1173–1182.

Bickham, D.S., Wright, J.C., & Huston, A.C. (2001). Attention, comprehension, and the educational influences of television. In D.G. Singer & J.L Singer (Eds.), *Handbook of children and the media* (pp. 101–120). Thousand Oaks, CA: Sage.

Bus, A.G. (2001). Early book reading in the family: A route to literacy. In S. Neuman & D. Dickinson (Eds.), *Handbook on research in early literacy* (pp. 179–191). New York: Guilford Publications.

Bus, A.G., Leseman, P.P.M., & Keultjes, P. (2000). Joint book reading across cultures: A comparison of Surinamese-Dutch, Turkish-Dutch, and Dutch parent–child dyads. *Journal of Literacy Research, 32*, 53–76.

Bus, A.G., van IJzendoorn, M.H., & Pellegrini, A.D. (1995). Joint book reading makes for success in learning to read: A meta-analysis on intergenerational transmission of literacy. *Review of Educational Research, 65*, 1–21.

Calvert, S.L., Huston, A.C., Watkins, B.A., & Wright, J.C. (1982). The relation between selective attention to television forms and children's comprehension of content. *Child Development, 53*, 601–610.

Calvert, S.L., Rideout, V.J., Woolard, J.L., Barr, R.F., & Strouse, G.A. (2005). Age, ethnicity, and socioeconomic patterns in early computer use. *American Behavioral Scientist, 48*, 590–607.

Dawson, M.D., Schell, A.M., & Filion, D.L. (2000). The electrodermal system. In J.T. Cacioppo, L.G. Tassinary, & G.G. Berntson (Eds.), *Handbook of psychophysiology* (pp. 200–223). Cambridge, UK: Cambridge University Press.

de Jong, M.T., & Bus, A.G. (2002). Quality of book-reading matters for emergent readers: An experiment with the same book in a regular or electronic format. *Journal of Educational Psychology, 94*, 145–155.

de Jong, M.T., & Bus, A.G. (2003). How well suited are electronic books to supporting literacy? *Journal of Early Childhood Literacy, 3*, 147–164.

de Jong, M.T., & Bus, A.G. (2004). The efficacy of electronic books in fostering kindergarten children's emergent story understanding. *Reading Research Quarterly, 39*, 378–393.

Gibbons, J., Anderson, D.R., Smith, R., Field, D.E., & Fischer, C. (1986). Young children's recall and reconstruction of audio and audiovisual narratives. *Child Development, 57*, 1014–1023.

Greenfield, P.M., Camaioni, L., Ercolani, P., Weiss, L., Lauber, B.A., & Perucchini, P. (1996). Cognitive socialization by computer games in two cultures: Inductive discovery or mastery of an iconic code? In I.E. Sigel (Series Ed.), P.M. Greenfield, & R.R. Cocking (Vol. Eds.), *Advances in applied developmental psychology: Vol. 11. Interacting with video* (pp. 141–167). Norwood, NJ: Ablex.

Hayes, D.S., & Birnbaum, D.W. (1980). Preschoolers' retention of televised events: Is a picture worth a thousand words? *Developmental Psychology, 16*, 410–416.

Hayes, D.S., Chemelski, B.E., & Birnbaum, D.W. (1981). Young children's incidental and intentional retention of televised events. *Developmental Psychology, 17*, 230.

Huston, A., & Wright, J. (1983). Children's processing of television: The information functions of formal features. In J. Bryant & D.R. Anderson (Eds.), *Children's understanding of television: Research on attention and comprehension* (pp. 35–68). New York: Academic Press.

Juel, C. (2006). The impact of early school experiences on initial reading. In D.K. Dickinson & S.B. Neuman (Eds.), *Handbook of early literacy research*, volume 2 (pp. 410–426). New York: Guilford Press.

Labbo, L.D., & Kuhn, M.R. (2000). Weaving chains of affect and cognition: A young child's understanding of CD-ROM talking books. *Journal of Literacy Research, 32*, 187–210.

Lewin, T. (2003). A growing number of video viewers watch from crib. *New York Times*, October 29.

Mayer, R.E., & Moreno, R. (1998). A split-attention effect in multimedia learning: Evidence for dual processing systems in working memory. *Journal of Educational Psychology, 90*, 312–320.

Mullis, I.V.S., Martin, M.O., Gonzalez, E.J., & Kennedy, A.M. (2003). *PIRLS 2001 International Report: IEA's study of reading literacy achievement in primary schools*. Chestnut Hill, MA: Boston College.

Neuman, S.B., & Koskinen, P. (1992). Captioned television as comprehensible input: Effects of incidental word learning from context for language minority students. *Reading Research Quarterly, 27*, 94–106.

Paivio, A. (1986). *Mental representations. A dual coding approach*. Oxford, UK: Oxford University Press.

Papert, S. (1996). *The connected family: Bridging the digital generation gap*. Atlanta, GA: Longstreet Press.

Pecchinenda, A., & Smith, C.A. (1996). The affective significance of skin conductance activity during a difficult problem-solving task. *Cognition and Emotion, 10*, 481–503.

Ravaja, N. (2004). Contributions of psychophysiology to media research: Review and recommendations. *Media Psychology, 6*, 193–235.

Reinking, D. (1994). *Electronic Literacy* (Perspectives Series No. 1-PS-N-07). Athens, GA and College Park, MD: National Reading Research Center.

Reinking D., Labbo L., & McKenna, M. (1997). Navigating the changing landscape of literacy: Current theory and research in computer-based reading and writing. In J. Flood, S.B. Heath, & D. Lapp. (Eds.), *Research on teaching literacy through the communicative and visual arts* (pp. 77–92). New York: Simon & Schuster Macmillan.

Rideout, V.J., Vandewater, E.A., & Wartella, E.A. (2003). *Zero to six. Electronic media in the lives of infants, toddlers and preschoolers*. Menlo Park, CA: The Kaiser Family Foundation.

Salomon, G. (1984). Television is "easy" and print is "tough": The differential investment of mental effort as a function of perceptions and attributions. *Journal of Educational Psychology, 76*, 647–658.

Salomon, G., & Leigh, T. (1984). Predispositions about learning from print and television. *Journal of Communication, 34*, 119–135.

Sharp, D.L.M., Bransford, J.D., Goldman, S.R., Risko, V.J., Kinzer, C.K., & Vye, N.J. (1995). Dynamic visual support for story comprehension and mental model building by young, at-risk children. *Educational Technology Research and Development, 43*, 25–40.

Stanovich, K. (1986). Matthew effects in reading: Some consequences of individual differences in the acquisition of literacy. *Reading Research Quarterly, 21,* 360–407.

Verhallen, M.J.A.J., & Bus, A.G. (2007). Video storybooks create new possibilities to linguistically disadvantaged kindergarten children. Unpublished manuscript.

Verhallen, M.J.A.J., Bus, A.G., & de Jong, M.T. (2006). The promise of multimedia stories for kindergarten children at risk. *Journal of Educational Psychology, 98,* 410–419.

Wright, J.C., & Huston, A.C. (1983). A matter of form. Potentials of television for young viewers. *American Psychologist, 38,* 835–843.

Zeijl, E., Crone, M., Wiefferink, K., Keuzekamp, S., & Reijneveld, M. (2005). *Kinderen in Nederland* [Children in the Netherlands]. The Hague: SCP publication 2005/4.

11
The Educational Electronic Book as a Tool for Supporting Children's Emergent Literacy

Adina Shamir and Ofra Korat

With computers penetrating ever more areas of everyday life, including that of children in all age groups, today's teachers are facing a new challenge: the effective use of innovative CD-ROM storybooks (eBooks) with young children in a classroom who have already been exposed to computers. In addition to their acquaintance with computers, these young children appear to be more cognitively receptive to written language than previous generations, a result we can attribute to changes embedded in the contemporary socio-cultural environment (Neuman & Dickenson, 2001; Whitehurst & Lonigan, 2001). Yet, the creators of these books often overlook the need to integrate educational goals with the developmental capacities of young children (Haugland & Wright, 1997; Shamir & Korat, 2006). The purpose of this chapter is, therefore, to provide teachers with some guidance regarding eBook use in the kindergarten classroom.

Viewed from the perspective of the educator interested in adapting this tool to pedagogical work with young children, this combination of educational and developmental functions is difficult to evaluate. As Wood, Rawlings, and Ozturk (2003) rightly argue: "This is not surprising ... as teachers are not expected to be multimedia experts..." (p. 91). The current chapter therefore discusses some of the respective issues. Its conclusions are based on two experiments. The first explores the relationship of activation modes with emergent literacy acquisition, using an educational eBook specially designed by the authors. The second examines the educational efficacy of paired or collaborative learning with the same educational eBook in a kindergarten setting.

Many of the eBooks that teachers use are designed to improve emergent literacy skills (de Jong & Bus, 2002, 2003; Eagleton & Hamilton, 2001; Lehrer, Erickson, & Connel, 1994; Leu & Kinzer, 2000; McKenna & Watkins, 1996; Shamir & Korat, 2006). These skills, while important in themselves, are also considered to be effective predictors of later reading and writing achievement in elementary school (Scarborough, 2001; Shatil, Share, & Levin, 2001; Whitehurst, 1999). Choosing an appropriate eBook and using it in an appropriate learning context, therefore, has repercussions on various levels of the child's educational progress. With respect to learning context, educators continue to explore whether eBooks will be equally effective when used by pairs or by individual young learners.

Because of the eBook's newness as a learning tool, teachers of young children need guidance when selecting and using eBooks (de Jong & Bus, 2003; Labbo, 1996, 2000; McKenna & Watkins, 1996). These guidelines should help teachers identify the features that match the developmental level of the child's physical, emotional, and cognitive characteristics in general and how the eBook's structure and activations support emergent literacy in particular.

In recognition of the eBook's features and its potential for enhancing literacy acquisition, study of this new technology has shown steady progress over the last decade (Glasgow, 1996–1997; Matthew, 1996; Reinking, 1997; Smith, 2001). Yet, much additional research remains to be conducted on the relationship between the eBook's special features and the appropriate conditions for its use with a young audience (see Roskos, this volume, for example; Shamir & Korat, 2006). In focusing on the eBook's educational features, this chapter's direct purpose is threefold: (1) to provide teachers with some guidelines for eBook use that best contribute to enhancing *emergent literacy* in light of the contemporary young child's *developmental needs*; (2) to present research findings regarding the effectiveness of three eBook modes for the acquisition of selected emergent literacy skills; and (3) to ascertain eBook effectiveness in different *learning settings*.

Stories and eBooks: Updating a Recognized Educational Tool

Stories appear to be fundamental, timeless methods for achieving educational purposes (Bruner, 1990; Chen, Ferdig, & Wood, 2003; Gudmundsdottir, 1995; Heath, 1994; Jonassen & Hernandez-Serrano, 2002; McEwan & Egan, 1995; Schank, 1999). Due to their narrative structure, stories are exceptional repositories of experience, a feature that enables them to support the acquisition of primary problem-solving skills while improving their comprehension and interpretation of events. Stories have thus retained their traditional features even after being updated or transformed into software-supported narratives or eBooks. When multimedia elements augment oral methods of delivery, as they do in eBooks, students can respond on various levels (Labbo & Kuhn, 2000; see Matthew, 1996 regarding third-graders). They can improve their verbal abilities (Johnston, 1995), or maintain motivation for reading or listening to stories (Glasgow, 1996–1997), all while having fun. And so, a new category of literature—*edutainment*, the neologism capturing the combination of educational and entertainment features that characterizes much of the new software (Wood et al., 2003)—has become part of children's educational literature. Because this combination attracts children, teachers are often tempted to introduce eBooks into preschool and kindergarten classrooms as supplemental pedagogic tools.

A major stream of research on eBook use in school grew out of the suggestion that the child's experience of the eBook's interactive features resembles his or her response to adult mediation, a process activated when adults jointly read books with children (Dixon-Krauss, 1996; Zellermier & Kuzulin, 2004). Hearing an adult reading aloud is considered a promising method, in itself, for fostering language acquisition (Bus, van IJzendoorn, & Pellegrini, 1995; van Kleeck, 2003; Whitehurst & Lonigan, 2001) and emergent literacy development (Haden, Reese, & Fivush, 1996; Leseman & de Jong, 1998; Reese, 1995), especially among young children.

Even if only implicitly, eBooks directed at young children incorporate this understanding about the role of narrative and adult mediation of reading skills in their software and application modes. As multimedia devices, eBooks expand mediation by integrating different types of expression—visual, audio, and written formats—within a digital "package" activated with a range of process-oriented modes. One such mode—user-activated hidden hotspots—has indeed become quite standard. These devices, embedded at various screen locations, are intended to provide additional information about the characters, to repeat or elaborate text (words or themes), to explain a word, duplicate a sound, and switch screens (equivalent to flipping pages containing pictures or animation), or to provide entry into games and other activities meant to promote the story's understanding. Such software features transform reading eBooks into an enjoyable, interactive experience (Chera & Wood, 2003; Underwood & Underwood, 1996).

The kindergarten teacher, as the primary classroom storyteller or mediator, is in a good position to take advantage of the full range of eBook options to further pedagogical goals. To do so effectively, the teacher must exercise considerable discretion in choosing the eBook as well as assigning the multimedia applications to be activated during a lesson (Shamir & Korat, 2006). This point is underscored by the fact that although multimedia features are directed primarily at arousing or maintaining the child's interest and motivation to read, these same effects can distract the child from the eBook's narrative and educational substance (Burrel & Trushell, 1997; de Jong and Bus, 2002; Labbo & Kuhn, 2000; Matthew, 1996; Turbill, 2001; Underwood & Underwood, 1996).

Research on the efficacy of eBooks for literacy development among school beginners and young children has revealed, however, some promising results in several domains—despite these qualms. For example, the word recognition skills of preschoolers (Miller, Blackstock, & Miller, 1994; de Jong & Bus, 2002) and school children (Lewin, 2000) were observed to improve following eBook experiences. eBooks were also found to enhance children's phonological awareness (Chera & Wood, 2003; Wise et al., 1989) whether they worked individually or in pairs (Shamir & Korat, 2007). Chera and Wood (2003), for instance, found that kindergarteners aged 3–6 who had been exposed to eBooks during a 4-week program were more advanced in their phonological awareness than were control group children. Verbal knowledge was also found to improve with eBook use (Lewin, 2000), as was story recall ability (Underwood & Underwood, 1998). Equally important, children attending Head Start programs that incorporated developmentally appropriate eBooks showed significant improvement in their emergent literacy levels in kindergarten (Talley, 1994).

eBooks as Tools for Enhancing Young Children's Emergent Literacy

Despite the accumulating research literature showing the positive effects of well-designed software on children's cognitive and social development (Clements, 1991; Hannafin & Sullivan, 1995), one cannot assume that all eBooks meet the required standards (Shamir & Korat, 2006). For example, recent evaluations of the eBooks commercially available in the Netherlands (de Jong & Bus, 2003) and in Israel (Korat & Shamir, 2004) revealed a disappointing picture regarding their educational quality and literacy-supporting potential. Even if unintentionally, most of the commercial Hebrew and Dutch eBooks stress amusement to the detriment of literacy development. For instance, by combining the read and play options in the same mode, children can be easily distracted from the storyline (de Jong & Bus, 2002, 2003; Korat & Shamir, 2004).

From these studies, it was evident that several instructional design features could improve eBooks. For example, games should be designed on a separate track from instruction to avoid the immediate availability of distracting activations. Further, additional features—such as highlighting of written text and an animated dictionary—should be incorporated to extend young children's vocabulary and story comprehension. In addition, more hotspots are generally needed to promote story understanding and expand children's knowledge about the story's background. Allowing children to choose between reading the text by themselves or together with the narrator might add to the interactivity of the book.

Because our target population here is young children, the developmental elements required for inclusion in an appropriate eBook should be considered. Earlier studies by Haugland and Shade (1994) as well as by Haugland and Wright (1997) found that software targeted for young children often did not respond to the developmental capacities of its young users (see also National Association for the Education of Young Children, 2003). Haugland and Wright (1997) subsequently identified what they considered to be developmentally appropriate software. Their guidelines suggest:

- Software should reflect realistic performance expectations, taking into consideration the child's emerging cognitive, physical, emotional, and social skills.

- It should contain no violent behavior.
- Software should allow children to control and navigate between tasks independently with clear instructions to facilitate autonomy.
- It should allow for creative exploration.

Based on the developmental scale suggested by Haugland and Wright (1997) and the criteria regarding eBook quality for enhancing literacy developed by de Jong and Bus (2003), we recently proposed a set of guidelines to assist educators dealing with these issues in the area of emergent literacy (Shamir & Korat, 2006). The guidelines relate to the age appropriateness of the materials; whether or not it is child controlled, has clear instructions, is process-oriented, and contains technical features that operate consistently (for the complete guidelines see Shamir & Korat, 2006).

For example, an eBook's *age appropriateness* is expressed by the content's relevance for young children, e.g., its plot should be simple and structured according to one main problem followed by a solution, text (sentences or/and words) that is highlighted as it is read aloud as well as the user's timely and easy access to a lexicon or dictionary. The amount of text on each screen should avoid information overload and font size should be sufficiently large and formed for ready recognition, based on the child's age. Consideration of the *child control capacities* in eBooks is expressed by the separate modes offered, which allow for active learning and navigation according to the teacher's pedagogic goals (e.g., focusing on learning tasks). The software should include reading functions such as forward and backward buttons, interruption and restart options, (re)reading of text segments, and a print option. eBooks should contain *clear instructions* accompanied by pictures that facilitate the child's mastery of the program in addition to features explicitly oriented to learning. A *process-oriented* eBook therefore contains activations that are congruent with the story content as well as amusing so that working with the eBook will reinforce the child's sense of discovery in addition to his story understanding. The eBook's *technical quality* is expressed in software that operates consistently and installs easily. Such technical quality attracts the child's attention to the screen and saves valuable learning time. This array of elements, when attuned to the child's emotional maturity, self-esteem, and physical aptitudes (e.g., manual dexterity), appear to augment cognitive development (for an expanded discussion see Shamir & Korat, 2006). Allowing children to control the eBook's applications by means of electronic modes so they can independently solve problems may also support their learning.

However, to date, there is little research on the relationship between the eBook's different multimedia modes and children's literacy acquisition. In addition, research is also needed about the effect of educational setting on eBook use in classrooms. The two studies reported below were designed to begin to fill in some of these gaps.

Evaluation of an Educational eBook: Modes and Contexts

The two studies described here employed the same educational eBook, specially designed to enhance emergent literacy in kindergarten settings. In the first study, our purpose was to examine the educational effectiveness of the modes used to activate an eBook; in the second study, the focus was on the learning context with children working in pairs as opposed to children working individually.

With respect to the eBook's modes, we should reiterate that all three modes were designed to comply with the age-appropriate eInteractive elements meant to motivate and amuse children on the one hand, and those reported to support children's emergent literacy and language on the other (Shamir & Korat, 2006). Each mode represented a different application option—"Read story only," "Read story with Dictionary," and "Read story and Play"—and was programmed to be activated separately. The "Read story only" mode initiated an oral reading of the printed text, accompanied by automatic dynamic visuals together with additional music and film effects meant to dramatize narrative segments. The "Read story with Dictionary" mode supplemented the oral reading with explanations of difficult words, and appeared automatically following the narrator's reading of each page. The "Read story and Play" mode allowed activation of hotspots on the screen. To avoid distraction, children could activate the hotspots only after the entire text had been read from the screen.

Like many other eBooks intended for a young audience, the special 25-page educational eBook utilized the text and graphics of a well-known and popular print book, in this case, *The Tractor in the Sand Box* (in Hebrew: *Ha tractor Be'argaz Hachol*), authored by Meir Shalev (1995). The story tells of the relationship between a grandfather and his ancient tractor. Like the original, a large colored drawing covered more than half of each screen page, with the remainder of the screen containing three to five written sentences (about 40 words per screen). The book was selected due to its age-appropriate developmental qualities, such as simple narrative elements (Mandler & Johnson, 1977).

Several important software features were introduced into the educational eBook. These included forward and backward buttons on each screen to allow children to return to previous screens or to continue onto the next one. These features support an orientation to reading and active involvement in the task. Another function allowed the children to reread/relisten to text by clicking on an arrow that initiated text repetition. The relationship between the visual text and its oral reading was stressed by highlighting written phrases as they were uttered by the narrator, a function aimed at supporting exposure to written text and, perhaps, word recognition (de Jong & Bus, 2002). An overview screen showing all optional screens in reduced format was introduced to further a pro-reading orientation as well as print knowledge.

Study 1

Two fundamental research questions were posed in this study. (1) Would emergent literacy scores improve from pre- to post-test sessions? Which skills showed improvement and by how much? We assumed that children would show the greatest advances in the areas of word meaning, word recognition, and phonological awareness because the software's design was aimed directly at these skills rather than word writing and knowledge of letter names. (2) Was the degree of improvement related to the eBook mode it activated? If yes, which emergent literacy skills were affected? The "Read story only" mode was expected to be less effective than either the "Read story and Play" or the "Read story with Dictionary" mode because this was the simplest, most straightforward activation mode, free of any additional tasks. Since all the modes were designed to promote emergent literacy we hypothesized that the experimental children, who used the specially designed eBook, would show higher levels of improved performance than would the control group, which worked with traditional material having the same purpose.

Participants in the first study were 120 children aged 5–6, randomly selected from eight kindergarten classes located in various neighborhoods in Tel-Aviv. At this age, children are usually able to read and write their names independently. In Israeli kindergartens, children are frequently read to and encouraged to browse through books. Classrooms are generally equipped with one or two computers; hence, children tend to be acquainted with eBooks as well as other software.

The children in the sample were randomly assigned by the researcher to four different groups. Three groups were assigned to work with only one mode each: "Read story only," "Read story with Dictionary," or "Read story and Play." A fourth group, representing the control group, worked with the standard non-computerized emergent literacy program. All the children selected had prior classroom experience with computers. After being shown how the software operates, the experimental children worked individually during three different sessions, given on different days over 1 week. Each session lasted for about 30 minutes. At the beginning of each session, the children were given general instructions on how to use the mode to which they were assigned. Children were free to activate the hotspots associated with each mode at will.

All sample participants were assessed before and after working with the eBook for *word meaning, word recognition,* and *phonological awareness.* With respect to the first question, as hypothesized, the findings of the research revealed that the three groups of experimental children demonstrated significant ($p < 0.01$) improvement in pre- to post-test scores for word meaning (Partial eta square = 0.30, $p < 0.001$), word recognition (Partial eta square = 0.24, $p < 0.001$), syllable segmentation (Partial eta square = 0.19, $p < 0.001$), and sub-syllabic segmentation (Partial eta square = 0.19, $p < 0.001$) as compared to the control group.

With respect to the second question, which pertained to the effectiveness of the specific modes, a significant interaction between Time and Mode (F (12, 214) = 3.70, $p < 0.001$) was found. This interaction appeared for word meaning (Partial eta square = 0.24, $p < 0.001$) and for word recognition (Partial eta square = 0.09, $p < 0.001$). A further analysis indicated that word meaning improved after the "Read and Play" mode (F [1, 38] = 11.76, Partial eta square = 0.24, $p < 0.001$) and the "Dictionary" mode (F [1, 39] = 56.63, Partial eta square = 0.59, $p < 0.001$), but not after the "Read only" mode (F [1, 35] = 0.30, Partial eta square = 0.01, $p > 0.05$). As to word recognition, the children's word reading improved after working in the "Dictionary" mode (F [1, 39] = 26.80, Partial eta square = 0.41, $p < 0.001$) and the "Read only" mode (F [1, 35] = 8.00, Partial eta square = 0.19, $p < 0.01$) but not after the "Read and Play" mode (F [1, 38] = 3.81, $p > 0.05$).

These findings indicate that when using an age-appropriate educational eBook that includes features aimed at supporting literacy development, children can improve their emergent literacy skills. The findings also indicate that not all activation modes are equally effective for skill acquisition: "Read story with Dictionary" and "Read story and Play" were the most effective of the modes tested. These results should not be surprising when we recall that the educational eBook used was specially designed with multimedia modes that capture the child's developmental capacities at the same time that they exhibit features believed to enhance literacy.

Because software dictionaries are so crucial for vocabulary acquisition, we made sure that the dictionary placed in the special eBook allowed exposure to words in two ways: first, as words appear automatically on the screen, children learned how they are spelled; later, they could reactivate the dictionary by clicking on the desired word as often and as long as they chose. Furthermore, each difficult word that appeared written in a large balloon was pronounced clearly by the narrator and was associated with pictures that supported its meaning. This may explain why these young children could grasp—relatively easily—the meanings of infrequently used new words.

The great improvement observed in word recognition after the children had worked with the "Read story and Dictionary" mode implies that text activation, by whatever mode, may affect cognitive processes and thereby increase the child's general responsiveness to written text. Exposure to the hotspots in the "Read story and Play" mode, which was targeted specifically at improving word recognition, may likewise have triggered other language skills (note: hotspots were unavailable in the "Read story only" mode).

We should note that these findings contradict previous findings regarding activations embedded within reading modes. For example, de Jong and Bus (2002) found that 4- to 5-year-old children's story comprehension was not as well supported by the electronic version compared to the regular book format read to them by an adult. Following Labbo and Kuhn (2000), they concluded that "the many attractive options of electronic-books seem to distract children's attention from text and number of readings of the text in favor of iconic and pictorial explorations" (p. 154). It appears that when activations are designed to transcend story content and plot (e.g., by including additional comments, made by the main characters) as well as targeted at emergent literacy (e.g., the "Read story and Dictionary" mode), children are not distracted but, quite the contrary, are benefited.

The fact that the control group showed a small improvement in its word recognition scores with a standard, non-computerized emergent literacy program may indicate that the improvement obtained on this measure by the experimental groups may not have been due solely to eBook use. The improvement may, in effect, point to a somewhat different but related phenomenon. According to Neuman and Dickenson (2001), today's young children are better prepared for cognitive processing of written language. These authors attribute this development to cultural changes observed in greater exposure to electronic media, from television to eBooks, at increasingly younger ages. This implies that whatever learning tools or programs they are exposed to, very young children's word recognition scores will improve after completing a wide-range learning task simply because they are already prepared to learn. Methods for testing as well as teaching emergent literacy skills—such as word recognition—should therefore be adapted to the children's greater preparedness for this visually based capacity.

We can therefore conclude that the findings of the first study support other research indicating the eBook's contribution to emergent literacy skills, particularly to verbal knowledge (Lewin, 2000; Segers & Verhoeven, 2002), word recognition (de Jong & Bus, 2002; Lewin, 2000), and phonological awareness (Chera & Wood, 2003). They likewise show that carefully designed multimedia eBooks can avoid the disadvantages—especially distraction (Burrel & Trushell, 1997; de Jong and Bus, 2002; Labbo & Kuhn, 2000; Matthew, 1996; Turbill, 2001; Underwood & Underwood, 1996)—of some activity modes.

Study 2

The second study focused on a different aspect of teaching emergent literacy: the learning context. Because classroom conditions often make it necessary for children to work on computers in pairs (Lewin, 1998), the study investigated whether collaborative learning with computers is effective for enhancing emergent literacy among kindergarteners. Although the positive effects of peer (or paired) learning with computers have been studied for more than 20 years (Topping & Ehly, 1998), the research on peer learning with computers among young children is limited.

Many questions remain regarding the effectiveness of collaborative learning when compared with individual learning for this age group. (1) Are young children capable of working collaboratively? That is, do very young children exhibit the requisite developmental capacities for productive interaction in paired learning (see Crook, 1998, 2002; Hyun, 2005)? (2) If so, is collaboration effective? Therefore, the second study explored whether joint activity with computers, carried out in pairs, fostered young children's emergent literacy compared to children with individualized instruction.

In the present case, the sample consisted of 72 children from three kindergartens; 24 children were randomly assigned to work individually and 48 children (24 pairs) were randomly assigned to work in pairs. No formal educational program for teaching reading and writing was used in these kindergartens. All the children who participated in the study were Hebrew speakers, and their mean age was 5.5 years. All participants had some initial experiences with computers individually and in small groups as part of the kindergarten curriculum. Children also participated in games promoting phonemic awareness, with time devoted to recitation of the alphabet or to letter naming (Shatil et al., 2001).

Like the previous study, the children were tested for word meaning, word recognition, and phonological awareness. In addition, they were also tested for emergent writing and letter naming. All of the participants took part in three eBook activity sessions and experienced the three possible eBook modes (each mode once): first, "Read only," then "Read only with dictionary," and finally "Read and play."

Preliminary analyses of the emergent literacy scores showed no significant differences between the scores of children working individually and those working in pairs. As expected, across both groups and across all measures, the children's post-test scores were higher than their pre-test scores. However, no differences in the pre- to post-intervention improvements were obtained between children who worked individually compared with children who worked in pairs.

Considering the limited findings about the effectiveness of collaborative learning with computers among young children, the findings of this study are of special importance. They indicate that children, even at this age, can work in pairs and still improve their emergent literacy skills. The research therefore shows that paired learning, as a practical solution to scarcity, does not interfere and may even support the teacher's attempts to achieve various educational objectives.

Conclusion

As educational tools become more technologically sophisticated and young children become increasingly adept at using them, increasingly teachers will be compelled to investigate whether an eBook's design features are appropriate for their educational aims. This applies to the activation modes, the child's developmental capacities, in addition to the learning context. The first study reported here provided some understanding of the association between electronic activation modes and the teacher's emergent literacy agenda. For example, educators should be aware of how to select eBooks that contain the appropriate features, such as the content of written text, oral reading, oral discourse, music, sound effects, and animations.

Several features are especially important for young learners. For example, the narrator's oral reading of the text should be accompanied by highlighted written text aimed at providing users with insights into the nature of the written text. Hotspot activation should be directly associated with the written text; meaning that clicking on specific words, phrases, or sentences will provide children with opportunities to hear the written text as often as they wish. To support word recognition and vocabulary acquisition, a dictionary option combining multimedia explanations for difficult words is extremely important. Hotspots should also support story content, illustrations, and written text by adding information to expand the original narrative. Of special importance is the separation of play mode to avoid distraction (Korat & Shamir, 2004).

The second study's findings support previous research indicating that working in pairs with educational eBooks, a common practice in kindergarten classes (Lewin, 1998), may enhance children's learning no less than will working individually. The findings essentially dispute common expectations that young children find it difficult to concentrate on a task in the presence of a partner. If the educational eBook is sufficiently well designed in terms of content and opportunities for amusement, children are less likely to be distracted from the cognitive tasks by amusement-oriented activations. Training for paired learning may therefore be worth considering (Shamir & Tzuriel, 2004; Topping & Ehly, 1998). In light of the lack of research on young children and collaborative learning with computers, further studies on this topic are urgently needed.

In conclusion, eBooks represent an important new learning tool for young children. When teachers select these materials wisely, and use them to support children's learning, eBooks may potentially empower children and motivate them to develop key emergent literacy skills in the early years.

References

Bruner, J. (1990). *Acts of meaning*. Cambridge, MA: Harvard University Press.

Burrel, C., & Trushell, J. (1997). "Eye-candy" in "interactive books"—A wholesome diet? *Reading, 31*, 3–6.

Bus, A.G., van IJzendoorn, M.H., & Pellegrini, A.D. (1995). Joint book reading makes for success in learning to read: A meta-analysis on intergenerational transmission of literacy. *Review of Educational Research, 65*, 1–21.

Chen, M., Ferdig, R., & Wood, A. (2003). Understanding technology-enhanced storybooks and their roles in teaching and learning: An investigation of electronic storybooks in education. *Journal of Literacy and Technology, 3.* Retrieved September 13, 2005, from www.literacyandtechnology.org/v3n1/chenferdigwood.htm.

Chera, P., & Wood, C. (2003). Animated multimedia "talking books" can promote phonological awareness in children beginning to read. *Learning and Instruction, 13*, 33–52.

Clements, D.H. (1991). Enhancement of creativity in computer environments. *American Educational Research Journal, 28*, 173–187.

Crook, C. (1998). Children as computer users: The case of collaborative learning. *Computers & Education, 30*, 237–247.

Crook, C. (2002). Deferring to resources: Collaborations around traditional vs. computer-based notes. *Journal of Computer Assisted Learning, 18*, 64–76.

de Jong, M.T., & Bus, A.G. (2002). Quality of book-reading matters for emergent readers: An experiment with the same book in a regular or electronic format. *Journal of Educational Psychology, 94*, 145–155.

de Jong, M.T., & Bus, A.G. (2003). How suitable are electronic books to support literacy? *Journal of Early Childhood Literacy, 3*, 147–164.

Dixon-Krauss, L. (Ed.) (1996). *Vygotsky in the classroom: Mediated literacy instruction and assessment.* White Plains, NY: Longman.

Eagleton, M., & Hamilton, M. (2001). *New genres in literacy: Classroom Webzine projects.* Retrieved November 20, 2003, from www.nereading.org/webzinearticle/article.htm.

Glasgow, J. (1996–1997). It's my turn! Part 2: Motivating young readers using CD-ROM storybooks. *Learning and Leading with Technology, 24*, 18–22.

Gudmundsdottir, S. (1995). The narrative nature of pedagogical content knowledge. In H. McEwan & K. Egan (Eds.), *Narrative in teaching, learning and research.* New York: Teachers College Press.

Haden, C.A., Reese, E., & Fivush, R. (1996). Mothers' extratextual comments during storybook reading: Stylistic differences over time and across texts. *Discourse Processes, 21*, 135–169.

Hannafin, R., & Sullivan, H. (1995). Learner control in full and lean CAI programs. *Educational Technology Research and Development, 43*, 19–30.

Haugland, S.W., & Shade, D. (1994). Early childhood computer software. *Journal of Computing in Childhood Education, 5*, 83–92.

Haugland, S.W., & Wright, L. (1997). *Young children and technology a world of discovery.* London: Allyn and Bacon.

Heath, S.B. (1994). Stories as ways of acting together. In A.H. Dyson & C. Genishi (Eds.), *The need for story: Cultural diversity in classroom and community* (pp. 206–220). Urbana, IL: National Council of Teachers of English.

Hyun, E. (2005). A study of 5- to 6-year old children's peer dynamic and dialectical learning in a computer-based technology-rich classroom environment. *Computers & Education, 44*, 69–91.

Johnston, C. (1995). Interactive storybooks software and kindergarten children: The effect on verbal ability and emergent storybook reading behavior (unpublished Doctoral dissertation, Florida State University, 1995). *Dissertation Abstracts International, 56*(11): A4270.

Jonassen, D.H., & Hernandez-Serrano, J. (2002). Case-based reasoning and instructional design: Using stories to support problem solving. *Educational Technology, Research and Development, 50*, 65–77.

Korat, O., & Shamir, A. (2004). Do Hebrew electronic books differ from Dutch electronic books? A replication of a Dutch content analysis. *Journal of Computer Assisted Learning, 20*, 257–268.

Labbo, L.D. (1996). A semiotic analysis of young children's symbol making in a classroom computer center. *Reading Research Quarterly, 31*, 356–385.

Labbo, L.D. (2000). Twelve things young children can do with a talking book in a classroom computer center. *Reading Teacher, 53*, 542–546.

Labbo, L.D., & Kuhn, M.R. (2000). Weaving chains of affect and cognition: A young child's understanding of CD-ROM talking books. *Journal of Literacy Research, 32*, 187–210.

Lehrer, R., Erickson, J., & Connel, T. (1994). Learning by designing hypermedia documents. *Computers in the Schools, 10*, 227–254.

Leseman, P.P.M., & de Jong, P.F. (1998). Home literacy: Opportunity, instruction, cooperation and social-emotional quality predicting early reading achievement. *Reading Research Quarterly, 33,* 294–318.

Leu, D.J., & Kinzer, C.K. (2000). The convergence of literacy instruction and networked technologies for information and communication. *Reading Research Quarterly, 35,* 108–127.

Lewin, C. (1998). Talking book design: What do practitioners want? *Computers & Education, 30,* 87–94.

Lewin, C. (2000). Exploring the effects of talking book software in UK primary classrooms. *Journal of Research in Reading, 23,* 149–157.

McEwan, H., & Egan, K. (Eds.) (1995). *Narrative in teaching, learning and research.* New York: Teachers College Press.

McKenna, M.C., & Watkins, J. (1996). The effect of computer-mediated trade books on sight word acquisition and the development of phonics ability. Paper presented at the meeting of the National Reading Conference, Charleston, SC.

Mandler, J.M., & Johnson, N.S. (1977). Remembrance of things parsed: Story structure and recall. *Cognitive Psychology, 9,* 111–115.

Matthew, K.I. (1996). The impact of CD-ROM storybooks on children's reading comprehension and reading attitude. *Journal of Educational Multimedia and Hypermedia, 5,* 379–394.

Miller, L., Blackstock, J., & Miller, R. (1994). An exploratory study into the use of CD-ROM storybooks. *Computers & Education, 22,* 187–204.

National Association for the Education of Young Children (NAEYC). (November 2003). *NAEYC position statement on technology and young children—ages 3 through 8.* Retrieved October 20, 2003, from www.journal.naeyc.org/btj/200311/links.asp.

Neuman, S.B., & Dickenson, D. (Eds.) (2001). *Handbook of early literacy research.* New York: Guilford Press.

Reese, E. (1995). Predicting children's literacy from mother–child conversations. *Cognitive Development, 10,* 381–405.

Reinking, D. (1997). Me and my hypertext: A multiple digression analysis of technology and literacy (sic). *Reading Teacher, 50,* 626–643.

Scarborough, H.S. (2001). Connecting early language and literacy to later reading (dis)abilities: Evidence, theory, and practice. In S.B. Neuman & D. Dickenson (Eds.), *Handbook of early literacy research* (pp. 97–110). New York: The Guilford Press.

Schank, R.C. (1999). *Dynamic memory revisited.* Cambridge, UK: Cambridge University Press.

Segers, E., & Verhoeven, L. (2002). Multimedia support of early literacy learning. *Computers & Education, 39,* 207–221.

Shalev, M. (1995). *The tractor in the sand box* (In Hebrew Ha tractor Be'argaz Hachol). Tel-Aviv.

Shamir, A., & Korat, O. (2006). How to select CD-Rom storybooks for young children: The teacher role. *Reading Teacher, 59,* 532–543.

Shamir, A., & Korat, O. (2007). Developing an educational e-book for fostering kindergarten children's emergent literacy. *Computers in the Schools, 24,* 125–145.

Shamir, A., & Tzuriel, D. (2004). Characteristics of children's mediational teaching style as a function of intervention for cross-age peer mediation with computers. *School Psychology International, 25,* 106–116.

Shamir, A., Tzuriel, D. & Rosen, M. (2006). Peer mediation: The effects of program intervention, math level, and verbal ability on mediation style and improvement in math problem solving. *School Psychology International, 27,* 209–231.

Shatil, E., Share, D.C., & Levin, I. (2001). On the contribution of kindergarten writing to grade one literacy: A longitudinal study in Hebrew. *Applied Psycholinguistics, 21,* 1–21.

Smith, C.R. (2001). Click and turn the page: An exploration of multiple storybook literacy. *Reading Research Quarterly, 36,* 152–183.

Talley, S. (1994). The effect of CD-ROM computer storybook program on Head Start children's emergent literacy (Master's Thesis, Utah State University, 1994). *Master's Abstracts International, 33–06,* 1638.

Topping, K., & Ehly, S. (1998). Introduction to peer-assisted learning. In K. Topping & S. Ehly (Eds.), *Peer-assisted learning* (pp. 1–23). Mahwah, NJ: Erlbaum.

Turbill, J. (2001). A researcher goes to school: Using technology in the kindergarten literacy curriculum. *Journal of Early Childhood Literacy, 1,* 225–279.

Underwood, G., & Underwood, J. (1996). Gender differences in children's learning from interactive books? Technology and communications: Catalyst for educational change, Vol. 1. In *Proceedings of the Twelfth International Conference on Technology and Education*, New Orleans, Grande Prairie: ICTE, Texas.

Underwood, G., & Underwood, J.D.M. (1998). Children's interactions and learning outcomes with interactive talking books. *Computers and Education, 30*, 95–102.

van Kleeck, A. (2003). Research on book-sharing: Another critical look. In A. van Kleeck, S.A. Stahl, & E.B. Bauer (Eds.), *On reading books to children: Parents and teachers* (pp. 16–36). Mahwah, NJ: Erlbaum.

Wise, D., Olson, R., Annsett, M., Andrews, L., Terjak, M., Schneider, V. et al., & Kriho, L. (1989). Implementing a long term computerized remedial reading program with syntactic speech feedback: Hardware, software and read world issues. *Behavior Research Method Instruction and Computers, 21*, 173–180.

Whitehurst, G.J. (1999). The role of inside-out skills in reading readiness of children from low income families. In C.J. Lonigan (Chair), *From prereaders to readers: The role of phonological processing skills in at risk typically developing children.* Symposium conducted at the meeting of the Society for Research in Child Development, Albuquerque, NM.

Whitehurst, G.J., & Longian, C.J. (2001). Emergent literacy: Development from prereaders to readers. In S.B. Neuman & D. Dickenson (Eds.), *Handbook of early literacy research* (pp. 11–30). New York: Guilford Press.

Wood, R., Rawlings, A., & Ozturk, A. (2003). Towards a new understanding: The "Books Alive! multimedia project." *Reading Literacy and Language, 37*, 90–93.

Zellermier, M., & Kuzulin, A. (2004). *Learning in social context: The development of high psychological process.* Tel-Aviv: Hakibbutz Hameuhad (Hebrew).

12

Effects of Television on Language and Literacy Development

Yuuko Uchikoshi

Television, in particular educational television, is inexpensive, easily accessible, and has the potential utility for scalable intervention. Moreover, it is a popular medium used daily by many children of all ages. A Kaiser Foundation study (Wartella & Richert, this volume) concluded that 4- to 6-year-olds in the United States spend an average of slightly over two hours a day with screen media. Furthermore, on a typical day, 79% of children between the ages of 4 and 6 watch television, 32% watch videos and DVDs, and 13% read electronic books (Marsh, this volume; Rideout & Hamel, 2006). The fact is that many children are using screen media, particularly television. As such, we need to understand how viewing might influence children's language and literacy development. Can children learn language and literacy skills from television?

Paivio's (1986) dual coding theory has had a powerful influence on what we know about verbal (i.e., language) and visual (i.e., imagery) processing. The verbal subsystem processes and stores linguistic information while the visual subsystem stores images and pictorial information. While the two subsystems can be activated independently, the interrelations and connections of the two systems allow dual coding of information. Through educational television both the verbal and visual processing systems are stimulated. Viewers are required to integrate both the language and images from television. The activation of both the verbal and visual processing systems may be particularly helpful for English language learners (ELL) who may have difficulties with just verbal processing.

This chapter will explore children's language and literacy learning from a dual coding perspective. There has been much research on language and literacy development as well as research on television, yet there is not a significant amount of literature on the convergence of these two topics. This chapter will be organized in the following way. First, I will examine the features of educational television that activate the verbal and visual processing systems simultaneously and how children react to those features. Second, I will cover empirical studies that look at television's effects on language and literacy development. This will focus mainly on studies that examine vocabulary development. Third, I will cover empirical studies that look at television's effects on literacy development: this will also cover phonological awareness, early reading, and narrative development. Finally, I will present some suggestions for future research.

My main focus will be on educational television. Educational television refers to shows that have a core educational or informational purpose. In 1990, the Federal Communications Commission (FCC) passed the Children's Television Act (CTA), which required commercial broadcasters to air programming that has a core educational and informational purpose targeted to children under age 16 (Hill-Scott, 2001). The program must be a regularly scheduled, weekly program of at least 30 minutes aired between 7:00 a.m. and 10:00 p.m.

Educational Television Features

Language acquisition researchers show that language is best learned through direct interaction and modeling (Snow, 1972). Adults often use special speech directed to children, known as motherese or child-directed speech. The adult modifies his or her speech, particularly at the levels of paralinguistic features (e.g., higher pitch, exaggerated intonation), syntactic features (e.g., shorter sentences, fewer verbs), and discourse features (e.g., clear articulation, more repetitions). Through joint interactions with adults, children imitate what they hear and acquire the correct grammatical and lexical forms. Additionally, social development researchers show that language is best learned when the new material is in the child's *zone of proximal development* (Vygotsky, 1978). Children learn to speak by listening and imitating adult speech that is geared to their level and attention span. As the adult provides the child with appropriate speech at an appropriate pace, the child gradually learns the target language.

Can television enhance children's language development? Some researchers believe that it can (e.g., Rice, Huston, Truglio, & Wright, 1990; Van Evra, 1998; Linebarger, 2000). Rice (1983), for example, found that language was learned from television under the following conditions: (1) the program was appropriate to the child's linguistic abilities; (2) the child was older than a toddler, as preschoolers are able to gain linguistics skills without intensive one on one conversational interaction; and (3) the program was targeted to children's comprehension level in terms of dialogue and content. Through the use of the dialogue heard and the use of the objects seen, the child was able to learn language from television programs.

There is precedence for analyzing the dialogue used in educational television. For example, pioneering this work, Rice (1983) pointed out the differences in language use in programs between *Mr. Roger's Neighborhood* (targeted for a younger child audience) and *Electric Company* (targeted for an older child audience). Compared to the latter program, the former had more repetition of key words and phrases, which were emphasized by being presented in isolation or with vocal stress. Further, *Mr. Roger's Neighborhood* avoided novel words and nonliteral meanings, whereas such words were used in *Electric Company*. In a later study, Rice and Haught (1986) found that *Sesame Street*, also targeted for a younger child audience, used similar dialogue to *Mr. Roger's Neighborhood*. The features seen in these educational programs targeted for younger children are those typical of child-directed speech, i.e., speech that is geared to their level and attention span (Hoff-Ginsberg, 1986; Snow, 1984; Wells, 1985). Additionally, Rice and Haught (1986) show that approximately 60% of utterances in *Mr. Roger's Neighborhood* and *Sesame Street* referred to objects or events that were simultaneously shown on the screen. This implies that the viewer could see the object and hear the label of the object at the same time. This reinforcement and repetition by verbal and visual processing allows for dual coding of the new information.

This stimulation of both the verbal and visual processing systems is also used in more recent educational television programs aired on the Public Broadcasting System, such as *Between the Lions* (Frith, 2000). *Between the Lions* uses both pictures and written words on the screen for visual stimulation, as well as both speech and written words for language input. In this program, children simultaneously hear the written words read aloud and see the imagery (pictures as well as letters) associated with the visual word. The show does this for the read-aloud stories, as well as for the phonics parts. For example, in the episode "Touching the Moon," the show introduces a story about a queen trying to reach the moon. The story starts off with the following narration: "There once was a queen named Oona Cartoon/who gazed at the moon over her lagoon." As the narrator reads, the highlighted script is shown on the screen. At the same time, there is a picture of a woman looking at the moon in front of a lagoon. As the story continues, the viewer hears: "The queen climbed up." As the narrator speaks, the script is shown on the screen and highlighted. The picture is of a queen climbing up on objects piled on top of each other. The story continues to say that the queen "could not reach the moon." Along with the highlighted script is a picture of a queen reaching but not touching the moon as there is an apparent gap between the queen and the moon.

In the phonics section for this episode, one segment focuses on the *oo* vowel. The show introduces the word *balloon* by first showing a character, Fred, blowing up a real balloon and letting the air out of the balloon. Then the word *balloon* appears on the screen. Fred then says the two parts of the word *balloon—bal loon—*before saying the word. As Fred reads the word, he places emphasis on the *oo* vowel. Fred then pretends to let the word go as if the air in the word *balloon* is going out. The reinforcement of verbal and visual cues as described above assist young viewers to understand the content of the program.

Camera effects can also assist in creating a joint attention environment between the television and viewer (Salomon, 1981). The camera can zoom in on the object being discussed for emphasis. Sound effects also assist in capturing the audience's attention. As such, advanced technology also supports the dual coding theory.

Children as Active Participants

Despite these features, early researchers on television, such as Brown, Cramond, and Wilde (1974) claimed that children are passive nonparticipants in front of the television and that television displaced other learning and interaction time. This displacement theory states that television displaces the time that children could spend on out of school activities that might facilitate reading, such as leisure reading. However, television does not appear to displace leisure reading (Neuman 1988, 1991, this volume). In a synthesis of eight statewide reading assessments and a secondary analysis of the 1984 National Assessment of Educational Progress, Neuman shows that the displacement theory did not successfully predict the amount of television that children watch. Rather, the amount of television viewing decreased as the children got older and they became more involved in school and sports activities. Neuman also found differences in reading scores to be very small for children watching between two and four hours of television daily, yet beyond four hours per day television produced negative reading results. At the same time, results from a longitudinal study showed that watching educational television, in particular *Sesame Street* and *Mr. Roger's Neighborhood*, during the preschool years contributes positively to high school grades and academic behaviors, such as leisure reading (Anderson, Huston, Schmitt, Linebarger, & Wright, 2001).

Additionally, later research shows that young children frequently are active participants in television viewing (Labbo, this volume; Lemish & Rice, 1986; Singer & Singer, 1998; Crawley et al., 2002), thereby allowing for dual coding to happen. Preschoolers are often attentive and engaging during television viewing. They frequently laugh at the appropriate points, repeat parts of the dialogue, and talk back to the characters on the screen when the characters call out to the viewers. There is also evidence that familiarity with the format of the program improves participation. A study that compared regular, experienced viewers and new, inexperienced viewers of *Blue's Clues* shows that the former overly interacted more with a new episode and this effect was most marked during recurrent format portions of the episode (Crawley et al., 2002). Moreover, many children's shows make multiple attempts to evoke responses from the viewers (Crawley et al., 2002; Rice & Haught, 1986). For example, *Blue's Clues* has segments where Steve, the host, asks questions to the viewer and pauses with his hand to his ear as if he is listening for responses from the viewer. Through words and actions, children are expected to interact and they respond, especially when they are familiar with the segments.

Moreover, television, when viewed with a parent, has been proposed as a model of a talking picture book with both imagery and language input (Lemish & Rice, 1986). The rich verbal interactions that children see on educational television and experience with a co-viewer have been compared to parent–child book reading experiences in a classic study conducted by Lemish and Rice (1986). They collected longitudinal data of 16 children and their parents over a period of 6–8 months. At the beginning, the children's ages ranged from 0.6 to 2.5 years. They found that the frequency of utterances made by the child when viewing is roughly the same for book reading contexts. The kinds of utterances made by both parents and children were also very similar to those seen in joint book reading interactions. The four main categories of children's and parental verbalizations were: (1) labeling objects on the screen; (2) questioning about the content; (3) repetition of television dialogue or in the case of the child, parental comments about program content; (4) description of the content. It should be noted that this study did not focus on educational television. From this similarity in outcomes, it can be concluded that television provides opportunity for rich verbal interactions that promote language acquisition.

In sum, educational television has features that allow learning from television to occur under certain conditions. Dialogue can be designed for particular target audiences with object referents or events shown simultaneously on screen. Often camera angles and special sound effects may help young viewers focus on the object of concern though there is mostly additional visual information to distract children. Additionally when co-viewed with a parent, educational television can potentially provide opportunities for rich dialogues between the parent and the child, which could further promote language development. Moreover, children are more likely to be active participants when programs are age and level appropriate. Empirical studies that examine the effects of educational television's features on children's vocabulary acquisition will now be examined.

Vocabulary and Television

Research conducted on monolingual English-speaking children shows that educational television has the potential to serve as a facilitator of young children's language acquisition (e.g., Rice et al., 1990; Van Evra, 1998; Wright et al., 2001). In particular, studies show that monolingual preschoolers can learn new vocabulary while viewing educational television programs (Rice & Woodsmall, 1988). For example, pioneering this work, Rice and Woodsmall (1988) found that preschoolers could learn novel object, action, and attribute words in a viewing situation, with 5-year-olds gaining more words than 3-year-olds. The easiest words to learn were object words (e.g., *artisan, vessel*) and attribute words (e.g., *malicious, radiant*). Children were shown a 12-minute program with 20 new novel words. With two exceptions, each target word appeared five times within a 6–7 minute period. The novel words appeared a total of 114 times in a 12-minute period. In all, the 5-year-olds learned on average 4.86 words out of 20 words, the 3-year-olds 1.56 words after viewing the 12-minute program once.

Another study also shows that preschoolers can learn new vocabulary through educational television. Preschoolers who watched ten preselected episodes of *Barney & Friends* showed significant gains in their vocabulary test scores on nouns from pretest to posttest (Singer & Singer, 1998). The chosen nouns were mostly part of the central theme and were repeated often throughout the episode.

Furthermore, Naigles et al. (1995) found that preschoolers who viewed ten episodes of *Barney & Friends* increased their understanding of familiar intransitive verbs (e.g., *come, go*). They learned that *come* and *go* cannot take an object in the same way as *bring* and *take*.

One cannot review the educational television literature without mentioning the early studies conducted on *Sesame Street*. Consistent *Sesame Street* viewing has also been associated with increased English vocabulary scores among monolingual children (Rice et al., 1990). Children between the ages of 3 and 3.5 who were frequent viewers, performed significantly better on the vocabulary test at age 5 than those who were not, controlling for initial vocabulary scores. While this study suggests that viewing *Sesame Street* influences vocabulary development, the authors acknowledge that the data are correlational and more evidence is necessary to establish causality.

Almost all of the studies on educational television viewing and children's language development have been conducted with monolingual children (e.g., Rice & Woodsmall, 1988; Rice et al., 1990). There have only been a few studies on English language learners. Uchikoshi (2006b) found no educational television effect on incidental vocabulary learning for bilingual Spanish-speaking ELL kindergartners. Vocabulary was measured with the Peabody Picture Vocabulary Test (Dunn & Dunn, 1997). A total of 150 children (70 girls, 80 boys), attending ten public schools in a large urban district located on the East Coast participated in the study. Based on a stratified random sampling, half of the students in six classrooms (51 children) were assigned to watch *Arthur* during school hours, while the other half in the same six classrooms (57 children) were assigned to watch *Between the Lions* during school hours. The children watched three episodes per week, for a total of 54 episodes during the school year. The *Arthur* television series are based on storybooks and children are exposed to various stories with moral points of interest to children. The characters in *Arthur* learn to make thoughtful decisions and resolve problems in each episode. *Between the Lions* is a skills oriented program with intent to instruct the viewers with early literacy skills, such as phonological awareness and decoding. The show puts more emphasis on text structure, individual words, and other print features. Vocabulary was not particularly emphasized in both shows. Results show that there was no increase in receptive vocabulary from either of these educational programs. However, this does not rule out that there were effects on the target vocabulary in the programs.

This finding supports past research (e.g., Levin et al., this volume; Patterson, 2002) that found that television does not provide incidental vocabulary learning. However, at the same time, this finding suggests that standardized measurement of vocabulary used in this study may not have been sensitive enough to capture the growth. Children were not tested on the vocabulary shown on the programs. Results may have been different if the assessment had used specific vocabulary covering the episodes that the children watched. In a study of 60 5-year-olds learning Dutch as a second language, children in the group that watched the multimedia version of a storybook showed significant increases in understanding vocabulary while the children in the group that read the onscreen static picture book of the same story did not (Verhallen, Bus, & de Jong, 2006). In this Dutch multimedia study, vocabulary was measured with 42 content words from the story. Hence, results may have been different for the *Arthur/Between the Lions* study if researcher-created intervention-specific words had been tested.

Baby Viewers

The above studies have mainly looked at preschool age children. However, with the introduction of *Baby Einstein* video tapes (The Baby Einstein Company, 2003) and cable television channels for infants as young as 6 months, babies are being exposed to television from an early age. The American Academy of Pediatrics (n.d.) recommends that children younger than 24 months should not be exposed to television. Yet, do these programs provide infants with an early start in language development as they claim? There are only a few studies on this topic. One study found mixed positive and negative associations between television and language learning (Linebarger & Walker, 2005), while another found that infants learn object labels better in live situations than from television (Grela, Krcmar, & Lin, 2004; Wartella & Richert, this volume).

The study that found a positive relationship report that *Dora the Explorer*, *Blue's Clues*, *Arthur*, *Clifford*, and *Dragon Tales* support vocabulary development and expressive language use (Linebarger & Walker, 2005). Parents were asked to keep a viewing log and if at least 25% of the sample reported watching a particular show on at least two different occasions, that program was chosen for analysis. Vocabulary was measured with the MacArthur Communicative Development Inventory and expressive language use was measured by the Early Childhood Inventory. Combined *Arthur* and *Clifford* viewers had 8.6 more vocabulary words at 30 months and an increase in the rate of vocabulary growth at 0.61 words per month as compared to nonviewers. Combined *Arthur* and *Clifford* viewers also had 1.10 more single and multiple utterances at 30 months than nonviewers. Combined *Dora the Explorer* and *Blue's Clues* viewers had 8.6 more words at 30 months and an increase in the vocabulary growth rate at 1.35 words per month as compared to nonviewers. Additionally, combined *Dora the Explorer* and *Blue's Clues* viewers had 1.78 more single and multiple utterances at 30 months than nonviewers. Although there were no advantages to vocabulary growth, watching *Dragon Tales* was associated with having 1.70 more single and multiple utterances at 30 months than nonviewers. The authors suggest the characters in *Dora the Explorer* and *Blue's Clues* actively label objects and seek participation and verbalization from the viewers. At the same time, *Arthur, Clifford,* and *Dragon Tales* have strong narratives with stimulating visuals. The viewers hear vocabulary and the definitions, and see the visual representations on the screen. This dual encoding may assist children around 2-years-old to pick up vocabulary through viewing.

Interestingly there were negative relationships between *Sesame Street, Teletubbies,* and vocabulary acquisition (Linebarger & Walker, 2005). The authors note that the children were not the target age audiences for *Sesame Street.* The target audience for *Sesame Street* is 2 years and older. Thus, the children in their study may have been too young to understand the program. Additionally, they suggest that *Teletubbies* does not provide a rich vocabulary environment. Many characters give only vocalizations, thus encouraging the viewers to vocalize instead of utter words. This finding is in line with Grela et al.'s (2004) finding that children younger than 2.5 years old are able to learn object labels better in a live situation than by watching *Teletubbies.*

Summary

Taken together, these studies provide evidence that children can learn about words and their meanings from educational television programs. Through visual and verbal processing, children can develop their vocabulary by watching television. However, as with children learning words in a natural setting with their caregivers, the dialogue shown on television needs to be suited for the target children, with effective visuals and repetition.

Literacy Development

Like vocabulary acquisition, there appears to be evidence of positive effects of educational television on other literacy-related skills. Literacy is a broad field also encompassing phonological awareness, letter naming, decoding, storytelling, and retelling. Hereafter, educational television's dual coding effect on these aspects of children's literacy development will be discussed.

Phonological Awareness and Decoding

Past research has shown educational television programs, in particular *Between the Lions*, to be an effective intervention for phonological awareness and letter identification development (Linebarger, 2000; Linebarger, Kosanic, Greenwood, & Doku, 2004; Prince, Grace, Linebarger, Atkinson, & Huffman, 2002). Linebarger and colleagues (Linebarger, 2000; Linebarger et al., 2004) investigated the effects of viewing *Between the Lions* on 164 kindergarten and first grade children. After watching 17 episodes, kindergarten viewers had significantly higher mean scores as well as greater rates of growth on phonological awareness tasks when compared to classmates who had not viewed *Between the Lions*. Additionally, kindergarten viewers had significantly higher mean scores and greater rates of growth on letter-sound correspondence tasks when compared to classmates who had not viewed the show.

This study was replicated with Spanish-speaking ELL kindergarten children (Uchikoshi, 2006a). After viewing 54 30-minute episodes of *Between the Lions*, the Spanish-speaking ELL children showed significantly steeper growth curves for elision and blending words areas of phonological awareness than the control group of Spanish-speaking ELL children who watched equal hours of *Arthur*. The tests used were from the Comprehensive Test of Phonological Processing (Wagner, Torgesen, & Rashotte, 1999). Many of the segments in *Between the Lions* focus on these two phonological awareness skills. For example, in "Gawain's Word," two knights carrying parts of the word (e.g., Knight *h* and Knight *ug*) joust and crash into each other to create one word (e.g., *hug*). Through visual and audio means, the child sees the two sounds merging. From the left side of the screen Knight *h* appears and starts running towards Knight *ug* who is coming from the right side of the screen. As the knights run towards each other, the child hears the sounds *h* and *ug* repeatedly. Concurrently, the children see the letters *h* and *ug* in the speech balloons that show what the knights are chanting. The chants of *h* and *ug* continue until the knights crash, at which point the child hears *hug* and sees the knights hugging as well as the word *hug* in big black font on a white speech balloon. My study supports one of the goals of the program, i.e., to improve phonological awareness.

Another study with older children in the Netherlands found that the development of decoding skills was promoted by watching subtitled foreign films (Koolstra, van der Voort, & van der Kamp, 1997). Two groups of children were followed for 3 years; one cohort beginning at grade 2 and the other beginning at grade 4. However, it should be noted that this study did not focus on educational television and collected television-viewing frequency counts through questionnaires. Children were asked how much time they spend watching television. Additionally, children's decoding skills were measured with a standardized test consisting of a list of 116 increasingly complex, unrelated words and not with the words that were shown on the subtitled foreign films. Although the study did not test the exact words that the children had seen on the subtitled foreign films, this study suggests that subtitles on television promote the development of reading skills.

Subtitling in the same language was also shown to lead to syllable and word reading improvement, particularly mono-syllables, with low income fourth and fifth graders in India (Kothari, Takeda, Joshi, & Pandey, 2002). In this study, experimental children were shown five subtitled Hindi film songs in each session, three sessions per week, for a period of 3 months. There were two control groups. One group saw the same Hindi film songs but without subtitles, and the other did not see any songs. The authors suggest that songs have some advantages above ordinary dialogue. Songs have many repetitions and many people want to know the lyrics to songs. Especially for the verses that contained repetitions, children could anticipate the lyrics and this may have allowed them to focus on the written word on the screen, thus enabling them to improve their decoding skills. Moreover, hearing the word and seeing the word simultaneously allows for stimulation of both the verbal and visual processing systems.

Subtitling, or having captions, in English were also shown to be effective for beginning readers (Linebarger, 2001). Children who had just completed second grade recognized more words when they had viewed *Pinwheel*, a Nickelodeon show aired during the early 1980s, with captions, suggesting that the combination of pictures, sounds, and captions helped the children to make a connection between speech and print. It allowed them to recognize visually the word and connect it to the pictures they saw on the screen and the sound effects they heard from the television. Exposure to a word on the television screen as a caption for four to five times spread over 4–6 minutes was enough to help children retain the written words up to 15 days later. Additionally, the authors report that captions helped children concentrate on the central theme of the story. When captions were not present, children retained incidental facts and not the central story elements.

Story Telling

Studies also report positive effects of television on story telling (e.g., Uchikoshi, 2005). Through verbal and visual cues, children can learn narrative structure and glean the main points of a story.

Spanish-speaking ELL kindergarten children were reported to learn narrative skills by viewing *Arthur*, a show that follows the traditional narrative structure with a beginning, conflict, and resolution (Uchikoshi, 2005). A group of children who viewed 108 15-minute episodes of *Arthur* throughout the school year showed significantly steeper growth curves for story structure and evaluation than the children who viewed equivalent hours of *Between the Lions.* Story structure includes abstract, introduction, orientation, character delineation, problem, resolution, and coda. These are elements that appear in each 15-minute episode of *Arthur* where Arthur faces a dilemma and finds a happy resolution. Evaluation, which signals the point of the story from the narrator's perspective, includes intensifiers, adjectives, negative or defeats of expectation, references to emotional states or cognition, references to physical states, intentions, causal markers, and words with high evaluative content. Much of this is shown through the various characters' words and actions. Thus, viewing well-structured narratives on television by looking at the animation and hearing the narration and dialogue assisted ELL children's development of their own narrative stories.

Television has also been shown to have an impact on written retellings. Beentjes and van der Voort (1991), comparing the written retellings of students who had read a print version of the story with those who had watched the video version of the same story, show that children who watched the film version recalled more scenes in their written retelling. Out of a total of nine scenes, the viewers reported an average of 7.37, while the readers reported an average of 6.50. They also made fewer errors than the children who read the story. The readers made an average of 3.61 errors, while the viewers had 1.74. However, although there were no significant differences in number of action verbs used in the retellings, children who read the story referred to a greater variety of action than the children who viewed the story. On average, the readers reproduced 55.33 different action verbs, while the viewers only used 46.16 different words. Additionally, children who read the story had detailed descriptions of story elements and made more specific references to story characters in their written retellings. The children in this study were in grades 4 through 6 in the Netherlands. This study suggests that watching the film version leads to more complete and more accurate story recall. On the other hand, reading the story leads to more specific and clearer essays.

Summary

Together, these studies provide evidence that children can develop their literacy skills, including phonological awareness, letter naming, decoding, storytelling, and retelling from television programs. Literacy learning from television can be explained by Paivio's dual coding theory. Verbal and visual cues from educational programs that are age and level appropriate can assist in literacy development. Through effects such as subtitling in the same language or in the child's language (when the language of the program is a foreign language to the child), children can practice their reading skills. By seeing written words and hearing someone read the word to them via the television is effective in assisting children to learn the alphabet and to decode the words. Additionally, by viewing well-written narratives, children, even ELL children, can learn narrating skills.

Conclusion

Can children learn language and literacy skills from television? The review of the literature suggests that it is possible for children to learn language and literacy skills from educational television. Through reinforcement and repetition by verbal and visual processing, television can facilitate the language and literacy learning for children, including ELL children. Past research shows that children can learn vocabulary, decoding skills, narrative skills, and retelling skills from television, particularly if that is also the focus of the program. If the program is highly focused on vocabulary, it can teach vocabulary. If word recognition is required to understand the program, it can support decoding skills. Thus, in order to be effective, educational television programs need to be tailored to the target population's language and literacy needs.

Given the popularity of television, more research also needs to be conducted on the pedagogical potential of television. Although television has been in many households for over 30 years, there is still a significant gap in the educational television literature, especially where it concerns its effects on children's language and literacy development. The media's role in helping children learn language and literacy skills can be especially helpful for ELL children who may otherwise not get the target language exposure (see also Bus et al., this volume). Nationally, the number of ELL students in public schools increased by approximately one million students in 6 years to a total of three million students in 1999–2000, representing approximately 7% of the national public school population (Meyer, Madden, & McGrath, 2005). However, most of the television research has been done with monolingual children. More research needs to be conducted on this rapidly increasing population.

There is a popular misconception that television cannot add any linguistic value. It is true that it should not be the only tool to teach language and literacy to children and it cannot replace the learning that takes place in schools and homes. Yet, educational television has the potential to reach all children and it can motivate children to learn. Watching educational television can assist these children to reinforce and expand the language and literacy instruction they have received both at home and at school.

References

American Academy of Pediatrics (n.d.). *Television and the family.* Retrieved May 19, 2007 from www.aap.org/family/tv1.htm.
Anderson, D.R., Huston, A.C., Schmitt, K.L., Linebarger, D.L., & Wright, J.C. (2001). Early childhood television viewing and adolescent behavior: The recontact study. *Monographs of the Society for Research in Child Development, 66* (1, Serial No. 264).

Beentjes, J.W.J., & van der Voort, T.H.A. (1991). Children's written accounts of televised and printed stories. *Educational Technology Research and Development, 39,* 15–26.

Brown, J., Cramond, J., & Wilde, R. (1974). Displacement effects of television and the child's functional orientation to media. In J.G. Blumler & E. Katz (Eds.), *The uses of mass communications* (pp. 93–112). Beverly Hills, CA: Sage Publications.

Crawley, A.M., Anderson, D.R., Santomero, A., Wilder, A., Williams, M., Evans, M.K., et al., (2002). Do children learn how to watch television? The impact of extensive experience with *Blue's Clues* on preschool children's television viewing behavior. *Journal of Communication, 52,* 264–280.

Dunn, L.M., & Dunn, L.M. (1997). *Peabody Picture Vocabulary Test* (3rd ed.). Circle Pines, MN: American Guidance Service.

Frith, M.K. (Producer) (2000). *Between the Lions* [Television series]. Boston, MA: WGBH.

Grela, B.G., Krcmar, M. & Lin, Y.J. (2004). *Can television help toddlers acquire new words?* Retrieved June 11, 2007 from www.speechpathology.com/articles/article_detail. asp?article_id=72.

Hill-Scott, K. (2001). Industry standards and practices. In D.G. Singer & J.L. Singer (Eds.), *Handbook of children and the media* (pp. 605–620). Thousand Oaks, CA: Sage.

Hoff-Ginsberg, E. (1986). Function and structure in maternal speech: Their relation to the child's development of syntax. *Developmental Psychology, 22,* 155–163.

Koolstra, C.M., van der Voort, T.H.A., & van der Kamp, L.J.T. (1997). Television's impact on children's reading comprehension and decoding skills: A 3-year panel study. *Reading Research Quarterly, 32,* 128–152.

Kothari, B., Takeda, J., Joshi, A., & Pandey, A. (2002). Same language subtitling: A butterfly for literacy? *International Journal of Lifelong Education, 21,* 55–66.

Lemish, D., & Rice, M. (1986). Television as a talking picture book: A prop for language acquisition. *Journal of Child Language, 13,* 251–274.

Linebarger, D.L. (2000). *Summative evaluation of "Between the Lions": A final report to WGBH Educational Foundation.* Boston: WGBH.

Linebarger, D.L. (2001). Learning to read from television: The effects of using captions and narration. *Journal of Educational Psychology, 93,* 288–298.

Linebarger, D.L., Kosanic, A.Z., Greenwood, C.R., & Doku, N.S. (2004). Effects of viewing the television program *Between the Lions* on the emergent literacy skills of young children. *Journal of Educational Psychology, 96,* 297–308.

Linebarger, D.L., & Walker, D. (2005). Infants' and toddlers' television viewing and language outcomes. *American Behavioral Scientist, 48,* 624–645.

Neuman, S.B. (1988). The displacement effect: Assessing the relation between television viewing and reading performance. *Reading Research Quarterly, 23,* 414–440.

Neuman, S.B. (1991). *Literacy in the television age: The myth of the TV effect.* Norwood, NJ: Ablex.

Meyer, D., Madden, D., & McGrath, D.J. (2005, July 16). Elementary and secondary education English language learner students in U.S. public schools: 1994 and 2000. *Educational Statistics Quarterly, 6.* Retrieved May 19, 2007, from http://nces.ed.gov/programs/quarterly/vol_6/6_3/3_4.asp.

Naigles, L.R., Singer, J., Singer, D., Jean-Louis, B., Sells, D., & Rosen, C. (1995). *Barney & Friends as education and entertainment—the language study: Barney says, "Come, go think, know."* Hartford: Connecticut Public Broadcasting.

Paivio, A. (1986). *Mental Representations.* New York: Oxford University Press.

Patterson, J. (2002). Relationships of expressive vocabulary to frequency of reading and television experience among bilingual toddlers. *Applied Psycholinguistics, 23,* 493–508.

Prince, D.L., Grace, C., Linebarger, D.L., Atkinson, R., & Huffman, J.D. (2002). A *Final Report to Mississippi Educational Television.* Retrieved February 29, 2004, from http://pbskids.org/lions/about/pdf/BTL-Mississippi.pdf.

Rice, M. (1983). The role of television in language acquisition. *Developmental Review, 3,* 211–224.

Rice, M.L., & Haught, P.L. (1986). Motherese of Mr. Rogers: A description of the dialogue of educational television programs. *Journal of Speech and Hearing Disorders, 41,* 282–287.

Rice, M.L., Huston, A.C., Truglio, R., & Wright, J.C. (1990). Words from "Sesame Street": Learning vocabulary while viewing. *Developmental Psychology, 26,* 421–428.

Rice, M.L., & Woodsmall, L. (1988). Lessons from television: Children's word learning when viewing. *Child Development, 59*, 420–429.

Rideout, V., & Hamel, E. (2006, May). *The media family: Electronic media in the lives of infants, toddlers, preschoolers, and their parents.* Menlo Park, CA: Kaiser Family Foundation.

Salomon, G. (1981). *Communication and education.* Beverly Hills, CA: Sage.

Singer, D., & Singer, J. (1998). Barney & Friends as entertainment and education: Evaluating the quality and effectiveness of a television series for preschool children. In J. Asamen & G. Berry (Eds.), *Research paradigms, television, and social behavior* (pp. 205–367). Thousand Oaks, CA: Sage Publications.

Snow, C.E. (1972). Mother's speech to children learning language. *Child Development, 43*, 549–565.

Snow, C.E. (1984). Parent–child interactions and the development of communicative ability. In R.L. Schiefelbusch & J. Pickar (Eds.), *Communicative competence: Acquisition and intervention* (pp. 69–108). Baltimore: University Park Press.

Baby Einstein Company (2003). *Baby Einstein* [DVD series]. Burbank, CA: Buena Visa Home Entertainment.

Uchikoshi, Y. (2005). Narrative development in bilingual kindergarteners: Can Arthur help? *Developmental Psychology, 41*, 464–478.

Uchikoshi, Y. (2006a). Early reading development in bilingual kindergarteners: Can educational television help? *Scientific Studies of Reading, 10*, 89–120.

Uchikoshi, Y. (2006b). English vocabulary development in bilingual kindergartners: What are the best predictors? *Bilingualism: Language and Cognition, 9*, 33–49.

Van Evra, J. (1998). *Television and child development.* Mahwah, NJ: Erlbaum.

Verhallen, M.J.A.J., Bus, A.G., & de Jong, M.T. (2006). The promise of multimedia stories for kindergarten children at risk. *Journal of Educational Psychology, 98*, 410–419.

Vygotsky, L.S. (1978). *Mind in society: The development of higher psychological processes.* Cambridge, MA: Harvard University Press.

Wagner, R.K., Torgesen, J.K., & Rashotte, C.A. (1999). *Comprehensive test of phonological processing.* Austin, TX: Pro-Ed.

Wells, G. (1985). *Language development in the pre-school years. Language at home and at school (Vol. 2).* Cambridge, UK: Cambridge University Press.

Wright, J.C., Huston, A.C., Murphy, K.C., St. Peters, M., Piñon, M., Scantlin, R., et al. (2001). The relations of early television viewing to school readiness and vocabulary of children from low-income families: The early window project. *Child Development, 72*, 1347–1366.

13

"Let's *do* the Computer Story Again, Nana"

A Case Study of how a 2-Year-Old and his Grandmother Shared Thinking Spaces during Multiple Shared Readings of an Electronic Story

Linda D. Labbo

I watched from across the room as my 2-year-old grandson Griffin carefully settled into his Grandfather's big leather chair with two toys. He placed one toy, a favorite stuffed, red Elmo character, at his side. He placed the other toy, a small, yellow plastic computer, on his outstretched legs. He opened the monitor of the hinged toy laptop and pretended to turn on the computer by saying, "Click! [pause] Bong!" (The sound of an Apple computer being turned on). Next, he moved his Elmo toy onto his lap, nestling it safely between his tummy and the computer keyboard. "Can you see it?" he whispered softly into Elmo's ear. "See up here?" He pointed to the opened computer screen before continuing his pretend conversation. "Let's do a story together. Would you like to see a little story with me?"

I was immediately impressed with Griffin's playful behavior, which indicated to me his growing knowledge of the functions and forms of computer meaning making. However, I was also intrigued by the words he had used in his pretend conversation. In the past, I recalled that when Griffin sat in his Grandfather's chair to read one of his favorite books to his Elmo stuffed animal, he had consistently asked, "Would you like to *read* a book with me?" Yet, when he'd talked about computer-related story reading, he used phrases such as, "Let's *do* a story" and "Would you like to *see* a little story?"

I wondered how Griffin's and my ongoing, shared interactions with electronic books during his weekly visits to my house might be providing him with unique occasions to develop language and literacy. What was he learning about stories, language, and the new literacies that are involved in reading electronic stories? It was at the precise moment when I overheard Griffin's pretend conversation with his Elmo stuffed animal that I decided to join the ranks of other researchers, who are also parents or grandparents, (e.g., Baghban, 1984; Bissex, 1980; Butler, 1975; Crago & Crago, 1976; Smith, 2001;

White, 1954) by conducting a short term case study that focused on what and how Griffin was learning about language and literacy as we read the same electronic story when he visited my home once a week for 10 weeks.

What Do We Know about the Nature of Young Children's Early Literacy Development with Various Forms of Media?

Journalists love to opine about the "end of print" in traditional forms. For example, some suggest that eBooks usurp the role of the parent by reading aloud the story and prompting children's responses. Others have noted the positive influence of televised media (Gladwell, 2000) and electronic books (Labbo & Kuhn, 2000) on young children's literacy development. Clearly parents, caregivers, researchers, and educators are divided on whether or not to introduce infants, toddlers, and preschoolers to computer technologies. Here, I provide a brief overview of relevant research about features of media that support or do not support young children's early literacy development. I organize this into two: Preschool Educational Television and Electronic Books.

Preschool Educational Television

Television has been touted as a *low involvement* media that fosters passive viewing among young children. For young children, television is primarily a visual medium that is supported by sounds, music, and talking. The frequently held assumption is that youngsters will become mesmerized, staring at a television screen for hours and mentally zoning out as they view a quickly moving series of choppy visual images, zooming video, and harsh sounds effects that bombard and overwhelm their senses. Summarizing research conducted in the 1960s and 1970s on how preschoolers watch television, Uchikoshi (this volume) reports that preschoolers routinely distribute their attention between other activities and television viewing. They do not stare at the screen for hours. They primarily watch programs with short, strategic glimpses at the most informative parts of the televised shows.

This strategic viewing allows them to make sense of the key ideas and content. Other research (Kirkorian & Anderson, in press) on what parts of the screen preschoolers attend to suggest that what's in the middle of the viewing screen is the most compelling location for displaying important content. Additionally, when text and animations are presented simultaneously on the television, youngsters tend to focus exclusively on the animations. Distance between words and graphics or animations also serve as a distracter from the printed word for younger viewers. Are the lessons learned from what young children attend to on television screens relevant for understanding their interactions with electronic books delivered on computer screens?

Linebarger (2006) explored young children's multiple viewings of educational television programs (e.g., *Sesame Street, Clifford the Big Red Dog, Dora* the *Explorer*, *Blue's Clues*, *Barney and Friends*, *Teletubbies*, *Arthur and Friends*, and *Dragon Tales*) in an attempt to determine the programs' contributions to infants' and toddlers' linguistic development, expressive language use, and vocabulary size. She found that specific types of communication strategies inherent to each program inhibit or promote infants' and toddlers' use of language. Televised programs such as *Arthur and Friends* and *Clifford the Big Red Dog*, offer coherent content (e.g., follow a tightly structured story narrative framework), are engaging (e.g., have visual appeal), and are word rich (e.g., utilize vocabulary terms that are embedded in the meaningful conversation of characters), in ways that contribute positively to early language development. These findings have implications for selecting age-appropriate media in other venues besides television. To be effectively educational and appropriately entertaining to toddlers, electronic stories may also need to offer coherent storylines, present engaging visual content, and utilize meaningful vocabulary words within meaningful social and communicative situations.

Other televised programs, such as *Dora the Explorer* and *Blue's Clues*, that offer participation by prompting responses from viewers, providing definitions after posing a question, and presenting animations or visualizations of vocabulary words, are likely to support vocabulary acquisition among young viewers. Additionally, *Blue's Clues* has a deliberately slower pace than other televised educational programs. The program focuses on a single storyline and the goal is to find clues to solve a mystery presented by one live actor who interacts with various animated characters. Children who watch *Blue's Clues* show significant growth in problem solving and flexible thinking. Steve, the main character, serves as a caregiver on the screen, one who supports young viewers' thinking. He poses questions, waits several seconds for young viewers to grapple intellectually with the issue, and then provides the answer along with a rationale and explanation. As youngsters view the same show over several days, they begin to appropriate Steve's thinking. They *predict* what will happen next or they provide the answer to a clue that is based on knowledge acquired in previous viewings. Interestingly, the young children act as if the answer was completely the result of their own thinking, not the result of Steve's modeling. Thus, Steve's scaffolding was made available to children through repetitive viewings. The repetition made not only the answer to specific questions memorable, but it made visible the thinking process involved in problem solving.

Additionally, writers of early shows in the *Blue's Clues* series deliberately fashioned the type of clues presented for children's consideration to be easy and obvious. They did so in an effort to build children's confidence and cognitive inclinations towards problem solving. Later in the series, writers shifted the clues to become more of an adventure of discovery that involved more complex thinking. Children who were regular viewers were able to make the adjustments and engage in higher-level problem solving.

On the other hand, Linebarger (2006) posits that programs such as *Barney and Friends* and *Teletubbies*, which present loosely organized narrative structures, organize the show into quickly paced magazine segments of content, provide little or no reinforcement for child verbal engagement, and do not consistently provide character demonstrations of communication skills, may negatively impact infants' and toddlers' language development. She notes that *Barney and Friends* did support young children's vocabulary acquisition when an adult also watched and talked about the program. Indeed, Desmond, Singer, Singer, Calam, and Calimore (1985) note that parent/child co-viewing of televised programs fosters children's abilities to make sense of storylines and complex messages.

Electronic Books

Recent reports indicate that 70% of families with children in America have at least one computer (Woodard & Gridina, 2000). Digital versions of stories that are presented on computer screens, are dynamic in nature and may include some or all of the following interactive multimedia features: printed text, narration, graphics, animations, movie clips, music, sound effects, hypertextual links, or highlighted text (Bus, de Jong, & Verhallen, 2006; McKenna, 1998). Bus, de Jong and Verhallen (2006) note that CD-ROM talking books, electronic versions of books delivered on CD-ROMs, may be used as a joint activity between caregivers and children at home or as a child's independent and exploratory activity. In other words, multimedia features of electronic books may scaffold children's independent story comprehension, if they are able to listen to text read aloud, view animations that are cohesively related to story content, and navigate through the page screens by clicking on directional arrows.

Research indicates that CD-ROM storybooks can positively impact young children's emerging literacy development (Bus et al., 2006; Greenlee-Moore & Smith, 1996; Labbo & Kuhn, 2000; Turbill, 2001; see also chapters throughout volume). Chera and Wood (2003) conducted a 4-week study on effect of computerized animated CD-ROM stories on the phonological, letter sounds, and word onsets awareness of 3- to 6-year-old children. Daily ten-minute exposure to the story, as presented in animations that were accompanied by narrated text, resulted in improvement in all areas for the intervention group. Ricci and Beal 7-year-old students who either heard the story, viewed a video of the story, passively viewed a CD-ROM of the story on a computer, or participated in an interactive CD-ROM version. Students in the audio-only treatment did not perform as well as students in other treatment groups on a story knowledge questionnaire. The authors posit that students' comprehension is affected by the manner in which the narrative is presented. Young children benefit from a simultaneous presentation of visual, audio, and print. For the most part, research on electronic stories has focused on understanding their impact on the story comprehension of preschoolers (de Jong & Bus, 2002), first-grade students (Ricci & Beale, 2002), and students in the primary grades (McKenna, 1998).

Notable is Smith's (2001) case study research of how her son, James, spent a year (age $2\frac{1}{2}$ to $3\frac{1}{2}$) sharing CD-ROM storybooks with his mother. She records how his interactions with the hypertext configuration of electronic stories influenced his playtime and social behaviors. In fact, by paying systematic attention to James' playtime behaviors, she was able to gain insights into his understandings of technological concepts and the content of the electronic stories. This fascinating study serves as a starting point for my own case study research into my 2-year-old grandson's experiences with multiple exposures to one electronic story.

A Case Study

In this case study, I explored how my 2-year-old grandson made meaning of an electronic story. Specifically, I asked, "How does the nature of meaning-making change over ten read-aloud experiences during a three-month period?"

The study occurred in two phases. Phase one involved the selection and analysis of the content and multimedia features of an electronic story. Phase two involved data collection and analysis of the adult and child's conversations while reading the eStory. Data for this study consisted of videotapes, transcripts, observational and reflective notes, and data analysis charts.

Phase 1: Selecting and Analyzing the eStory's Content and Interactive Features

Following guidelines and hunches derived from research on television media and electronic story features that foster positive language and literacy effects for toddlers, I selected an online electronic story titled, *Elmo Goes to the Doctor* (www.sesameworkshop.org/sesamestreet/stories/flash.php?contentId=108867, retrieved January 20, 2007). I conducted a content analysis to summarize the narrative and to determine if the following multimedia characteristics and qualities were present in the electronic story: coherent content, engaging visual content, meaningful vocabulary, communicative situations, prompts for participation, control of the pace of the story, models of thinking, and ease of navigation.

SUMMARY OF THE STORY

Elmo Goes to the Doctor is a humorously and sensitively told slice of life story that addresses young children's concerns about going to the doctor. The story unfolds through a series of events that involve friendship, shared experiences, humor, and gentle text that unfold in a non-threatening environment. The focalization or point of view is designed to pull the reader into the story. In other words, readers get a sense that they are accompanying Elmo on his visit through visual techniques that replicate cinematic camera angles. For example, Elmo's cartoon friends look directly at the viewers, not at Elmo, as the viewers go about discovering why each character needs to see the doctor. Cinematic effects also invite readers to enter virtually into the doctor's office environment. For example, a video camera-type span across the waiting room suggests that viewers are also moving across the room. Viewers virtually go through a door, hearing it open and close. The gentle ending of the story, a screen that depicts Elmo taking a nap in his room, is reminiscent of Peter's Rabbit's experience in the classic English fairy tale, *Peter Cotton Tail*, when Peter is tucked into bed with a cup of chamomile tea.

MULTIMEDIA CHARACTERISTICS AND QUALITIES

The story is presented screen-by-screen, and not in a way that resembles the two-page spread of a story. Other electronic books have the visual onscreen appearance of a two-page open spread of a picture book. As McKenna (1998) predicted, over time the need to constrain electronic stories into a book format will be diminished because new multimedia forms of story telling will ultimately burst out of the page and onto the screen. However, the length of sentences and number of words per screen are similar to preschool children's literature.

Overall, my content analysis of *Elmo Goes to the Doctor* suggests that it is a "considerate" electronic story (Labbo & Kuhn, 2000). Considerate electronic storybooks include coherence among a tightly structured story narrative that is supported by multimedia. In other words, interactive animations are congruent with the story in a fundamental way (e.g., main characters state related information that is not in the text, animations carry out an action that is logical to the story). Stannard (1996) used the phrase polysemic to describe how texts "signal and support multiple meanings through a single set or combination of words and other symbols" (p. 12). The story also has engaging visual content that includes static graphics and charming animations. The key story actions follow guidelines drawn from educational preschool television research by occurring primarily in the middle of the screen. Supplemental actions and information occur in the outer edges of the screen.

I selected an electronic story that embedded meaningful words and thoughts that relate to the story. The electronic story also allows for the adult or child to have some control over the pace at which the story is presented. Drawing cues from *Blue's Clues*, televised episodes in which the main character, Steve, asks prompting questions and then provides a significant wait time before moving on, I wanted to be able to control the pace of the story. I wanted to be able to pause at key story events to make comments or to ask Griffin questions. Thus, the story I selected did not read the text aloud. Text was presented at the bottom of the screen or in talk or thought bubbles that appeared by characters' heads. The story did not move forward automatically without some decision by the reader to click on a green arrow to change the scene. This feature also allowed me to have some control over the pace with which the story proceeded. Additionally, the text boxes themselves provide prompts to be read aloud. For example, on the third screen/page of the story, the text reads "Elmo sees some friends in the waiting room": clicking on the green arrow results in new text appearing in the text box. "Why are they at the doctor's office?": clicking on the green arrow results in new text appearing in the text box. "Click on Elmo's friends to find out."

For the most part, hotspots, points of interactivity on screen, were integral to the storyline. All of the above mentioned components adhere to McKenna's (1998) recommendation that effective electronic books should provide readers with intuitive or easy navigation. Taken as a whole, *Elmo Goes to the Doctor* consists of nine screens, 17 automatic animations, 40 text boxes, 27 navigational arrows, and 48 hotspots that result in 48 animations, 26 sounds, and 25 additional text boxes. A total of 96% of the multimedia features and hotspots are congruent with the story.

Phase 2: Collecting and Analyzing Data

Data for this study consisted of videotapes, transcripts, researcher reflective notes, observational field notes, and data analysis charts. Data set: electronic story reading episodes included: video of ten eStory readings (timed), once a week for 10 weeks; ten transcripts describing what was occurring on the computer screen, supplemented with adult/child talk and actions; researcher observational and reflective notes that were written while viewing the videos and before transcription.

DATA ANALYSIS

I decided to use the focus of topics of discussion (TD) as the unit for analysis because I wanted to examine which elements on the screen we targeted. Thus, I could capture a variety of topics for discussion that might range from animated actions of characters to the meanings of words presented in the text. I coded all of the utterances and conversational turn taking (Sinclair & Coulthard, 1975) that occurred around one TD as message units (Mus) (Roser & Martinez, 2004) that I identified in transcripts by speaker (Grandma or Griffin). This fine-grained level of coding also allowed me to determine how many message units related to content or interactive features of the electronic story.

Continued data analysis of shared electronic book readings included creating conceptual categories derived from the constant comparative method (Glaser & Strauss, 1967) within the data collected for the first reading. I utilized the initial categories to analyze data for the second electronic book reading, also noting any new categories. This process continued across the ten reading events in order to gain insights into how the nature of book reading changed, or did not change, over time. I created a profile of each shared reading event (Sipe & Brightman, 2006) by noting on a chart the numbers and percent of Grandmother's or Griffin's talk that related to each conceptual category. Thus, I could trace the nature of any differences that occurred throughout the multiple readings of the electronic storybook.

Findings

Martinez and Roser (1985) have identified shared storybook reading from three perspectives: a book, a child, and a more capable reader. Shared electronic story multiple readings also consist of three key components: an eStory, a child, and a more capable reader whose interactions are mitigated by interactivity and multimedia. Figure 13.1 illustrates the convergence of influences that result in an act of mediation when a more capable reader and a child interact with an electronic story.

The term *mediation* is based on a pragmatist/sociohistorical framework that recognizes the mutual influences of participants within specific social learning environments. The environment, the participants, and the objects within the environment mediate what is learned and how it is learned as the participants (adult and child) collaboratively build knowledge that is scaffolded by the objects (cultural tools, multimedia, interactivity) as well as

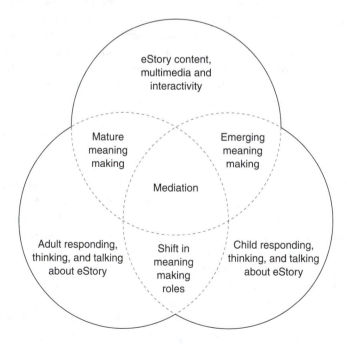

Figure 13.1 Multiple adult/child shared eBook readings as mediation.

cultural forces at play (what is valued or sanctioned, and how the events are interpreted) (Salomon & Perkins, 1998). Multiple adult and child shared readings of an electronic story, that is presented within a computer screen environment, rely on multimedia components to function as cognitive tools (Jonassen, Davidson, Collins, Campbell, & Haag, 1995). Fisch, Shulman, Akerman, and Levin (2002) found that parent–child readings of online storybooks provided ample occasions for labeling, making life connections, predicting, and explaining story events.

In the current study, the meaning making tools helped the participants, Griffin and me, to determine the direction, content, and substance of our learning. We shaped and were shaped by the multimedia, cognitive tools through a process of negotiated mediation. The next parts of the chapter describe how, over time, the key leadership roles of the adult as the primary meaning maker shifted through a transfer of authority for meaning making to the child.

Adult Roles in Meaning Making of eStory

During the first three readings of the eStory, I assumed the role of a more capable, mature meaning maker, who interpreted the story of Elmo's world as it appeared on the screen. During shared readings I attempted to reconcile Elmo's world with the world of my grandson. As I read the electronic story, I created a holistic interpretation of onscreen events that mingled the author's craft (linguistic representation of thoughts) with my own linguistic representations that transformed into cognitive and affective responses for Griffin and myself. Images of (visual graphic components) and animations (multimodal components) on screen allowed me to notice, discuss, describe, and interpret the different aspects of the story. As I invited my grandson to step into the story with me, to some degree the world we entered was transformed by our presence. Other voices and minds of the behind-the-scenes craftsmen, animators, sound effects experts, story boarders, directors, illustrators, and programming experts contributed to the way we experienced the unfolding story.

Table 13.1 describes the six roles I played to interpret and negotiate meaning with and for Griffin. The six roles to support Griffin's ability to make sense of the eStory include (1) Focuser, (2) Questioner, (3) Connector, (4) Navigator, (5) Pacer, and (6) Relationship builder. I focused his attention on aspects of the multimedia story components that I deemed relevant. For example, at times the subtle animated actions of a character illustrated the mood of the story or a character's state of mind. On other occasions I was a Questioner who drew Griffin's attention to vocabulary words and extended his ability to describe actions or sound effects revealed through multimedia. As a Connector, I helped Griffin think beyond the story and to connect story events with events in his own life. For example, when we viewed an aquarium

Table 13.1 Adult roles of first three shared eStory readings

Role	Description	Example
Focuser	Drawing attention to multimedia or text	Pointing "Look at this." "See these words?" "That's a funny dance"
Questioner	Asking for Labeling, describing, identifying, predicting, Inferencing	"Where is Elmo?" "How does he feel?" "What's the nurse wearing?" "What will happen next?" "Why did Elmo wish that?"
Connector	Thinking beyond the story through text-to-life and intertextual connections	"You sit in your car seat just like Elmo sits in his car seat."
Navigator	Demonstrating and/or sharing the mouse to interact with the story metacognitively	"We click this arrow to go to the next screen." "Let's click this to see what happens next."
Pacer	Gauging interest, following e-prompts, dwelling or moving on in the eStory. Providing answer	"Do you want to see more on this screen?" "Let's learn more in this room scene before we move on to the next scene."
Relationship builder	Engaging affectively in response to eStory	Shared hugs, smiles, performance reading.

sitting on a bookshelf in Elmo's doctor's waiting room, I saw an opportunity to help Griffin make a connection with his life experiences.

NANA: [Points to an animated swimming fish.] What's that, Griffin?
GRIFFIN: Nemo.
NANA: It is a fish like Nemo on the movie you like to watch, isn't it? He's sorta' orangy colors. What do the fish live in?
GRIFFIN: 'quarium.
NANA: That's right, smart boy. An aquarium just like the one you got for your birthday, remember?
GRIFFIN: Uh huh [yes—leans back and strokes Nana's hair]. (Transcript 1)

As a Navigator and Pacer I modeled for Griffin how to utilize interactive features of the eStory. Finally, as a Relationship Builder, I built on Griffin's affective stance towards reading storybooks. We continued to snuggle, laugh, and share moments of mirth related to building Griffin's enjoyment of reading making both on the page and on the screen.

Adult/Child's Shifting Roles in Meaning Making of an eStory Over Time

Initially, when Griffin wasn't sure of an answer to my questions, he would repeat them, verbatim. This was an action on his part that in turn prompted me to provide the answer. When asked to do so, he would provide labels for objects, descriptions of actions, and echoes of sounds. On occasion he would spontaneously mimic the actions of characters on screen or move rhythmically to music. During the final two readings of the eStory, Griffin and I both assumed the roles that I had previously taken in the initial read alouds; however he frequently assumed the role of the guide or leader through the story by determining which hotspots to select and which events to discuss. Table 13.2 describes the seven roles we played to negotiate meaning: Co-Questioner, Co-Answerer, Co-Connector, Co-Navigator, Co-Pacer, Relationship builder, and Celebrator.

It is worth noting that Griffin began to use the language that I had previously used in interpreting the story during our earlier readings in subsequent

Table 13.2 Adult/child roles in the last two shared eStory readings

Role	Description	Example
Co-Questioner	Asking for Labeling, describing, identifying, predicting, inferencing	"Where is Elmo?" "How does he feel?" "What's the nurse wearing?" "What will happen next?" "Why did Elmo wish that?"
Co-Answerer	Providing answers Adult-generated questions or child-generated questions	"That's a nurse. I know she has that white hat." "That's a stettosoap [*sic*]."
Co-Connector	Thinking beyond the story through text-to-life and intertextual connections	"I sit in my car seat just like Elmo sits in his car seat."
Co-Navigator	Sharing the mouse	"Okay, click on that one." "Where to next?
Co-Pacer	Gauging interest, following e-prompts, dwelling or moving on in the eStory.	"I want to see more on this screen?" "Let's go on." "No, I don't want to see that one [animated hotspot]."
Relationship builder	Engaging affectively in response to eStory	Shared hugs, smiles, snuggles, laughter, exaggerated performance reading.
Celebrator	Noticing child's accomplishments with meaning making and new literacies	"Wow, that was a great prediction!" "You're so smart. How did you know what to click on to see that toy pop up?"

readings of the electronic story. For example, on initial readings I had asked Griffin to name (provide a label) for the nurse character, to describe what the nurse was wearing, and to make a connection between the animated figure on screen to the nurse he knows from his own doctor's office. In the last two readings, Griffin labeled the nurse, described her uniform, and made a connection to the nurse he knows without any prompting or questioning from me.

GRIFFIN: That's the nurse Nana [pointing to the screen]. She's got her a white hat on her, like Ms. Judy at my's [sic] doctors. (Transcript 4)

At the onset of the tenth and final shared reading of the electronic story, as Griffin came running across the room to sit on my lap, he began "predicting," in a breathless rush of words, what he would be seeing and hearing on the computer screen.

GRIFFIN: Elmo's riding to doctors with mommy and his friends are there and the nurse is there and there's toys like my's [sic] toys at my's [sic] doctors and he's got tickles on his tummys [sic] and his laughs [sic]. (Transcript 5)

Shift in Roles: The total number of utterances made by Griffin (G) and myself (N for his nickname for me, Nana) remained fairly stable over the course of the ten readings. As depicted in Table 13.3, the first reading generated 285 total utterances and the tenth reading generated a total of 260 utterances. The interesting and subtle shift in patterns occurred in the percent of utterances made by the adult and the child, a shift across ten readings that denotes a decrease of 15% for the adult and an increase of 15% for the child. This change in percentage of utterances indicates an exchange in the roles of mediating the story meaning that occurred over time. Initially, the more

Table 13.3 Number of message unit utterances by Grandmother and Griffin during five multiple readings of *Elmo Goes to the Doctor* electronic story

Reading #	1		2		3		4		5		6		7		8		9		10	
Speaker	N	G	N	G	N	G	N	G	N	G	N	G	N	G	N	G	N	G	N	G
Utterances	150	135	151	137	141	142	145	149	137	151	130	140	111	154	120	163	110	167	98	162
Total utterances	285		288		283		294		288		270		265		283		277		260	
Percent of talk	53	47	53	47	50	50	49	51	48	52	48	52	42	47	52	47	40	60	38	62

Notes
N = Nana (Griffin's name for Grandmother).
G = Griffin.

capable reader provided most of the observations and prompts, while the child consistently responded to or repeated questions raised by the adult. During the final reading, the child took the lead by co-leading or by leading through making comments or asking questions about the story.

Discussion

OBSERVATIONS ABOUT THE eSTORY

Elmo Visits the Doctor seems to fit well with *Sesame Street*'s philosophy of inviting adults to co-participate in entertainment experiences with children. The eStory appears to have been culturally interpreted, through animations, music, sound effects, and text in ways that closely align with Griffin's experiences in visiting the doctor and the experiences of other children who are from middle to high SES families. It is unclear how well the story might be culturally interpreted by adults and children from other nations or those from lower SES families.

PACING MATTERS

Part of the eStory proceeded at its own pace; however, there were ample occasions for pausing, selecting, predicting, responding to onscreen prompts, and asking our own questions. The design of the eStory allowed us, the viewers, to determine to some extent the pace through which the story was read. This feature, unlike many other eBooks on the market, allowed me to slow or quicken the pace, based on Griffin's level of interest. I recommend that authors and publishers of eBooks that are intended for shared readings with toddlers build in similar moments for pausing, thinking, and discussing.

PLAYFUL RESPONSES

Griffin demonstrated his growing understanding of the content and contexts of electronic stories in various decontextualized ways during text-to-life connections. He talked about eStory events while giving his Elmo stuffed animal a check-up with his toy medical kit. When he used a toy stethoscope to listen to Elmo's heart, Griffin repeated a sound effect he'd heard in the eStory, "Elmo, I hear bumpity, bumpity, bumpity, bump like a little drum. Do you want to hear it?" On a visit to his own doctor's office, Griffin commented on how the toys in the waiting room were like the toys in the electronic story. Like Smith's (2001) son, Griffin playfully explored and expressed his understanding of electronic stories in various settings.

In closing, when Griffin and I share a story in the pages of a book or on the computer screen, we share a thinking space with each other and with the authors, illustrators, and other craftsmen who work together to create the stories we read. As the more capable reader, I enrich Griffin's experiences and help him learn how to enter into a story world by thinking aloud, wondering, and inviting him to begin weaving his own experiences and insights into the story. In addition, we read the stories for entertainment. We share an affective bond of laughter, comfort, attachment, and appreciation for wonderful stories. However, when reading electronic stories, the shared experience is transformed to some degree by the convergence of the multimedia we encounter as we mediate meaning. The richness of the animations, sound, and cinematic effects provide unique opportunities for me, as the adult and more capable reader, to provide descriptive language of the characters' appearance, actions, reactions, and moods. Over time, my grandson has been able to appropriate my words and my strategies, making them his own as he comments on and points to multimedia actions that he observes on screen. There are also unique occasions for Griffin to gain new literacies that include strategic navigation through hotspots and changing the screen by clicking on arrows with the computer mouse or touchpad. By the tenth shared reading, Griffin had taken responsibility for navigating through the story at a pace that suited his interests.

Two-year-old Griffin and his peers will enter kindergarten knowing that computers are unique spaces for thinking, communicating, and seeking entertainment. Literacy educators of the present and the future will soon be teaching a generation of students who do not know what it's like to live in a world without the presence of computers. Clearly, with the growing presence of computers in the lives of very young children, we need more research in this area. Despite some reservations, most parents, caregivers, and educators are interested in finding ways to utilize engaging electronic stories to entertain and introduce young children to print-based and new literacies. Electronic story publishers would do well to take recommendations to allow the control of pacing and the option for parental reading aloud of text to heart. As the format of eStories continues to blur the distinctions between stories told on paper and stories told on screens, educators and researchers must consider how computer technologies impact the ways in which adults and children mediate meaning with multimedia. We must also grapple with how to create learning environments in primary grades and beyond that utilize interactive multimedia as thinking tools.

References

Baghban, M. (1984). *Our daughter learns to read and write.* Newark, DE: International Reading Association.

Bissex, G. (1980). *GYNS AT WRK: A child learns to write and read.* Cambridge, MA: Harvard University Press.

Bus, A.G., de Jong, M.T., & Verhallen, M. (2006). CD-ROM talking books: A way to enhance early literacy? In M.C. McKenna, L.D. Labbo, R.D. Kieffer, & D. Reinking (Eds.), *International handbook of literacy and technology, Vol II*, (pp. 129–142), Mahwah, NJ: Lawrence Erlbaum Associates, Publishers.

Butler, D. (1975). *Cushla and her books.* Sevenoaks, UK: Hodder and Stoughton.

Chera, P., & Wood, C. (2003). Animated multimedia "talking books" can promote phonological awareness: Effects of spoken language experience and orthography. *Cognition, 81*, 227–241.

Crago, H., & Crago, M. (1976). The untrained eye? A preschool child explores Felix Hoffman's Rapunzel. *Children's Literature in Education, 22,* 135–151.

de Jong, M.T., & Bus, A.G. (2002). Quality of book reading matters for emergent readers: An experiment with the same book in a regular or electronic format. *Journal of Educational Psychology, 94,* 145–155.

Desmond, R.J., Singer, J.L., Singer, D.G., Calam, R., & Calimore, K. (1985). Family mediation patterns and television viewing: Young children's use and grasp of the medium. *Human Communication Research, 11,* 461–480.

Fisch, S.M., Shulman, J.S., Akerman, A., & Levin, G.A. (2002). Reading between the pixels: Parent–child interaction while reading online storybooks. *Early Education & Development, 13*(4), 435–451.

Gladwell, M. (2000). *The tipping point.* Boston: Little Brown and Company.

Glaser, B.G., & Strauss, A. (1967). *Discovery of grounded theory: Strategies for qualitative research.* Chicago: Aldine.

Greenlee-Moore, M.E., & Smith, L.L. (1996). Interactive computer software: The effects on young children's reading achievement. *Reading Psychology: An International Quarterly, 17,* 43–64.

Jonassen, D., Davidson, M., Collins, M., Campbell, J., & Haag, B.B. (1995). Constructivism and computer-mediated communication in distance education. *American Journal of Distance Education, 9,* 7–26.

Kirkorian, H., & Anderson, D. (in press). Attention to television: A predictor for learning. In S.B. Neuman, *Pathways to literacy achievement for high poverty children.* Baltimore: Brookes.

Labbo, L.D., & Kuhn, M.R. (2000). Weaving chains of affect and cognition: A young child's understanding of CD-ROM talking books. *Journal of Literacy Research, 32,* 187–210.

Linebarger, D. (2006). Young children, language, and television. *National Literacy Trust.* Retrieved May 9, 2007, from www.educationpublishing.com/index.html.

McKenna, M.C. (1998). Electronic texts and the transformation of beginning reading. In D. Reinking, M.C. McKenna, L.D. Labbo, & R.D. Kieffer (Eds.), *Handbook of literacy and technology: Transformations in a post-typographic world* (pp. 45–59). Mahwah, NJ: Lawrence Erlbaum Associates, Publishers.

Martinez, M., & Roser, N. (1985). Read it again: The value of repeated readings during story time. *Reading Teacher, 38,* 782–786.

Ricci, C.M., & Beal, C.R. (2002). The effect of interactive media on children's story memory. *Journal of Educational Psychology, 94,* 138–144.

Roser, N., & Martinez, M. (2004, December). Helping young children learn to read chapter books: The role of the teacher in reading aloud. Paper presented at the National Reading Conference, San Antonio, TX.

Salomon, G., & Perkins, D. (1988). Transfer of cognitive skills from programming: When and how. *Journal of Educational Computing Research, 3,* 149–170.

Salomon, G., Perkins, D.N., & Globerson, T. (1991). Partners in cognition extending human intelligence with intelligent technology. *Educational Researcher, 20,* 29.

Sinclair, J., & Coulthard, M. (1975). *Towards an analysis of discourse: The English used by teachers and pupils.* London: Oxford University Press.

Sipe, L.R., & Brightman, A.E., (2006). Teacher scaffolding of first-graders' literary understanding during read alouds of fairytale variants. In J.V. Hoffman, D.L., Schallert, C.M. Fairbanks, J. Worthy, & B. Maloch (Eds.), *55th Yearbook of the National Reading Conference,* Oak Creek, WI: National Reading Conference, Inc.

Smith, C.R. (2001). Click and turn the page: An exploration of multiple storybook literacy. *Reading Research Quarterly, 36,* 152–183.

Stannard, R. (1996). Texts, language, literacy and digital technologies. *English and Media Magazine, 34,* 4–63.

Turbill, J. (2001). A researcher goes to school: Using technology in the kindergarten literacy curriculum. *Journal of Early Childhood Literacy, 1,* 255–279.

White, D. (1954). *Books before five.* Wellington, New Zealand: Council for Educational Research.

Woodard, E.H., & Gridina, N. (2000). *Media in the home 2000: The fifth annual survey of parents and children.* Philadelphia University of Pennsylvania, Annenberg Public Policy Center. Retrieved August 2, 2007, from www.appepenn.org/mediainhome/survey7.pdf.

IV
Multimedia Applications in Classroom Instruction

14

Embedded Multimedia

Using Video to Enhance Reading Outcomes in Success for All[1]

Bette Chambers, Alan Cheung, Nancy A. Madden,
Robert E. Slavin, and Richard Gifford

For more than 50 years, educators and policymakers have been expectantly waiting for the video[2] revolution in education. Indeed, research on educational programs such as *Sesame Street* (Bogatz & Ball, 1971; Fisch & Truglio, 2000; Rice, Huston, Truglio, & Wright, 1990) and *Between the Lions* (Linebarger, Kosanic, Greenwood, & Doku, 2004; Uchikoshi, this volume) has shown positive effects of educational television for the reading and language development of young children. Yet video has remained a minor medium in the classroom, where it has been seen as a replacement for teacher instruction rather than a tool for teachers.

In recent years, however, video has begun to appear in educational practice in a new form that has great potential for education reform. Video is one example of what Mayer (2001) calls "multimedia," instructional formats that combine words and pictures. Instead of replacing instruction, multimedia can be embedded in classroom instruction to enhance teachers' lessons (see for an illustration Levin et al., this volume). This "embedded multimedia" application is not widely known or used, but research on the practice has shown initial promise. In embedded multimedia, brief multimedia segments are threaded throughout teachers' lessons. In one sense, embedded multimedia should at least share the impacts on achievement found in studies of the use of pictures, illustrations, diagrams, and other graphic content to enhance the effects of class lessons and text (see Carney & Levin, 2002; Schnotz, 2002; Shah, Mayer, & Hegarty, 1999; Vekiri, 2002). Yet well-designed embedded multimedia using video has properties that go beyond static graphics. First, video can model skills or content for students, giving them clear demonstrations of proficient performance. For example, videos can show children modeling advanced problem-solving strategies, sounding out words, thinking out loud about their creative writing, or working through a scientific investigation. Further, any multimedia that models for children also models for teachers, providing "just-in-time" professional development. For example, showing children working in cooperative groups to solve particular kinds of problems may provide teachers with a clear idea of what cooperative learning should look like, just as it would for students.

Theoretical Background

The theoretical basis for embedded multimedia begins with Paivio's dual coding theory (Clark & Paivio, 1991), which demonstrated that information held both in verbal memory and in visual memory is retained better than information held in only one memory system. For example, Mayer (2001) and his colleagues carried out a series of experiments in which students were taught how lightning works. Teaching about lightning using narration alone or text alone teaches only to verbal memory. Adding diagrams or moving pictures to illustrate the concept teaches to visual memory. Adding the pictures to narration or text greatly increased initial learning of the concept, as well as both retention and transfer, as long as the pictures and text or narration were closely aligned with each other and focused on the instructional objective (Mayer & Moreno, 2003).

Another key concept in multimedia learning is cognitive load. It has long been known that working memory places a severe limitation on the amount of information that can be absorbed at any given time (Solso, 2001). Each learning objective has a given intrinsic cognitive load, and if this exceeds the working memory capacity of children of a given age or level of knowledge, the objective must be broken into components that "fit" within the child's working memory capacity (Paas, Renkl, & Sweller, 2003). However, each memory system has its own limitations, which may be fairly independent of one another. That is, a learner has a limited working memory capacity for words and a limit for pictures, but "using up" the word limit does not "use up" the picture limit. Therefore, Mayer and Moreno (2003) suggest that instructors or designers can "off-load" meaningful information from one channel to the other, by using fewer words and more pictures when verbal working memory would otherwise be overloaded. Again, this "off-loading" only works if the pictures and words directly support each other. Pictures that are interesting but irrelevant to the words, containing "seductive details," can be detrimental because they fill limited working memory with irrelevant content (Hoeffler & Leutner, 2006; Mayer, 2001). Based on Neuman's (1997, this volume) theory of synergy, Verhallen, Bus, and de Jong (2006) demonstrated that repeated presentations of multimedia versions of the same story increased children's comprehension of the story and vocabulary more than did static presentations.

The complementary nature of words and moving pictures has been demonstrated in a series of studies in which instructional video material was broken into audio and silent video components and compared to the full video with audio (see Kozma, 1991, for a review). In most cases children learned significantly more from the video–audio presentations, and in no case did they learn less. This supports the concept that narrative and picture information do not interfere with each other, but instead support each other.

When both memory systems are in danger of overload, Mayer and Moreno's (2003) research suggests segmentation of combined word–picture content, organizing content in "bite-size segments" with opportunities to integrate and organize new information between segments (Mayer & Chandler, 2001).

Success for All and Embedded Multimedia

The Success for All embedded multimedia, called Reading Reels, takes advantage of these theoretical principles, combining verbal and visual content (words and moving pictures) to give learners multiple pathways to retention and comprehension and interspersing "bite-sized segments" with opportunities to practice and apply new learning. For example, a key problem in early reading instruction is teaching associations between letter shapes and letter sounds. The embedded multimedia strategy described in this chapter contains a series of animations designed to link the letter shape and letter sound in a brief, memorable story. In introducing the /p/ sound, for instance, a parrot eats some watermelon, and then spits out the seeds, making the sound /p/, /p/, /p/. The seeds fall in the shape of the letter "p." This 30-second story, which 5-year-olds readily learn and remember, gives them a link in their visual memory between the shape "p" and the sound /p/ that they can easily access, adding to the verbal and tactile learning the teacher provides by having children look at a picture of the parrot in the shape of the letter "p," writing "p" in the air, and having them make the /p/ sound and noticing how their lips form when they do so.

In English reading, children must learn 44 phonemes (letter sounds) represented by more than 58 graphemes (letters and letter combinations) (Adams, 1990). For example, the long /a/ sound can be represented by "ay," "ai," or "a_e." In order to recognize each quickly and automatically, and avoid confusions among them, children need to practice them separately and in words and sentences. Practice in cooperative groups, working with the teacher, and practice in other formats, is necessary to solidify learning from "bite-sized segments," which is why the multimedia segments by themselves are insufficient.

Similar theories underlie other multimedia applications in beginning reading (see Pailliotet & Mosenthal, 2000). To teach sound blending, the Success for All conducted experiments using video skits showing puppets sounding out words, creating both visual and auditory representations in memory. To teach vocabulary, live-action skits acted out the meanings of key words, both in context and then out of context (see for examples Segers, this volume). Again, students were expected to recall the skits (in their visual memories) to gain access to word meanings (needed in their verbal memories).

Reading Reels includes the *Animated Alphabet, The Sound and the Furry, Word Plays,* and *Between the Lions* segments, which are described below.

Animated Alphabet

Animations teach and reinforce sound/symbol relationships. For example, the animation introducing the short /e/ sound features an elephant pushing a rock with an "e" on it up a hill, making an /e/ sound with each push. At the top, the rock rolls down, and the exhausted elephant says "ehhhh" in frustration. The pairing of the memorable images, the letter sound, and the letter shape gives students many mental pathways to link the letter with its sound. There are animations for 58 different graphemes that comprise most of the phonemes used in the English language. Each animation is between 30 seconds and 1 minute long.

The Sound and the Furry

Multimedia skits, using SFA puppet characters, model the word blending process, phonemic awareness, spelling, fluency, reading strategies, and cooperative learning routines. For example, a puppet sees a sign, "Watch out for stick." He sounds out the word "stick" phonetically. Then he notices a stick, which he picks up. The stick sticks to his fur, and in trying to get it off he bites it—and then realizes he's in real trouble. After the skit, the sounding out section is repeated, and children sound out the word along with the puppets. More than 100 such vignettes illustrate sound blending strategies from simple CVC words to multi-syllable words. The average puppet skit is about 2 minutes long.

Word Plays

Live action multimedia skits dramatize important vocabulary concepts from the Success for All beginning reading texts. These skits are particularly designed to help English language learners build the specific vocabulary for the books they will be reading. For example, when children are about to read a story about China, they first see a skit that introduces words such as "chopsticks," "fireworks," "beautiful," and "ugly." The average Word Play is about 3 minutes long.

Between the Lions

Puppet skits and animations from the award-winning PBS program, *Between the Lions,* help teach phonemic awareness, sound/symbol correspondence, and sound blending. *Between the Lions* segments are about 1 minute long. A sample *Between the Lions* segment shows a funny man drawing lips and writing the word "lipstick" with lipstick on clear glass in front of him and sounding it out. After he finishes he puts his face up to the glass with his lips behind the lipstick, looking very silly.

The embedded multimedia materials were developed to be particularly beneficial to English language learners. In particular, the vocabulary skits demonstrating the vocabulary emphasized in each story children are about to read were designed to ensure that all children know the vocabulary in advance so that they can focus on the decoding and comprehension tasks required to master and enjoy each book. The alphabet and sound-blending segments are also designed to build children's language skills as well as their reading skills.

Each daily 90-minute reading lesson contains about five Reading Reels 30-second to three-minute skits. No additional time is added to the lessons to accommodate the multimedia. Rather, they are integrated into each lesson and replace teacher presentation of the concepts with materials such as picture cards.

During training, teachers are taught to play the video skits when they teach the associated component of the lesson. The teacher manuals also indicate where each segment should be played. For example, when introducing a particular phoneme, the teacher is instructed to play the *Animated Alphabet* skit for that phoneme. When a new phonetic story is introduced, the teacher is instructed to play the *Word Play* for that story, which introduces the vocabulary that the children will encounter in reading that story. It takes a bit of practice to integrate smoothly the videos into the appropriate time slot but with DVDs it is not difficult to master.

Research on Reading Reels

In 2001, researchers and developers at the nonprofit Success for All Foundation and Johns Hopkins University began a project to enhance the Success for All reading program with embedded multimedia. Success for All teaches beginning reading using a systematic phonics approach (see Slavin & Madden, 2001, for a program description). Fifty experimental–control comparisons of 1 or more years' duration have found, on average, positive effects of Success for All on children's reading achievement (see Borman, Hewes, Overman, & Brown, 2003; Borman, Slavin, Cheung, Chamberlain, Madden, & Chambers, 2007; Herman, 1999; Slavin & Madden, 2001).

The addition of embedded multimedia to Success for All's beginning reading program was intended to enhance the effectiveness of the program by giving children compelling, memorable demonstrations of letter sounds, sound blending strategies, vocabulary, and comprehension strategies. A particular focus was on the needs of English language learners, who were felt to be in particular need of visual models for vocabulary and sound blending.

Study 1

A preliminary study of the embedded multimedia strategy was carried out by Chambers and her colleagues (Chambers, Slavin, Madden, Cheng, & Gifford,

2005). In that study, four schools primarily serving Hispanic students were compared with four matched schools with similar demographics and achievement histories. The experimental schools used Success for All with embedded multimedia, while the control schools used traditional basal approaches. After a 1-year implementation, students in the Success for All/embedded multimedia treatment scored significantly higher than those in the matched control group, controlling for Peabody Picture Vocabulary Test pretests, on the Woodcock Word Identification, Word Attack, and Passage Comprehension scales. There were no differences on Letter Identification.

This experiment established the combined effect of Success for All reading and embedded multimedia on reading achievement, but it did not allow for a test of the unique contribution of the embedded multimedia content.

Study 2

The definitive study of embedded multimedia was carried out by Chambers, Cheung, Madden, Slavin, and Gifford (2006). This study was a cluster randomized trial, with random assignment of schools to embedded multimedia or control treatments. Ten schools in the Hartford (CT) Public Schools participated in the study ensuring similarity between experimental and control schools on all factors other than the embedded multimedia treatment. All schools used the Success for All reading program so experimental and control schools differed only in the use or nonuse of the multimedia content. Random assignment eliminated selection bias from the experiment, as all schools had an equal chance of being assigned to the experimental or control groups. All school staffs were willing to implement the embedded multimedia program; those randomly assigned to the control group were given the materials and training in the year following the experiment, as a delayed treatment control procedure.

The 450 first graders participated in the study, of whom 394 completed pre- and posttests. Almost all students qualified for free- or reduced-price lunches, and 62% of students were Hispanic and 35% African-American. Pretests were used as covariates in the main analyses to adjust for any initial difference between the two groups and to increase statistical power. Because the unit of random assignment and treatment was the school, the school was also the unit of analysis.

The experimental group used the multimedia content embedded in teachers' daily 90-minute Success for All reading lessons. This material consisted of 30-second to 3-minute skits and other demonstrations integrated with teachers' lessons, for a total of about 5 minutes per lesson. No additional time was added to the lessons to accommodate the multimedia. The purpose of the multimedia content was to present directly to students compelling demonstrations of key elements of beginning reading: letter sounds, sound blending strategies, and vocabulary. In addition, it was hoped that by showing multimedia content in class, teachers would have constant reinforcement of effective teaching strategies.

In this study, the experimental classes viewed Reading Reels embedded multimedia skits for about 5 minutes per day, integrated throughout the 90-minute Success for All reading lesson. Control schools used the regular 90-minute Success for All reading program without the embedded multimedia content. In place of the multimedia content, teachers used picture cards to illustrate the letter shapes and vocabulary in the student books. Demonstrations and games were used to teach word-level blending.

The findings from this study demonstrated that the experimental group scored significantly higher than the control group on the Word Attack subtest of the Woodcock-Johnson III Tests of Achievement (Woodcock, McGrew, & Mather, 2001) with an effect size of +0.47. Although the experimental group also scored higher than the control on other measures of reading these differences were not statistically significant in the HLM analysis. Individual-level ANCOVAs also found significant differences on Word Attack ($p < 0.001$) and Word Identification ($p < 0.02$), but not Passage Comprehension.

Study 3

A third study evaluating the effects of embedded multimedia was carried out by Chambers and her colleagues (Chambers et al., in press). This study used random assignment of individual students to conditions. Low-achieving first graders who qualified for tutoring received a computer-assisted tutoring intervention in addition to embedded multimedia. However, students who did not qualify for tutoring were randomly assigned to embedded multimedia or control conditions, within Success for All schools.

This study took place in two large, multitrack year-round schools in high poverty communities in Las Vegas and Los Angeles that had been implementing Success for All for several years. On entry to first grade, 159 children within the two schools were assigned at random to tracks. Then one track was randomly assigned to the experimental or technology-infused instruction condition and one track was randomly assigned to be the control or no technology, regular SFA instruction condition. Teachers assigned to the no technology control group were given the technology and training at the end of the year-long study, so this was a delayed treatment control group comparison.

Within the sample, the 60 lowest-achieving students received tutoring, and were therefore not included in the study of embedded multimedia alone. The remaining 99 students (43 experimental, 56 control) were the subjects for this multimedia study.

In the experimental group, all students were instructed in reading using Success for All with embedded multimedia, as described previously. Students in the control treatment experienced Success for All, without the multimedia content. The use or nonuse of the videos was the only factor differentiating experimental and control treatments.

This study also used the reading subtests of the Woodcock-Johnson III Tests of Achievement (Woodcock et al., 2001), as well as the Gray Oral Reading Tests—4th Edition (Gray & Robinson, 2001). It employed a similar methodology as in the previously described studies. On adjusted posttests, students in the experimental tracks scored significantly better than control students on Letter–Word Identification ($ES=+0.35$), Word Attack ($ES=+0.27$), Gray Oral Fluency ($ES=+0.27$), and Gray Oral Reading Test Total ($ES=+0.22$).

Discussion

The results of the three Chambers et al. studies (2005, 2006, in press) support the expectation that the addition of embedded multimedia content to a beginning reading program would enhance children's reading achievement. In these studies, schools or tracks were randomly assigned to conditions and all used the same Success for All reading strategies, so the use of embedded multimedia content was the only factor differentiating experimental and control conditions. In Study 2, a conservative HLM analysis found that only one of the four outcome measures, Word Attack, showed significant experimental–control differences, but this is in line with theoretical expectations. Three of the four multimedia segments dealt primarily with letter sounds and sound blending, which are key components of Word Attack. The fourth, *Word Plays*, focused on vocabulary. The other measures, especially Passage Comprehension and DIBELS, are more logically related to reading of connected text, which was emphasized equally in both treatments. In the Chambers et al. (in press) study, positive effects were found on Letter–Word Identification, Word Attack, and Fluency, but not Comprehension.

The findings of these studies suggest that the use of embedded multimedia has potential to enhance the effectiveness of beginning reading instruction for disadvantaged children. The individual-level effect size of +0.32 for Word Attack in Chambers et al. (2006) and +0.27 in Chambers et al. (in press) is educationally important, particularly given the minimal cost of the intervention. Adding the DVDs to an existing Success for All school costs $129 per classroom (plus the cost of a DVD player and television) and occupies an average of about five minutes per day out of a 90-minute reading period.

From these studies, it is not clear what processes were most influential in improving children's reading achievement. It may be that the combined audio and visual content of the Reading Reels is retained better because it is held in both verbal memory and in visual memory, as Clark and Paivio (1991) and Mayer and Moreno (2003) demonstrated.

It may be that the humorous, vivid images provided mnemonic cues for the children, making the graphemes more memorable for the children

(Slavin, 2006). The authors have heard numerous examples of children who learned to identify the letter sounds with the videos, referring to the images from the videos. For example, a girl named Erika complained to her mother that someone spelled her name with a caterpillar instead of a kangaroo, icons used for the /c/ and /k/ graphemes in the *Animated Alphabet*.

It may be that the teachers learned effective strategies for teaching reading from the "just-in-time" professional development aspect of the videos. For example, the videos model for teachers the precise sounds the letters make and show them how the word-blending process works. This may have improved their teaching of this skill to their students.

Much research remains to be done to understand these effects further. It would be important to study the program's effects on teachers' practices, to assess the validity of the theory that multimedia modeling of effective teaching practices would improve teachers' implementations of the reading program and their overall teaching skill. Further, small-scale studies are needed to examine the separate impacts of the multimedia components, and to vary elements of the interventions. Such studies could help build a theoretical base for embedded multimedia in reading instruction and suggest design principles for further development.

It is interesting to note that the video segments were designed to be totally integrated into the teachers' lessons, with the teachers playing each segment at the exact time when they were teaching the associated content to the class. While most teachers did this a number of them found it too difficult to start and stop the DVD player throughout the lesson so they played all of a particular lesson's video skits at the end of the lesson. We will need further research to see whether playing the videos at the end of the lesson is less or more effective than embedding them throughout the lesson as they were designed to be used.

The potential applications of embedded multimedia are numerous. As of this writing, the Success for All Foundation is evaluating the use of embedded multimedia in writing instruction for grades 3 to 5. The media is used to model cooperative learning and the writing process. Another avenue of application is in upper elementary math instruction, with brief skits introducing mathematical concepts. An extension of the use of multimedia is embedding it in lessons that are presented on interactive whiteboards. This is also being developed and evaluated for beginning reading and elementary math instruction.

Research on multimedia learning (e.g., Mayer, 2001) shows that specific design elements matter a great deal in determining learning outcomes. Using design principles known to contribute to learning, multimedia embedded in literacy instruction may have significant potential to improve reading outcomes for children.

Notes

1. Adapted from Chambers, Cheung, Madden, Slavin, and Gifford (2006), Chambers, B., Slavin, R.E., Madden, N.A., Abrami, P.C., Tucker, B.J., Cheung, A., and Gifford, R. (in press) and Chambers, B., Slavin, R.E., Madden, N.A., Cheung, A., and Gifford, R. (2005).

   This research was funded by the Interagency Educational Research Initiative (IERI), a collaboration among the National Science Foundation, the Institute of Education Sciences, and the National Institute of Child Health and Human Development (Grant No. REC 0115659). However, any opinions expressed are those of the authors and do not necessarily represent the positions or policies of our funders.
2. Throughout this chapter, the term "video" is assumed to include DVD and CD formats as well as VHS unless otherwise noted.

References

Adams, M.J. (1990). *Beginning to read: Thinking and learning about print.* Cambridge, MA: MIT Press.

Bogatz, G.A., & Ball, S. (1971). *The second year of Sesame Street.* Princeton, NJ: Educational Testing Service.

Borman, G.D., Hewes, G.M., Overman, L.T., & Brown, S. (2003). Comprehensive school reform and achievement: A meta-analysis. *Review of Educational Research, 73*, 125–230.

Borman, G., Slavin, R.E., Cheung, A., Chamberlain, A., Madden, N.A., & Chambers, B. (2007). Final reading outcomes of the national randomized field trial of Success for All. *American Educational Research Journal, 44*(3), 701–703.

Carney, R.N., & Levin, J.R. (2002). Pictorial illustrations still improve students' learning from text. *Educational Psychology Review, 14*, 5–26.

Chambers, B., Cheung, A., Madden, N.A., Slavin, R.E., & Gifford, G. (2006). Achievement effects of embedded multimedia in a Success for All reading program. *Journal of Educational Psychology, 98*, 232–237.

Chambers, B., Slavin, R.E., Madden, N.A., Abrami, P., Tucker, B., Cheung, A., et al. (in press). *Technology infusion in Success for All: Reading outcomes for first graders.* Manuscript submitted for publication.

Chambers, B., Slavin, R.E., Madden, N.A., Cheung, A., & Gifford, R. (2005). Effects of Success for All with embedded video on the beginning reading achievement of Hispanic children. Technical Report. Center for Research and Reform in Education, Johns Hopkins University, Baltimore, MD.

Clark, J.M., & Paivio, A. (1991). Dual coding theory and education. *Educational Psychology Review, 3*, 149–210.

Fisch, S., & Truglio, R. (2000). *G is for growing: 30 years of research on* Sesame Street. New York: Lea's Communications Series.

Gray, W.S., & Robinson, H. (2001). *Gray oral reading tests* (4th ed.). Austin, TX: PRO-ED.

Herman, R. (1999). *An educator's guide to schoolwide reform.* Arlington, VA: Educational Research Service.

Hoeffler, T., & Leutner, D. (2006). Instructional animation vs. static pictures: A meta-analysis. Paper presented at the annual meeting of the American Educational Research Association, San Francisco, CA.

Kozma, R. (1991). Learning with media. *Review of Educational Research, 61*, 179–211.

Linebarger, D.L., Kosanic, A.Z., Greenwood, C.R., & Doku, N.S. (2004). Effects of viewing the television program *Between the Lions* on the emergent literacy skills of young children. *Journal of Educational Psychology, 96*, 297–308.

Mayer, R.E. (2001). *Multimedia learning.* New York: Cambridge University Press.

Mayer, R.E., & Chandler, P. (2001). When learning is just a click away: Does simple user interaction foster deeper understanding of multimedia messages? *Journal of Educational Psychology, 93*, 390–397.

Mayer, R.E., & Moreno, R. (2003). Nine ways to reduce cognitive load in multimedia learning. *Educational Psychologist, 38*, 43–52.

Neuman, S.B. (1997). Television as a learning environment: A theory of synergy. In J. Flood, S.

Brice Heath, & D. Lapp (Eds.), *Handbook of research on teaching literacy through the communicative and visual arts* (pp. 15–30). New York: Simon & Schuster.

Paas, F., Renkl, A., & Sweller, J. (2003). Cognitive load theory and instructional design: Recent developments. *Educational Psychologist, 38,* 1–4.

Pailliotet, A.W., & Mosenthal, P.B. (Eds.) (2000). *Reconceptualizing literacy in the age of media, multimedia, and hypermedia.* Norwood, NJ: JAI/Ablex.

Rice, M.L., Huston, A.C., Truglio, R., & Wright, L.C. (1990). Words from *Sesame Street:* Learning vocabulary while viewing. *Developmental Psychology, 26,* 421–428.

Schnotz, W. (2002). Towards an integrated view of learning from text and visual displays. *Educational Psychology Review, 14,* 101–120.

Shah, P., Mayer, R., & Hegarty, M. (1999). Graphs as aids to knowledge construction: Signaling techniques for guiding the process of graph comprehension. *Journal of Educational Psychology, 91,* 690–702.

Slavin, R.E. (2006). *Educational psychology: Theory into practice* (8th ed.). Boston: Allyn & Bacon.

Slavin, R.E., & Madden, N.A. (Eds.) (2001). *One million children: Success for All.* Thousand Oaks, CA: Corwin.

Solso, R.L. (2001). *Cognitive psychology* (6th ed.). Boston: Allyn & Bacon.

Vekiri, I. (2002). What is the value of graphical displays in learning? *Educational Psychology Review, 14,* 261–312.

Verhallen, M.J.A.J., Bus, A., & de Jong, M. (2006). The promise of multimedia stories for kindergarten children at risk. *Journal of Educational Psychology, 98,* 410–419.

Woodcock, R.W., McGrew, K.S., & Mather, N. (2001). *Woodcock-Johnson III Tests of Achievement.* Itasca, IL: Riverside Publishing.

15

Computer-Assisted Tutoring in Success for All

Two Studies of Reading Outcomes for First Graders[1]

Bette Chambers, Robert E. Slavin, Nancy A. Madden,
Philip C. Abrami, Bradley J. Tucker, and Alan Cheung

For the past 30 years, the computer revolution in education has been eagerly anticipated, but never realized (Cuban, 2001). As the cost of computers has decreased and as computers have become commonplace in homes and businesses, the numbers of computers in America's schools have steadily grown, with a 1998 estimate of 69 computers in every elementary school (see Becker, 2001). Yet computers remain largely separate from core instruction in classrooms. They are typically used by students for word processing, enrichment, skill practice, remediation, or reference, all applications that have little role for the teacher (Becker & Ravitz, 2001).

This chapter presents a novel approach to using computers to support, rather than replace reading tutors. A computer-assisted tutoring program, called Alphie's Alley, provides reading tutors with animated activities for students, assessment tools, and professional development. The chapter reports on two randomized experiments evaluating Alphie's Alley and discusses the potential this approach has for teaching.

Computer-Assisted Instruction

In beginning reading instruction, computers are often used for skill practice and remediation, but there is limited evidence of their effectiveness (see also McKenna & Zucker, this volume). In a recent meta-analysis, Kulik (2003) found that most studies reported no difference between computer-assisted instruction and traditional reading lessons. There have been some promising applications of computers in teaching skills such as phonological awareness (Foster, Erickson, Foster, Brinkman, & Torgeson, 1994; Segers & Verhoeven, 2005; Wise, Ring, and Olson, 1999), letter and word recognition (Mioduser, Tur-Kaspa, & Leitner, 2000), and other specific reading skills (Greenlee-Moore & Smith, 1996; Torgeson & Barker, 1995). However, much remains to be learned about how computers can help improve children's reading outcomes.

In reading, computers are frequently used to provide one-to-one tutorial instruction to supplement classroom instruction, especially to children who are at risk or performing below expectations (Van Daal, this volume). In this application, computers may be seen as less costly alternatives to human tutors. However, human tutors are far more effective. Studies of one-to-one tutoring find substantial positive effects on the reading performance of at-risk first graders (Wasik & Slavin, 1993; Torgeson, Wagner, & Rashotte, 1997; Pinnell, Lyons, DeFord, Bryk, & Seltzer, 1994; Hock, Schumaker, & Deshler, 2001; Morris, Tyner, & Perney, 2000).

One possible reason for the often-disappointing results of computer-assisted instruction is that the computers are expected to replace teachers in providing one-to-one instruction to students. Computers can provide outstanding graphics, excellent assessments, and precise diagnosis and prescription, but they may not be very good tutors, especially for young children. No computer can perceive children's difficulties, explain difficult concepts, or motivate children like a caring, capable tutor. Young children work in school because they want to please their teachers, who are valued adults. Computers cannot replace the human relationship between teacher and child.

The present research was undertaken to test the idea that tutors and computers working together could enhance the reading achievement of at-risk first graders better than tutors alone. This strategy, which we call *embedded technology*, is intended to enhance the effectiveness of human tutors by providing children with compelling multimedia presentations, frequent assessments, and evidence-based diagnosis and prescription, and providing tutors with just-in-time professional development, planning tools, and record-keeping applications. In other words, the intention was to integrate the strengths of both tutors and computers to make tutoring consistently effective for at-risk first graders.

Success for All

This chapter reports two randomized, year-long evaluations of an approach to computer-assisted tutoring that took place within schools using the Success for All comprehensive reform model (Slavin & Madden, 2000, 2001). Success for All provides high-poverty elementary schools with well-structured, phonetic materials in beginning reading. It makes extensive use of cooperative learning, a rapid pace of instruction, and frequent assessment. Most importantly for the present research, Success for All provides daily tutoring for children in grades 1–3 who are experiencing difficulties in learning to read. More than 50 experimental–control comparison studies have evaluated the reading impacts of Success for All, and have found overall positive effects (Borman, Hewes, Overman, & Brown, 2003; Herman, 1999; Slavin & Madden, 2000). A recent longitudinal randomized evaluation involving 38 schools has also found positive effects of the program (Borman, Slavin, Cheung, Chamberlain, Madden, & Chambers, 2007). The present studies do not evaluate Success for All, which was a constant in both treatment conditions, but Success for All provided important context for both experiments.

Computer-Assisted Tutoring in Success for All

The Success for All daily 20-minute tutoring sessions in foundational reading are provided to approximately one-third of first graders who are struggling in reading. Students are excused from tutoring when they reach grade level on formal assessments given every 9 weeks. Originally, Success for All required certified teachers as tutors, but due to limitations on the availability of certified tutors, as well as their cost, most schools now use paraprofessionals to do much or most of their tutoring. Having tutors use computer-assisted tutoring software tailored to the SFA tutoring program was expected to improve the tutoring that students experience and get students up to grade level more quickly.

Based on previous research and experience, computers were expected to improve the outcomes of tutoring in three main areas. In presenting content to children, the computer provided engaging animations to engage students' attention and motivation, to give them greater control over their own learning, and to give them immediate feedback on their performance. In assessment and prescription, the computer enabled tutors to diagnose reading difficulties through multiple means, track children's progress carefully, and provide detailed suggestions to tutors for next steps, based on each child's unique needs. In professional development, the computer provided demonstrations of effective instruction precisely attuned to the tutor's immediate needs and helped increase implementation fidelity.

The computer-assisted tutoring model, called "Alphie's Alley" (Danis et al, 2005) was designed to help tutors make effective use of tutoring sessions to help at-risk children make adequate progress in reading. Alphie's Alley structures the entire 20-minute tutoring session. The computer helps assess children, and suggests individually tailored plans based on the assessments. It provides students with multimedia screens containing 12 types of activities designed to build skills such as phonemic awareness, sound blending, comprehension monitoring, and connected reading. The tutor has an active role in guiding the child, assessing his or her ongoing progress, and modifying plans in light of the child's needs, so the computer serves as an aid, not a replacement for the tutor.

Making learning relevant, understandable, and engaging so that time on task increases is especially important for students struggling to read. Alphie's Alley was designed to increase students' task engagement and self-efficacy beliefs.

The computer also provides a performance support system for the tutor, including video clips showing expert tutors implementing each type of activity with children with various strengths and weaknesses (Gery, 2002). This "just-in-time" professional development is expected to help tutors to become more thoughtful and strategic in working with their at-risk students (Chambers, Abrami, McWhaw, & Therrien, 2001). It builds on models of cognitive apprenticeship (Collins, Brown, & Newman, 1989) and self-regulated learning (Randi & Corno, 2000).

Alphie's Alley was designed to support the human tutor rather than replace the tutor (Everson, 1995; Mitchell & Grogono, 1993). It contains a complex database that allows the computer to make "intelligent" decisions on interventions, based on the individual performance of each student, both between and within sessions (Everson, 1995; Mitchell & Grogono, 1993). The computer analyzes the student's responses and provides to the tutor suggested templates of instruction for that individual student. The tutor can choose to have the student engage in the suggested activities or can choose other activities, based on his or her knowledge of the student's abilities. The computerized diagnostic and assessment activities simplify record-keeping so the tutor's full attention can be devoted to the student.

There are several key concepts that underlie the design of Alphie's Alley. One is the use of embedded multimedia. Embedded multimedia (Chambers, Cheung, Madden, Slavin, & Gifford, 2006) refers to strategies in which animations and other video are woven into teachers' lessons. The use of embedded multimedia is based on theoretical work by Mayer (2001) and his colleagues demonstrating that well-designed multimedia can greatly enhance learning and retention of concepts. Other research has found multimedia to be effective in enhancing learners' comprehension and vocabulary (Hoeffler & Leutner, 2006; Verhallen, Bus, & de Jong, 2006; Uchikoshi, this volume).

Three studies of this application in classroom (not tutorial) instruction have found that adding brief video content on letter sounds and sound blending to class lessons in first grade reading enhances decoding outcomes (See Chambers, Cheung et al., this volume; Chambers et al., 2006; Chambers, Slavin, Madden, Cheung, & Gifford, 2005). Giving the students animated representations of concepts such as letter sounds, sound blending, and sequence of events in a story is expected to help children master reading skills. For example, the computer progressively moves letters closer to each other to represent sound blending. In another activity the computer shows illustrations from stories out of order for children to put in proper sequence.

Second, as noted earlier, the interaction of tutor and computer builds on the strengths of each. The computer organizes and presents attractive animations, keeps records, and so on, but the tutor listens to children, gives them feedback, and most importantly, forms human relationships with them. Finally, the computer's professional development capacity is expected to help tutors build their own understandings of how to implement the program and, more importantly, how to reach a broad range of children with diverse learning strengths and difficulties.

In developing Alphie's Alley, a combination of existing research, surveys, focus groups, consultations, observations, and annual testing for formative evaluation were used to create a tool that was theoretically sound, practically useful, and empirically supported. Initial reports from a year-long pilot test include a limited amount of quantitative data collected in a quasi-experimental design in a pilot year. Students in regular Success for All tutoring were compared to students who participated in Success for All tutoring with Alphie's Alley. A significant multivariate effect size of +0.39 ($N = 27$ tutees) was found in favor of those who were tutored using Alphie's Alley on Word Identification, Word Attack, and Passage Comprehension subtests of the Woodcock Reading Mastery Tests-Revised and DIBELS Oral Reading Fluency, when pretest scores on the Peabody Picture Vocabulary Tests were used as a covariate.

Schmid et al. (2005) examined tutor reactions to Alphie's Alley versus traditional "paper and pencil" forms of tutoring support within SFA, using pretest and posttest surveys. They concluded that Alphie's Alley assumed and maintained a central role throughout the year. Tutors consistently reported that students were highly motivated to come to tutoring and appeared to learn at a rapid pace.

Study 1

Study 1 was undertaken to determine the independent effects of the Alphie's Alley computer-assisted tutoring model. The study took place in 25 Success for All schools located in high-poverty communities in eight states throughout the USA. In each school, first graders who were identified for tutoring due to low scores on curriculum-based measures were assigned at random to tutors who themselves were randomly assigned to use either Alphie's Alley or to continue their usual tutoring strategies, as specified in the Success for All program. A total of 412 low-achieving first graders who received tutoring across the 25 high-poverty schools participated in the study.

Experimental Treatment: Computer-Assisted Tutoring

Students who experienced difficulties in reading in Success for All were assigned to daily 20-minute one-to-one tutoring sessions. In the experimental group, tutors used Alphie's Alley, the computer-assisted tutoring program, designed specifically to align with the SFA curriculum. The program has four components: assessment, planning, computer activities, and just-in-time professional development.

ASSESSMENT

Alphie's Alley assesses children's reading strengths and difficulties in the areas of phonemic awareness, phonics, fluency, and comprehension. For example, in assessing phonemic awareness, the computer presents the student with the discrete sounds of a word (e.g., /d/ /o/ /g/) and the student is asked to say the word. The tutor records on the computer whether the response is correct or not. The computer summarizes the student's performance and communicates this information on an assessment report for each student. The program continuously updates information relevant to the student's progress.

PLANNING

The program suggests a 2-week tutoring plan based on the child's assessment. The tutor may modify the plan in light of the child's performance and needs. From the tutoring plan, the student and tutor choose a goal for the student to focus on each week. At the end of the 2-week period, a new plan is generated based on the student's performance on the activities.

COMPUTER ACTIVITIES

Alphie's Alley is a computer-based learning environment built around Alphie the Alligator and his friends. Students work on Alphie's Alley computer activities specifically designed to reinforce skills taught in their core reading program. In each activity, students have an opportunity to respond, but if they cannot produce a correct answer, the computer gives them progressive scaffolding until they can reach the right answer. For some activities the student responds directly on the computer. For others, the student responds orally to the tutor, who records on the computer whether the student's response was correct or not, and either the tutor or the computer provides individualized explanations and scaffolded support to the student. In this way the computer can track the student's progress on all of the subskills associated with reading.

Specific activities that students encounter are as follows.

1. *Letter Identification.* The computer gives a sound, and the student must select a letter or letter combination that makes that sound.
2. *Letter Writing.* Same as letter ID, except that the student must type or write the letter or letter combination.
3. *Auditory Blending.* The computer presents sounds for two, three, or four-phoneme words, which the student blends into a word for the tutor.
4. *Auditory Segmenting.* The computer says a word and the student must break it into its separate sounds for the tutor.
5. *Sight Words.* The computer displays sight words, which the student reads to the tutor.

6. *Word-Level Blending.* The computer displays a word and the student uses sound blending to decode it to the tutor.
7. *Spelling.* The computer says a word and the student types it. At higher levels, the computer reads a sentence that the student types.
8. *Story Preparation.* Before the child reads a decodable story, the computer displays story-related words (both phonetically regular and sight words) for the student to practice. This activity is particularly important for ELLs, who can learn the story vocabulary before they encounter it in a book or on screen.
9. *Tracking.* The student reads a storybook on the computer to the tutor, and uses an arrow key to track work by word. The computer models appropriate decoding strategies if the student cannot decode a word, and orally presents sight words that the student does not know.
10. *Fluency.* The student reads a story to the tutor, who notes errors and times to compute words correct per minute. Fluency practice and assessment focuses on accuracy, then smoothness, then expression, then rate.
11. *Comprehension Questions.* The computer displays questions about the stories that the student answers to the tutor.
12. *Graphic Organizers.* The student completes a graphic organizer to represent main ideas from the stories.

JUST-IN-TIME PROFESSIONAL DEVELOPMENT

Alphie's Alley offers just-in-time performance support for tutors in the form of video vignettes and written suggestions on how to help remediate students' particular problems. Once a diagnosis has been made about specific problems a student may have, the tutor can view a variety of intervention strategies to help remediate that problem. For example, if a tutor determines that a child has a problem with visual tracking, then the tutor can view video vignettes of other tutors modeling ways to help children learn to track. Short audiovisual vignettes provide immediate expert guidance to the tutors focused on the exact problem they are confronting.

Control Treatment

Students in the control treatment experienced Success for All including tutoring without the technology elements. The use or nonuse of the technology was the only factor differentiating experimental and control treatments.

Training

Tutors in both conditions received a 1-day initial training in tutoring. For the Alphie's Alley tutors, about a third of the day was devoted to learning to implement the Alphie's Alley computer-assisted tutoring program. Tutors in both conditions received a tutoring manual, and follow-up visits by trainers throughout the school year to support them in implementing the program, either the regular SFA tutoring or tutoring with Alphie's Alley.

Students were individually pretested in September, 2004 on the Letter-Word Identification scale of the Woodcock–Johnson III Tests of Achievement and post-tested in May, 2005 on it again, along with the Woodcock Word Attack scale and the Gray Oral Reading Tests of Fluency and Comprehension. The data were analyzed using analyses of covariance, controlling for Letter-Word Identification pretests.

Overall Findings

There were no differences at pretest ($p < 0.99$). At posttest, there were also no significant differences across the five outcome measures.

High Implementers

In this first study of Alphie's Alley, implementation was highly variable. Some tutors assigned to the experimental group never implemented Alphie's Alley at all, and some did so very poorly. Others implemented the program very well. The use of random assignment of tutors to computer and non-computer conditions within schools created particular problems, as it sometimes created confusion about what each tutor was expected to do. For this reason, a separate analysis of the schools that did fully implement the experimental treatment was carried out.

SFA trainers, who were responsible to oversee program training and follow-up implementation, rated program implementation for all experimental schools on a three-point scale: "fully implemented" to "poorly implemented." Tutors in 13 schools, teaching 203 students (49% of the student sample), were rated as "fully implementing." Those in nine schools were rated "partially implementing" and three schools were rated as "poorly implementing."

Separate analyses by implementation rating showed sharply differing outcomes. There were no program impacts for partial and poor implementers. However, for fully implementing schools, results were generally positive.

Pretest differences among experimental and control students in fully implementing schools were not significant. At posttest, there were significant positive effects on three of the four independent measures. Effect sizes (adjusted mean differences divided by unadjusted standard deviations) and p-values were as follows: Woodcock Letter-Word Identification (ES = +0.45, $p < 0.001$), Woodcock Word Attack (ES = +0.31, $p < 0.05$), and GORT Fluency (ES = +0.23, $p < 0.05$). There were no differences on GORT Comprehension (ES = +0.05, n.s.) or GORT Total (ES = +0.18, n.s.).

Study 2

Study 2 (Chambers et al., in press-a) was undertaken to evaluate the combined effects of the Reading Reels embedded multimedia content and the

Alphie's Alley computer-assisted tutoring model. Because only tutored children receive Alphie's Alley, the study allowed for a test of Reading Reels alone among non-tutored children, as well as a test of the combined programs among tutored children, reported here. See Chambers, Cheung, et al. (this volume) for a description of the results for the non-tutored children. Study 2 used an experimental design in which children in multitrack year-round schools were randomly assigned to tracks, and then tracks were randomly assigned to conditions. This was expected to facilitate more distinct implementations of experimental and control conditions than was possible in Study 1, because tracks within multitrack year-round schools are essentially separate schools-within-schools.

As in Study 1, because the study used random assignment of students and teachers to treatments within the same schools, it eliminated selection bias as a possible confound. The study schools were experienced Success for All schools, so instruction, curriculum, grouping, and other factors were identical in all groups. The only factor differentiating experimental and control group was the use or nonuse of the embedded multimedia treatment in reading classes and of computer-assisted tutoring in one-to-one tutoring sessions.

The study took place in two large, multitrack year-round schools that had been implementing Success for All for several years. As described in Chambers, Cheung et al. (this volume) Study 3, first graders were assigned at random to tracks and randomly assigned to implement technology or not.

There were a few children who could not be randomly assigned to tracks because they had a sibling in a given track, 20% of the experimental group and 26% of control. A test for differences between these students and those who were randomly assigned found nearly identical scores, so these children were included in the analyses.

Subjects were the first graders who were struggling readers in the two high-poverty multitrack, schools described in Study 3 (see Chambers, Cheung et al., this volume). The lowest 30% of first graders (60 students) were designated to receive tutoring in both experimental and control conditions. Students generally remain in tutoring until they are reading at the level of their class. It takes on average two 9-week tutoring sessions to bring them up to their class level.

Experimental Treatments

In the experimental group, all students were instructed in reading using Success for All with embedded multimedia (i.e., Reading Reels described in Chambers, Cheung et al., this volume) during their reading classes. Students who needed tutoring were also provided one-to-one tutoring with a tutor using Alphie's Alley.

COMPUTER-ASSISTED TUTORING

Students who experienced difficulties in reading in Success for All were assigned to daily 20-minute one-to-one tutoring sessions. In the experimental group, tutors used Alphie's Alley, as described above.

CONTROL TREATMENT

Students in the control treatment experienced Success for All, including tutoring without the technology elements. The use or nonuse of the technology was the only factor differentiating experimental and control treatments.

Participants were individually pretested in September and posttested in May, as described in Study 1. The data were analyzed using analyses of covariance, controlling for Letter-Word Identification pretests.

The numbers of children tutored in the experimental and control groups were somewhat different, even though the number of tutors and the number of available tutoring slots were equal between the two groups. Among students with pre- and posttests, 43% of experimental and 33% of control students were tutored. This difference, also seen in the Chambers et al. (in press-a) study of computer-assisted tutoring, came about because tutored children in the experimental group caught up to their grade level faster than those in the control group and were therefore excused from tutoring earlier and at a higher rate. This allowed the tutors in the experimental group to tutor a higher percentage of their struggling students.

At pretest, there were no differences between experimental and control groups ($p < 0.52$). On posttests, adjusted for pretests, experimental students scored significantly higher than controls on all measures. Effect sizes and p values were as follows: Letter-Word Identification ($ES = +0.47$, $p < 0.05$), Word Attack ($ES = +0.39$, $p < 0.05$), Fluency ($ES = +0.58$, $p < 0.05$), Comprehension ($ES = +1.02$, $p < 0.02$), and GORT Total ($ES = +0.76$, $p < 0.02$). The median effect size across the four independent measures was $ES = +0.53$.

Discussion

The findings of the two randomized experimental evaluations of the Alphie's Alley computer-assisted tutoring program indicate that the outcomes depended on quality of implementation. In Study 1, schools with high implementation quality had significant positive achievement effects on three out of four independent measures, with a median effect size of +0.27. However, there were no significant effects for partial or poor implementers, or for all schools taken together.

Study 2, by Chambers et al. (in press-b), also involved a randomized experiment that evaluated Alphie's Alley, but experimental students experienced the Reading Reels embedded multimedia content in their regular reading classes as well as Alphie's Alley in their tutoring sessions. Implementation quality was high, and the problem of having experimental and control tutors in the same schools was largely solved by locating the study in multi-track year-round schools in which students were randomly assigned from a common pool to distinct tracks or "mini-schools." In Study 2, treatment effects for tutored students on the same Woodcock and GORT measures used in Study 1 were very positive and significant, with a median effect size of +0.53.

Beyond the overall effects, the two studies differ in patterns of reading outcomes. In Study 2, the largest impacts were seen on the GORT Comprehension measure, with an effect size of +1.02. In contrast, Comprehension was the only measure that showed no differences between experimental and control groups among students in high implementing schools in Study 1.

The different findings in these two similar studies could be due to the use of Reading Reels in Study 2 (which had positive separate effects in two studies, by Chambers et al., 2006, and Chambers et al., in press-b [see Chambers, Cheung et al., this volume]). It could also be the case that implementation quality in Study 2 made the difference, as the tutors varied somewhat in their implementation of the program in Study 1. Further research is under way to understand more fully these effects.

Both studies of the reading effects of the Alphie's Alley computer-assisted tutoring model agree that when well implemented, this program can have a significant and educationally meaningful impact on the reading performance of at-risk first graders. This suggests that integrating technology to enhance the work of human tutors can lead to greater reading impacts than those likely to be achieved by tutors alone. More attention needs to be paid to implementation quality, however. Over time, tutors using the tool are likely to come to resemble the high implementers who achieved excellent outcomes in both studies. The studies to date establish the principle that adding well-designed computer activities can make tutors more effective. Given the expense of one-to-one tutoring, anything that can enhance tutoring outcomes is an important contribution to enhancing overall cost effectiveness.

It is important to recall that both studies compared two versions of SFA tutoring, one using Alphie's Alley and a second using traditional "paper and pencil" SFA tutoring. The traditional version of SFA has already demonstrated its effectiveness compared to non-SFA controls (see Slavin & Madden, 2001; Borman et al., 2006, 2007). Had the present study also used non-SFA controls as the comparison group, it is likely that the treatment effect would have been substantially larger.

Future investigations should focus on understanding the cognitive and motivational processes by which computer-assisted tutoring enhances learning. Do the self-efficacy and self-regulation of students and tutors increase over time with use of the technology-enhanced SFA curriculum? Do tutors become more effective by using computer-assisted tutoring?

Another application of this computer-assisted tutoring model that combines cooperative learning is being explored by the Success for All Foundation as of this writing. In this model, pairs of students work together on the computer, with a tutor supporting between three and four pairs of students. Students take turns performing the activities on the computer and act as a recorder for each other for activities that require a verbal response. Tutors monitor students' work and verify when they master levels of different skills. There are other potential applications of this computer-assisted instruction that draw on the unique abilities of both computers and humans, which future development and research will explore.

The present studies, and related studies by Chambers et al. (2006, in press-b), suggest a new role for technology in education: enhancing rather than replacing teachers' instruction. This concept may have much broader implications than its application in first grade reading instruction, and is worth exploring on a broader scale. Perhaps the technology revolution will finally come in education when the computer becomes the teacher's partner, rather than the teacher's replacement.

Note

1. Adapted from Chambers et al. (in press-a), and Chambers et al. (in press-b).

This research was funded by the Interagency Educational Research Initiative (IERI), a collaboration among the National Science Foundation, the Institute of Education Sciences, and the National Institute of Child Health and Human Development (Grant No. REC 0115659). However, any opinions expressed are those of the authors and do not necessarily represent the positions or policies of our funders.

The authors would like to acknowledge the contributions of the following individuals for their contribution in the creation of the technological enhancements: Jennifer Chong, Georges Côté, Benoît Danis, Caroline Dumont, Emily Gam, Barry Gordemer, Luis Guadarrama, Tonia Hawkins, Sally Heldrich, Ane Jorgensen, Francis Longpré, Mónica López, Roberto Muzard, Alexandra Olsen, Sébastien Rainville, Jane Strausbaugh, Micha Therrien, David Wells, and Mimi Zhou.

References

Becker, H.J. (2001, April). How are teachers using computers in instruction? Paper presented at the annual meetings of the American Educational Research Association, Seattle, WA.

Becker, H.J., & Ravitz, J.L. (2001, April). Computer use by teachers: Are Cuban's predictions correct? Paper presented at the annual meetings of the American Educational Research Association, Seattle, WA.

Borman, G.D., Hewes, G.M., Overman, L.T., & Brown, S. (2003) Comprehensive school reform and achievement: A meta-analysis. *Review of Educational Research, 73*, 125–230.

Borman, G.D., Slavin, R.E., Cheung, A., Chamberlain, A., Madden, N.A., & Chambers, B. (2006). The national randomized field trial of Success for All: Second-year outcomes. *American Educational Research Journal, 42*, 673–696.

Borman, G., Slavin, R.E., Cheung, A., Chamberlain, A., Madden, N.A., & Chambers, B. (2007). Final reading outcomes of the national randomized field trial of Success for All. *American Educational Research Journal, 44*(3), 701–703.

Chambers, B., Abrami, P., McWhaw, K., & Therrien, M.C. (2001). Developing a computer-assisted tutoring program to help children at risk learn to read. In P. Abrami (Ed.), Understanding and promoting complex learning using technology. *Educational Research and Evaluation, 7*, 223–239.

Chambers, B., Cheung, A., Madden, N.A., Slavin, R.E., & Gifford, G. (2006). Achievement effects of embedded multimedia in a Success for All reading program. *Journal of Educational Psychology, 98*, 232–237.

Chambers, B., Slavin, R.E., Madden, N.A., Abrami, P., Tucker, B., Cheung, A., et al. (in press-a). *Computer-assisted tutoring in Success for All: Reading outcomes.* Manuscript submitted for publication.

Chambers, B., Slavin, R.E., Madden, N.A., Abrami, P.C., Tucker, B.J., Cheung, A., et al. (in press-b). Technology infusion in Success for All: Reading outcomes for first graders. *Elementary School Journal.*

Chambers, B., Slavin, R.E., Madden, N.A., Cheung, A., & Gifford, R. (2005). *Effects of* Success for All *with embedded video on the beginning reading achievement of Hispanic children.* Technical Report. Center for Research and Reform in Education, Johns Hopkins University, Baltimore, MD.

Cuban, L. (2001). *Oversold and underused: Reforming schools through technology, 1980–2000.* Cambridge, MA: Harvard University Press.

Collins, A., Brown, J.S., & Newman, S.E. (1989). Cognitive apprenticeship: Teaching the crafts of reading, writing, and mathematics. In L.B. Resnick (Ed.), *Knowing, learning, and instruction. Essays in honor of Robert Glaser* (pp. 453–494). Hillsdale, NJ: Erlbaum.

Danis, B., Rainville, S., Therrien, M., Tucker, B., Abrami, P.C., & Chambers, B. (2005, July). Alphie's Alley early literacy tutoring software. Paper presented at the EDMedia Conference, Montreal, QC.

Everson, H.T. (1995). Modeling the student in intelligent tutoring systems: The promise of a new psychometrics. *Instructional Science, 23*, 433–452.

Foster, K.C., Erickson, G.C., Foster, D.F., Brinkman, D., & Torgeson, J.K. (1994). Computer administered instruction in phonological awareness: Evaluation of the DaisyQuest program. *Journal of Research and Development in Education, 27*, 126–137.

Gery, G. (2002). Achieving performance and learning through performance centered systems. *Advances in Developing Resources, 4*(4), 464–478.

Greenlee-Moore, M.E., & Smith, L.L. (1996). Interactive computer software: The effects on young children's reading achievement. *Reading Psychology, 17*, 43–64.

Herman, R. (1999). *An educator's guide to schoolwide reform.* Arlington, VA: Educational Research Service.

Hock, M., Schumaker B., & Deshler, D. (2001). The case for strategic tutoring. *Educational Leadership, 58*, 50–52.

Hoeffler, T., & Leutner, D. (2006). Instructional animation vs. static pictures: A meta-analysis. Paper presented at the annual meeting of the American Educational Research Association, San Francisco, CA.

Kulik, J.A. (2003). *Effects of using instructional technology in elementary and secondary schools: What controlled evaluation studies say. SRI Project Number P10446.001.* Arlington, VA: SRI International.

Mayer, R.E. (2001). *Multimedia learning.* New York: Cambridge University Press.

Mioduser, D., Tur-Kaspa, H., & Leitner, I. (2000). The learning value of computer-based instruction of early reading skills. *Journal of Computer Assisted Learning, 16*, 54–63.

Mitchell, P.D., & Grogono, P.D. (1993). Modeling techniques for tutoring systems. *Computers in Education, 20*, 55–61.

Morris, D., Tyner, B., & Perney, J. (2000). Early steps: Replicating the effects of a first-grade reading intervention program. *Journal of Educational Psychology, 92*, 681–693.

Pinnell, G.S., Lyons, C.A., DeFord, D.E., Bryk, A.S., & Seltzer, M. (1994). Comparing instructional models for the literacy education of high risk first graders. *Reading Research Quarterly, 29*, 9–40.

Randi, J., & Corno, L. (2000). Teacher innovations in self-regulated learning. In M. Boekaerts, P.R. Pintrich, & M. Zeidner (Eds.), *Handbook of self-regulation.* San Diego, CA: Academic Press.

Schmid, R.F., Tucker, B.J., Jorgensen, A., Abrami, P.C., Lacroix, G., & Nicolaidou, I. (August, 2005). Tutor-based data on implementation fidelity of SFA Program using technology versus no technology. Paper submitted for presentation at the 2006 Annual Meeting of the American Educational Research Association, Anaheim, CA.

Segers, E., & Verhoeven, L. (2005). Long-term effects of computer training of phonological awareness in kindergarten. *Journal of Computer Assisted Learning, 21,* 17–27.

Slavin, R.E., & Madden, N.A. (2000). Research on achievement outcomes of Success for All: A summary and response to critics. *Phi Delta Kappan, 82,* 38–40, 59–66.

Slavin, R.E., & Madden, N.A. (Eds.) (2001). *One million children: Success for All.* Thousand Oaks, CA: Corwin.

Torgeson, J.K., & Barker, T.A. (1995). Computers as aids in the prevention and remediation of reading disabilities. *Learning Disability Quarterly, 18,* 76–87.

Torgeson, J.K., Wagner, R.K., & Rashotte, C.A. (1997). Prevention and remediation of severe reading disabilities. *Scientific Studies of Reading, 1,* 217–234.

Verhallen, M.J.A.J., Bus, A., & de Jong, M. (2006). The promise of multimedia stories for kindergarten children at risk. *Journal of Educational Psychology, 98,* 410–419.

Wasik, B.A., & Slavin, R.E. (1993). Preventing early reading failure with one-to-one tutoring: A review of five programs. *Reading Research Quarterly, 28,* 178–200.

Wise, B.W., Ring, J., & Olson, R.K. (1999). Training phonological awareness with and without explicit attention to articulation. *Journal of Experimental Child Psychology, 72,* 271–304.

16

Can an Intervention Program in Kindergarten Augment the Effects of Educational TV and Websites in Promoting Literacy?

Iris Levin, Michal Schleifer, Rachel Levin, and Tali Freund

There is ample evidence that early literacy in kindergarten predicts the acquisition of literacy in the first years of school. Results, however, are not entirely consistent across measures. For example, the best predictors have been found to be phonological awareness, rapid naming, invented spelling, and letter knowledge (see e.g., Badian, 1998; Kirby, Parrila, & Pfeiffer, 2003; Levin, Share, & Shatil, 1996; McBride-Chang & Kail, 2002; Morris, Bloodgood, & Perney, 2003; Parrila, Kirby, & McQuarrie, 2004; Scanlon & Vellutino, 1996). Linguistic skills like vocabulary or morphological awareness, however, have been found to be inconsistently associated with later school literacy (see e.g., Aram, 2005; Chaney, 1998; Levin, Ravid, & Rapaport, 2001; Schatschneider, Fletcher, Francis, Carison, & Foorman, 2004; Storch & Whitehurst, 2002). Still, the indisputable conclusion is that literacy from an early age on is highly predictive for the later learning of reading, spelling, and language in school.

The continuity between kindergarten and school grades in literacy is believed to be causal. Consequently, numerous training or intervention studies have been designed to promote early literacy in preschools or kindergartens and most have proved advantageous for literacy achievement later in school (Bus & van IJzendoorn, 1999; Ehri, Nunes, Willows, Yaghoub-Zadeh, & Shanahan, 2001). Three groups of children have been mainly targeted in these studies: children performing poorly at a young age on literate skills (see, e.g., Vellutino, Scanlon, Small, & Fanuele, 2006; O'Connor, Harty, & Fulmer, 2005), children at risk due to familial dyslexia (see e.g., Elbro & Petersen, 2004), or children from socio-culturally disadvantaged populations (see e.g., Gunn, Smolkowsky, Biglan, Black, & Blair, 2005). These studies recognize that it is particularly important to determine how best to promote the literacy skills of socially disadvantaged children because they, by definition, comprise a high proportion of their cohort, and also because they often belong to discriminated sectors on either ethnic–religious or cultural grounds.

A different and new vehicle for promoting literacy, namely educational television programs, has been in use in the last 30 years. In comparison with other more traditional types of intervention programs, this vehicle can be highly cost effective because television is accessible to almost all children rather than only to the small samples used in intervention programs. Moreover, educational programs can be used repeatedly for years without additional cost.

However, there are very few studies on the effects of educational television programs on literacy among preschoolers or kindergarten children. Wright et al. (2001) found a positive association between frequency of viewing child-oriented informative programs like *Sesame Street* at the very young age of 2–3 years and later scores on letter-word skills, receptive vocabulary, and school readiness. In preschool or kindergarten age the frequency of viewing ceased to be related to literacy skills probably because these programs are less attractive for preschoolers and kindergarteners as can be derived from a decline in viewing time.

In contrast, the viewing of the television program *Between the Lions* has been found to promote phonological awareness in kindergarteners (Linebarger, Kosanic, Greenwood, & Doku, 2004; Uchikoshi, 2006; this volume) even though there are certain constraints. For example, Uchikoshi (this volume) found that viewers of *Between the Lions* made more gains in phonological awareness than viewers of the narrative enriching program *Arthur*. Linebarger et al. (2004) found greater gains in phonological awareness among viewers of *Between the Lions* than nonviewers, but the effects were moderated by children's preliminary reading risk status. Those who gained significantly from viewing the program were moderately at risk for reading failure, as assessed by their pretest phonemic awareness. Gains were lower and statistically insignificant for children highly at risk or not at risk for reading failure. Linebarger and colleagues suggest that high-risk children were unable to profit from viewing the program because their teachers were asked to refrain from giving any support in comprehending the program or its print.

In another study by Uchikoshi (2005), gains in narrative skills were found among viewers of *Arthur*, compared with viewers of *Between the Lions*. The results of the aforementioned studies suggest that some educational television programs can enhance code-related skills, like phonological awareness, whereas other programs may promote supra-lexical linguistic skills, like narrative skills.

The study reported in this chapter tests whether support by teachers can improve the effects of a high-tech educational package including a television series and a website. This public package included an educational broadcast on cable television, short interactive interstitials, and a website aimed to improve both code-related and linguistic skills. We wondered whether any effects of this package on kindergarteners' literacy growth could be expended when there was a synergy of information sources (Neuman, this volume) and when teachers' initiated activitiés were designed to build on the package.

In this study, at the time teachers were introduced to the package, they were simultaneously instructed in how to use it in the kindergarten by scaffolding children's learning. They were also equipped with literacy-enriching games, as well as print materials with content similar to the rest of the program. Parents were also introduced to the package, and encouraged to share the activities with their children. Comparisons were made between children involved with the teacher intervention program in the kindergarten who also had access at home to the public domain package (i.e., intervention group) and children who only had access at home to the same public domain package on the TV and the website (i.e., comparison group) but no support in school.

Children from the intervention and comparison groups were recruited from kindergartens serving the low socioeconomic strata, with relatively low parental education levels and poor home literacy. These factors are known to hinder growth of early literacy (Aram & Levin, 2001; Christian, Morrison, & Bryant 1998; Roberts, Jurgens, & Burchinal, 2005) as well as the acquisition of reading, spelling, and language in school (Korat & Levin, 2001; Sénéchal, 2006; Yuet-Han-Lau & McBride-Chang, 2005). Separate analyses were carried out for two groups with an additional at-risk factor, namely new immigrants and kindergarten children with special needs.

Two institutions, the Center for Educational Technology (CET) and Hop! joined forces to make possible this ambitious project. CET is a leading Israeli, nonprofit, nongovernmental organization, established to improve Israel's educational system. The organization's mission is the introduction of innovation, change, and large-scale implementation of general educational initiatives and, specifically, of educational technology. CET develops traditional devices like games and books, as well as programs for promoting literacy in a broad age range. Hop! is a commercial company that established itself as the major nursery–preschool TV channel in Israel. It is ranked as the fourth most viewed channel among the 120 cable channels in Israel. An educational psychologist from Tel Aviv University with expertise on early literacy served as the project's academic consultant.

The Public Projects' Components

Children in the intervention and the comparison groups had access at home to a *television series, interactive television interstitials* on the Hop! channel, and a *website with educational games* developed by CET. Broadcasting started about 5 months earlier than implementation of the intervention program in kindergarten and continued then for a 7-month period. Each of the components listed above are described in detail below.

TV series

Forty TV broadcasts, 15 minutes each, comprised the series entitled *Nachshon Can Do All.* The series was developed by Hop! based on discussions with CET experts and the academic consultant. A program from this series was launched five times a week during the channel's prime time of late afternoon. As mentioned above, the intervention group had access to the program in advance of the kindergarten intervention program.

The TV series had a leading figure named Nachshon. According to Talmudic literature, Nachshon was the first to walk into the Red Sea, upon which the sea separated as promised by God, letting the Israel people escape to liberty. In the present context, Nachshon solves problems related to literacy and language. The basic idea of the series was to introduce the children to metalinguistic knowledge and motivate them to acquire skills in this domain. The playful games featured in the series were premised on the assumption that learning about language and literacy can be fun and useful. Each broadcast, Nachshon runs into a problem and solves it successfully using insights related to language and literacy. The programs cover a wide range of topics, including subsystems of Hebrew morphology, genre distinctions, enrichment of lexicon, and phonological awareness.

One broadcast, for instance, aims at increasing sensitivity to the morphological structure of Hebrew (Ravid, 2004; Ravid & Bar-On, 2005). In this edition, Nachshon discovers that names of colors relate to names of objects with this color. He discovers that the word "rose" is related to the name of the color "pink" (*vered* to *varod*), "ash" to "gray" (*efer* to *afor*), and "vegetable" to "green" (*jerek* to *jarok*). Insight into root structure helps Hebrew speakers grasp the meaning of new lexical items as well as how to spell regular words (Ravid, 2001; Ravid & Schiff, 2006).

Another edition introduced children to the metaphorical use of language. Nachshon tries to find a child while playing "hide and seek." However, he does not understand helpful suggestions rich in metaphorical idiom, such as "to look for a needle in a haystack" or "he lost his hands and feet" (confused). By first taking the metaphorical language too literally and therefore making mistakes, children are made aware of metaphorical and literal use of language, a distinction that is significant for comprehending spoken and written language (Berman & Ravid, 2006).

In yet another edition, Nachshon tries to understand instructions via a telephone but it is not working properly. As the initial syllables of words keep fading he has to guess them. The situation alerts the children to the sound structure of words, an important precursor of reading, thus promoting children's phonological awareness (Bus & van IJzendoorn, 1999; Ehri et al., 2001).

An attempt was made to make Nachshon into a figure with which the children could identify to increase their interest in language and literacy.

Nachshon is therefore depicted on the games and other materials to strengthen the link between the intervention program and the television series.

Interactive Television Interstitials

More than 100 interactive quiz games were developed, each lasting 5 minutes. They served as interstitials and were broadcasted about eight to ten times a day, sometimes using an interactive technology. As previously mentioned, the children in the intervention group had access to these interstitials before the intervention program in the kindergarten started. The interstitials dealt mainly with naming or sounding out letters. For instance, the Hebrew alphabet was presented and each letter was highlighted and named. Many interstitials showed a letter that was simultaneously named in addition to three words in print with matching pictures. Children are instructed to click on the picture with a name starting (or ending) with the focal letter. When children click on one of the wrong pictures the letter name is repeated, till the correct response is selected and approved.

Website Educational Games

A website developed by CET included seven interactive games practicing code-related skills: letter knowledge, phonological awareness (e.g., retrieval of initial or final sounds), and grapho-phonemic awareness (e.g., retrieval of initial or final letters). Text production and word spelling were encouraged via a creative center: the children could compose texts by selecting letters from the keyboard or by dragging items from a file of preprinted words and phrases (e.g., "How are you?" or "Happy birthday") that were pronounced when touched by the cursor. Colorful drawings and decorative patterns could be dragged from another file. The program enabled children to print their text.

Most participating families had access to this rich package either through cable television (83%) or through internet-connected computers (62%). However, the effects of this package were dependent on scaffolding by parents or siblings. Children who were left alone to watch a television series, to manipulate interactive television, or to use a website of educational games, if not supported through family interaction, might gain little because of a lack of understanding, discouragement, or frustration. Consequently, another aim of our study was to assess if the intervention program in school stimulating similar skills added to the effects of this package. Teachers in the intervention group encouraged parents to take a scaffolding role at home.

The Project in Kindergartens

Teachers' Scaffolding

The teachers had via video cassettes access to the *Nachshon Can Do All* series and to the interactive interstitials, and were instructed in how to support children while watching or playing. Children also had access to the website of games and the creative center. In addition, the teachers got feedback about the child users: how often and how long individual children used each game and how well they did on a time scale. The teacher could watch and present on the web children's products in the creative center and assess their spelling and text production. With the help of this rich source of information teachers could decide who needed additional help and in which area. The website also had features that enabled communication between teachers and parents and between teachers and consulting CET experts.

Printed Material

Kindergartens were enriched with printed devices to train code-related skills: cards with Hebrew letters, card games, activity books, and posters. Other print materials were present to enhance language: posters that invite story production and communication with teachers and classmates, 24 storybooks with folk tales and short stories, and a dictionary for young children.

Parental Involvement

Parents were invited to attend two presentations by the teachers with suggestions on how to enhance literacy skills at home. Parents received a special parent–child activity guide for sharing fun games related to the TV broadcasts. Parents were encouraged to watch the TV broadcasts jointly with their children and to participate with their children playing games on the website. Parents had access to the parents' forum on the website that enabled them to share experiences and ideas.

Teachers' Study Group

The teachers participated in seven sessions of about 4 hours, spread over the period of the intervention but mainly taking place in the first 3 months of the project. A CET expert on language and literacy planned and guided the course. Teacher training was considered essential for deepening teachers' knowledge of literacy and language, strengthening their professional skills as educators, and encouraging their cooperation with and commitment to the implementation of the program (e.g., Dickinson & McCabe, 2001). Topics were: development of emergent literacy; incorporating the educational materials into the regular curriculum; guidance of parents in promoting literacy at home; using different genres as reading materials in the kindergarten; developing their own materials and activities to enhance literacy;

and clarification of the goals of the current literacy curricula in Israeli preschools and kindergartens.

Devices Assisting Implementation

To help teachers with pedagogical and technical matters they were visited four times by the expert responsible for the teachers' study group and weekly by CET experts during the first 3 months of the project. Throughout the year CET experts were available by phone or email for any personal assistance needed by the teachers. Teachers used the teachers' forum on the program's website, to share problems and ideas with other teachers and with the experts. In addition, every teacher received written materials concerning the rationale of the program.

Evaluation Study

Participants

Children in 15 kindergartens formed the intervention group and children in 14 kindergartens formed the comparison group. Altogether the sample numbered 449 children, divided between the intervention (233 children) and comparison (216 children) group. All participating kindergartens served primarily low socioeconomic strata, according to criteria developed by the Israeli Ministry of Education.

Evaluation Components

The evaluation included four components: *testing children* in the intervention and comparison groups, *observations* in the kindergartens of the intervention group, *interviewing teachers*, and *interviewing parents* involved in the intervention. A group of university graduates was trained for about 10 hours on testing children and interviewing parents and teachers as well as on documenting responses.

Children's Performance on Tests

Children were tested twice with a period of about 5 months in between, once at the beginning and once at the end of the program. Children who attended the kindergartens on the testing dates took part in the evaluation study. Seven tests were used to assess letter knowledge, phonological awareness, morpho-phonological awareness, and vocabulary. Each type of test has been used in previous studies and found to be reliable and informative. On *Naming Letters* children were asked to name each Hebrew letter printed on a card (see e.g., Treiman, Levin, & Kessler, 2006b). On *Retrieval of Initial Letter* children named the first letter of the stimulus words presented to them orally, and on *Retrieval of Final Letter* they named the last letter of the words (see e.g., Levin, Patel, Margalit, & Barad, 2002; Treiman, Tincoff, & Richmond-Welty, 1996). On *Isolating Initial CV* children isolated the first two phonemes of monosyllabic spoken words with a CVC structure, and on *Isolating Final VC* they did the same for final VC sounds (see e.g., Levin, Shatil-Carmon, & Asif-Rave, 2005; Share & Blum, 2005). On *Pluralization of Nouns* children were asked to provide the plural form of an orally presented noun in singular form (see e.g., Ravid & Schiff, in press). On the *Vocabulary Antonym Test* children were asked to supply the antonym of given lexical items (see e.g., Peyser, Shimborsky, Wolf, & Hazany, 1996).

Both groups exhibited "growth" because all children attended kindergarten, had access at home to the *Nachshon Can Do All* series and the interstitials on cable television, and were able to access the games on the public website on the internet.

Comparisons between the intervention and comparison groups were carried out on each test separately. Mean scores at the start of the program

Table 16.1 Pretest, posttest and progress scores for each test and t-values as indicators of differences in progress

Test and timing	Intervention group			Comparison group			t-value and significance
	M	SD	N	M	SD	N	
Naming letters: Pretest	35	30	193	37	31	214	
Naming letters: Posttest	76	25	194	70	27	211	
Naming letters: Progress	40	24	185	33	23	209	$t = 2.99$**
Retrieval of Initial Letter: Pretest	22	25	201	26	31	210	
Retrieval of Initial Letter: Posttest	68	33	194	61	33	212	
Retrieval of Initial Letter: Progress	46	30	193	34	29	206	$t = 3.89$**
Retrieval of Final Letter: Pretest	8	15	199	11	20	213	
Retrieval of Final Letter: Posttest	52	36	188	39	31	208	
Retrieval of Final Letter: Progress	44	33	186	28	27	206	$t = 5.25$**
Retrieval of Initial Sound: Pretest	33	27	199	30	29	213	
Retrieval of Initial Sound: Posttest	64	30	191	54	29	211	
Retrieval of Initial Sound: Progress	32	31	188	25	30	209	$t = 2.52$*
Retrieval of Final Sound: Pretest	13	26	200	14	25	211	
Retrieval of Final Sound: Posttest	58	41	189	45	37	208	
Retrieval of Final Sound: Progress	45	39	187	31	33	204	$t = 3.95$**
Vocabulary (Antonyms): Pretest	41	16	202	41	17	216	
Vocabulary (Antonyms): Posttest	56	15	193	56	19	212	
Vocabulary (Antonyms): Progress	15	13	193	14	15	212	$t = 0.20$ ns
Morphology (Plurality): Pretest	72	13	202	73	12	216	
Morphology (Plurality): Posttest	81	11	194	80	10	208	
Morphology (Plurality): Progress	9	11	194	7	9	208	$t = 1.46$ ns
Total Score: Pretest	32	15	202	34	18	216	
Total Score: Posttest	65	23	194	58	21	212	
Total Score: Progress	33	17	194	24	14	212	$t = 5.40$**

Notes
Progress scores are based on scores of children tested on pre- and on posttest.
*$p < 0.05$; **$p < 0.01$.

and at the end, as well as progress from beginning to end, for each test and each group separately, appear in Table 16.1. Analyses by t-tests contrasting progress in the intervention and comparison group revealed that the intervention enhanced growth in all code-related skills (i.e., letter naming, retrieval of initial and final letters, and isolating initial CV and final VC sounds) but not in vocabulary and morphology (i.e., vocabulary antonym test and pluralization of nouns). Hebrew morpho-phonology and vocabulary, key focus points in a few episodes of the *Nachshon Can Do All* series, were promoted by posters and storybooks. The reasons for less growth may therefore not be that the program overlooked these skills but may lie in the density and complexity to practice and assess these skills.

This project targeted children at academic risk since they were recruited from classrooms mainly attended by children from low SES. However, children with additional risk factors attended the same classrooms: immigrants and children with special needs. To analyze whether high-risk children gained from the program as much as low SES mainstream children, the impact of the intervention program on mainstream children was compared to that on high-risk children.

Immigrants came from two main sources: Asian Republics of the former Soviet Union and Ethiopia. Immigrants to Israel in general and from Ethiopia in particular are at risk in terms of academic achievements in school (Levin, Shohami, & Spolsky, 2003). Shany (2006) documented that Israeli kindergarten children from an Ethiopian background were relatively poor on many measures of language and literacy relative to their classmates and to the normative cohort in Israel. Schleifer (2003) did not find statistically significant differences between Ethiopian and native Israeli low SES students in grades 5–11 but both groups performed worse than their middle SES counterparts. The children with special needs were mainly slow learners or pupils who received professional remedial help for diagnosed behavioral problems.

Table 16.2 presents mean scores across all tests at the beginning and the end of the intervention period among the four groups. Three Way Analysis of Variance (ANOVA) with as independent variables Time (pretest and posttest), Group (intervention and comparison), and Population (mainstreamers, immigrants, children with special needs) revealed the following picture. Overall performance improved from pretest to posttest, (F (1, 398) = 412.05, $p < 0.001$). Most importantly, there was more improvement in the intervention than in the comparison group, as reflected by a Time by Group interaction (F (1, 398) = 6.29, $p < 0.02$). Overall, the four populations differed significantly from each other: mainstreamers and immigrants gained more than Israeli born or immigrants with special needs, (F (3, 398) = 4.86, $p < 0.002$). No significant difference emerged between Israeli mainstreamers or immigrants. In the same vein, no difference emerged between Israeli born and immigrants, both of which had special needs. Population did not interact

Table 16.2 Mean scores on pre- and posttests across all tests, by population, group and time

Population	Pretest		Posttest	
	M	SD	M	SD
Intervention group				
Mainstream children (*n* = 117)	35	16	67	23
Immigrants (*n* = 46)	30	14	65	21
Children with special needs (*n* =27)	27	12	58	24
Immigrants with special needs (*n* = 4)	32	10	56	20
Comparison group				
Mainstream children (*n* = 121)	36	19	60	21
Immigrants (*n* = 46)	32	16	59	20
Children with special needs (*n* = 35)	26	15	50	21
Immigrants with special needs (*n* = 10)	35	23	56	23

with Group, with Time, or with Group and Time, suggesting that the intervention had a similar effect on all populations suggesting that children with special needs who possibly may have greater difficulty in using the educational materials make similar gains as their mainstream counterparts. However, the gains in literacy skills exhibited by the children with special needs, though promising, did not narrow the gap between the risk group and mainstream children (see Table 16.2).

Observations in Kindergartens

Planned visits took place twice in each kindergarten: 2 months after the beginning of the intervention program and close to the end of the program. Each visit lasted for about 2 hours. Observations focused on one of the following activities: watching videocassettes of the *Nachshon* series, playing games on the website, and using printed materials.

Small groups of 14–20 children watched the *Nachshon* series together on a regular basis. The observers reported that children appeared interested and as having fun. Many sang along with the opening song of the broadcast. The level of scaffolding varied across teachers. Most teachers watched the video with the children and stopped it from time to time for questions or clarification of issues. A few teachers remained passive or occupied themselves with something else. One teacher during the first visit and two during the second prepared printed material or organized a game providing additional practice of the skill taught in the program.

The website games were carried out either by a single child or jointly by two children for about 20 minutes. The teachers who mostly designated children to play games had a preference for weak children to promote their motivation to learn and advance language and literacy skills. On the other hand, they were careful to give turns to all children. Sometimes they comprised dyads varying in academic skills to facilitate and encourage peer teaching. At one extreme, the teachers were totally uninvolved; in the moderate involvement range, teachers approached the children when a problem arose or to suggest changing games; and at the other extreme, teachers sat with the children, made suggestions, and provided help and encouragement. The observers reported that children were highly motivated about using the website and, in general, exhibited no recurrent difficulties or frustrations.

Groups of five to eight children played together with the printed games. Often, the children were highly involved in the games and interacted extensively with each other. The teachers always participated and guided the children in problem solving. The games observed dealt mostly with code-related skills.

Teachers' interviews. Most teachers mentioned that they utilized the materials. The website presenting games and a creativity center was unanimously perceived as most attractive to children. Some children often arrived earlier than usual at school "to be the first in line." Some parents reported buying a computer so that their children had access to the games at home.

The teachers found the videocassettes broadcasting the *Nachshon Can Do All* series to be enjoyable and stimulating. As many children watched the television series at home, to the extent that they cited sections of the text by heart, they were not as eager to watch them as often in school.

The printed materials, including cards, literacy games, books, and a dictionary, were used several times a week. Teachers developed a classroom library where children could borrow the provided storybooks.

Teachers were asked an open-ended question about how successful they thought the program had been in their kindergartens. All teachers expressed a high level of satisfaction with the program and its impact on children's development and their own professional development and motivation. One teacher said:

> My children's literacy is at a more advanced level, earlier than in the previous years. The ideas in the guidebook for teachers led me to invent new materials. The program increased my motivation to work harder and aspire for higher levels of achievement. It heightened my sense of responsibility concerning children's achievements.

A second teacher commented: "Although I worked on literacy in kindergarten for many years, the program updated me and made me demand more from the kids. Now I am computer-literate and can use the internet." A third teacher said: "The contents were delivered in a game-like atmosphere. It was a delight for the entire class."

Parents' interviews. A total of 95 parents, randomly selected of the children in the intervention group (40%) were interviewed. Most parents (85%) had access to cable television at home. Among those parents, 87% reported that their children watched the *Nachshon Can Do All* series at home on cable television, a highly impressive number—40% reported a high rate of five to six times a week, 28% a rate of three to four times a week, and the rest a low rate of once or twice a week. Access to the internet website with games, the creativity center, and the communication center for parents was present in 64% of the homes. Among those parents, 84% reported that their children were using the website, again, a highly impressive number—21% reported a high rate of five to six times a week, 27% reported a rate of three to four times a week, and the rest a low rate of once or twice a week. The intensive use of TV and the website may be promoted by the intervention program in school. Children probably improved on the trained skills, were motivated to deepen their learning, a motivation that corroborated the motivation of parents to get involved.

A total of 97% of the interviewed sample reported working on the parent–child activity book, a remarkable high rate of involvement. This result suggests that exclusion of print materials like activity books and working sheets is not desirable taking into account that the device is simple and inexpensive and can easily be developed by teachers.

Overall parents responded positively to an open-ended question about how successful they thought the project in the kindergartens has been, perhaps more positively than they really felt because of social desirability. Nevertheless, the degree of support and the variety of issues praised were encouraging. One mother said: "Since the project started, my child has made great progress, recognizes letters, and almost reads. I am very satisfied. The project is a success." Another mother referred to spelling and school readiness:

The program is very good. It helped my son. Thanks to the program, he now knows how to spell words aloud … thanks to the program he is well prepared for first grade. It's too bad that such a program did not exist before.

A third mother mentioned discourse skills as well as code-related skills: "The program is excellent and contributes greatly to learning how to follow instructions, listening, learning the alphabet, and rhyming." A fourth mother talked about parental involvement:

It's good that there is a program that involves the parents. It is very important to get ready for first grade. My daughter already knows all of the letters and is very good with letters. It's important that the parents take part. Usually, in kindergarten, parents don't participate.

Discussion

This study is unique in that it examined the impact of an intervention program in kindergarten that was planned to enhance the effects of programs on television and the internet that were accessible at home. The program was as effective in promoting code skills for mainstream children as for immigrants and for children with special needs, all of whom were at risk academically to some extent because of their low SES background.

The results of our study can be compared with those of Linebarger et al. (2004) who, unlike us, found no positive effects on high-risk children who watched the television literacy-related program *Between the Lions*. They concluded that high-risk children probably need scaffolding in understanding the program and its print. In our study, the more positive results can be explained by the fact that the children in the intervention group got a high amount of scaffolding by teachers and by parents.

Our program was effective in promoting code-related skills but did not seem to enhance the children's vocabulary or morphology skills. The failure of the program to boost vocabulary and morphological awareness is perhaps related to the density, complexity, and difficulty of the competencies tested. It has been claimed that learning to name letters follows the same principles as those involved in learning new words (Treiman, Kessler, & Pollo, 2006a; Treiman et al., 2006b). However, letter names in many alphabets form a close class of 20 to 30 items whereas the lexicon is an open class of a huge number of items. Therefore, it may be easier to trace growth in letter names by asking the children to name all the letters in the alphabet than to show growth in vocabulary by testing them on a sample of lexical items, not necessarily those that were dealt with in the program. In an evaluation study of an intervention program in kindergarten, Levin, Aram, Biron, and Shemesh (2003) reported that vocabulary growth was found to occur when children were tested on words practiced by the program but not when they were tested on children using the Antonym Vocabulary Test that we administered in the current study. It is possible that our intervention program may have familiarized children with new words or helped them in understanding other words having the same roots, but that it had no effect on children's scores obtained in a general test of vocabulary.

Phonological awareness at the level used here (CV or VC sound isolation) develops from preschool to first grade (Levin et al., 2005; Share & Blum, 2005) and, therefore, suitable for training in kindergarten. Pluralization in Hebrew as measured in our study taps knowledge of the complex morphophonological system of Hebrew, a skill that develops later (Ravid & Schiff, in press). Our program perhaps enhanced children's acquisition of plural forms, but at a preliminary level rather than at the more complex level in the test. Our observations and teachers' reports clearly show that interacting with computers is attractive to young children. A new medium of electronic books used on the computer might have had an added impact on vocabulary and related competencies (Bus et al., this volume; Korat & Shamir, this volume; Verhallen, Bus, & de Jong, 2006).

A main limitation of this study is that the intervention comprised a multitude of components. We do not know which component or combination of components accounted for the positive effects we found on literacy in kindergarten. The conclusion that the educational effects of TV programs and websites in the public domain can be expanded by related interventions in school is a fascinating result awaiting further systematic research.

References

Aram, D. (2005). The continuity in children's literacy achievements: A longitudinal perspective from kindergarten to second grade. *First Language, 25*, 259–289.

Aram, D., & Levin, I. (2001). Mother–child joint writing in low SES: Sociocultural factors, maternal mediation, and emergent literacy. *Cognitive Development, 16*, 831–852.

Badian, N.A. (1998). A validation of the role of preschool phonological and orthographic skills in the prediction of reading. *Journal of Reading Disabilities, 31*, 472–481.

Berman, R., & Ravid, D. (2006, July 6–8). Children's knowledge of novel and traditional sayings: The impact of schooling. Paper presented at the 2006 Conference of the Society for the Scientific Study of Reading, Vancouver, Canada.

Bus, A.G., & van IJzendoorn, M.H. (1999). Phonological awareness and early reading: A meta-analysis of experimental training studies. *Journal of Educational Psychology, 91*, 403–414.

Chaney, C. (1998). Preschool language and metalinguistic skills are links to reading success. *Applied Psycholinguistics, 19*, 433–446.

Christian, K., Morrison, F., & Bryant, F.B. (1998). Predicting kindergarten academic skills: Interactions among child care, maternal education, and family literacy environments. *Early Childhood Literacy Research Quarterly, 13*, 501–521.

Dickinson, D.K., & McCabe, A. (2001). Bringing it all together: The multiple origins, skills, and environmental supports of early literacy. *Learning Disabilities Research & Practice, 16*, 186–202.

Ehri, L.C., Nunes, S.R., Willows, D.M., Yaghoub-Zadeh, Z., & Shanahan, T. (2001). Phonemic awareness instruction helps children learn to read: Evidence from the National Reading Panel's meta-analysis. *Reading Research Quarterly, 36*, 250–287.

Elbro, C., & Petersen, D.K. (2004). Long-term effects of phoneme awareness and letter sound training: An intervention study with children at risk for dyslexia. *Journal of Educational Psychology, 96*, 660–670.

Gunn, B., Smolkowsky, K., Biglan, A., Black, C., & Blair, J. (2005). Fostering the development of reading skills through supplemental instruction: Results for Hispanic and non-Hispanic students. *Journal of Special Education, 39*, 66–85.

Kirby, J.R., Parrila, R.K., & Pfeiffer, S.L. (2003). Naming speed and phonological awareness as predictors of reading achievement. *Journal of Educational Psychology, 95*, 453–464.

Korat, O., & Levin, I. (2001). Maternal beliefs, mother–child interaction, and child's literacy: Comparison of independent and collaborative text writing between two social groups. *Applied Developmental Psychology, 22*, 397–420.

Levin, I., Aram, D., Biron, S., & Shemesh, K. (2003). Tochnijot lekidum orjanut beganei jeladim bejafo [Programs for promoting literacy in preschools in Japha]. *Hed Hagan, 2*, 4–24 (Hebrew).

Levin, I., Patel, S., Margalit, T., & Barad, N. (2002). Letter-names: Effect on letter saying, spelling and word recognition in Hebrew. *Applied Psycholinguistics, 23*, 269–300.

Levin, I., Ravid, D., & Rapaport, S. (2001). Morphology and spelling among Hebrew-speaking children: From kindergarten to first grade. *Journal of Child Language, 28*, 741–772.

Levin, I., Share, D.L., & Shatil, E. (1996). A qualitative–quantitative study of preschool writing:

Its development and contribution to school literacy. In M. Levy & S. Ransdell (Eds.), *The science of writing* (pp. 271–293). Mahwah, NJ: Erlbaum.

Levin, I., Shatil-Carmon, S., & Asif-Rave, O. (2005). Learning of letter names and sounds and contribution to word reading. *Journal of Experimental Child Psychology, 93*, 139–165.

Levin, T., Shohami, E., & Spolsky, D. (2003). *Matzavam ha'limudi shel talmidim olim: Mimtzaim ve'hamlatzot le'mekablei haxlatot* [*Academic achievements of immigrant students: Findings and recommendations for decision makers*]. Jerusalem, Israel: Department of the Chief Scientist, Ministry of Education (Hebrew).

Linebarger, D.L., Kosanic, A.Z., Greenwood, C.R., & Doku, N.S. (2004). Effects of viewing the television program *Between the Lions* on the emergent literacy skills of young children. *Journal of Educational Psychology, 96*, 297–308.

McBride-Chang, C., & Kail, R.V. (2002). Cross-cultural similarities in predictors of reading acquisition. *Child Development, 73*, 1392–1407.

Morris, D., Bloodgood, J., & Perney, J. (2003). Kindergarten predictors of first- and second-grade reading achievement. *Elementary School Journal, 104*, 93–109.

O'Connor, R.E., Harty, K.R., & Fulmer, D. (2005). Tiers of intervention in kindergarten through third grade. *Journal of Learning Disabilities, 38*, 523–538.

Parrila, R., Kirby, J.R., & McQuarrie, L. (2004). Articulation rate, naming speed, verbal short-term memory, and phonological awareness: Longitudinal predictors of early reading development? *Scientific Studies of Reading, 8*, 3–26.

Peyser, M., Shimborsky, G., Wolf, N., & Hazany, I. (19965). *Israeli version: Kauffman Assessment Battery for Children.* Jerusalem, Israel: Ministry of Education, Culture & Sports, Henrietta Szold Institute for Research in Behavioral Sciences.

Ravid, D. (2001). Learning to spell in Hebrew: Phonological and morphological factors. *Reading and Writing, 14*, 459–485.

Ravid, D. (2004). Hebrew orthography and literacy. In R.M. Joshi & P.G. Aaron (Eds.), *Handbook of orthography and literacy* (pp. 339–363). Mahwah, NJ: Lawrence Erlbaum Associates.

Ravid, D., & Bar-On, A. (2005). Manipulating written Hebrew roots across development: The interface of semantic, phonological and orthographic factors. *Reading and Writing, 18*, 231–256.

Ravid, D., & Schiff, R. (2006). Roots and patterns in Hebrew language development: evidence from written morphological analogies. *Reading and Writing, 19*, 789–818.

Ravid, D., & Schiff, R. (in press). Morpho-phonological categories of noun plurals in Hebrew: A developmental study. *Linguistics.*

Roberts, J., Jurgens, J., & Burchinal, M. (2005). The role of home literacy practices in preschool children's language and emergent literacy skills. *Journal of Speech, Language and Hearing Research, 48*, 345–359.

Scanlon, D.M., & Vellutino, F.R. (1996). Prereading skills, early instruction, and success in first-grade reading: Selected results from a longitudinal study. *Mental Retardation and Developmental Disabilities Research Reviews, 2*, 54–63.

Schatschneider, C., Fletcher, J.M., Francis, D.J., Carison, C.D., & Foorman, B.R. (2004). Kindergarten prediction of reading skills: A longitudinal comparative analysis. *Journal of Educational Psychology, 96*, 265–282.

Schleifer, M. (2003). Development of written text production of native Israeli and Ethiopian immigrant schoolchildren and adolescents: Linguistic and socio-cultural perspectives. Unpublished doctoral dissertation, Tel-Aviv University, Tel-Aviv, Israel.

Sénéchal, M. (2006). Testing the home literacy model: Parent involvement in kindergarten is differentially related to Grade 4 reading comprehension, fluency, spelling, and reading for pleasure. *Scientific Studies of Reading, 10*, 59–87.

Shany, M. (2006). Rexishat ha'safa ha'ktuva be'kerev jaledei ha'eda ha'etjopit be'Israel, mi'gil ha'gan ve'ad kita vav: Heibetim cognitivijim, orjaniim-svivatijim u'lshonijim [Acquisition of written language in Ethiopian children in Israel from kindergarten to grade 6: Cognitive, literate-environmental and linguistic aspects]. Scientific report submitted to the Israeli Ministry of Education (Hebrew).

Share, D.L., & Blum, P. (2005). Syllable splitting in literate and pre-literate Hebrew speakers:

Onsets and rimes or bodies and codas. *Journal of Experimental Child Psychology, 92*, 182–202.

Storch, S.A., & Whitehurst, G.J. (2002). Oral language and code-related precursors to reading: Evidence from a longitudinal structural model. *Developmental Psychology, 38*, 934–947.

Treiman, R., Kessler, B., & Pollo, T.C. (2006a). Learning about the letter name subset of the vocabulary: Evidence from US and Brazilian preschoolers. *Applied Psycholinguistics, 27*, 211–227.

Treiman, R., Levin, I., & Kessler, B. (2006b). Learning of letter names follows similar principles across languages: Evidence from Hebrew. *Journal of Experimental Child Psychology, 93*, 139–165.

Treiman, R., Tincoff, R., & Richmond-Welty, E.D. (1996). Letter names help children connect print and speech. *Developmental Psychology, 32*, 505–514.

Uchikoshi, Y. (2005). Narrative development in bilingual kindergartners: Can Arthur help? *Developmental Psychology, 41*, 464–478.

Uchikoshi, Y. (2006). Early reading in bilingual kindergartners: Can educational television help? *Scientific Studies of Reading, 10*, 89–120.

Vellutino, F.R., Scanlon, D.M., Small, S., & Fanuele, D.P. (2006). Response to intervention as a vehicle for distinguishing between children with and without reading disabilities: Evidence for the role of kindergarten and first grade interventions. *Journal of Learning Disabilities, 39*, 157–169.

Verhallen, M., Bus, A.G., & de Jong, M. (2006). The promise of multimedia stories for kindergarten children at risk. *Journal of Educational Psychology, 98*, 410–419.

Wright, J.C., Huston, A.C., Murphy, K.C., St. Peters, M., Piñon, M., Scantlin, R., et al. (2001). The relations of early television viewing to school readiness and vocabulary of children from low income families: The early windows project. *Child Development, 72*, 1347–1366.

Yuet-Han-Lau, J., & McBride-Chang, C. (2005). Home literacy and Chinese reading in Hong Kong children. *Early Education and Development, 16*, 5–22.

17

Use of Electronic Storybooks in Reading Instruction

From Theory to Practice

Michael C. McKenna and Tricia A. Zucker

It seems fair to say that the market-driven genesis of electronic storybooks has relied more on evidence of commercial appeal than evidence of efficacy. If we assume the presence of eStorybooks in classrooms for the foreseeable future, it is important that literacy researchers systematically produce the latter kind of evidence, asking questions that are key to determining the most effective ways of using these promising resources. Such questions include how best to integrate eStorybooks into classroom instruction and which features are likely to aid particular students, both those who struggle and those who do not. Research agendas devised to address these questions must be grounded in theory. Some of the theoretical underpinnings of these lines of inquiry are extensions of those used in print settings; some are unique to hypermedia contexts (see also Neuman, this volume). Our goals in this chapter are to examine how theory can inform investigations into the effectiveness of eStorybooks, to summarize the evidence presently available, and to derive recommendations for practice on the basis of both theory and research.

Problems of Characterizing eStorybook Features

In their discussion of eStorybook features, de Jong & Bus (2003) point out that many of them enrich the reading experience, making it qualitatively different from the print version. Such features include overview screens that might include read-to-me versus let-me-play options, animations that dramatize the story, music and cinematic effects that create mood, interactive activities that might support learning, and hotspots that might facilitate comprehension. Identifying features is a first step toward framing a theoretical basis for investigating eStorybooks and implementing them to best effect in classrooms. However, it is also important to consider the readers most likely to benefit from digital features and under what circumstances.

One way to categorize digital features is according to whether they are useful to struggling versus developmental readers. We do not find this approach to be very useful. This is because most features can support both kinds of readers, depending on the relationship between text demands and a reader's proficiency. For example, point-and-click definitions might support a child with vocabulary too weak to comprehend grade-level text, but they might also support a better reader who is attempting to read more challenging text. Likewise, a listening version might support a child with limited decoding skills, but it might also be chosen by a child who prefers the dramatic story-telling within the read-aloud function. It is true that a few features, such as American Sign Language pop-ups, appear to be useful only to those who read with difficulty; it is likewise true that hyperlinks to more advanced sources are likely to be useful only to more able readers. However, the majority of features may be used by readers of differing abilities for different purposes. This fact has implications for the designers of commercial eStorybooks, for the teachers who integrate them into instruction, and for researchers interested in how such features are used. Figure 17.1 illustrates how some of the more common digital features might be categorized on the basis of reader ability.

A second approach to categorizing features involves their capacity to support the reader in comprehending the text versus their capacity to provide incidental or explicit instruction as the child reads. We find this approach equally problematic because most supportive features have at least some instructional value. Figure 17.2 categorizes a nonexhaustive set of such features as to whether they are instructive or supportive (or both or neither). Embedded instructional devices that are not instrumental to comprehension, such as decoding minilessons, are one of the few examples of features that are purely instructive, while print enlargement is among the few that support without instructing. Some features, such as amusing but irrelevant links and hotspots, seem to have neither a supportive nor an instructive function. Consequently, it is probably best to consider features in light of the goals of reading and of reading instruction.

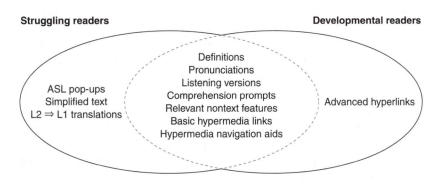

Figure 17.1 Categorizing digital features by their usefulness to readers of differing ability.

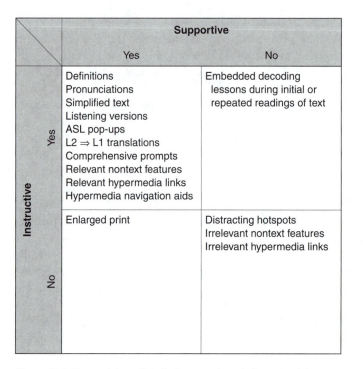

		Supportive	
		Yes	No
Instructive	Yes	Definitions Pronunciations Simplified text Listening versions ASL pop-ups L2 ⇒ L1 translations Comprehensive prompts Relevant nontext features Relevant hypermedia links Hypermedia navigation aids	Embedded decoding lessons during initial or repeated readings of text
	No	Enlarged print	Distracting hotspots Irrelevant nontext features Irrelevant hypermedia links

Figure 17.2 Categorizing digital features by their potential to support and instruct.

The Simple View for the Complex World of eStorybooks

As evidenced by this brief discussion of eStorybook features, it is clear that multimedia texts create a complex world with many factors for educators to consider. Yet, two models of reading provide a particularly useful structure for interpreting and simplifying the eStorybook research because these models make clear the reading processes that electronic texts can most effectively support. First is Gough and Tunmer's (1986) simple view of reading and next is Stanovich's (1980) interactive-compensatory model of reading. The simple view postulates that both decoding (D) skills and oral language comprehension (LC) abilities are necessary for successful reading (R). Thus, successful reading can be represented by the equation, $R = D \times LC$, where D and LC range from 0 (no ability) to 1 (highest ability). According to this equation, even perfect proficiency in one area cannot compensate for no proficiency in the other. That is, the product of 1 and 0 will always be 0. This model can be applied two decades later to the specific case of eStorybooks because the features embedded in these digital texts generally seek to bolster either decoding or oral language (listening) comprehension abilities. Given the framework of the simple view, we will consider research regarding code-related and comprehension-related opportunities of eStorybooks in turn.

Like the simple view, the interactive-compensatory model (Stanovich, 1980) proposes that it is not enough to have orthographic knowledge for successful reading. This model goes further by suggesting that automatic decoding is necessary for skilled reading and that if readers lack these word level skills, they will attempt to compensate by accessing alternative knowledge sources, such as considering the semantic context of the sentence, to aid in decoding. But this model is not limited to decoding. Stanovich (1980) explains that a "deficit in any knowledge source results in heavier reliance on other knowledge sources, *regardless* of their level in the processing hierarchy," or regardless of whether it is a low- or high-level cognitive process (p. 63). The problem with compensating for deficiencies in an area such as automatic word recognition is that accessing additional cognitive resources occurs "at a cost" (p. 64) because fewer cognitive resources are available for comprehension processes (see also LaBerge & Samuels, 1974).

Several features of electronic texts are designed to provide a type of automatic compensatory mechanism to support a reader's deficits in either low- or high-level processes at a minimal "cost" to the cognitive resource supply. Thus, a child who would normally rely on context to compensate for poor decoding skills can instead use an on-demand text-to-speech feature to hear the word pronounced; similarly, a child who does not know the meaning of a word can access embedded word definitions or animations to understand the word's meaning in context. The presence of these digital scaffolds challenges conventional notions of the independent, instructional, and frustrational reading levels (McKenna, 1998). For a beginning reader with limited decoding skills, for example, word recognition supports might mean that the independent level is equal to the listening level. Likewise, with conceptual supports (background knowledge, simplified text, definitions on demand, audio commentary, etc.), the independent level might actually exceed the listening level. Still, to be effective, support features must be within the child's zone of proximal development (de Jong & Bus, 2002; McKenna, Reinking, & Bradley, 2003; Talley, Lancy, & Lee, 1997) and, as stated above, must align with a child's instructional needs as determined by systematic assessment (Stahl, Kuhn, & Pickle, 1999; McKenna, Stahl, & Stahl, 2008).

By applying the interactive-compensatory model to eStorybooks, we can view them as one type of assistive technology (AT) in that their digital supports help to compensate for skill deficits until the child reaches the point at which assistance is no longer needed. For this reason, it also makes sense to consider eStorybooks as a potential intervention when the use of compensatory supports is deemed appropriate and/or instructive (see also Van Daal, this volume). Accordingly, eStorybooks may have an important role to play in the response to intervention (RTI) applications that are arising in special education. (For a discussion of the potential of AT in reading clinics see McKenna & Walpole, 2007.)

Although we believe that the simple view and the interactive-compensatory model provide a good theoretical fit to both print and electronic books, one more issue must be mentioned. The dynamic and evolving nature of all new literacies means that eStorybooks "are not just new today, they will be newer tomorrow, and even newer next week, and continuously renewed as new technologies for literacy regularly appear" (Leu, 2006, p. 13). Because of this rapidly changing nature of the new technologies, Leu (2000, 2006) defines the new literacies as a deictic construct in which meanings change quickly. Thus, it is necessary to ground all of our thinking in the notion that effective ways to use eStorybooks today and the features that provide an interactive-compensatory scaffold may be outdated in the future.

Breaking the Code: Supportive Digital Practices for Struggling Readers

Perhaps the clearest application of the interactive-compensatory model to eStorybooks is considering how digital decoding supports allow readers to devote their attention and cognitive resources to comprehension (LaBerge & Samuels, 1974). Before examining this research, we should state that we agree with Stanovich (1984) that "there is no substitute for automatic, efficient data-driven processing at the word level" for comprehension to occur (p. 15). We do not support the indefinite use of electronic decoding supports, but rather view this as a scaffold to provide while the reader receives instruction, and perhaps intervention, to develop automatic word recognition abilities (McKenna & Walpole, 2007).

Several researchers have explored ways to use computers to compensate for deficits in decoding skills (e.g., de Jong & Bus, 2002; Doty, Popplewell, & Byers, 2001; Matthew, 1997; McKenna, 1998; Olofsson, 1992; Reitsma, 1988). Findings from this research are mixed, with some studies showing comprehension benefits when using electronic texts with text-to-speech supports (e.g., Doty et al., 2001), and others finding no gains in comprehension despite use of eStorybooks that are designed to compensate for word decoding problems (e.g., Olofsson, 1992). Doty et al. (2001) found that second-grade children who read interactive eStorybooks scored significantly higher in answering oral comprehension questions compared with students who read a conventional text; however, no significant differences were found in oral retellings of these two groups. When Matthew (1997) asked third-grade students to produce a written retelling of three eStorybooks, their retellings were significantly more developed than students who read the print version of these storybooks. Yet Matthew (1997) found no significant group differences in the ability to answer reading comprehension questions. These differences in outcomes may reflect variations in measurement formats and text genres used more than differences in the efficacy of using electronic texts to support comprehension.

Electronic supports for decoding may have differential effects for more-

and less-skilled readers. With a group of first graders, Lefever-Davis and Pearman (2005) investigated the advantages and disadvantages of using electronic books to support oral reading practice. In this study, the researchers observed students' miscues and interactions with the *Reader Rabbit* series of CD-ROM storybooks and noted different behaviors for struggling versus stronger readers. For instance, struggling readers used the features of the electronic text only to support the actual reading process, such as using "digital pronunciations to familiarize themselves with a word, confirm their predictions, and gain meaning" (pp. 451–452). On the other hand, proficient readers used the digital pronunciation tool for more mature purposes such as fine-tuning their voice intonation and expression based on the computer's model. This finding is promising in that eStorybooks appear to have benefits for different levels of readers, but it also illustrates why mere access to electronic texts will not close the achievement gap between normal and struggling readers.

Interestingly, electronic decoding supports may not only serve as a compensatory mechanism, but may also increase students' word recognition skills. For example, accessing pronunciations in eStorybooks helps children add to their lexicon of automatically recognized sight words (e.g., Davidson, Coles, Noyes, & Terrell, 1991; McKenna et al., 2003; Shamir & Korat, this volume). But not all electronic features are equally effective in supporting decoding. Evidence suggests that electronic decoding resources must be unobtrusive so that young readers can activate these supports with enough ease that comprehension is not sacrificed in an effort to improve code-related skills (McKenna, 1998). For example, in a series of studies McKenna and Watkins (1994, 1995, 1996) found that embedding decoding minilessons at points where children clicked to hear a word pronounced (e.g., "Let's see, if c-a-t is cat, then h-a-t must be [pause] hat") can be too intrusive or cognitively demanding for beginning readers.

Nonetheless, research with conventional books suggests that adults can effectively embed explicit, print-related minilessons during read-alouds with preschool-age children by making verbal and nonverbal references to print (e.g., Justice & Ezell, 2000, 2002; Lovelace & Stewart, 2007). Likewise, research with traditional storybooks suggests that embedding explicit instruction in phonological awareness within read-alouds can be effective for preschoolers (e.g., Ukrainetz, Cooney, Dyer, Kysar, & Harris, 2000). Still, some researchers suggest that young children may not benefit from computer assistance in breaking the code (Goodwin, Goodwin, Nasel, & Helm, 1986; Olofsson, 1992), but others are more optimistic that children as young as preschool can foster early-developing print knowledge skills by using electronic texts (Talley et al., 1997). With a quasi-experimental design, Talley et al. (1997) found that Head Start children who were not read to at home made significant gains in print concepts and book convention knowledge when given access to eStorybooks for 8 weeks. Some evidence suggests that eStorybooks can support development of young children's phonological skills as well (Wood, 2005).

Further research is needed to determine how code-related supports can be effectively embedded in eStorybooks for increasing both early-developing print skills, such as understanding book and print conventions, and later-developing print skills, including sight word recognition and decoding. Although positive outcomes for improving children's code-based skills with eStorybook use have been cited, others have failed to find effects for increasing students' decoding and word recognition skills when reading eStorybooks (e.g., Davidson et al., 1991). A recent study examining the impact of reading eStorybooks on young readers' recognition of target words from eStorybooks suggests that animations and hotspots can distract children from attending to print (de Jong & Bus, 2002). Perhaps these competing features of the electronic reading environment can explain the inconsistent findings in this area; perhaps, like traditional print books, simply providing young children access to electronic read-alouds of eStorybooks will only have limited effects on their code-related skills without a deliberate adult- or computer-mediated focus on print (Stahl, 2003). Additional research is needed to determine if and at what stages of reading development explicit code-based minilessons detract from students' enjoyment and comprehension of eStorybooks. Given that comprehension proficiency becomes more important in later stages when children read texts requiring higher levels of inferencing and more sophisticated conceptual knowledge (Storch & Whitehurst, 2002; Vellutino, Tunmer, Jaccard, & Chen, 2007), it is plausible that decoding minilessons, fluency minilessons, or even features that highlight the printed words in eStorybooks could be a liability for more advanced readers, whose focus should be on improving comprehension and vocabulary during reading.

Applying the Interactive-Compensatory Model to Comprehension

The interactive-compensatory model (Stanovich, 1980) focuses primarily on individual differences in the ways young readers and struggling readers use context to facilitate and compensate for limited decoding abilities while reading. But as Stanovich makes clear, the implications of an interactive-compensatory model can be extended to the realm of comprehension as well. Where decoding and fluency are adequate, the model applies to comprehension insofar as eStorybook features can provide compensation *within* the comprehension process. By this we mean that less-skilled readers may also have comprehension deficits because they possess inadequate prior knowledge related to the subject or structure of the text, because they approach the text less actively or strategically as proficient readers, because they do not have full command of comprehension strategies, or because they do not know the meanings of crucial vocabulary (Pressley, 2000). Accordingly, interactive features within eStorybooks can improve comprehension for struggling readers by providing assistance when a reader reaches a problematic word or phrase (Anderson-Inman & Horney, 1998), by offering immediate support for unknown vocabulary words (Greenlee-Moore & Smith, 1996), or by suggesting appropriate comprehension strategies to employ at specific points in the text (Strangman, 2003). Further, some researchers posit that electronic media might improve comprehension by simultaneously stimulating the dual processing of visual and verbal material (Kamil, Intrator, & Kim, 2000), resulting in a richer and more memorable understanding of the story through the interactive technology.

We first consider multimodal design features of eStorybooks that might improve comprehension processes and the extent to which dynamic or interactive multimedia presentations differ from standard print texts. Many scholars and educators suggest that the new literacies, with their "flexible use of text, image, audio, video, animation, and virtual reality represent a new unique form of human discourse" (Eagleton, 2002). Jewitt (2002) examined the discourse of CD-ROM texts and compared the transformation of novels to electronic texts to the conversion experienced when a novel is made into a film. She described how subtle elements of multimodal texts, such as the characters' posture or physical distance during conversation, reshape the persona of characters in texts that did not originally contain any graphic representations. In addition, Jewitt described 14- and 15-year-old students' interactions while reading a CD-ROM version of Steinbeck's *Of Mice and Men*, noting that students engage with electronic texts in unique ways by accessing dramatically different resources than those available in the print novel. Others have studied the multimodal design features present when picture books are converted to eStorybooks and suggest that illustrations and animations can enhance comprehension of narrated eStorybooks (Bus et al., this volume; de Jong & Bus, 2003, 2004; Shamir & Korat, this volume; Verhallen, Bus, & de Jong, 2006). For example, Verhallen and colleagues (2006) compared young second language learners' understanding of an eStorybook containing static illustrations to children's understanding when the book contained animated illustrations and multimedia. The static eStorybook was presented on the computer but the pictures were motionless while the animated eStorybook included video, music, and sound that were generally congruent with the main story elements. The participants benefited somewhat from repeated exposures to static stories; however, multiple exposures to multimedia stories were more effective in promoting story understanding and language development for these 5-year-olds. Lessons from research with print storybooks demonstrate that graphic elements are supportive of comprehension processes if they reinforce or elaborate information in the text; however, graphic embellishments that are unrelated to the text are less desirable (Donovan & Smolkin, 2001). Similarly, Narayanan and Hegerty (2000) explain that possible benefits of animations for supporting comprehension can be overemphasized, particularly when dynamic computer graphics are not designed in accordance with cognitive processes of how readers are believed to construct mental models.

Other features of eStorybooks that might provide support within the comprehension process include prompts to use a comprehension strategy, instructive cues that define comprehension strategies or provide hints about how to apply the strategy to the text, and embedded vocabulary aids. Some research suggests that accessing links to vocabulary supports in electronic texts can interactively compensate for vocabulary deficits (Higgins & Cooks, 1999; Higgins & Hess, 1999) and can also result in the learning of new words (Collins, 2006). This positive finding for embedding word elaborations and explanations during reading mirrors research conducted with traditional read-alouds (e.g., Biemiller, 2004; Biemiller & Boote, 2006; Penno, Wilkinson, & Moore, 2002). However, the eStorybook evidence also exposes some potential problems with some unsupportive embedded vocabulary cues that may mislead students. While exploring the potential of electronic poems with animated cues for supporting vocabulary development, Higgins and Hess (1999) found that third-grade students who accessed animated vocabulary cues during eStorybook reading learned fewer meanings of six target vocabulary words ($M=2.91$) than students who accessed animated cues and received vocabulary support from an adult during eStorybook reading ($M=5.0$). The individualized adult support included providing synonyms when word meanings were unclear to the child after viewing the animation and generating questions that helped the student arrive at the word's meaning, whereas students in the no-support condition simply listened to the text read aloud by the computer and accessed the animation cues without additional conversation with the researcher. It is unclear whether this level of adult support would have been required if more helpful animation cues had been embedded in the software. Specifically, some animations appeared inadequate and perhaps misleading, such as this cue: "When *Plumbing* is selected, a character beats on a maze of pipes with drum sticks" (Higgins & Cooks, 1999, p. 5). This cue does little to characterize pipes as long tubes for transporting liquid or gas and instead presents pipes as a type of musical instrument. Thus, it is understandable that the more student-friendly definitions provided by the researcher, such as "Plumbing is the pipes that carry water and waste in your home," (Higgins & Hess, 1999, pp. 427–428), were more useful. The researcher's definition met the criteria for student-friendly definitions favored by Beck, McKeown, and Kucan (2002) because it characterized the word accurately and used it in everyday language, whereas the animation may have led students astray. When the goal of using eStorybooks is to increase vocabulary for students with low initial vocabulary levels, it is likely that techniques used with traditional texts, such as discussing the meanings of target words with a more knowledgeable partner and providing student-friendly definitions, will facilitate word learning (e.g., Beck et al., 2002; Ewers & Brownson, 1999; Justice, Meier, & Walpole, 2005). Further research is needed to characterize vocabulary and comprehension strategy cues that can be effectively embedded in eStorybooks as compensatory mechanisms for comprehension processes.

eStorybooks as Assistive Technology

Because the interactive-compensatory model predicts that readers will use available resources to make up for deficiencies in knowledge and skills and because eStorybooks have the potential to make many of these resources available, eStorybooks hold the promise of elevating the performance of struggling readers to a level comparable to that of their normally progressing peers. This is the goal of AT, and eStorybooks equipped with digital supports appropriate to address a reader's deficits can be viewed as a viable form of AT. Dalton and Strangman (2006) use the metaphor of "universal access" in comparing the availability of digital supports to barrier-free architecture, designed to permit access by physically disabled individuals.

Figure 17.3 displays how digital supports, when present, can elevate reading performance to a point at which comprehension is adequate. The figure also suggests that when such supports are not present (e.g., when a child attempts to read a print book), comprehension can be predicted to fall to an unacceptable level, compared with age peers. With respect to the simple view of reading, supports can be categorized into two broad areas: those that address deficits in word recognition (e.g., digitized pronunciations) and those intended to address comprehension difficulties (e.g., word meanings on demand, simplified paraphrases, and background information assumed by

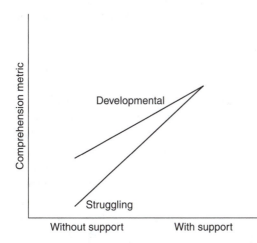

Figure 17.3 Theoretical effect of supportive features on struggling and developmental readers of similar age and cognitive development.

	Word recognition supports	
	Yes	No
Comprehension supports — Yes	Wide-ranging supports that might include pronunciations on demand and listening options for weak decoders, plus comprehension scaffolds such as vocabulary, background information, text simplifications, translations.	Adequate decoding proficiency is assumed, but comprehension supports are provided, possibly including vocabulary, background information, text simplifications, translations, etc.
Comprehension supports — No	Decoding supports, such as point-and-click pronunciations, listening options, etc., are available. Adequate comprehension is assumed when the child is given adequate decoding support.	Support for weak decoding and/or comprehension is not available.

Figure 17.4 Possible combinations of compensatory digital support features.

the author). Figure 17.4 illustrates how supports might be present or absent in each of these two broad areas. eStorybooks can range from very limited support (neither word recognition nor comprehension support is available) to unidimensional support (one but not the other type is available) to full support (both word recognition and comprehension support is available).

A hope of most AT applications is that their continued use will eventually preclude the need for them. As a child practices skills and strategies in concert in various reading contexts, the expectation is that proficiency will improve to the point at which comprehension without the supports will differ neither from unsupported comprehension nor from the comprehension of age peers. When this goal is attained, AT has served its purpose. Figure 17.5 illustrates this hoped-for trajectory over time. Like the scaffolds used during the construction of a building, the digital supports offered by eStorybooks can eventually be removed and the child will be able to comprehend without them.

Contrast this situation with one in which a child's comprehension is adequate given the use of scaffolds, but the dependence on them does not diminish over time (see also Van Daal, this volume). An extreme example is the use of enlarged print by a visually impaired reader. No amount of additional exposures will result in diminished reliance on the use of this feature. Figure

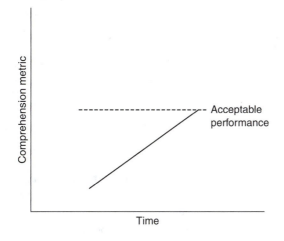

Figure 17.5 Student trajectory without supports when supports serve as scaffolds.

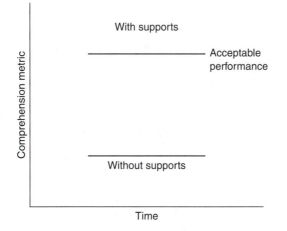

Figure 17.6 Student trajectory with and without supports when supports serve as prosthesis.

17.6 illustrates this "flat" pattern. McKenna and Walpole (2007) offer another metaphor to describe such a pattern—that of the prosthesis. In the case of a permanent physical impairment, the prosthetic use of scaffolds might be viewed as a godsend. When, however, such a trajectory reflects inadequate instruction, we have cause for concern. Consider the case in which a child's limited decoding proficiency requires frequent access to on-demand pronunciations. The idea that this scaffold might always be needed is unacceptable and says much about the effectiveness of the instruction this child is receiving.

These notions form a bridge between the theory offered by the simple view and the interactive-compensatory model, on the one hand, and theories related to response to intervention, on the other. They converge in the support system offered to readers in the context of eStorybooks, and we suggest that they constitute ways of grounding systematic inquiry into their uses with students who need support.

The Affective Promise of eStorybooks

So far, we have confined our discussion to cognitive elements associated with eStorybooks. Were we to leave the discussion at that, we would ignore important affective questions associated with their use, questions that can be grounded in available theory. In a model of reading attitude development proposed by McKenna, Kear, and Ellsworth (1995; see also McKenna, 2001), three factors affecting attitude change were postulated. They include (1) the long-term cumulative impact of each reading experience, (2) the beliefs a child harbors toward the outcome of an impending reading episode (i.e., whether the child believes that it is likely to be pleasurable, boring, frustrating, etc.), and (3) the beliefs the child has concerning how significant others (e.g., peers, siblings) view reading. Research into the affective impact of eStorybooks can be framed within this model by testing and refining its three premises. An example involving the first factor might be inquiry into whether exposures to many eStorybooks would, over time, foster more positive attitudes than conventional teaching approaches through which the print counterparts of eStorybooks are used. Likewise, investigations might examine whether and which compensatory supports lead the child to believe that reading eStorybooks need not be frustrating, and whether this belief contributes to more positive attitudes toward reading, both in digital and print environments. Researchers might examine the extent to which collaborative activities involving eStorybooks affect children's beliefs about social norms and whether altered beliefs foster more positive attitudes. Further, such models could be extended to assess whether use of electronic texts can serve to counteract negative attitudes toward reading and if any compensatory affective benefits persist when the novelty of the technology wears off.

Electronic texts appear to be a particularly motivating context for supporting literacy development. In a review of technology applications for literacy learning, Kamil et al. (2000) identified two categories of motivational effects of technology use: (a) effects compared with traditional literacy formats, and (b) effects for special populations of learners such as struggling readers or young, preliterate children. Regarding the first type of motivational effects, eStorybooks often fall into a category that "attempt[s] to motivate through fun, glitzy, arcade-like edutainment" rather than more authentic educational tasks (Kamil et al., 2000, p. 779). However, McKenna and Watkins (1994) found that kindergartners and first graders overwhelmingly preferred eStorybooks equipped with digitized pronunciations but without animations to print versions of the same books. Reinking and Watkins' (2000) work suggests that students' attitude toward reading can increase when they are given opportunities to create multimedia book reviews to share with their peers. Some work on peer-to-peer collaboration with electronic texts has already begun with beginning readers (e.g., Wood, Littleton, & Chera, 2005) and older readers (e.g., Jewitt, 2002; Strangman, 2003). These students reviewed traditional print books, but it is likely that providing opportunities to use and review eStorybooks could also produce increased motivation and reading for enjoyment. Despite the attractiveness of eStorybooks for motivating young readers, some research suggests educators should be cautious that too much "edutainment," or whistles and bells, may overshadow literacy goals because young learners may become so engrossed in exploring these features they may not attend sufficiently to the language of the story (de Jong & Bus, 2002). Smolkin. McTigue, and Donovan (2008) maintain that similar problems can occur in print versions of information books, such as the Dorling Kindersley style found in their Eyewitness science series, when so many graphic images appear on a single two-page spread that it results in cognitive overload. Another potential downside is that children may passively watch the screen as "incongruent" hotspots take the reader on a tangent of elaborate animation that is unrelated to the narrative (Labbo & Kuhn, 2000) or students may "watch" designers' constructions of characters rather than creating their own understanding of characters (Jewitt, 2002). However, Bangert-Drowns and Pyke (2001) report observing higher-level engagement and literate behaviors with eStorybooks than with other types of computer-assisted instruction and tutorial software.

As for the second type of motivational effects, many struggling or reluctant readers show a greater interest in reading when they are given opportunities to use multiple literacies, including electronic texts (Snow, Griffin, & Burns, 2005). Adam and Wild (1997) examined the use of interactive CD-ROM multimedia books for supporting struggling, reluctant readers in third grade. They suggested that multimedia books and their embedded supports can create a nonthreatening environment for struggling readers to explore literacy. Their findings suggest that "reluctant readers" developed strong positive attitudes toward eStorybooks and also toward traditional reading materials as a result of a 4-week intervention with 11 eStorybooks. The group of "willing readers" in this study did not show such dramatic attitudinal effects as the more reluctant students. However, children's overall attitude toward reading did not significantly differ between the experimental group that used CD-ROM books and the no-treatment control group. Still, taken together, these results strengthen the case that eStorybooks may provide a remarkable context for motivating readers, especially those who struggle. Further inquiry, designed to gauge the effects of these and other supports (e.g., background knowledge, simplified versions) may eventually inform the efforts of software producers and educators alike.

Extending Theoretical Perspectives: Final Thoughts

Digital features lead to experiences that may differ considerably from reading print books or listening to read-alouds (Smith, 2001, 2002). The interactive-compensatory model is a good place to begin, permitting grounded inquiry designed to describe children's use of digital supports and to gauge the effects, both cognitive and affective; however, additional theories can help focus such inquiry and may ultimately play an explanatory role as well. For example, the presence of supports may create a metacognitive dilemma for readers, who must determine when to access them (Duke, Schmar-Dobler, & Zhang, 2006). It may be that explicit instruction in their use (actually, a type of comprehension strategy) followed by continual practice in novel settings will make these supports "disappear," in that they become part of the given landscape of digital text and lose their distracting novelty (Bruce & Hogan, 1998). It may also be that some of the monitoring strategies children learn through their experiences with supported text will transfer not only to other digital texts but to print situations as well, where conventional supports (footnotes, glossary entries, etc.) are available. This "high road to transfer," requiring conscious attention to resources irrespective of mode (Salomon & Perkins, 1989), is an important instructional goal for educators implementing eStorybooks.

Such models have the potential to help researchers frame their investigations in appropriate theory in order to answer questions central to understanding how best to use eStorybooks. Throughout this chapter we have suggested numerous questions grounded in theory and likely to advance our understanding. We close with a few further questions that help to round out a comprehensive research agenda. What combinations of electronic scaffolds work best for various profiles of struggling readers? How can eStorybooks best be integrated into the daily instruction of such readers? Would a steady diet of static and dynamic illustrations curtail children's ability to form mental images when reading text? How can prosthetic trajectories be detected and avoided? Can trackware and keylogging be used reliably to record student actions? Does reading eStorybooks foster more positive attitudes toward reading in general? Toward reading in print settings? What effect will eStorybooks have when they "disappear?" These questions constitute an important and timely agenda for research as current policy and learning standards increasingly require teachers to use technology to support literacy instruction (Edyburn, 2003).

References

Adam, N., & Wild, M. (1997). Applying CD-ROM interactive storybooks to learning to read. *Journal of Computer Assisted Learning, 13*, 119–132.

Anderson-Inman, L., & Horney, M.A. (1998). Transforming text for at-risk readers. In D. Reinking, M.C. McKenna, L.D. Labbo, & R.D. Kieffer (Eds.), *Handbook of literacy and technology: Transformations in a post-typographic world*. Mahwah, NJ: Erlbaum.

Bangert-Drowns, R.L., & Pyke, C. (2001). A taxonomy of student engagement with educational software: An exploration of literate thinking with electronic text. *Journal of Educational Computing Research, 24,* 213–234.

Beck, I.L., McKeowen, M.G., & Kucan, L. (2002). *Bringing words to life: Robust vocabulary instruction.* New York: Guilford.

Biemiller, A. (2004). Teaching vocabulary in the primary grades. In J.F. Baumann & E.J. Kame'enui (Eds.), *Vocabulary instruction: Research to practice* (pp. 28–40). New York: Guilford.

Biemiller, A., & Boote, C. (2006). An effective method for building meaning vocabulary in the primary grades. *Journal of Educational Psychology, 98,* 44–62.

Bruce, B.C., & Hogan, M.P. (1998). The disappearance of technology: Toward an ecological model of literacy. In D. Reinking, M.C. McKenna, L.D. Labbo, & R.D. Kieffer (Eds.), *Handbook of literacy and technology: Transformations in a part-typographic world* (Vol. 1, pp. 269–282). Hillsdale, NJ: Laurence Erlbaum.

Collins, M.F. (2006). Raising the bar on vocabulary learning from storybook reading: Using illustrations and extratextual comments to foster preschoolers' rare vocabulary learning. Paper presented at the Colloquium of the Royal Netherlands Academy of Arts and Sciences, Amsterdam, the Netherlands.

Dalton, B., & Strangman, N. (2006). Improving struggling readers' comprehension through scaffolded hypertexts and other computer-based literacy programs. In M.C. McKenna, L.D. Labbo, R. Kieffer, & D. Reinking (Eds.), *International handbook of literacy and technology* (Vol. 2, pp. 75–92). Mahwah, NJ: Laurence Erlbaum.

Davidson, J., Coles, D., Noyes, P., & Terrell, C. (1991). Using computer-delivered natural speech to assist in the teaching of reading. *British Journal of Educational Technology, 22,* 110–118.

de Jong, M.T., & Bus, A.G. (2002). Quality of book-reading matters for emergent readers: An experiment with the same book in regular or electronic format. *Journal of Educational Psychology, 94,* 145–155.

de Jong, M.T., & Bus, A.G. (2003). How well suited are electronic books to supporting literacy? *Journal of Early Childhood Literacy, 3,* 147–164.

de Jong, M.T., & Bus, A.G. (2004). The efficacy of electronic books in fostering kindergarten children's emergent story understanding. *Reading Research Quarterly, 39,* 378–393.

Donovan, C.A., & Smolkin, L.B (2001). Genre and other factors influencing teachers' book selections for science instruction. *Reading Research Quarterly, 36,* 412–440.

Doty, D., Popplewell, S., & Byers, G. (2001). Interactive CD-ROM storybooks and young readers' reading comprehension. *Journal of Research on Computing on Education, 33,* 374–384.

Duke, N.K., Schmar-Dobler, E., & Zhang, S. (2006). Comprehension and technology: In M.C. McKenna, L.D. Labbo, R. Kieffer, & D. Reinking (Eds.), *International handbook of literacy and technology* (Vol. 2, pp. 317–326). Mahwah, NJ: Laurence Erlbaum.

Eagleton, M. (2002). Making text come to life on the computer: Toward an understanding of hypermedia literacy. *Reading Online, 6.* Retrieved May 27, 2007, from www.readingonline.org/articles/art_index.asp?HREF=eagleton2/index.html.

Edyburn, D.L. (2003). Rethinking assistive technology. *Special Education Technology Practice, 5,* 16–22.

Ewers, C.A. & Brownson, S.M. (1999). Kindergarteners' vocabulary as a function of active vs. passive storybook reading, prior vocabulary, and working memory. *Journal of Reading Psychology, 20,* 11–20.

Goodwin, L.D., Goodwin, W.L., Nasel, A., & Helm, C.P. (1986). Cognitive and affective effects of various types of microcomputer use by preschoolers. *American Educational Research Journal, 23,* 348–356.

Gough, P.B., & Tunmer, W.E. (1986). Decoding, reading, and reading disability. *Remedial and Special Education, 7,* 6–10.

Greenlee-Moore, M.E., & Smith, L.L. (1996). Interactive computer software: The effects on young children's reading achievement. *Reading Psychology, 17,* 43–64.

Higgins, N.C., & Cooks, P. (1999). The effects of animation cues on vocabulary development. *Journal of Reading Psychology, 20,* 1–10.

Higgins, N.C., & Hess, L. (1999). Using electronic books to promote vocabulary development. *Journal of Research on Computing in Education, 31,* 425–430.

Jewitt, C. (2002). The move from page to screen: The multimodal reshaping of school English. *Visual Communication, 1,* 171–195.

Justice, L.M., & Ezell, H.K. (2000). Enhancing children's print and word awareness through home-based parent intervention. *American Journal of Speech-Language Pathology, 9,* 257–269.

Justice, L.M., & Ezell, H.K. (2002). Use of storybook reading to increase print awareness in at-risk children. *American Journal of Speech-Language Pathology, 11,* 17–29.

Justice, L.M., Meier, J., & Walpole, S. (2005). Learning new words from storybooks: An efficacy study with at-risk kindergarteners. *Language, Speech, and Hearing Services in Schools, 36,* 17–32.

Kamil, M.L., Intrator, S., & Kim, H.S. (2000). Effects of other technologies on literacy and learning. In M.L. Kamil, P.B. Mosenthal, P.D. Pearson, & R. Barr (Eds.), *handbook of reading research* (Vol. 3, pp. 771–788). Mahwah, NJ: Erlbaum.

Labbo, L.D., & Kuhn, M.R. (2000). Weaving chains of affect and cognition: A young child's understanding of CD-ROM talking books. *Journal of Literacy Research, 32,* 187–210.

LaBerge, D., & Samuels, S. (1974). Toward a theory of automatic information processing in reading. *Cognitive Psychology, 6,* 293–323.

Lefever-Davis, S., & Pearman, C. (2005). Early readers and electronic texts: CD-ROM storybook features that influence reading behaviors. *Reading Teacher, 58,* 446–454.

Leu, D.J. (2000). Literacy and technology: Deictic consequences for literacy education in an information age. In M.L. Kamil, P.B. Mosenthal, P.D. Pearson, & R. Barr (Eds.), *Handbook of reading research* (Vol. 3, pp. 745–772). Mahwah, NJ: Erlbaum.

Leu, D.J. (2006). New literacies, reading research, and the challenges of change: A deictic perspective. In J.V. Hoffman, D.L. Schallert, C.M. Fairbanks, J. Worthy, & B. Maloch (Eds.), *55th yearbook of the National Reading Conference* (pp. 1–20). Oak Creek, WI: National Reading Conference.

Lovelace, S., & Stewart, S.R. (2007). Increasing print awareness in preschoolers with language impairments using non-evocative print referencing. *Language, Speech, and Hearing Services in Schools, 38,* 16–30.

McKenna, M.C. (1998). Electronic texts and the transformation of beginning reading. In D. Reinking, M.C. McKenna, L.D. Labbo, & R.D. Kieffer (Eds.), *Handbook of literacy and technology: Transformations in a post-typographic world* (pp. 45–59). Mahwah, NJ: Erlbaum.

McKenna, M.C. (2001). Development of reading attitudes. In L. Verhoeven & C. Snow (Eds.), *Literacy and motivation: Reading engagement in individuals and groups* (pp. 135–158). Mahwah, NJ: Laurence Erlbaum.

McKenna, M.C., Kear, D.J., & Ellsworth, R.A. (1995). Children's attitudes toward reading: A national survey. *Reading Research Quarterly, 30,* 934–956.

McKenna, M.C., Reinking, D., & Bradley, B.A. (2003). The effects of electronic trade books on the decoding growth of beginning readers. In R. Malatesha Joshi, C.K. Leong, & B.L.J. Kaczmarek (Eds.), *Literacy acquisition: The role of phonology, morphology, and orthography* (pp. 193–202). Amsterdam: IOS Press.

McKenna, M.C., Stahl, K.A.D., & Stahl, S.A. (2008). *Assessment for reading instruction* (2nd ed.). New York: Guilford.

McKenna, M.C., & Walpole, S. (2007). Assistive technology in the reading clinic: Its emerging potential. *Reading Research Quarterly, 42,* 140–145.

McKenna, M.C., & Watkins, J.H. (1994, December). Effects of a program of computer-mediated books on the progress of beginning readers. Paper presented at the meeting of the National Reading Conference, San Diego, CA.

McKenna, M.C., & Watkins, J.H. (1995, November). Effects of computer-mediated books on the development of beginning readers. Paper presented at the meeting of the National Reading Conference, New Orleans, LA.

McKenna, M.C., & Watkins, J.H. (1996, December). The effects of computer-mediated trade books on sight word acquisition and the development of phonics ability. Paper presented at the meeting of the National Reading Conference, Charleston, SC.

Matthew, K. (1997). A comparison of the influence of interactive CD-ROM storybooks and traditional print storybooks on reading comprehension. *Journal of Research on Computing in Education, 29,* 263–275.

Narayanan, N.H., & Hegerty, M. (2000). Communicating dynamic behaviors: Are interactive multimedia presentations better than static mixed-mode presentations? In M. Anderson, P. Cheng, & V. Haarslev (Eds.), *Theory and application of diagrams: First international conference, Diagrams 2000* (pp. 178–193). Berlin, Germany: Springer-Verlag.

Olofsson, A. (1992). Synthetic speech and computer aided reading for reading disabled children. *Reading and Writing: An Interdisciplinary Journal, 4,* 165–178.

Penno, J.F., Wilkinson, I.A.G., Moore, D.W. (2002). Vocabulary acquisition from teacher explanation and repeated listening to stories: Do they overcome the Matthew effect? *Journal of Educational Psychology, 94,* 23–33.

Pressley, M. (2000). What should comprehension instruction be the instruction of? In M.L. Kamil, P.B. Mosenthal, P.D. Pearson, & R. Barr (Eds.), *Handbook of reading research* (Vol. 3, pp. 545–561). Mahwah, NJ: Erlbaum.

Reinking, D., & Watkins, J. (2000). A formative experiment investigating the use of multimedia book reviews to increase elementary students' independent reading. *Reading Research Quarterly, 35,* 384–419.

Reitsma, P. (1988). Reading practice for beginners: Effects of guided reading, reading-while-listening, and independent reading with computer-based speech feedback. *Reading Research Quarterly, 23,* 219–235.

Salomon, G., & Perkins, D.N. (1989). Rocky roads to transfer: Rethinking mechanisms of a neglected phenomenon. *Educational Psychologist, 24,* 113–142.

Smith, C.R. (2001). "Click and turn the page": An exploration of multiple storybook literacy. *Reading Research Quarterly, 36,* 152–183.

Smith, C.R. (2002). Click on me! An example of how a toddler used technology in play. *Journal of Early Childhood Literacy, 2,* 5–20.

Smolkin, L.B., McTigue, E.M., & Donovan, C.A. (2008). Explanation and science text: Overcoming the comprehension challenges in nonfiction text for elementary students. In C.C. Block, S. Paris, & P. Afflerbach (Eds.), *Comprehension instruction: Research-based best practices* (2nd ed., pp. 183–195). New York: Guilford.

Snow, C.E., Griffin, P., & Burns, M.S. (2005). *Knowledge to support the teaching of reading: Preparing teachers for a changing world.* San Francisco: Jossey-Bass.

Stahl, S.A. (2003). What do we expect storybook reading to do? How storybook reading impacts word recognition. In A. van Kleeck, S.A. Stahl, & E.B. Bauer (Eds.), *On reading books to children: Parents and teachers* (pp. 363–383). Mahwah, NJ: Erlbaum.

Stahl, S.A., Kuhn, M.R., & Pickle, J.M. (1999). An educational model of assessment and targeted instruction for children with reading problems. In D.H. Evensen & P.B. Mosenthal (Eds.), *Reconsidering the role of the reading clinic in a new age of literacy* (pp. 249–272). Stamford, CT: JAI Press. [Volume 6 of *Advances in Reading/Language Arts*].

Stanovich, K.E. (1980). Toward an interactive-compensatory model of individual differences in development of reading fluency. *Reading Research Quarterly, 16,* 32–71.

Stanovich, K.E. (1984). The interactive-compensatory model of reading: A confluence of developmental, experimental, and educational psychology. *Remedial and Special Education, 5,* 11–19.

Storch, S.A., & Whitehurst, G.J. (2002). Oral language and code-related precursors to reading: Evidence from a longitudinal structural model. *Developmental Psychology, 38,* 934–947.

Strangman, N. (2003). Strategy instruction goes digital: Two teachers' perspectives on digital texts with embedded learning supports. *Reading Online, 6.* Retrieved May 27, 2007 from www.readingonline.org/articles/art_index.asp?HREF= voices/winslow_previte/index.html.

Talley, S., Lancy, D.F., & Lee, T.R. (1997). Children, storybooks, and computers. *Reading Horizons, 38,* 116–128.

Ukrainetz, T.A., Cooney, M.H., Dyer, S.K., Kysar, A.J., & Harris, T.J. (2000). An investigation into teaching phonemic awareness through shared reading and writing. *Early Childhood Research Quarterly, 15,* 331–355.

Vellutino, F.R., Tunmer, W.E., Jaccard, J.J., & Chen, R. (2007). Components of reading ability:

Multivariate evidence for a convergent skills model of reading development. *Scientific Studies of Reading, 11*, 3–32.

Verhallen, M.J.A.J., Bus, A.G., & de Jong, M.T. (2006). The promise of multimedia stories for kindergarten children at risk. *Journal of Educational Psychology, 98*, 410–419.

Wood, C. (2005). Beginning readers' use of "talking books" software can affect their reading strategies. *Journal of Research in Reading, 28*, 170–182.

Wood, C., Littleton, K., & Chera, P. (2005). Beginning readers' use of talking books: Styles of working. *Literacy, 39*, 135–141.

Afterword

Adriana G. Bus and Susan B. Neuman

I am convinced that the way children learn will improve dramatically and often find myself fighting fiercely with those who say computers have little to offer in this area.

(Papert, 1996, p. 18)

Computers and technological tools have become ubiquitous in children's worlds. Today, children are exposed to rich linguistic stimulation not only through books but through multimedia technologies that engage them in the prototypical and iconic aspect of literacy. Increasingly interactions with electronic media influence playtime and social behaviors. How these technologies might support children's learning, and growing achievement in literacy has been the focus of a growing body of research and serious investigation. The present infusion of computers in homes and early childhood classrooms enables the research community to gain new insights into new ways to develop literacy.

This volume was designed to address this important topic—to examine the state-of-the-art research on how multimedia contribute to early literacy. It came about as a result of an historic meeting, funded by the Royal Netherlands Academy of Arts and Sciences to bring together world-class scholars all of whom shared an interest and cutting edge research in literacy and multimedia. Throughout the 3-day conference, lively discussions followed each research presentation. Below, we highlight the gist of these conversations, as we move toward a comprehensive research agenda for the future.

Facilitators of Basic Reading Skills

Traditionally, media have often been blamed for displacing reading and, as low involvement media, blocking development. In contrast, this conference reported on the many studies that demonstrated the *added* value of media—filmic images, cinematic techniques, music, and sounds—to support children's literacy development. New media have a high attractivity to young children but this is not the only explanation for learning. When multimedia additions are supportive of story content, and not merely affectations, children seem to learn important early literacy skills. In fact, one common theme throughout many of the chapters is that a synergistic treatment is especially profitable for linguistically disadvantaged preschoolers from low educated families and minorities and for struggling beginning readers. Multimedia embedded in instructional formats and storybooks can enhance preschoolers' specific skills for literacy development including phonological awareness, letter names, and decoding and, later on, word recognition and comprehension skills.

The interactive-compensatory model predicts that linguistically disadvantaged children and struggling readers will use all available resources in books to counterbalance their deficiencies in knowledge and skills. Because onscreen storybooks make more resources available than traditional print books, especially groups who lag behind the average can profit from onscreen storybooks that include visual, sound, and music effects. For instance, when multiple information sources are added to stories, resulting in visually challenging digitized storybooks, children with non-mainstream heritage languages better understand the storyline than they do with static pictures alone. And, as importantly, they learn more new words and sentence structures from the animated stories. Additional information sources can also elevate the performance of struggling beginning readers by making up for deficits in word recognition or comprehension difficulties and, more importantly, the strategies children learn through their experiences with supported text in electronic books will transfer not only to other digital texts but to print situations as well. This and other findings discussed throughout this volume open up an exciting new perspective for intervention and for treatment programs. This new perspective on learning and instruction is grounded in reading and memory theories.

The Importance of Learning from Multiple Channels

Children benefit from additions like video clips, music, and sounds. This research finding is not terribly surprising, especially for those who have studied educational television's effects on children's learning. Studies have shown that by watching televisual narratives children learn to use nonverbal information sources to create rich comprehension-supporting imagery of digitized stories. More surprising, however, is that several studies report that not only story comprehension but language and literacy skills benefit from a synergy of information sources (i.e., narration, filmatic images, music, and sounds).

The interactive-compensatory model predicts that readers will use visual resources to make up for deficiencies in word recognition and comprehension and that preschoolers can grapple with age-appropriate storybooks even when they belong to a linguistically "poor" group (Stanovich, 1980). Electronic books remedy the "limitations" of traditional texts and storybooks: by simultaneously stimulating the dual processing of visual and verbal material, electronic media might improve comprehension resulting in a richer and more memorable understanding of the story through the interactive technology. This seems especially true when one delivery system is "blocked" as is the case with linguistically disadvantaged children or children struggling with decoding skills. There is also evidence that multiple deliveries "grade up" psychological energy invested in processing information when children lag behind.

Paivio's (1986) dual coding model is brought up to explain that readers can use various resources simultaneously without bothering each other: nonverbal information added to digitized storybooks does not distract attention from the language. Quite the reverse, it supports the development of words and phrases. Paivio's memory model postulates that different channels process information, one specialized for information concerning nonverbal objects and events and the other for dealing with language. The nonverbal information channel can only be profitable for language learning when it does not "elbow out" the channel dealing with linguistically coded information, and vice versa. Here we come to the second main assumption postulated by Paivio's dual coding model: the two channels for language and nonverbal information can operate simultaneously without cutting down the effective memory capacity for each channel separately.

The outcomes of various experiments with digitized storybooks reported throughout this book show a perfect match with the theory of dual coding. Nonverbal information does not "use up" the capacity for storing language in short-term memory but enables children to figure out the meaning of unknown words and store it in long-term memory. Far from being a distraction, multiple representations of favorite stories help deepen children's understanding of the text. Multiple deliveries of information, instead of just one, bootstrap development of language, basic skills of decoding, and comprehension.

Scaffolding of a Different Form

Alternate forms of books are put forward as assets, rather than a problem. They have a promise as potential scaffolds when word recognition skills interfere with reading fluently or comprehension skills do not suffice for text understanding. New media have the capacity to be used constructively for learning: a good choice of digitized storybooks enables students who struggle in reading to experience independently electronic versions of books. Until recently picture storybooks were only accessible for the young—not yet conventional readers—when they were read to by grown-ups. A minimum multimedia feature, i.e., text spoken out loud, for example, allows nonreaders to have access to text without adult intervention. And this seems to work. An outcome of experiments with digitized storybooks is that these books have the potential to effect a literal interaction between emergent readers and the story and make children learn without adult intervention. Game-like computer programs for the youngest can stimulate basic reading skills. To some extent they can be made adaptive to children's responses. They give feedback and provide some form of support when children fail a task.

The research suggests that digitized scaffolding can stimulate to some extent the adult role in learning to shrink back and let the technology take over. This does not degrade the importance of the role of grown-ups. There is plenty of evidence supporting the hypothesis that programs do not work unless adults create and maintain a context that is fit to interest children and keep them motivated. Parent–child co-viewing of television shows boosts children's understanding of storylines. The intimacy and comfort of traditional literacy-related activities between parents and children are definitely not lost. Moreover, current designs of multimedia stories and other literacy programs incorporate, in an increasing degree, features of adult behavior when they adapt the task to children's level and actually scaffold children's learning. For instance, Steve in *Blue's Clues* serves as a caregiver on the screen, one who supports young viewers' thinking.

Electronic scaffolds can look like a computer pal who from time to time interrupts the story to interact with the audience through questions or encouragement. It can also include a set of rules that enable the selection of new tasks on the basis of how children did in the previous tasks. Scrutinizing the effects of such additional features of computer programs for young children should be high on our research agenda since they may make programs not only cognitively but also emotionally more rewarding. Future work may employ sophisticated eye-movement equipment to pinpoint what children are attending to on screen, when the information is presented as static illustrations, animated illustrations, animated illustrations supported by sound, etc. Eye tracking is a window on children's cognitive engagement while interacting with electronic materials. By building in possibilities to record the child's mouse behavior during sessions on the computer we may also dispose of information showing how they proceed, whether or not they are able to solve subtasks, and which electronic scaffolds challenge their skills in solving problems.

In theory, registration of computer behavior may enable us to construct rules for a built-in processor to adapt computer tasks to children's needs but, as far as we know, the present generation of programs is still far removed from the realization of trackware and keylogging to be used reliably to record student actions and adaptivity. As Reinking (1994) suggested in his seminal report on *Electronic Literacy*, monitoring physiological changes in skin conductance responses as indicators of comprehension difficulty and anxiety during processing the onscreen storybook can be an instrument to adapt programs to children's needs in the near future. Based on such input, the story presentation could be adapted accordingly in the future.

The Digital Divide

Computerization may level the playing field for children from different family backgrounds. After all, many programs have free access through television or

Internet, and storybooks on CD-ROMs or DVDs are often cheaper and—even more than print books—accessible to almost everyone, and, more importantly, children can learn about words and their meaning from these educational materials. As there hardly is any variety in availability, this may reduce the pedagogical divide between groups varying in educational background.

Conference attenders offered one note of caution, however. *High quality* computer programs may not be equally accessible to everyone. Traditional as well as newer media offer highly promising opportunities for language and literacy learning in the early years but the use of media differs strongly between families. Trying to appeal to multiple audiences, commercial enterprises may promote materials that have little educational content. Parent education seems critically important for selecting programs. Low income groups have traditionally been vulnerable to the more commercialized world of media applications. As young children show an almost universal preference for the exciting commercial programs on television and on the computer, it often depends on parents' involvement and determination to make choices. In low socioeconomic communities, parents may lack access to the possibilities and qualities of quality media, and allow their children to be in charge of making selections. The result is that these children, to a lesser degree than their middle and upper income peers benefit from new opportunities offered by high quality educational programs. For instance, a brief questionnaire was completed by all visitors of the Dutch website *Bereslim* with a selection of award-winning animated picture storybooks for 3- to 6-year-olds (Mansens, 2007). Most visitors were from high educated families and grew up in a cornucopian home literacy environment. If this type of free access Internet site is indeed chiefly used by a privileged group as Mansens' data suggest we may expect that, as a result of the new sources for learning, differences between low income and higher income groups in language and other literacy skills will increase rather than decrease. Without active attempts to overcome the knowledge deficit, media influences may further widen the digital divide between children.

Final Thoughts

This is an exciting time for those involved in multimedia applications and research. Throughout this volume, we see a new generation of materials and interventions to support early literacy and to compensate for the language gap between linguistically advantaged and disadvantaged children. These multimedia applications suggest that rather than developing "new literacies" multimedia are enabling children to learn traditional literacy skills, albeit in new ways. And, this suggests that multimedia might be an important tool for not only closing the achievement gap, but promoting higher levels of literacy for all.

References

Mansens, T. (2007). Elektronische boeken op internet: Nieuwe kansen voor risicokinderen? [Electronic stories through the Internet: New chances for children at-risk?] Master thesis, Leiden University, the Netherlands.

Paivio, A. (1986). *Mental representations. A dual coding approach.* Oxford, UK: Oxford University Press.

Papert, S. (1996). *The connected family: Bridging the digital generation gap.* Atlanta, GA: Longstreet Press.

Reinking, D. (1994). *Electronic literacy.* Perspectives in reading research No. 4. National Reading Research Center.

Stanovich, K.E. (1980). Toward an interactive-compensatory model of individual differences in development of reading fluency. *Reading Research Quarterly, 16,* 32–71.

Contributors

Philip C. Abrami is the Director of the Centre for the Study of Learning and Performance at the University of Concordia. Currently he is researching ways to use technology to support the emerging literacy skills of young children, especially those at risk of school failure. Email: abrami@education.concordia.ca.

Jeremy Brueck serves as the Web Services Manager for e-Read Ohio at the University of Akron. He provides strategic direction and coordination of web services in the design of online professional development in the area of literacy for pre-K-12 teachers across Ohio. Prior to that, he spent 5 years as a Curriculum and Technology Specialist in the local schools with a focus on designing standards-based integrated lessons for grades K-3. Email: jbruek@uakron.edu.

Adriana G. Bus is professor of education and child studies at Leiden University in the Netherlands. She focuses on impact of attachment theory on children's emergent literacy development, and on developmental changes in storybook reading among parents and children. Currently she is developing, in close collaboration with computer experts and instructional designers, an internet environment for young learners to promote rich literacy experiences. Email: bus@fsw.leidenuniv.nl.

Bette Chambers is a professor in the Institute for Effective Education at the University of York in England and at the Center for Research and Reform in Education at Johns Hopkins University, where she conducts research in early childhood education and early literacy. She also directs the development and dissemination of the early childhood education and technology-embedded programs at the Success for All Foundation in Baltimore, MD. Email: bchambers@jhu.edu or bc512@york.ac.uk.

Alan Cheung is an Associate Professor in the Center for Data-Driven Reform in Education at Johns Hopkins University and most recently from the Hong Kong Institute of Education. His research areas include private education, school reform, research reviews, and quantitative methods. Email: acheung@jhu.edu.

Maria T. de Jong, a former teacher in special education, is now an assistant professor at Leiden University in the Netherlands. Her recent studies of electronic media include young first and second language learners low in language proficiency. Email: jongtm@fsw.leidenuniv.nl.

Mary Ann Evans is a Professor of Psychology and Director of Clinical Training at the University of Guelph. Since its inception, she has been a project leader in the Canadian Language and Literacy Research Network, from which some studies are reported in this volume. Her research deals primarily with literacy and communication development, social and cognitive aspects of shyness, shared book reading, and home literacy experiences. Email: evans@psy.uoguelph.ca.

Tali Freund is Vice President of the Planning, Information and Evaluation division at the Center for Educational Technology (CET). Her division provides assessment and evaluation services for the Israeli government, local municipalities, foundations, and schools. Email: talif@cet.ac.il.

Richard Gifford is the Project Coordinator for Educational Technology at the Success for All Foundation, in Baltimore, MD. His expertise is in reading instruction and embedding technology in instruction. Email: rgifford@jhu.edu.

Panayiota Kendeou is Assistant Professor in the Department of Educational and Counselling Psychology at McGill University in Canada. Her research program entails the investigation of the cognitive processes that support learning and memory in the context of reading comprehension. Email: panayiota.kendeou@mcgill.ca.

Ofra Korat is a senior lecturer and the head of the Early Childhood Program in the School of Education of Bar-Ilan University, Israel. Her main research subjects focus on emergent literacy, socio-cultural context as a support for literacy development, and technology as a support for children's language and literacy. Email: korato@mail.biu.ac.il.

Linda D. Labbo is Professor in the Department of Language and Literacy Education at the University of Georgia, Athens, GA, USA, specializing in computers in literacy education. She is the recipient of several awards including an American Library Association Award for an Outstanding Academic Book. She received a National Science Foundation to explore the use of multimedia, classroom anchor cases in pre-service teacher literacy education in the primary grades. Email: lindalabbo@gmail.com.

Paul P.M. Leseman is a professor of special education at Utrecht University, the Netherlands. His research interests concern biological and cultural influences on language and literacy development and developmental approaches to learning disabilities. Currently he studies language demands for cognitively complex, decontextualized communication in school context. Email: P.P.M.Leseman@uu.nl.

Iris Levin is Professor of Education at Tel Aviv University, Israel. She studies early literacy and language, and especially children's alphabetic skills, early writing, and reading. Her current analyses refer to linguistic variations, to socio-cultural effects and to intervention studies at home and in school. Email: irisl@post.tau.ac.il.

Rachel Levin is a researcher at the Center for Educational Technology (CET) in Israel. She participates in several projects that involve large-scale assessment, classroom assessment, and programs evaluation. Email: rachelle@cet.ac.il.

Michael C. McKenna is Thomas G. Jewell Professor of Reading at the University of Virginia. His research focuses on the use of technology in supporting text for beginning readers, and he has co-edited both volumes of the *International handbook of literacy and technology*. Email: mcm7g@virginia.edu.

Nancy A. Madden is president and co-founder of the Success for All Foundation, and professor in the Center for Research and Reform in Education at Johns Hopkins University and the Institute for Effective Education at the University of York. An expert in literacy and instruction, she is the author or co-author of many articles and books on cooperative learning, mainstreaming, and education of disadvantaged students. Email: nmadden@jhu.edu or nm536@york.ac.uk.

Jackie Marsh is Professor of Education at the University of Sheffield, where she is involved in research relating to the nature and role of popular culture, media, and new technologies in young children's literacy development. She is immediate past president of the United Kingdom Literacy Association and is a co-editor of the *Journal of Early Childhood Literacy*. Jackie maintains a blog relating to young children's media literacy: www.digitalbeginnings.blogspot.com. Email: j.a.marsh@sheffield.ac.uk.

Aziza Y. Mayo is a post doctoral researcher at the University of Utrecht, the Netherlands. Her research focuses on language development of immigrant and Dutch 3- to 6-year-olds. Email: A.Y.Mayo@fss.uu.nl.

Susan B. Neuman is a Professor of Education at the University of Michigan specializing in early literacy development. Previously, she directed the Center for the Improvement of Early Reading Ability (CIERA). Her research and teaching interests include early childhood policy, curriculum, and early reading instruction. She has served as the US Assistant Secretary for Elementary and Secondary Education. Email: sbneuman@umich.edu.

Rebekah A. Richert received her PhD at the University of Virginia and is now Assistant Professor at the University of California, Riverside. Email: rebekah.richert@ucr.edu.

Kathleen Roskos is Professor of Education at John Carroll University in Cleveland. Her areas of research include early literacy development, teacher cognition, and the design of professional education for teachers. She is currently a member of the e-Learning Committee and the Early Childhood Commission of the International Reading Association and a leader in the Literacy Development for Young Children SIG of that organization. Email: pdroskos@suite224.net.

Annie Roy-Charland is Assistant Professor in Psychology at Laurentian University, Sudbury, Canada and member of the Canadian Language and Literacy Research Network. Her main research interests are eye movements in cognitive tasks. She currently studies the missing-letter effect and cognitive processes involved in reading, shared book reading, and selective attention, and implicit cognitions in addiction. Email: aroycharland@laurentian.ca.

Jean Saint-Aubin is a professor at Université de Moncton in New Brunswick, Canada, and a project leader in the Canadian Language and Literary Research Network. His research is in the field of experimental psychology in which he investigates short-term memory and reading. With an equipment grant from the Canadian Language and Literacy Research Network he established at Université de Moncton a high-tech laboratory for investigating eye movements in reading. Email: jean.saint-aubin@umoncton.ca.

Anna F. Scheele is a doctoral candidate at Utrecht University in the Netherlands. Her research focus is language development of young immigrant children. Email: A.F.Scheele@uu.nl.

Michal Schleifer is a division head of the Literacy and Language Arts Department at the Center for Educational Technology (CET) in Israel. She is an expert on literacy in multi-cultural environments. Email: michals@cet.ac.il.

Eliane Segers is Assistant Professor at the Behavioral Science Institute at the Radboud University in the Netherlands. Her research focuses on multimedia learning, reading problems, specific language impairment, and ICT interventions. Email: e.segers@pwo.ru.nl.

Adina Shamir is a lecturer at Bar-Ilan University in Israel. She is currently serving as head of the Special Interest Group on Children with Special Needs of the European Association for Learning and Instruction (EARLI). Her research has incorporated development of innovative educational programs including educational eBooks as supports for children's language and literacy development. Email: Shamir_a@netvision.net.il.

Robert E. Slavin is a Professor at Johns Hopkins University, and serves as the Co-Director of the Center for Research on the Education of Students

Placed at Risk and Chairman of the Success for All Foundation. He received several awards among which the Palmer O. Johnson award for the best article in an AERA journal in 1988, and the Outstanding Educator award from the Horace Mann League in 1999. Email: rslavin@jhu.edu or rs553@york.ac.uk.

Bradley J. Tucker is the Director of Institutional Planning at Concordia University, Montreal, Canada. His expertise is in instruction and the use of technology in education. Email: tucker@education.concordia.ca.

Yuuko Uchikoshi is Assistant Professor of Education at the University of California, Davis. Her research interests include language and literacy development in young children and the influence of television on children's language development. Email: yuchikoshi@ucdavis.edu.

Victor H.P. van Daal is Professor of Special Education at the University of Stavanger in Norway, affiliated with the National Center for Reading Education and Reading Research. His work concentrates on the nature and origin of cognitive problems in children and adults with learning disabilities. His applied research deals with international comparisons of reading comprehension (PIRLS) and with good praxis for struggling adolescent readers (core partner in a European Erasmus project). Email: victor.v.daal@uis.no.

Paul van den Broek is Professor of Education and Child Studies at Leiden University and most recently Guy Bond Professor in Reading Research at the University of Minnesota. His research interests focus on the cognitive processes involved in text comprehension and in the development of these processes. He pursues these interests using behavioral methodologies, computational modelling, and, recently, neuro-imaging techniques. Email: broekpwvanden@fsw.leidenuniv.nl.

Marian J.A.J. Verhallen, a former teacher in primary education, is pursuing her doctorate at Leiden University in the Netherlands. Her research focuses on the use of video storybooks with the aim to enhance vocabulary in young immigrant children from low socioeconomic status families. Email: Verhallen@fsw.leidenuniv.nl.

Ellen Wartella is a distinguished professor of Psychology at University of California, Riverside. Currently she is co-principal Investigator on a 5-year multi-site research project entitled: "IRADS Collaborative Research: Influence of Digital Media on Very Young Children." She serves on several boards among which the National Academy of Sciences Board on Children Youth and Families and the Board for Sesame Workshop. Email: wartella@ucr.edu.

Mary Jane White recently received her PhD from the University of Minnesota in the Department of Educational Psychology. In her research she examines cognitive processes in reading and writing. Email: whit0782@umn.edu.

Tricia A. Zucker is a doctoral candidate in Reading Education at the University of Virginia's Curry School of Education. She currently serves as a research coordinator for the Children's Learning Institute at the University of Texas Health Science Center, Houston. Email: taz3m@virginia.edu.

Index